Study Guide

Child and Adolescent development

tuesday and thursday

@

11 am

STUDY GUIDE

Richard O. Straub

University of Michigan, Dearborn

to accompany

Kathleen Stassen Berger

The Developing Person Through Childhood and Adolescence

Sixth Edition

WORTH PUBLISHERS

Study Guide
by Richard O. Straub
to accompany
Berger: **The Developing Person Through Childhood and Adolescence**, Sixth Edition

ISBN: 0-7167-5282-4 (EAN: 9780716752820)

Third Printing

Worth Publishers
41 Madison Avenue
New York, New York 10010
www.worthpublishers.com

Contents

Preface   vii

CHAPTER   1   Introduction   1

CHAPTER   2   Theories of Development   19

CHAPTER   3   Heredity and Environment   37

CHAPTER   4   Prenatal Development and Birth   577

CHAPTER   5   The First 2 Years: Biosocial Development   75

CHAPTER   6   The First 2 Years: Cognitive Development   91

CHAPTER   7   The First 2 Years: Psychosocial Development   107

CHAPTER   8   The Play Years: Biosocial Development   123

CHAPTER   9   The Play Years: Cognitive Development   139

CHAPTER   10   The Play Years: Psychosocial Development   155

CHAPTER   11   The School Years: Biosocial Development   171

CHAPTER   12   The School Years: Cognitive Development   187

CHAPTER   13   The School Years: Psychosocial Development   203

CHAPTER   14   Adolescence: Biosocial Development   219

CHAPTER   15   Adolescence: Cognitive Development   239

CHAPTER   16   Adolescence: Psychosocial Development   253

APPENDIX   B   More About Research Methods   269

Preface

This Study Guide is designed for use with *The Developing Person Through Childhood and Adolescence*, Sixth Edition, by Kathleen Stassen Berger. It is intended to help you to evaluate your understanding of that material, and then to review any problem areas. "How to Manage Your Time Efficiently, Study More Effectively, and Think Critically" provides detailed instructions on how to use the textbook and this Study Guide for maximum benefit. It also offers additional study suggestions based on principles of time management, effective note-taking, evaluation of exam performance, and an effective program for improving your comprehension while studying from textbooks.

Each chapter of the Study Guide includes a Chapter Overview, a set of Guided Study questions to pace your reading of the text chapter, a Chapter Review section to be completed after you have read the text chapter, and three review tests. One chapter in most sections of the text includes a crossword puzzle that provides an alternative way of testing your understanding of the terms and concepts. The review tests are of two types: Progress Tests that consist of questions focusing on facts and definitions and a Thinking Critically Test that evaluates your understanding of the text chapter's broader conceptual material and its application to real-world situations. For all three review tests, the correct answers are given, followed by textbook page references (so you can easily go back and reread the material), and complete explanations not only of why the answer is correct but also of why the other choices are incorrect.

I would like to thank Betty and Don Probert of The Special Projects Group for their exceptional work in all phases of this project. My thanks also to Graig Donini and Stacey Alexander for their skillful assistance in the preparation of this Study Guide. We hope that our work will help you to achieve your highest level of academic performance in this course and to acquire a keen appreciation of human development.

Richard O. Straub
September 2002

How to Manage Your Time Efficiently, Study More Effectively, and Think Critically

How effectively do you study? Good study habits make the job of being a college student much easier. Many students, who *could* succeed in college, fail or drop out because they have never learned to manage their time efficiently. Even the best students can usually benefit from an in-depth evaluation of their current study habits.

There are many ways to achieve academic success, of course, but your approach may not be the most effective or efficient. Are you sacrificing your social life or your physical or mental health in order to get A's on your exams? Good study habits result in better grades *and* more time for other activities.

Evaluate Your Current Study Habits

To improve your study habits, you must first have an accurate picture of how you currently spend your time. Begin by putting together a profile of your present living and studying habits. Answer the following questions by writing *yes* or *no* on each line.

_____ 1. Do you usually set up a schedule to budget your time for studying, recreation, and other activities?

_____ 2. Do you often put off studying until time pressures force you to cram?

_____ 3. Do other students seem to study less than you do, but get better grades?

_____ 4. Do you usually spend hours at a time studying one subject, rather than dividing that time between several subjects?

_____ 5. Do you often have trouble remembering what you have just read in a textbook?

_____ 6. Before reading a chapter in a textbook, do you skim through it and read the section headings?

_____ 7. Do you try to predict exam questions from your lecture notes and reading?

_____ 8. Do you usually attempt to paraphrase or summarize what you have just finished reading?

_____ 9. Do you find it difficult to concentrate very long when you study?

_____ 10. Do you often feel that you studied the wrong material for an exam?

Thousands of college students have participated in similar surveys. Students who are fully realizing their academic potential usually respond as follows: (1) yes, (2) no, (3) no, (4) no, (5) no, (6) yes, (7) yes, (8) yes, (9) no, (10) no.

Compare your responses to those of successful students. The greater the discrepancy, the more you could benefit from a program to improve your study habits. The questions are designed to identify areas of weakness. Once you have identified your weaknesses, you will be able to set specific goals for improvement and implement a program for reaching them.

Manage Your Time

Do you often feel frustrated because there isn't enough time to do all the things you must and want to do? Take heart. Even the most productive and successful people feel this way at times. But they establish priorities for their activities and they learn to budget time for each of them. There's much in the saying "If you want something done, ask a busy person to do it." A busy person knows how to get things done.

If you don't now have a system for budgeting your time, develop one. Not only will your academic accomplishments increase, but you will actually find more time in your schedule for other activities. And you won't have to feel guilty about "taking time off," because all your obligations will be covered.

Establish a Baseline

As a first step in preparing to budget your time, keep a diary for a few days to establish a summary, or baseline, of the time you spend in studying, socializing, working, and so on. If you are like many students, much of your "study" time is nonproductive; you may sit at your desk and leaf through a book, but the time is actually wasted. Or you may procrastinate. You are always getting ready to study, but you rarely do.

Besides revealing where you waste time, your diary will give you a realistic picture of how much time you need to allot for meals, commuting, and other fixed activities. In addition, careful records should indicate the times of the day when you are consistently most productive. A sample time-management diary is shown in Table 1.

Plan the Term

Having established and evaluated your baseline, you are ready to devise a more efficient schedule. Buy a calendar that covers the entire school term and has ample space for each day. Using the course outlines provided by your instructors, enter the dates of all exams, term paper deadlines, and other important academic obligations. If you have any long-range personal plans (concerts, weekend trips, etc.), enter the dates on the calendar as well. Keep your calendar up to date and refer to it often. I recommend carrying it with you at all times.

Develop a Weekly Calendar

Now that you have a general picture of the school term, develop a weekly schedule that includes all of your activities. Aim for a schedule that you can live with for the entire school term. A sample weekly schedule, incorporating the following guidelines, is shown in Table 2.

1. Enter your class times, work hours, and any other fixed obligations first. *Be thorough.* Using information from your time-management diary, allow plenty of time for such things as commuting, meals, laundry, and the like.

Table 1   Sample Time-Management Diary

Activity	Time Completed	Duration Hours: Minutes
Sleep	7:00	7:30
Dressing	7:25	:25
Breakfast	7:45	:20
Commute	8:20	:35
Coffee	9:00	:40
French	10:00	1:00
Socialize	10:15	:15
Videogame	10:35	:20
Coffee	11:00	:25
Psychology	12:00	1:00
Lunch	12:25	:25
Study Lab	1:00	:35
Psych. Lab	4:00	3:00
Work	5:30	1:30
Commute	6:10	:40
Dinner	6:45	:35
TV	7:30	:45
Study Psych.	10:00	2:30
Socialize	11:30	1:30
Sleep		

Prepare a similar chart for each day of the week. When you finish an activity, note it on the chart and write down the time it was completed. Then determine its duration by subtracting the time the previous activity was finished from the newly entered time.

2. Set up a study schedule for each of your courses. The study habits survey and your time-management diary will direct you. The following guidelines should also be useful.

(a) Establish regular study times for each course. The 4 hours needed to study one subject, for example, are most profitable when divided into shorter periods spaced over several days. If you cram your studying into one 4-hour block, what you attempt to learn in the third or fourth hour will interfere with what you studied in the first 2 hours. Newly acquired knowledge is like wet cement. It needs some time to "harden" to become memory.

(b) Alternate subjects. The type of interference just mentioned is greatest between similar topics. Set up a schedule in which you spend time on several *different* courses during each study session. Besides reducing the potential for interference, alternating subjects will help to prevent mental fatigue with one topic.

(c) Set weekly goals to determine the amount of study time you need to do well in each course. This will

Table 2   Sample Weekly Schedule

Time	Mon.	Tues.	Wed.	Thurs.	Fri.	Sat.
7–8	Dress Eat	Dress Eat	Dress Eat	Dress Eat	Dress Eat	
8–9	Psych.	Study Psych.	Psych.	Study Psych.	Psych.	Dress Eat
9–10	Eng.	Study Eng.	Eng.	Study Eng.	Eng.	Study Eng.
10–11	Study French	Free	Study French	Open Study	Study French	Study Stats.
11–12	French	Study Psych. Lab	French	Open Study	French	Study Stats.
12–1	Lunch	Lunch	Lunch	Lunch	Lunch	Lunch
1–2	Stats.	Psych. Lab	Stats.	Study or Free	Stats.	Free
2–3	Bio.	Psych. Lab	Bio.	Free	Bio.	Free
3–4	Free	Psych.	Free	Free	Free	Free
4–5	Job	Job	Job	Job	Job	Free
5–6	Job	Job	Job	Job	Job	Free
6–7	Dinner	Dinner	Dinner	Dinner	Dinner	Dinner
7–8	Study Bio.	Study Bio.	Study Bio.	Study Bio.	Free	Free
8–9	Study Eng.	Study Stats.	Study Psych.	Open Study	Open Study	Free
9–10	Open Study	Open Study	Open Study	Open Study	Free	Free

This is a sample schedule for a student with a 16-credit load and a 10-hour-per-week part-time job. Using this chart as an illustration, make up a weekly schedule, following the guidelines outlined here.

depend on, among other things, the difficulty of your courses and the effectiveness of your methods. Many professors recommend studying at least 1 to 2 hours for each hour in class. If your time-management diary indicates that you presently study less time than that, do not plan to jump immediately to a much higher level. Increase study time from your baseline by setting weekly goals [see (4)] that will gradually bring you up to the desired level. As an initial schedule, for example, you might set aside an amount of study time for each course that matches class time.

(d) Schedule for maximum effectiveness. Tailor your schedule to meet the demands of each course. For the course that emphasizes lecture notes, schedule time for a daily review soon after the class. This will give you a chance to revise your notes and clean up any hard-to-decipher shorthand while the material is still fresh in your mind. If you are evaluated for class participation (for example, in a language course), allow time for a review just before the class meets. Schedule study time for your most difficult (or least motivat-ing) courses during hours when you are the most alert and distractions are fewest.

(e) Schedule open study time. Emergencies, additional obligations, and the like could throw off your schedule. And you may simply need some extra time periodically for a project or for review in one of your courses. Schedule several hours each week for such purposes.

3. After you have budgeted time for studying, fill in slots for recreation, hobbies, relaxation, household errands, and the like.

4. Set specific goals. Before each study session, make a list of specific goals. The simple note "7–8 PM: study psychology" is too broad to ensure the most effective use of the time. Formulate your daily goals according to what you know you must accomplish during the term. If you have course outlines with advance assignments, set systematic daily goals that will allow you, for example, to cover fifteen chapters before the exam. And be realistic: Can you actually

expect to cover a 78-page chapter in one session? Divide large tasks into smaller units; stop at the most logical resting points. When you complete a specific goal, take a 5- or 10-minute break before tackling the next goal.

5. Evaluate how successful or unsuccessful your studying has been on a daily or weekly basis. Did you reach most of your goals? If so, reward yourself immediately. You might even make a list of five to ten rewards to choose from. If you have trouble studying regularly, you may be able to motivate yourself by making such rewards contingent on completing specific goals.

6. Finally, until you have lived with your schedule for several weeks, don't hesitate to revise it. You may need to allow more time for chemistry, for example, and less for some other course. If you are trying to study regularly for the first time and are feeling burned out, you probably have set your initial goals too high. Don't let failure cause you to despair and abandon the program. Accept your limitations and revise your schedule so that you are studying only 15 to 20 minutes more each evening than you are used to. The point is to identify a regular schedule with which you can achieve some success. Time management, like any skill, must be practiced to become effective.

Techniques for Effective Study

Knowing how to put study time to best use is, of course, as important as finding a place for it in your schedule. Here are some suggestions that should enable you to increase your reading comprehension and improve your note-taking. A few study tips are included as well.

Using SQ3R to Increase Reading Comprehension

How do you study from a textbook? If you are like many students, you simply read and reread in a *passive* manner. Studies have shown, however, that most students who simply read a textbook cannot remember more than half the material ten minutes after they have finished. Often, what is retained is the unessential material rather than the important points upon which exam questions will be based.

This *Study Guide* employs a program known as SQ3R (Survey, Question, Read, Recite, and Review) to facilitate, and allow you to assess, your comprehension of the important facts and concepts in *The Developing Person Through Childhood and Adolescence*, Sixth Edition, by Kathleen Stassen Berger.

Research has shown that students using SQ3R achieve significantly greater comprehension of textbooks than students reading in the more traditional passive manner. Once you have learned this program, you can improve your comprehension of any textbook.

Survey Before reading a chapter, determine whether the text or the study guide has an outline or list of objectives. Read this material and the summary at the end of the chapter. Next, read the textbook chapter fairly quickly, paying special attention to the major headings and subheadings. This survey will give you an idea of the chapter's contents and organization. You will then be able to divide the chapter into logical sections in order to formulate specific goals for a more careful reading of the chapter.

In this Study Guide, the *Chapter Overview* summarizes the major topics of the textbook chapter. This section also provides a few suggestions for approaching topics you may find difficult.

Question You will retain material longer when you have a use for it. If you look up a word's definition in order to solve a crossword puzzle, for example, you will remember it longer than if you merely fill in the letters as a result of putting other words in. Surveying the chapter will allow you to generate important questions that the chapter will proceed to answer. These question correspond to "mental files" into which knowledge will be sorted for easy access.

As you survey, jot down several questions for each chapter section. One simple technique is to generate questions by rephrasing a section heading. For example, the "Preoperational Thought" head could be turned into "What is preoperational thought?" Good questions will allow you to focus on the important points in the text. Examples of good questions are those that begin as follows: "List two examples of . . . ." "What is the function of . . . ?" "What is the significance of . . . ?" Such questions give a purpose to your reading. Similarly, you can formulate questions based on the chapter outline.

The *Guided Study* section of this Study Guide provides the types of questions you might formulate while surveying each chapter. This section is a detailed set of objectives covering the points made in the text.

Read When you have established "files" for each section of the chapter, review your first question, begin reading, and continue until you have discovered its answer. If you come to material that seems to answer an important question you don't have a file for, stop and write down the question.

Using this Study Guide, read the chapter one section at a time. First, preview the section by skimming it, noting headings and boldface items. Next, study the appropriate section objectives in the *Guided Study*. Then, as you read the chapter section, search for the answer to each objective.

Be sure to read everything. Don't skip photo or art captions, graphs, marginal notes. In some cases, what may seem vague in reading will be made clear by a simple graph. Keep in mind that test questions are sometimes drawn from illustrations and charts.

Recite When you have found the answer to a question, close your eyes and mentally recite the question and its answer. Then *write* the answer next to the question. It is important that you recite an answer in your own words rather than the author's. Don't rely on your short-term memory to repeat the author's words verbatim.

In responding to the objectives, pay close attention to what is called for. If you are asked to identify or list, do just that. If asked to compare, contrast, or do both, you should focus on the similarities (compare) and differences (contrast) between the concepts or theories. Answering the objectives carefully will not only help you to focus your attention on the important concepts of the text, but it will also provide excellent practice for essay exams.

Recitation is an extremely effective study technique, recommended by many learning experts. In addition to increasing reading comprehension, it is useful for review. Trying to explain something in your own words clarifies your knowledge, often by revealing aspects of your answer that are vague or incomplete. If you repeatedly rely upon "I know" in recitation, you really may not know.

Recitation has the additional advantage of simulating an exam, especially an essay exam; the same skills are required in both cases. Too often students study without ever putting the book and notes aside, which makes it easy for them to develop false confidence in their knowledge. When the material is in front of you, you may be able to recognize an answer, but will you be able to recall it later, when you take an exam that does not provide these retrieval cues?

After you have recited and written your answer, continue with your next question. Read, recite, and so on.

Review When you have answered the last question on the material you have designated as a study goal, go back and review. Read over each question and your written answer to it. Your review might also include a brief written summary that integrates all of your questions and answers. This review need not

take longer than a few minutes, but it is important. It will help you retain the material longer and will greatly facilitate a final review of each chapter before the exam.

In this Study Guide, the *Chapter Review* section contains fill-in and one- or two-sentence essay questions for you to complete after you have finished reading the text and have written answers to the objectives. The correct answers are given at the end of the chapter. Generally, your answer to a fill-in question should match exactly (as in the case of important terms, theories, or people). In some cases, the answer is not a term or name, so a word close in meaning will suffice. You should go through the Chapter Review several times before taking an exam, so it is a good idea to mentally fill in the answers until you are ready for a final pretest review. Textbook page references are provided with each section title, in case you need to reread any of the material.

Also provided to facilitate your review are two *Progress Tests* that include multiple-choice questions and, where appropriate, matching or true–false questions. These tests are not to be taken until you have read the chapter, written answers to the objectives, and completed the *Chapter Review*. Correct answers, along with explanations of why each alternative is correct or incorrect, are provided at the end of the chapter. The relevant text page numbers for each question are also given. If you miss a question, read these explanations and, if necessary, review the text pages to further understand why. The *Progress Tests* do not test every aspect of a concept, so you should treat an incorrect answer as an indication that you need to review the concept.

Following the two Progress Tests is a *Thinking Critically Test*, which should be taken just prior to an exam. It includes questions that test your ability to analyze, integrate, and apply the concepts in the chapter. As with the *Progress Tests*, answers for the *Thinking Critically Test* are provided at the end of each chapter, along with relevant page numbers.

The chapter concludes with *Key Terms*, either in list form only or also in a crossword puzzle. In either form, as with the *Guided Study* objectives, it is important that the answers be written from memory, and in list form, in your own words. The *Answers* section at the end of the chapter gives a definition of each term, sometimes along with an example of its usage and/or a tip to help you remember its meaning.

One final suggestion: Incorporate SQ3R into your time-management calendar. Set specific goals for completing SQ3R with each assigned chapter. Keep a record of chapters completed, and reward yourself for being conscientious. Initially, it takes more time and effort to "read" using SQ3R, but with practice, the steps will become automatic. More importantly, you will comprehend significantly more material and retain what you have learned longer than passive readers do.

Taking Lecture Notes

Are your class notes as useful as they might be? One way to determine their worth is to compare them with those taken by other good students. Are yours as thorough? Do they provide you with a comprehensible outline of each lecture? If not, then the following suggestions might increase the effectiveness of your note-taking.

1. Keep a separate notebook for each course. Use 8 1/2 × 11-inch pages. Consider using a ring binder, which would allow you to revise and insert notes while still preserving lecture order.

2. Take notes in the format of a lecture outline. Use roman numerals for major points, letters for supporting arguments, and so on. Some instructors will make this easy by delivering organized lectures and, in some cases, by outlining their lectures on the board. If a lecture is disorganized, you will probably want to reorganize your notes soon after the class.

3. As you take notes in class, leave a wide margin on one side of each page. After the lecture, expand or clarify any shorthand notes while the material is fresh in your mind. Use this time to write important questions in the margin next to notes that answer them. This will facilitate later review and will allow you to anticipate similar exam questions.

Evaluate Your Exam Performance

How often have you received a grade on an exam that did not do justice to the effort you spent preparing for the exam? This is a common experience that can leave one feeling bewildered and abused. "What do I have to do to get an A?" "The test was unfair!" "I studied the wrong material!"

The chances of this happening are greatly reduced if you have an effective time-management schedule and use the study techniques described here. But it can happen to the best-prepared student and is most likely to occur on your first exam with a new professor.

Remember that there are two main reasons for studying. One is to learn for your own general academic development. Many people believe that such knowledge is all that really matters. Of course, it is possible, though unlikely, to be an expert on a topic without achieving commensurate grades, just as one can, occasionally, earn an excellent grade without truly mastering the course material. During a job interview or in the workplace, however, your A in Cobol won't mean much if you can't actually program a computer.

In order to keep career options open after you graduate, you must know the material and maintain competitive grades. In the short run, this means performing well on exams, which is the second main objective in studying.

Probably the single best piece of advice to keep in mind when studying for exams is to *try to predict exam questions*. This means ignoring the trivia and focusing on the important questions and their answers (with your instructor's emphasis in mind).

A second point is obvious. How well you do on exams is determined by your mastery of both lecture and textbook material. Many students (partly because of poor time management) concentrate too much on one at the expense of the other.

To evaluate how well you are learning lecture and textbook material, analyze the questions you missed on the first exam. If your instructor does not review exams during class, you can easily do it yourself. Divide the questions into two categories: those drawn primarily from lectures and those drawn primarily from the textbook. Determine the percentage of questions you missed in each category. If your errors are evenly distributed and you are satisfied with your grade, you have no problem. If you are weaker in one area, you will need to set future goals for increasing and/or improving your study of that area.

Similarly, note the percentage of test questions drawn from each category. Although exams in most courses cover both lecture notes and the textbook, the relative emphasis of each may vary from instructor to instructor. While your instructors may not be entirely consistent in making up future exams, you may be able to tailor your studying for each course by placing additional emphasis on the appropriate area.

Exam evaluation will also point out the types of questions your instructor prefers. Does the exam consist primarily of multiple-choice, true–false, or essay questions? You may also discover that an instructor is fond of wording questions in certain ways. For example, an instructor may rely heavily on questions that require you to draw an analogy between a theory or concept and a real-world example. Evaluate both your instructor's style and how well you do with each format. Use this information to guide your future exam preparation.

Important aids, not only in studying for exams but also in determining how well prepared you are, are the Progress and Thinking Critically Tests provided in this Study Guide. If these tests don't include all of the types of questions your instructor typically writes, make up your own practice exam questions. Spend extra time testing yourself with question formats that are most difficult for you. There is no better way to evaluate your preparation for an upcoming exam than by testing yourself under the conditions most likely to be in effect during the actual test.

A Few Practical Tips

Even the best intentions for studying sometimes fail. Some of these failures occur because students attempt to work under conditions that are simply not conducive to concentrated study. To help ensure the success of your time-management program, here are a few suggestions that should assist you in reducing the possibility of procrastination or distraction.

1. If you have set up a schedule for studying, make your roommate, family, and friends aware of this commitment, and ask them to honor your quiet study time. Close your door and post a "Do Not Disturb" sign.

2. Set up a place to study that minimizes potential distractions. Use a desk or table, not your bed or an extremely comfortable chair. Keep your desk and the walls around it free from clutter. If you need a place other than your room, find one that meets as many of the above requirements as possible—for example, in the library stacks.

3. Do nothing but study in this place. It should become associated with studying so that it "triggers" this activity, just as a mouth-watering aroma elicits an appetite.

4. Never study with the television on or with other distracting noises present. If you must have music in the background in order to mask outside noise, for example, play soft instrumental music. Don't pick vocal selections; your mind will be drawn to the lyrics.

5. Study by yourself. Other students can be distracting or can break the pace at which your learning is most efficient. In addition, there is always the possibility that group studying will become a social gathering. Reserve that for its own place in your schedule.

If you continue to have difficulty concentrating for very long, try the following suggestions.

6. Study your most difficult or most challenging subjects first, when you are most alert.

7. Start with relatively short periods of concentrated study, with breaks in between. If your attention starts to wander, get up immediately and take a break. It is better to study effectively for 15 minutes and then take a break than to fritter away 45 minutes out of an hour. Gradually increase the length of study periods, using your attention span as an indicator of successful pacing.

Critical Thinking

Having discussed a number of specific techniques for managing your time efficiently and studying effectively, let us now turn to a much broader topic: What exactly should you expect to learn as a student of developmental psychology?

Most developmental psychology courses have two major goals: (1) to help you acquire a basic understanding of the discipline's knowledge base, and (2) to help you learn to think like a psychologist. Many students devote all of their efforts to the first of these goals, concentrating on memorizing as much of the course's material as possible.

The second goal—learning to think like a psychologist—has to do with critical thinking. Critical thinking has many meanings. On one level, it refers to an attitude of healthy skepticism that should guide your study of psychology. As a critical thinker, you learn not to accept any explanation or conclusion about behavior as true until you have evaluated the evidence. On another level, critical thinking refers to a systematic process for examining the conclusions and arguments presented by others. In this regard, many of the features of the SQ3R technique for improving reading comprehension can be incorporated into an effective critical thinking system.

To learn to think critically, you must first recognize that psychological information is transmitted through the construction of persuasive arguments. An argument consists of three parts: an assertion, evidence, and an explanation (Mayer and Goodchild, 1990).

An assertion is a statement of relationship between some aspect of behavior, such as intelligence, and another factor, such as age. Learn to identify and evaluate the assertions about behavior and mental processes that you encounter as you read your textbook, listen to lectures, and engage in discussions with classmates. A good test of your understanding of an assertion is to try to restate it in your own words. As you do so, pay close attention to how important terms and concepts are defined. When a researcher asserts that "intelligence declines with age," for example, what does he or she mean by "intelligence"? Assertions such as this one may be true when a critical term ("intelligence") is defined one way (for example, "speed of thinking"), but not when defined in another way (for example, "general knowledge"). One of the strengths of psychology is the use of *operational* definitions that specify how key terms and concepts are measured, thus eliminating any ambiguity about their meaning. "Intelligence," for example, is often operationally defined as performance on a test measuring various cognitive skills. Whenever you encounter an assertion that is ambiguous, be skeptical of its accuracy.

When you have a clear understanding of an argument's assertion, evaluate its supporting evidence, the second component of an argument. Is it *empirical*? Does it, in fact, support the assertion? Psychologists accept only *empirical (observable) evidence* that is based on direct measurement of behavior. Hearsay, intuition, and personal experiences are not acceptable evidence. Chapter 1 discusses the various research methods used by developmental psychologists to gather empirical evidence. Some examples include surveys, observations of behavior in natural settings, and experiments.

As you study developmental psychology, you will become aware of another important issue in evaluating evidence—determining whether or not the research on which it is based is faulty. Research can be faulty for many reasons, including the use of an unrepresentative sample of subjects, experimenter bias, and inadequate control of unanticipated factors that might influence results. Evidence based on faulty research should be discounted.

The third component of an argument is the explanation provided for an assertion, which is based on the evidence that has been presented. While the argument's assertion merely *describes* how two things (such as intelligence and age) are related, the explanation tells *why*, often by proposing some theoretical mechanism that causes the relationship. Empirical evidence that thinking speed slows with age (the assertion), for example, may be explained as being caused by age-related changes in the activity of brain cells (a physiological explanation).

Be cautious in accepting explanations. In order to think critically about an argument's explanation, ask yourself three questions: (1) Can I restate the explanation in my own words?; (2) Does the explanation make sense based on the stated evidence?; and (3) Are there alternative explanations that adequately explain the assertion? Consider this last point in relation to our sample assertion: It is possible that the slower thinking speed of older adults is due to their having less recent experience than younger people with tasks that require quick thinking (a disuse explanation).

Because psychology is a relatively young science, its theoretical explanations are still emerging, and often change. For this reason, not all psychological arguments will offer explanations. Many arguments will only raise additional questions for further research to address.

Some Suggestions for Becoming a Critical Thinker

1. Adopt an attitude of healthy skepticism in evaluating psychological arguments.

2. Insist on unambiguous operational definitions of an argument's important concepts and terms.

3. Be cautious in accepting supporting evidence for an argument's assertion.

4. Refuse to accept evidence for an argument if it is based on faulty research.

5. Ask yourself if the theoretical explanation provided for an argument "makes sense" based on the empirical evidence.

6. Determine whether there are alternative explanations that adequately explain an assertion.

7. Use critical thinking to construct your own effective arguments when writing term papers, answering essay questions, and speaking.

8. Polish your critical-thinking skills by applying them to each of your college courses, and to other areas of life as well. Learn to think critically about advertising, political speeches, and the material presented in popular periodicals.

Some Closing Thoughts

I hope that these suggestions help make you more successful academically, and that they enhance the quality of your college life in general. Having the necessary skills makes any job a lot easier and more pleasant. Let me repeat my warning not to attempt to make too drastic a change in your life-style immediately. Good habits require time and self-discipline to develop. Once established they can last a lifetime.

Chapter One

Introduction

Chapter Overview

The first chapter introduces the study of human development. The first section defines development, introduces the life-span perspective, and describes the three domains into which development is often divided. It also makes clear that development is influenced as much by external factors as by internal factors, beginning with a discussion of the ecological model—Bronfenbrenner's description of how the individual is affected by, and affects, many other individuals, groups of individuals, and larger systems in the environment.

The second section describes different aspects of the overlapping contexts in which people develop. The story of David illustrates the effects of these contexts.

The next two sections discuss the strategies developmentalists use in their research, beginning with the scientific method and including scientific observation, correlational research, experiments, surveys, and case studies. To study people over time, developmentalists have created several research designs: cross-sectional, longitudinal, and cross-sequential.

The final section discusses the ethics of research with humans. In addition to ensuring confidentiality and safety, developmentalists who study children are especially concerned that the benefits of research outweigh the risks.

NOTE: Answer guidelines for all Chapter 1 questions begin on page 12.

Guided Study

The text chapter should be studied one section at a time. Before you read, preview each section by skimming it, noting headings and boldface items. Then read the appropriate section objectives from the following outline. Keep these objectives in mind and, as you read the chapter section, search for the information that will enable you to meet each objective. Once you have finished a section, write out answers for its objectives.

Definitions: Change Over Time (pp. 1–8)

1. Define the study of human development, and explain three important discoveries that developmentalists have made about change.

   • Seeks that understand the ways in which people change and remain the same as they grow older.

   3 insights about change.
   1. Interacting systems / change affect many things.
   2. The butterfly effect is small change becomes huge 3. Continuity

2. Describe the ecological model of human development, and explain how this approach leads to an understanding of the overlapping contexts in which people develop. Each person is significantly affected by interactions among a number of overlapping systems. Microsystems intimately and immediately affect development. Mesosystems refer to interactions among microsystems (as when parents coordinate w/ teachers) Exosystems include external networks such as community structures. Macrosystems are including cultural values political philosophs Chronosystem includes time.

3. Identify five characteristics of development identified by the life-span perspective.

   Multidirectional-change is not always linear
   Multicontextual-Every human life must be understood as embedded in many contexts
   Multicultural Many cultural settings each with a distinct set of values, traditions, and tools for living.
   Multidisciplinary many academic fields esp. psychology, biology, education, and sociology.
   Plastic -Every individual trait within each individual can be altered at any pt.

4. Identify and describe the three domains into which human development is often separated.

Bosocial
All growth and change to a persons body + the genetic nutritional + health factors that affect growth and change

Cognitive
Mental processes that a person uses to obtain knowledge or to think about the environment perception, imagination memory language think decide + learn

Psycho soc.
emotions temperment social skills Family + friends community + culture and the larger society are particically oricentral to this domain

The Contexts of Development (pp. 8–19)

5. Discuss the three broad, overlapping contexts that affect development throughout the life span.

The historical context – how history effects the lives and thoughts of a specific person depends on where in history he was born

Culture includes values, assumptions + customs not only physical items

Socioeconomic- An indicator of a person's social + economic standing measured thru a combo of family income, occupation in, education level, place of residence

6. (text and Thinking Like a Scientist) Discuss the relationship between race and ethnicity. other variab

Race is the biological treits that people use to distinguish one group from another. Ethnic identity is a product of social environment and individuals conciousness race

Developmental Study as a Science (pp. 19–29)

7. List and describe the basic steps of the scientific method.
1. Research question
2. Hypothesis
3. Test hypothesis
4. Draw conclusions
5. Make findings availible.

8. Identify several controversies that echo throughout the study of development.

Nature vs. Nuture. (genetics vs. environment)

Continuity vs. discontinuity (gradual vs. suddenly)

Difference vs. deficit Celebration vs. problem to be corrected.

9. Describe scientific observation and correlation as research strategies, noting at least one advantage (or strength) and one disadvantage (or weakness) of each.

Scientific observation observing and recording in a systemic and objective manner.

Correlation exists between 2 varibles if 1 varible is more or less likely to occur when the other occurs.

10. Describe the components of an experiment, and discuss the main advantage and some of the limitations of this research method.

dependant and independant varible control vs. experimental group.
subjects could try to produce the result they believe the researchers want, and skew the results

11. Describe surveys and case studies, noting at least one advantage (or strength) and one disadvantage (or weakness) of each.

Survey - questionare given to a large # of people
advantage large data sample
disadvantage - people lie.

case study- 1 individual is studied intensely
advantage longitudal study over yrs. dis- cannot generalize.

12. Describe three basic research designs used by developmental psychologists.

Cross sectional - differ in age but have similar characteristics being studied.
longitudinal - same individuals are studied over a long period of time.

cross-sequential
Both longitudinal + and cross- sectional

Ethics and Science (pp. 29–31)

13. Briefly summarize some of the ethical issues involved in conducting research with human subjects.

Chapter Review

When you have finished reading the chapter, work through the material that follows to review it. Complete the sentences and answer the questions. As you proceed, evaluate your performance for each section by consulting the answers on page 12. Do not continue with the next section until you understand each answer. If you need to, review or reread the appropriate section in the textbook before continuing.

Definitions: Change Over Time (pp. 1–8)

1. The scientific study of human development can be defined as the science that seeks to understand _the way that people change and stay the same over time_.

2. Although _linear_ _change_ is the easiest kind of change to envision, it is the _least_ (most/least) likely to occur.

3. To capture the idea that change is a continual process within each person and group, development is described as the product of _dynamic_ _systems_.

4. The approach that emphasizes the influence of the systems, or contexts, that support the developing person is called the _ecological_ model. This approach was emphasized by _interaction of the different system_

5. According to this model, the family, the peer group, and other aspects of the immediate social setting constitute the _microsystems_.

6. Systems that link one microsystem to another constitute the _mesosystems_.

7. Community structures and local educational, medical, employment, and communications systems make up the _exosystems_.

8. Cultural values, political philosophies, economic patterns, and social conditions make up the _macrosystems_.

9. A recent addition to this model is the _chronosystem_, which emphasizes the importance of historical time on development.

10. Three important insights of this model are the concepts of _interacting systems_, in which a change in one thing affects many other things; the _butterfly effect_, in which even a tiny change in one system can have a profound effect on the other systems of development; and the _power of continuity_, in which even large changes seemingly have no effect.

11. Central to the study of development is the _life-span perspective_, which recognizes the sources of continuity and discontinuity from the beginning of life to the end.

The five developmental characteristics embodied within the life-span perspective are that development is

a. _multidirectional_
b. _multicontextual_
c. _multicultural_
d. _multidisciplinary_
e. _plastic_

12. One of the most encouraging aspects of the life-span perspective is that development is characterized by _plasticity_, or the capability of change.

13. The study of human development can be separated into three domains: _biosocial_, _cognitive_, and _psychosocial_.

14. The study of the brain and body, as well as changes in our biological selves and the social influences that guide our physical growth, falls within the _biosocial_ domain.

15. Thinking, perception, and language learning fall mainly in the _cognitive_ domain of development.

16. The study of emotions, personality, and interpersonal relationships falls within the _psychosocial_ domain.

17. All three domains _are_ (are/are not) important at every age. Each of the domains _is_ (is/is not) affected by the other two.

The Contexts of Development (pp. 8–19)

18. Forces outside the individual that influence development make up the <u>Contexts</u> of development.

19. A group of people born within a few years of each other is called a <u>Cohort</u>. These people tend to be affected by history in <u>the same way</u> (the same way/different ways).

20. A widely shared idea that is built more on shared perceptions than on objective reality is a <u>social</u> <u>construction</u> An important point about such ideas is that they <u>often change</u> (often change/are very stable) over time.

21. The life stage of <u>childhood</u> is an example of a social construction.

22. The values, assumptions, and customs as well as the physical objects that a group of people have adopted as a design for living constitute a <u>Culture</u>.

23. One example of the impact of cultural values on development is the greater tendency for children to be viewed as an economic asset in <u>marginal</u> <u>agricultural</u> communities. In such communities, infant care is designed to maximize <u>Survival</u> and emphasize family <u>cooperation</u>. By contrast, middle-class parents in <u>post industrializatio</u> nations are less worried about infant mortality and thus focus care on fostering <u>intellectual</u> growth and emotional <u>independence</u>. For these reasons, most women in developed nations want <u>1-2</u> (how many?) children and most women in developing countries want <u>3-5</u> (how many?) children.

24. The impact of cultural variations in <u>sleeping</u> <u>Arrangements</u> can be seen in the fact that children who <u>sleep Alone</u> (sleep alone/sleep with parents) are taught to be independent of their families, while those who <u>sleep with</u> (sleep alone/sleep with parents) are taught to depend

on them for warmth and protection. A <u>Kibbutz</u> is a kind of farming commune developed in <u>Israel</u>, whose members share <u>work, meals, income and child care,</u>.

25. One example of a universal cultural value in child rearing is that raising children without a <u>dedicated</u> <u>caregiver</u> is never satisfactory.

26. A contextual influence that is determined by a person's income, education, place of residence, and occupation is called <u>social economic status</u>, which is often abbreviated <u>SES</u>.

27. The minimum income needed to pay for a family's basic necessities is called the <u>poverty</u> <u>Line</u>. Among the hazards and pressures of poverty are higher rates of <u>child</u> <u>neglect</u>, <u>infant</u> <u>mortality</u>, inadequate <u>schools</u>, and adolescent <u>violence</u>.

28. Today, poverty rates are highest in the <u>85 & up.</u> age group.

29. Although poverty is a useful signal for severe problems throughout life, other variables, such as the presence of <u>supportive</u> <u>Relationships</u> within a family, play a crucial role in determining individual development. For example, some children seem resilient to the hazards of poverty, especially those whose parents are <u>nurturant</u> and involved. As another example, there are likely to be fewer social problems among poor people who work to keep up their <u>morale</u>.

30. A collection of people who share certain attributes, such as ancestry, national origin, religion, and language and, as a result, tend to have similar beliefs, values, and cultural experiences is called a(n) <u>ethnic</u> <u>group</u>.

31. (Thinking Like a Scientist) Biological traits used to differentiate people whose ancestors come from different regions is the definition of <u>Race</u>. However, this

social _CONSTRUCTION_ is much less influential on development than a person's _ethnic_ _background_ is.

32. (In Person) Because his mother contracted the disease _Rubella_ during her pregnancy, David was born with a heart defect and cataracts over both eyes. Thus, his immediate problems centered on the _Biosocial_ domain. However, because he was born at a particular time, he was already influenced by the larger _HISTORICAL_ context. His physical handicaps later produced _severe disabilities_ and _mental_ handicaps.

Developmental Study as a Science (pp. 19–29)

33. In order, the basic steps of the scientific method are

   a. _Formulate a Research?_

   b. _Develop a hypothesis_

   c. _Test the hypothesis_

   d. _Draw Conclusions_

   e. _Make the findings availible_

34. A specific, testable prediction that forms the basis of a research project is called a _hypothesis_.

35. To repeat an experimental test procedure and obtain the same results is to _verify_ the test of the hypothesis.

36. Age, sex, education, and other qualities that may differ during an investigation are called _variables_. Developmental researchers deal with both _intrapersonal_ variation, which occurs from day to day in each person, and _interpersonal_ variation, which occurs between people or groups.

37. The nature–nurture controversy concerns how much and which aspects of development are affected by _genes_ and how much by _environment_. The _Continuity_ – _Discontinuity_ controversy concerns whether development is largely gradual in nature or characterized by sudden transformations. The _difference_ – _deficit_

controversy focuses on when individual differences in development are celebrated or considered problems that need correcting.

38. In designing research studies, scientists are concerned with four issues: _validity_, or whether a study measures what it purports to measure; _accuracy_, or whether its measurements are correct; _generalizability_ or whether the study applies to other populations and situations; and _usefulness_, or whether it solves real-life problems.

39. When researchers observe and record, in a systematic and unbiased manner, what research subjects do, they are using _Scientific Observation_. People may be observed in a _natural_ setting or in a _laboratory_.

40. A chief limitation of observation is that it does not indicate the _causes_ of the behavior being observed.

41. A number that indicates the degreee of relationship between two variables is a _correlation_. To say that two variables are related in this way _does not_ (does/does not) necessarily imply that one caused the other.

42. A correlation is _positive_ if the occurrence of one variable makes it more likely that the other will occur, and _negative_ if the occurrence of one makes it less likely that the other will occur.

43. The method that allows a scientist to determine cause and effect is the _experiment_. In this method, researchers manipulate a(n) _independent_ variable to determine its effect on a(n) _dependent_ variable.

44. In an experiment, the subjects who receive a particular treatment constitute the _experimental group_; the subjects who do not receive the treatment constitute the _control_ _group_.

45. To determine whether a difference between two groups occurred purely by coincidence, or

chance, researchers apply a mathematical test of statistical _analysis_ .

46. Experiments are sometimes criticized for studying behavior in a situation that is _hypothetical_ .

47. Another limitation is that participants in this research technique (except very young children) who know they are research subjects may attempt to _influence their answers toward what is being studied._ The most accurate and ethical way to conduct developmental research on children is the _natural_ _experiment_ .

48. In a(n) _survey_ , scientists collect information from a large group of people by personal interview, written questionnaire, or some other means.

49. A potential problem with this research method is that respondents may give answers they think the researcher _wants._ .

50. An intensive study of one individual is called a(n) _case_ _study_ . An advantage of this method is that it provides a rich _longitudinal_ description of development, rather than relying only on _quantitative_ data. Another important use is that it provides a good _starting_ _point_ for other research.

51. Research that involves the comparison of people of different ages is called a _cross_ - _sectional_ research design.

52. With cross-sectional research it is very difficult to ensure that the various groups differ only in their _studied characteristics_ In addition, every cross-sectional study will, to some degree, reflect _____ _____ .

53. Research that follows the same people over a relatively long period of time is called a _longitudinal_ research design.

State three drawbacks of this type of research design.

54. The research method that combines the longitudinal and cross-sectional methods is the _cross_ - _sequential_ research method.

Ethics and Science (pp. 29–31)

55. Developmental researchers work from a set of moral principles that constitute their _____ _____ _____ . Researchers who study humans must ensure that their subjects are not _____ and that their participation is _____ and _____ .

56. The most complex matter in research with humans is ensuring that the _____ of a proposed study outweigh its _____ . Complicating this issue is the fact that research with the greatest potential benefit often involves groups that are the most _____ .

57. A research study that is a compilation of data from many other sources is called a __ _____ - _____ .

Progress Test 1

Multiple-Choice Questions

Circle your answers to the following questions and check them against the answers on page 13. If your answer is incorrect, read the explanation for why it is incorrect and then consult the appropriate pages of the text (in parentheses following the correct answer).

1. The scientific study of human development is defined as the study of:
   a. how and why people change or remain the same over time.
   b. psychosocial influences on aging.
   c. individual differences in learning over the life span.
   d. all of the above.

2. The cognitive domain of development includes:
   a. perception.
   b. thinking.
   c. language.
   d. all of the above.

3. Changes in height, weight, and bone thickness are part of the _____ domain.
   a. cognitive
   b. biosocial
   c. psychosocial
   d. physical

4. Psychosocial development focuses primarily on personality, emotions, and:
   a. intellectual development.
   b. sexual maturation.
   c. relationships with others.
   d. perception.

5. The ecological model of developmental psychology focuses on the:
   a. biochemistry of the body systems.
   b. cognitive domain only.
   c. internal thinking processes.
   d. overall environment of development.

6. Researchers who take a life-span perspective on development focus on:
   a. the sources of continuity from the beginning of life to the end.
   b. the sources of discontinuity throughout life.
   c. the "nonlinear" character of human development.
   d. all of the above.

7. That fluctuations in body weight are affected by genes, appetite, caregiving, culture, and food supply indicates that body weight:
   a. is characterized by linear change.
   b. is a dynamic system.
   c. often has a butterfly effect.
   d. is characterized by all of the above.

8. A hypothesis is a:
   a. conclusion.
   b. prediction to be tested.
   c. statistical test.
   d. correlation.

9. A developmentalist who is interested in studying the influences of a person's immediate environment on his or her behavior is focusing on which system?
   a. mesosystem
   b. macrosystem
   c. microsystem
   d. exosystem

10. Socioeconomic status is determined by a combination of variables, including:
    a. age, education, and income.
    b. income, ethnicity, and occupation.
    c. income, education, and occupation.
    d. age, ethnicity, and occupation.

11. A disadvantage of experiments is that:
    a. people may behave differently in the artificial environment of the laboratory.
    b. control groups are too large to be accommodated in most laboratories.
    c. they are the method most vulnerable to bias on the part of the researcher.
    d. proponents of the ecological approach overuse them.

12. In an experiment testing the effects of group size on individual effort in a tug-of-war task, the number of people in each group is the:
    a. hypothesis.
    b. independent variable.
    c. dependent variable.
    d. level of significance.

13. Which research method would be most appropriate for investigating the relationship between parents' religious beliefs and their attitudes toward middle-school sex education?
    a. experimentation
    b. longitudinal research
    c. naturalistic observation
    d. the survey

14. In which type of community are children generally valued most highly as economic assets?
    a. marginal agricultural communities
    b. developed postindustrial nations
    c. low-income families in developed countries
    d. middle-income families in developing nations

15. Developmentalists who carefully observe the behavior of schoolchildren during recess are using a research method known as:
    a. the case study.
    b. cross-sectional research.
    c. scientific observation.
    d. cross-sequential research.

True or False Items

Write T (*true*) or F (*false*) on the line in front of each statement.

___T___ 1. Psychologists separate human development into three domains, or areas of study.

___F___ 2. (In Person) The case study of David clearly demonstrates that for some children only nature (or heredity) is important.

___F___ 3. Observation usually indicates a clear relationship between cause and effect.

___F___ 4. Each developmental domain influences development independently.

_____ 5. Cohort differences are an example of the impact of the social context on development.

___T___ 6. A study of history suggests that particularly well-defined periods of child and adult development have always existed.

___T___ 7. Socioeconomic status is rarely measured solely by family income.

_____ 8. The influences between and within Bronfenbrenner's systems are unidirectional and independent.

___T___ 9. People of different ethnic groups can all share one culture.

___T___ 10. Longitudinal research is particularly useful in studying development over a long age span.

_____ 11. Children who sleep with their parents are taught to depend on their parents for protection and typically become bold and independent as adults.

Progress Test 2

Progress Test 2 should be completed during a final chapter review. Answer the following questions after you thoroughly understand the correct answers for the Chapter Review and Progress Test 1.

Multiple-Choice Questions

1. An individual's context of development refers to his or her:
   a. microsystem and mesosystem.
   b. exosystem.
   c. macrosystem.
   d. microsystem, mesosystem, exosystem, and macrosystem.

2. The three domains of developmental psychology are:
   a. physical, cognitive, psychosocial.
   b. physical, biosocial, cognitive.
   c. biosocial, cognitive, psychosocial.
   d. biosocial, cognitive, emotional.

3. Which of the following is true of the three domains of development?
   a. They are important at every age.
   b. They interact in influencing development.
   c. They are more influential in some cultures than in others.
   d. a. and b. are true.

4. When developmentalist speak of the "butterfly effect," they are most directly referring to the idea that:
   a. a small event may have a powerful impact on development.
   b. development is fundamentally a nonlinear event.
   c. each of the three domains of development is a dynamic system.
   d. each of the three domains of development interacts with the other two.

5. According to the ecological model, the macrosystem would include:
   a. the peer group.
   b. the community.
   c. cultural values.
   d. the family.

6. When developmentalists speak of the "power of continuity," they are referring to the insight that:
   a. a change in one developmental system often affects many other things.
   b. a small change can become huge.
   c. a large change may have no perceptible effect.
   d. all of the above occur.

7. Professor Cohen predicts that because "baby boomers" grew up in an era that promoted independence and assertiveness, people in their 40s and 50s will respond differently to a political survey than will people in their 20s and 30s. The professor's prediction regarding political attitudes is an example of a(n):
   a. meta-analysis.
   b. hypothesis.
   c. independent variable.
   d. dependent variable.

8. A cohort is defined as a group of people:
   a. of similar national origin.
   b. who share a common language.
   c. born within a few years of each other.
   d. who share the same religion.

9. In a test of the effects of noise, groups of students performed a proofreading task in a noisy or a quiet room. To what group were students in the noisy room assigned?

   (a.) experimental   c. randomly assigned

   b. comparison   d. dependent

10. In differentiating ethnicity and culture, we note that:

   a. ethnicity is an exclusively biological phenomenon.

   b. an ethnic group is a group of people who were born within a few years of each other.

   (c.) people of many ethnic groups can share one culture, yet maintain their ethnic identities.

   d. racial identity is always an element of culture.

11. If developmentalists discovered that poor people are happier than wealthy people are, this would indicate that wealth and happiness are:

   a. unrelated.

   b. positively correlated.

   (c.) negatively correlated.

   d. causally related.

12. The plasticity of development refers to the fact that:

   a. development is not always linear.

   (b.) each human life must be understood as imbedded in many contexts.

   c. there are many reciprocal connections between childhood and adulthood.

   d. human characteristics can be molded into different forms and shapes.

13. In an experiment testing the effects of noise level on mood, mood is the:

   a. hypothesis.

   b. independent variable.

   (c.) dependent variable.

   d. scientific observation.

14. An important factor in the impact of living in poverty on development is:

   a. family size.

   (b.) the presence of supportive relationships within the family.

   c. the child's gender.

   d. the family's nationality.

15. Which of the following statements concerning ethnicity and culture is not true?

   a. Ethnicity is determined genetically.

   b. Race is a social construction.

   (c.) Racial identity is an element of ethnicity.

   d. Ethnic identity provides people with shared values and beliefs.

Matching Items

Match each definition or description with its corresponding term.

Terms

   _h_   1. independent variable

   _k_   2. dependent variable

   _f_   3. culture

   _j_   4. replicate

   _d_   5. biosocial domain

   _g_   6. cognitive domain

   _i_   7. psychosocial domain

   _b_   8. socioeconomic status

   _a_   9. cohort

   _e_   10. ethnic group

   _c_   11. cross-sectional research

   _l_   12. longitudinal research

Definitions or Descriptions

a. group of people born within a few years of each other

b. determined by a person's income, education, and occupation

c. research study comparing people of different ages at the same time

d. concerned with physical growth and development

e. collection of people who share certain attributes, such as national origin

f. shared values, attitudes, and customs maintained by people in a specific setting

g. concerned with thought processes

h. the variable manipulated in an experiment

i. concerned with emotions, personality traits, and relationships

j. to repeat a study and obtain the same findings

k. the variable measured in an experiment

l. research study retesting one group of people at several different times

Thinking Critically About Chapter 1

Answer these questions the day before an exam as a final check on your understanding of the chapter's terms and concepts.

1. Dr. Wong conducts research on the psychosocial domain of development. She is *most* likely to be interested in a child's:
   a. perceptual abilities.
   b. brain-wave patterns.
   c. emotions.
   d. use of language.

2. In order to study the effects of temperature on mood, Dr. Sanchez had students fill out questionnaires in very warm or very cool rooms. In this study, the independent variable consisted of:
   a. the number of subjects assigned to each group.
   b. the students' responses to the questionnaire.
   c. the room temperature.
   d. the subject matter of the questions.

3. Jahmal is writing a paper on the role of the social context in development. He would do well to consult the writings of:
   a. Piaget.   c. Bronfenbrenner.
   b. Freud.   d. Skinner.

4. Dr. Ramirez looks at human development in terms of the individual's supporting ecosystems. Evidently, Dr. Ramirez subscribes to the _____ model.
   a. psychosocial   c. biosocial
   b. ecological   d. cognitive

5. Esteban believes that high doses of caffeine slow a person's reaction time. In order to test his belief, he has five friends each drink three 8-ounce cups of coffee and then measures their reaction time on a learning task. What is wrong with Esteban's research strategy?
   a. No independent variable is specified.
   b. No dependent variable is specified.
   c. There is no comparison condition.
   d. There is no provision for replication of the findings.

6. When researchers find that the results of a study are statistically significant, this means that:
   a. they may have been caused purely by chance.
   b. it is unlikely they could be replicated.
   c. it is unlikely they could have occurred by chance.
   d. the sample population was representative of the general population.

7. When we say that the idea of old age as we know it is a "social construction," we are saying that:
   a. the idea is built on the shared perceptions of members of society.
   b. old age has only recently been regarded as a distinct period of life.
   c. old age cannot be defined.
   d. the idea is based on a well-tested hypothesis.

8. As compared with parents in developing countries, middle-class American parents emphasize cognitive and social stimulation in their child-rearing efforts because:
   a. they are more likely to regard children as an economic asset.
   b. their families are smaller.
   c. they do not have to be as concerned about infant mortality.
   d. of all the above reasons.

9. Karen's mother is puzzled by the numerous discrepancies between the developmental psychology textbook she used in 1976 and her daughter's contemporary text. Karen explains that the differences are the result of:
   a. the lack of regard by earlier researchers for the scientific method.
   b. changing social conditions and cohort effects.
   c. the widespread use of cross-sectional research today.
   d. the widespread use of longitudinal research today.

10. If height and body weight are positively correlated, which of the following is true?
    a. There is a cause-and-effect relationship between height and weight.
    b. Knowing a person's height, one can predict his or her weight.
    c. As height increases, weight decreases.
    d. All of the above are true.

11. An example of longitudinal research would be when an investigator compares the performance of:

    a. several different age groups on a memory test.
    b. the same group of people, at different ages, on a test of memory.
    c. an experimental group and a control group of subjects on a test of memory.
    d. several different age groups on a test of memory as each group is tested repeatedly over a period of years.

12. For her developmental psychology research project, Lakia decides she wants to focus primarily on qualitative data. You advise her to conduct:

    a. a survey.
    b. an experiment.
    c. a cross-sectional study.
    d. a case study.

13. Which of the following is *not* a major controversy in the study of development?

    a. nature vs. nurture
    b. difference vs. deficit
    c. continuity vs. discontinuity
    d. individual vs. society

14. Dr. Weston is comparing research findings for a group of 30-year-olds with findings for the same individuals at age 20, as well as with findings for groups who were 30 in 1990. Which research method is she using?

    a. longitudinal research
    b. cross-sectional research
    c. case study
    d. cross-sequential research

15. Professor Albertini wants to determine whether adopted children have personalities that are more similar to their biological parents or to their adoptive parents. In this instance, the professor is primarily concerned with the issue of:

    a. deficit–difference.
    b. continuity–discontinuity.
    c. nature–nurture.
    d. individual–society.

Key Terms

Writing Definitions

Using your own words, write a brief definition or explanation of each of the following terms on a separate piece of paper.

1. scientific study of human development
2. linear change
3. dynamic systems
4. butterfly effect
5. life-span perspective
6. multidirectional
7. multicontextual
8. multicultural
9. multidisciplinary
10. plastic
11. biosocial domain
12. cognitive domain
13. psychosocial domain
14. cohort
15. social construction
16. culture
17. socioeconomic status (SES)
18. poverty line
19. ethnic group
20. race
21. scientific method
22. hypothesis
23. replicate
24. variable
25. scientific observation
26. correlation
27. experiment
28. independent variable
29. dependent variable
30. experimental group
31. comparison group
32. survey
33. case study
34. cross-sectional research
35. longitudinal research
36. cross-sequential research
37. code of ethics

Cross-Check

After you have written the definitions of the key terms in this chapter, you should complete the crossword puzzle to ensure that you can
reverse the process—recognize the
term, given the definition.

ACROSS

2. Domain concerned with think-
    ing.
7. Group of people born at about
    the same time.
9. A subset of a population.
11. A measure of status.
13. Research design involving the
    study of different age groups
    over time.
14. Set of values shared by a
    group.

DOWN

1. Domain concerned with
    physical growth.
3. An _____ _____
    shares certain characteristics
    such as national origin.
4. The treatment-present group.
5. A testable prediction.
6. Research design in which peo-
    ple in different age groups are compared.
7. A measure of a statistical relationship.
8. Research design that follows a group of people over
    time.
10. All the members of a certain group.
12. An in-depth study of one person.

ANSWERS

CHAPTER REVIEW

1. the ways in which people change and remain the
    same as they grow older
2. linear change; least
3. dynamic systems
4. ecological; Urie Bronfenbrenner
5. microsystem
6. mesosystem
7. exosystem
8. macrosystem
9. chronosystem
10. interacting systems; butterfly effect; power of
    continuity
11. life-span perspective

    a. multidirectional
    b. multicontextual
    c. multicultural
    d. multidisciplinary
    e. plastic

12. plasticity
13. biosocial; cognitive; psychosocial
14. biosocial
15. cognitive
16. psychosocial
17. are; is
18. contexts (or systems or environments)
19. cohort; the same way
20. social construction; often change
21. childhood
22. culture
23. marginal agricultural; survival; interdependence;
    postindustrial; intellectual; independence, one or
    two; three to five

24. sleeping places; sleep alone; sleep with parents; kibbutz; Israel; work, meals, income, and child care
25. dedicated caregiver
26. socioeconomic status; SES
27. poverty level; child neglect; infant mortality; schools; violence
28. youngest
29. supportive relationships; nurturant; neighborhoods
30. ethnic group
31. race; social construction; ethnic group
32. rubella; biosocial; social; cognitive; psychosocial
33. a. formulate a research question;
    b. develop a hypothesis;
    c. test the hypothesis;
    d. draw conclusions;
    e. make the findings available.
34. hypothesis
35. replicate
36. variables; intrapersonal; interpersonal
37. genes; environment; continuity–discontinuity; difference–deficit
38. validity; accuracy; generalizability; usefulness
39. scientific observation; naturalistic; laboratory
40. cause
41. correlation; does not
42. positive; negative
43. experiment; independent; dependent
44. experimental group; comparison group
45. significance
46. artificial
47. produce the results they believe the experimenter is looking for; natural experiment
48. survey
49. expects (wants)
50. case study; qualitative; quantitative; starting point
51. cross-sectional
52. ages; cohort differences
53. longitudinal

Over time, some subjects may leave the study. Some people may change simply because they are part of the study. Longitudinal studies are time-consuming and expensive.

54. cross-sequential

55. code of ethics; harmed; confidential; voluntary
56. benefits; costs; vulnerable
57. meta-analysis

PROGRESS TEST 1

Multiple-Choice Questions

1. **a.** is the answer. (p. 1)

   b. & c. The study of development is concerned with a broader range of phenomena, including biosocial aspects of development, than these answers specify.

2. **d.** is the answer. (p. 6)
3. **b.** is the answer. (p. 6)

   a. This domain is concerned with thought processes.

   c. This domain is concerned with emotions, personality, and interpersonal relationships.

   d. This is not a domain of development.

4. **c.** is the answer. (p. 6)

   a. This falls within the cognitive and biosocial domains.

   b. This falls within the biosocial domain.

   d. This falls within the cognitive domain.

5. **d.** is the answer. This approach sees development as occurring within five interacting levels, or environments. (p. 3)

6. **d.** is the answer. (p. 5)
7. **b.** is the answer. (p. 2)

   a. Body weight does not always increase in a linear fashion.

   c. Although it is possible that a small change in a person's body weight could set off a series of changes that culminate in a major event, the question is concerned with the interconnectedness of body weight, nutrition, and other dynamic developmental systems.

8. **b.** is the answer. (p. 20)
9. **c.** is the answer. (p. 3)

   a. This refers to systems that link one microsystem to another.

   b. This refers to cultural values, political philosophies, economic patterns, and social conditions.

   d. This includes the community structures that affect the functioning of smaller systems.

10. **c.** is the answer. (p. 14)
11. **a.** is the answer. (pp. 23–24)

12. **b.** is the answer. (p. 23)

   a. A possible hypothesis for this experiment would be that the larger the group, the less hard a given individual will pull.

   c. The dependent variable is the measure of individual effort.

   d. Significance level refers to the numerical value specifying the possibility that the results of an experiment could have occurred by chance.

13. **d.** is the answer. (p. 25)

   a. Experimentation is appropriate when one is seeking to uncover cause-and-effect relationships; in this example the researcher is only interested in determining whether the parents' beliefs *predict* their attitudes.

   b. Longitudinal research would be appropriate if the researcher sought to examine the development of these attitudes over a long period of time.

   c. Mere observation would not allow the researcher to determine the attitudes of the subjects.

14. **a.** is the answer. (pp. 10–11)

15. **c.** is the answer. (p. 21)

   a. In this method, *one* subject is studied over a period of time.

   b. & d. In these research methods, two or more *groups* of subjects are studied and compared.

True or False Items

1. T (p. 6)
2. F   The case study of David shows that both nature and nurture are important in affecting outcome. (pp. 18–19)
3. F   A disadvantage of observation is that the variables are numerous and uncontrolled, and therefore cause-and-effect relationships are difficult to pinpoint. (p. 21)
4. F   Each domain is affected by the other two. (pp. 6–7)
5. T (p. 8)
6. F   Our ideas about the stages of childhood and adulthood are historical creations that have varied over the centuries. (pp. 8–9)
7. F   In government statistics it often is. (p. 14)
8. F   Quite the reverse is true. (pp. 2–3)
9. T (p. 16)
10. T (p. 28)
11. F   This is true of children who sleep alone. (pp. 11–12)

PROGRESS TEST 2

Multiple-Choice Questions

1. **d.** is the answer. (p. 3)
2. **c.** is the answer. (p. 6)
3. **d.** is the answer. (pp. 6-7)

   c. Research has not revealed cultural variations in the overall developmental influence of the three domains.

4. **a.** is the answer. (p. 2)

   b., c., & d. Although these are true, they are not the butterfly effect.

5. **c.** is the answer. (p. 3)

   a. & d. These are part of the microsystem.

   b. This is part of the exosystem.

6. **c.** is the answer. (p. 3)

   a. This is the insight of interacting systems.

   b. This insight is the butterfly effect.

7. **b.** is the answer. (p. 20)

   a. In a meta-analysis, the results of a number of separate research studies are combined.

   c. & d. Variables are treatments (independent) or behaviors (dependent) in *experiments*, which this situation clearly is not.

8. **c.** is the answer. (p. 8)

   a., b., & d. These are attributes of an ethnic group.

9. **a.** is the answer. The experimental group is the one in which the variable or treatment—in this case, nose—is present. (p. 23)

   b. Students in the quiet room would be in the comparison condition.

   c. Presumably, all students in both groups were randomly assigned to their groups.

   d. The word *dependent* refers to a kind of variable in experiments; groups are either experimental or control.

10. **c.** is the answer. (p. 16)

   a. & d. Ethnicity refers to shared attributes, such as ancestry, national origin, religion, and language.

   b. This describes a cohort.

11. **c.** is the answer. (p. 23)

   a. Wealth and happiness clearly *are* related.

   b. This answer would be correct if wealthy people were found to be happier than poor people.

   d. Correlation does not imply causation.

12. d. is the answer. (p. 5)

13. c. is the answer. (p. 23)

a. Hypotheses make *specific*, testable predictions.

b. Noise level is the independent variable.

d. Scientific observation is a research method in which subjects are watched, while their behavior is recorded unobtrusively.

14. b. is the answer. (p. 14)

a., c., & d. The text does not suggest that these variables affect poverty's influence on development.

15. a. is the answer. Ethnic identity is a product of the social environment and the individual's consciousness. (p. 16)

Matching Items

1. h (p. 23)	**5.** d (p. 6)	**9.** a (p. 8)
2. k (p. 23)	**6.** g (p. 6)	**10.** e (p. 16)
3. f (p. 10)	**7.** i (p. 6)	**11.** c (p. 26)
4. j (p. 20)	**8.** b (p. 14)	**12.** l (p. 28)

THINKING CRITICALLY ABOUT CHAPTER 1

1. c. is the answer. (p. 6)

a. & d. These pertain to the cognitive domain.

b. This pertains to the biosocial domain.

2. c. is the answer. Room temperature is the variable being manipulated. (p. 23)

a. & d. These answers are incorrect because they involve aspects of the experiment other than the variables.

b. This answer is the dependent, not the independent, variable.

3. c. is the answer. (p. 2)

a. Piaget is notable in the area of cognitive development.

b. Freud was a pioneer of psychoanalysis.

b. Skinner is notable in the history of learning theory.

4. b. is the answer. (pp. 2–3)

a., c., & d. These are the three domains of development.

5. c. is the answer. In order to determine the effects of caffeine on reaction time, Esteban needs to measure reaction time in a comparison group that does not receive caffeine. (p. 23)

a. Caffeine is the independent variable.

b. Reaction time is the dependent variable.

d. Whether or not Esteban's experiment can be replicated is determined by the precision with

which he reports his procedures, which is not an aspect of research strategy.

6. c. is the answer. (p. 23)

7. a. is the answer. (p. 9)

8. c. is the answer. (p. 11)

9. b. is the answer. (pp. 8–9)

a. Earlier developmentalists had no less regard for the scientific method.

c. & d. Both cross-sectional and longitudinal research were widely used in the 1970s.

10. b. is the answer. (p. 23)

a. Correlation does not imply causation.

c. If height and body weight are positively correlated, as one increases so does the other.

11. b. is the answer. (p. 28)

a. This is an example of cross-sectional research.

c. This is an example of an experiment.

d. This type of study is not described in the text.

12. d. is the answer. (p. 25)

a., b., & c. These research methods generally yield *quantitative*, rather than qualitative, data.

13. d. is the answer. On this issue, developmentalists are in agreement: individuals are inextricably involved with their social groups. (p. 21)

14. d. is the answer. (p. 29)

a. & c. In these research methods only one group of subjects is studied.

b. Dr. Weston's design includes comparison of groups of people of different ages *over time*.

15. c. is the answer. (p. 21)

a. This issue concerns whether individual differences are considered problems that need correcting or causes for celebration.

b. This issue concerns whether development builds gradually or occurs through sudden transformations.

d. This issue concerns whether individual people can be studied apart from the social groups to which they belong.

KEY TERMS

Writing Definitions

1. The **scientific study of human development** is the science that seeks to understand how and why people change, and how and why they remain the same, as they grow older. (p. 1)

2. **Linear change** is a process in which developmental change occurs in a gradual, regular, predictable sequence—in other words, in a "straight line." (p. 2)

3. **Dynamic systems** are systems that change continually, and in which changes in one area (or system) influences other systems as well. (p. 2)

4. The **butterfly effect** is the insight that even small events (such as the breeze created by the flap of a butterfly's wings) may set off a series of changes that culminate in a major event. (p. 2)

5. The **life-span perspective** on human development recognizes that human growth is lifelong and characterized by both continuity (as in personality) and discontinuity (as in the number of brain cells). (p. 4)

6. To say that development is **multidirectional** is to say that it progresses in a nonlinear sequence of predictable and unexpected changes. (p. 5)

7. To say that development is **multicontextual** means that it takes place within multiple contexts—cultural, historical, and socioeconomic. (p. 5)

8. The **multicultural** nature of human development indicates that it takes place within many cultural settings worldwide and reflects a variety of values and traditions. (p. 5)

9. The **multidisciplinary** nature of development means that many different academic fields contribute to our understanding of change. (p. 5)

10. **Plastic** is the capability of any human characteristics to be molded or reshaped by time and circumstances. (p. 5)

11. The **biosocial domain** is concerned with brain and body, as well as changes in our biological selves and in the social influences that guide our physical growth. (p. 6)

12. The **cognitive domain** is concerned with thought processes, perceptual abilities, and language mastery, and the educational institutions that encourage these aspects of development. (p. 6)

13. The **psychosocial domain** is concerned with emotions, personality, and interpersonal relationships with family, friends, and the wider community. (p. 6)

14. A **cohort** is a group of people who, because they were born within a few years of each other, experience many of the same historical changes. (p. 8)

15. A **social construction** is an idea that is built more on the shared perceptions of members of a society than on objective reality. (p. 9)

16. **Culture** refers to the set of shared values, assumptions, customs, and physical objects that a group of people have developed over the years as a design for living to structure their life together. (p. 10)

17. An individual's **socioeconomic status (SES)** is determined by his or her income, education, place of residence, and occupation. (p. 14)

18. The **poverty line** is the minimum dollar amount needed to pay for the basic necessities of living, as determined by the federal government. (p. 14)

19. An **ethnic group** is a collection of people who share certain attributes, such as national origin, religion, ancestry, and/or language and who, as a result, tend to identify with each other and have similar daily encounters with the social world. (p. 16)

20. **Race** is a misleading social construction that was originally based on biological differences between people whose ancestors came from different regions of the world. (p. 16)

21. The **scientific method** is a general procedural model that helps researchers remain objective as they study behavior. The five basic steps of the scientific method are (1) formulate a research question; (2) develop a hypothesis; (3) test the hypothesis; (4) draw conclusions; and (5) make the findings available. (p. 20)

22. In the scientific method, a **hypothesis** is a specific, testable prediction. (p. 20)

23. To use **replication** is to repeat a test of a research hypothesis and try to obtain the same results using a different but related set of subjects or procedures in order to test its validity. (p. 20)

24. A **variable** is any quality that may differ during a scientific investigation. (p. 20)

25. **Scientific observation** is the unobtrusive watching and recording of subjects' behavior in a situation that is being studied, either in the laboratory or in a natural setting. (p. 21)

26. **Correlation** is a number that indicates the degree of relationship between two variables such that one is likely (or unlikely) to occur when the other occurs or one is likely to increase (or decrease) when the other increases (or decreases). (p. 22)

27. The **experiment** is the research method designed to untangle cause from effect by manipulating variable to see the effect on another variable. (p. 23)

28. The **independent variable** is the variable that is manipulated in an experiment. (p. 23)

29. The **dependent variable** is the variable that is being studied in an experiment. (p. 23)

    Example: In the study of the effects of a new drug on memory, the subjects' memory is the dependent variable.

30. The **experimental group** of an experiment is one in which subjects are exposed to the independent variable being studied. (p. 23)

31. The **comparison group** of an experiment is one in which the treatment of interest, or independent variable, is withheld so that comparison to the experimental group can be made. (p. 23)

32. The **survey** is the research method in which information is collected from a large number of people, either through written questionnaires or through interviews. (p. 25)

33. The **case study** is the research method involving the intensive study of one person. (p. 25)

34. In **cross-sectional research**, groups of people who differ in age but share other important characteristics are compared with regard to the variable under investigation. (p. 26)

35. In **longitudinal research**, the same group of individuals is studied over a period of time to measure both change and stability as they age. (p. 28)

36. **Cross-sequential research** follows a group of people of different ages over time, thus combining the strengths of the cross-sectional and longitudinal methods. (p. 29)

37. Developmental psychologists and other scientists work from a **code of ethics**, which is a set of moral principles that guide their research. (p. 29)

Cross-Check

ACROSS

2. cognitive
7. cohort
9. sample
11. SES
13. cross-sequential
14. culture

DOWN

1. biosocial
3. ethnic group
4. experimental
5. hypothesis
6. cross-sectional
7. correlation
8. longitudinal
10. population
12. case study

Chapter Two

Theories of Development

Chapter Overview

Developmental theories are systematic statements of principles and generalizations that explain behavior and development and provide a framework for future research. Many such theories have influenced our understanding of human development. This chapter describes and evaluates five broad theories—psychoanalytic, behaviorism, cognitive, sociocultural, and epigenetic systems—that will be used throughout the book to present information and to provide a framework for interpreting events and issues in human development. Each of the theories has developed a unique vocabulary with which to describe and explain events as well as to organize ideas into a cohesive system of thought.

Three of the theories presented—psychoanalytic theory, behaviorism, and cognitive theory—are "grand theories" that are comprehensive in scope but inadequate in the face of recent research findings. Two of the theories—sociocultural and epigenetic systems—are considered "emergent theories" because they may become the comprehensive theories of the future. Rather than adopt any one theory exclusively, most developmentalists take an eclectic perspective and use many or all of the theories.

As you study this part of the chapter, consider what each of the theories has to say about your own development, as well as that of friends and relatives in other age groups. It is also a good idea to keep the following questions in mind as you study each theory: Which of the theory's principles are generally accepted by contemporary developmentalists? How has the theory been criticized? In what ways does this theory agree with the other theories? In what ways does it disagree?

NOTE: Answer guidelines for all Chapter 2 questions begin on page 31.

Guided Study

The text chapter should be studied one section at a time. Before you read, preview each section by skimming it, noting headings and boldface items. Then read the appropriate section objectives from the following outline. Keep these objectives in mind and, as you read the chapter section, search for the information that will enable you to meet each objective. Once you have finished a section, write out answers for its objectives.

What Theories Do (pp. 35–36)

1. Define developmental theory, and describe how developmental theories help explain human behavior and development. In your answer, be sure to differentiate grand theories, minitheories, and emergent theories. Developmental Theory is a systematic statement of principles + generalizations that provides a coherent framework for studying and explaining development.
Grand theories are comprehensive theories that have traditionally inspired + directed thinking about development. Minitheories - some specific area of development but are less general and comprehensive than grand ones. Emergent theories being together information from many minitheories but have not yet cohered to theories that are grand and

Grand Theories (pp. 36–48) systematic.

2. Discuss the major focus of psychoanalytic theories, and describe the conflicts that occur during Freud's stages of psychosexual development.
psychoanalytic theory - interprets human development in terms of intrinsic drives and motives many of which are unconscious hidden from awareness.
• Oral stage-mouth tongue focus of pleasure
• Anal stage- Anus focus of pleasure
• phallic stage phallus/penis most important body part.
• Latency- Nothing important happens.
• Genital period- genitals are pleasure point.

Behavioralism-focuses on the sequences and processes by which behavior is learned
Cognitive Theory focuses on structured development of thinking

3. Describe the crises of Erikson's theory of psychosocial development, and contrast them with Freud's stages.

Trust vs. Mistrust - Babies learn to trust that others will care for them, or lack confidence in the care of others. Autonomy vs. shame/doubt children learn to either be self-sufficient in many activities including toileting, feeding, walking or doubt their abilities. Initiative vs. guilt child want undertake many adult like activities sometimes overstepping the limits set by parents and feeling guilty. Industry vs. Inferiority children busily learn to be competent + productive in mastering new skills or feel inferior + unable to do anything well. Identity vs. Role diffusion establish who they are vs. role confusion Intimacy vs. Isolation young adults seek companionship and love w/others or become isolated. Generativity vs. stagnation contribute to next generation or remain stagnant.

4. Discuss the major focus of behaviorism, and explain the basic principles of classical and operant conditioning.

Focuses on the ways we learn specific behaviors ways that can be described and analyzed + predicted w/ far more scientific accuracy. classical conditioning is the process by which a neutral stimulus becomes assoc. with a meaningful stimulus so that the organism responds to the former stimulus as it were the latter. Operant conditioning is the process by which a response is gradually learned via reinforcement or punishment.

5. (Thinking Like a Scientist) Discuss Harlow's research with infant monkeys, and explain how it contributed to revisions of psychoanalytic theories and behaviorism.

Harlow decided to study attachment (mother-child bond) using monkeys. He set up a experiment baby cubs went to a wire mother on others wire covered in cloth. He found that the cloth mother was used for more than just nourishment but for comfort, and solace. This finding disproved the behaviorism and psychoanalytic theories b/c they contend that mother's satisfy the basic hunger needs and sucking needs but it is also about touching, comforting, and holding is a huge aspect of mothering.

6. Discuss social learning theory as an application of behaviorism.

The social learning theory is emphasizes that many human behaviors are learned thru observation and imitation of others. An integral part of social learning is modeling in which people observe and copy the behavior of others.
   It is an extension of the school of behaviorism because the question was thought provoking and studies and results followed.

7. Identify the primary focus of cognitive theory, and briefly describe Piaget's stages of cognitive development.

Focuses on structure & development of thinking which shapes people's attitudes and behaviors. Sensorimotor - senses and motor skill to understand the world. preoperational - uses symbolic thinking to understand the world. Understand from own perspective. concrete operational understands and applies logical explanations to help interpret things objectively. Formal operational abstract and hypothetical situations.

8. Discuss the process that, according to Piaget, guides cognitive development.

Cognitive equilibrium

equilibrium
|
learn something new
|
disequilibrium
|
use adaptation and assimilation
|
New equilibrium

9. Identify the major criticisms and contributions of each of the grand theories of development.

The theories seem much less comprehen. and inclusive as they once did. And this is apparent in the controversy of nature vs. nurture, difference deficient & continuity vs. discontinuity.

Emergent Theories (pp. 48–55)

10. Discuss the basic ideas of Vygotsky and the sociocultural theory of development.

Vygotsky believed in guided participation and an apprenticeship in thinking (A novice is taught by an experienced person to teach you.)

This ties into the sociocultural theory b/c it believes in a dynamic interaction between each person and the surrounding culture including social forces near & distant like apprenticeship in thinking.

11. Discuss the basic ideas of epigenetic systems theory. *emphasizes the interactions of genes and the environment, it is dynamic and reciprocal.*
- *Stresses powerful instincts and abilities that arise from a biological heritage.*
- *factors that effect expression of genes*
  - *Some are stress factors (injury temp, and crowding*
  - *Others are facilitating factors nourishing food, loving care + freedom to play.*

12. (In Person) Discuss the ethology of infant social instincts and adult caregiving impulses. *Study of animal behavior. Because so many women died in childbirth early in the century babies have the disposition to take care from anyone, that soon changes in toddlers who have formed attachments to certain people and are afraid of new people. Adults in the same way are genetically nuturing because logically no parent would put up with a baby's needs.*

Comparisons and Controversies (pp. 55–62)

13. Summarize the contributions and criticisms of the major developmental theories, and compare the position of the theories regarding three controversies of development. *Psychoanalytic Theory made us aware of early childhood experiences + the impact of hidden drama on everyday life* *Behaviorism—immediate effect of environment on behavior. Cognitive theory—Intellectual processes effect actions Sociocultural theory—development is embedded in a rich and multifaceted culture. Epigenetic systems theory inherited forces effect each person in a human context.*

14. Explain the nature–nurture controversy as it pertains to sexual orientation, and describe the eclectic perspective of contemporary developmentalists. *Nuture over Nature but also see that there is a genetic component.*

Chapter Review

When you have finished reading the chapter, work through the material that follows to review it. Complete the sentences and answer the questions. As you proceed, evaluate your performance for each section by consulting the answers on page 31. Do not continue with the next section until you understand each answer. If you need to, review or reread the appropriate section in the textbook before continuing.

What Theories Do (pp. 35–36)

1. A systematic set of principles and generalizations that explains behavior and development is called a(n) _developmental_ _Theory_.

2. Developmental theories provide a broad and _coherent_ view of the influences on development; they form the basis for educated guesses, or _hypotheses_, about behavior; and they provide a framework for future research.

3. Developmental theories fall into three categories: _grand_ theories, which traditionally offer a comprehensive view of development; _minitheories_ theories, which explain a specific area of development; and _emergent_ theories, which may be the comprehensive theories of the future.

Grand Theories (pp. 36–48)

4. Psychoanalytic theories interpret human development in terms of intrinsic _drives_ and _motives_, many of which are _unconscious_ (conscious/unconscious) and _hidden from awareness_.

5. According to Freud's _psychoanalytic_ theory, children experience sexual pleasures and desires during the first six years as they pass through three _psychosexual_ _stages_. From infancy to early childhood to the preschool years, these stages are the _Oral_ stage, the _Anal stage_ stage, and the _phallic stage_ stage. One of Freud's most influential ideas was that each stage includes its own potential _conflicts_ between child and parent. Another was his conception of personality as consisting of three systems: the _id_, which represents _unconscious_ psychic energy devoted to satisfying our basic urges; the _super ego_, which is a strict moral judge; and the _ego_ , which tries to make _Rational_ choices as it balances the demands of the other two systems.

Specify the focus of sexual pleasure and the major developmental need associated with each of Freud's stages.

oral _The mouth tongue and gums are the focus of the pleasurable sensations in the baby's body_

anal _Anus — pleasure point in baby's body + toilet training most important activity._

phallic _phallus/penis most important pleasure from genital stimulation_

genital _genital pleasure , young person seeks sexual stimulation._

6. Erik Erikson's theory of development, which focuses on social and cultural influences, is called a(n) _psychosocial_ theory. In this theory, there are _8_ (number) developmental stages, each characterized by a particular developmental _crises_ related to the person's relationship to the social environment. Unlike Freud, Erikson proposed stages of development that _span_ (span/do not span) a person's lifetime.

Complete the following chart regarding Erikson's stages of psychosocial development.

Age Period	Stage
Birth to 1 yr.	trust vs. _MISTRUST_
1–3 yrs.	autonomy vs. _shame/doubt_
3–6 yrs.	initiative vs. _guilt_
7–11 yrs.	_Industry_ vs. inferiority
Adolescence	identity vs. _Role Diffusion_
Young adulthood	_Intimacy_ vs. isolation
Middle adulthood	_generativity_ vs. stagnation
Older adulthood	_Integrity_ vs. despair

7. A major theory in American psychology, which directly opposed psychoanalytic theory, was _Behavioralism_ . This theory, which emerged early in the twentieth century under the influence of _Watson_ , is also called _learning_ theory because of its emphasis on how we learn specific behaviors.

8. Behaviorists have formulated laws of behavior that are believed to apply _at all ages_ (only at certain ages/at all ages). The learning process, which is called _conditioning_ , takes two forms: _classical_ _condition_ and _operant_ _conditioning_ .

9. In classical conditioning, which was discovered by the Russian scientist _Pavlov_ and is also called _respondent_ conditioning, a person or an animal learns to associate a(n) _neutral_ stimulus with a meaningful one.

10. According to _Skinner_ , the learning of more complex responses is the result of _operant_ conditioning, in which a person learns that a particular behavior produces a particular _Response_ , such as a reward. This type of learning is also called _instrumental_ conditioning.

11. The process of repeating a consequence to make it more likely that the behavior in question will recur is called _reinforcement_. The consequence that increases the likelihood that a behavior will be repeated is called the _positive reinforcement_.

12. (Thinking Like a Scientist) The behavior of infant monkeys separated from their mothers led researcher _Harry Harlow_ to investigate the origins of _attachment_ in infant monkeys. These studies, which demonstrated that infant monkeys clung more often to "surrogate" mothers that provided _comfort_ (food/contact comfort), disproved _psychoanalytic_ theory's idea that infants seek to satisfy oral needs and _behaviorism_ view that reinforcement directs behavior.

13. The application of behaviorism that emphasizes the ways that people learn new behaviors by observing others is called _social learning theory_ . The process whereby a child

patterns his or her behavior after a parent or teacher, for example, is called _modeling_ .

14. This process is most likely to occur when an observer is _uncertain_ and when the model is _admirable, powerful, and nurturing_ This type of learning is also affected by the individual's _____ . Self-confidence, developed from reinforcement by parents and teachers, leads to _self efficacy_ , which motivates people to change themselves and their environments.

15. The structure and development of the individual's thought processes and the way those thought processes affect the person's understanding of the world are the focus of _Cognitive_ theory. A major pioneer of this theory is _Piaget_ .

16. In Piaget's first stage of development, the _sensorimotor_ stage, children experience the world through their senses and motor abilities. This stage occurs between birth and age _2 yrs._ .

17. According to Piaget, during the preschool years (up to age _6_), children are in the _preoperational_ stage. A hallmark of this stage is that children begin to think _symbolically_ . Another hallmark is that sometimes the child's thinking is _egocentric_ , or focused on seeing the world solely from his or her own perspective.

18. Piaget believed that children begin to think logically in a consistent way at about _7_ years of age. At this time, they enter the _concrete operational_ stage.

19. In Piaget's final stage, the _formal operational_ stage, reasoning expands from the purely concrete to encompass _abstract and hypothetical_ thinking. Piaget believed most children enter this stage by age _12 yrs_ .

20. According to Piaget, cognitive development is guided by the need to maintain a state of mental balance, called _cognitive equilibrium_ .

21. When new experiences challenge existing understanding, creating a kind of imbalance, the individual experiences _cognitive disequilibrium_ , which eventually leads to mental growth.

22. According to Piaget, people adapt to new experiences either by reinterpreting them to fit into, or _adapt it_ with, old ideas. Some new experiences force people to revamp old ideas so that they can _accommodate_ new experiences.

23. The idea that every person passes through fixed stages, as proposed by _Freud_ , _Erikson_ , and _Piaget_ , cannot account for the diversity of human development worldwide. Similarly, the idea that every person can be conditioned in the same way, as proposed by _Skinner_ , _Watson_ , and _Pavlov_ , has also been refuted.

24. Today, the grand theories seem much _less_ (more/less) comprehensive than they once did. Psychoanalytic theory's focus on _human emotion_ behaviorism's focus on _actions_ , and cognitive theory's focus on _thoughts_ yield conflicting points of view on what should be studied and how.

25. The grand theories seem to ignore major _cultural_ differences and underestimate the power of _genetics_ .

Emergent Theories (pp. 48–55)

26. In contrast to the grand theories, the two emerging theories draw from the findings of _many_ (one/many) discipline(s).

27. Sociocultural theory sees human development as the result of _dynamic interaction_ _____ between developing persons and their surrounding _culture_ .

28. A major pioneer of this perspective was
Lev Vygotsky, who was primarily interested in the development of
cognitive competencies.

29. Vygotsky believed that these competencies result
from the interaction between _novices_
and more mature members of the society, acting
as _tutors_, in a process that has been
called an _apprenticeship in_
thinking.

30. In Vygotsky's view, the best way to accomplish
the goals of apprenticeship is through
guided _participation_, in
which the tutor engages the learner in joint activities.

31. According to Vygotsky, a mentor draws a child
into the _____
zone   of   proximal
development, which is defined as the
range of skills that the child can exercise with
help but cannot perform independently.

Cite a contribution and a criticism of sociocultural
theory. _Criticism— overlooked_
developmental processes that are
not primarily social.
Contribution

32. The newest of the emergent theories,
epigenetic   theory theory,
emphasizes the interaction between
genetics and the _environment_.

33. In using the word _genetic_, this theory emphasizes
that we have powerful _instincts_
and abilities that arise from our
biological heritage.

34. The prefix "epi" refers to the various
before, on, after factors that affect the expression of _genetic_
instructions. These include _stress_
factors such as injury, temperature, and crowding. Others are _facilitating_ factors such
as nourishing food and freedom to play.

35. Some epigenetic factors are the result of the evolutionary process called _selective_
adaptation, in which, over generations,
genes for useful traits that promote survival of
the species become more prevalent.

36. "Everything that seems to be genetic is actually
epigenetic." This statement highlights the fact
that _all_ (some/most/all) genetic
instructions are affected by the environment.

37. The "systems" aspect of this theory points out
that changes in one part of the individual's system _cause corresponding changes_
& adjustments in every other part.

38. (In Person) The study of animal behavior as it is
related to the evolution and survival of a species
is called _ethnology_. Newborn animals
and human infants are genetically programmed
for _social   contact_ as a
means of survival. Similarly, adult animals and
humans are genetically programmed for
infant   caregiving.

Comparisons and Controversies (pp. 55–62)

39. Which major theory of development emphasizes:

a. the importance of culture in fostering development? _sociocultural_

b. the ways in which thought processes affect
actions? _cognitive_

c. environmental influences? _behavioralism_

d. the impact of "hidden dramas" on development? _psychoanalytic_
theory

e. the interaction of genes and environment? _____
epigenetic systems

40. Which major theory of development has been criticized for:

    a. being too mechanistic?

    behavioralism

    b. undervaluing genetic differences?

    cognitive

    c. being too subjective?

    psychoanalytic

    d. neglecting society?

    epigenetic systems

    e. neglecting individuals?

    sociocultural

41. Regarding the controversy over whether development is continous or discontinuous, Freud, Erikson, and Piaget can be classified as stage theorists. Behaviorists do not (do/do not) subscribe to the idea of stages. Sociocultural theory proposes that cultures generally do (do/do not) define ideal settings of the social clock. Epigenetic systems theory includes intervals, or stages, but they are unlike those described in other theories.

42. Regarding the controversy over whether differences between children are normal differences or problematic decificit, none of the developmental theories suggest that there is only one correct way to raise a child.

43. Identify one example of a "deficit" from the perspective of each of the developmental theories.

    a. Psychoanalytic theory

    mother is unresponsive

    b. Behaviorism

    too much agression in school

    c. Cognitive theory

    slow to develop,

    d. Sociocultural theory

    Raised standard in 1 culture won't survive in another one.

    e. Epigenetic systems theory

    environmental condition that does not provide proper nurtuance.

44. The debate over the relative influence of heredity and environment in shaping personal traits and characteristics is called the nature – nurture controversy. Traits inherited at the moment of conception give evidence of the influence of genes; those that emerge in response to learning and environmental influences give evidence of the effect of nurture.

45. Developmentalists agree that, at every point, the interaction between nature and nurture is the crucial influence on any particular aspect of development.

46. All the grand theories tended to explain homosexuality in terms of nuture (nature/nurture). However, new research suggests that it is at least partly due to nature (nature/nurture).

47. Because no one theory can encompass all of human behavior, most developmentalists have a(n) eclectic perspective, which capitalizes on the strengths of all the theories.

Progress Test 1

Multiple-Choice Questions

Circle your answers to the following questions and check them with the answers on page 33. If your answer is incorrect, read the explanation for why it is incorrect and then consult the appropriate pages of the text (in parentheses following the correct answer).

1. The purpose of a developmental theory is to:
   a. provide a broad and coherent view of the complex influences on human development.
   b. offer guidance for practical issues encountered by parents, teachers, and therapists.
   c. generate testable hypotheses about development.
   d. do all of the above.

2. Which developmental theory emphasizes the influence of unconscious drives and motives on behavior?
   a. psychoanalytic   c. cognitive
   b. behaviorism   d. sociocultural

3. Which of the following is the correct order of the psychosexual stages proposed by Freud?
   a. oral stage; anal stage; phallic stage; latency; genital stage
   b. anal stage; oral stage; phallic stage; latency; genital stage
   c. oral stage; anal stage; genital stage; latency; phallic stage
   d. anal stage; oral stage; genital stage; latency; phallic stage

4. Erikson's psychosocial theory of human development describes:
   a. eight crises all people are thought to face.
   b. four psychosocial stages and a latency period.
   c. the same number of stages as Freud's, but with different names.
   d. a stage theory that is not psychoanalytic.

5. Which of the following theories does *not* belong with the others?
   a. psychoanalytic
   b. behaviorism
   c. sociocultural
   d. cognitive

6. An American psychologist who explained complex human behaviors in terms of operant conditioning was:
   a. Lev Vygotsky.
   b. Ivan Pavlov.
   c. B. F. Skinner.
   d. Jean Piaget.

7. Pavlov's dogs learned to salivate at the sound of a bell because they associated the bell with food. Pavlov's experiment with dogs was an early demonstration of:
   a. classical conditioning.
   b. operant conditioning.
   c. positive reinforcement.
   d. social learning.

8. The nature–nurture controversy considers the degree to which traits, characteristics, and behaviors are the result of:
   a. early or lifelong learning.
   b. genes or heredity.
   c. heredity or experience.
   d. different historical concepts of childhood.

9. Modeling, an integral part of social learning theory, is so called because it:
   a. follows the scientific model of learning.
   b. molds character.
   c. follows the immediate reinforcement model developed by Bandura.
   d. involves people's patterning their behavior after that of others.

10. Which developmental theory suggests that each person is born with genetic possibilities that must be nurtured in order to grow?
    a. sociocultural
    b. cognitive
    c. behaviorism
    d. epigenetic systems

11. Vygotsky's theory has been criticized for neglecting:
    a. the role of genes in guiding development.
    b. developmental processes that are not primarily biological.
    c. the importance of language in development.
    d. social factors in development.

12. Which is the correct sequence of stages in Piaget's theory of cognitive development?
    a. sensorimotor, preoperational, concrete operational, formal operational
    b. sensorimotor, preoperational, formal operational, concrete operational
    c. preoperational, sensorimotor, concrete operational, formal operational
    d. preoperational, sensorimotor, formal operational, concrete operational

13. When an individual's existing understanding no longer fits his or her present experiences, the result is called:
    a. a psychosocial crisis.
    b. equilibrium.
    c. disequilibrium.
    d. negative reinforcement.

14. In explaining the origins of homosexuality, the grand theories have traditionally emphasized:
    a. nature over nurture.
    b. nurture over nature.
    c. a warped mother–son or father–daughter relationship.
    d. the individual's voluntary choice.

15. The zone of proximal development refers to:
    a. a stage during which the child exhibits preoperational thinking.
    b. the influence of a pleasurable stimulus on behavior.
    c. the range of skills a child can exercise with assistance but cannot perform independently.
    d. the tendency of a child to model an admired adult's behavior.

True or False Items

Write T (*true*) or F (*false*) on the line in front of each statement.

_____ 1. Behaviorists study what people actually do, not what they might be thinking.

_____ 2. Erikson's eight developmental stages are centered not on a body part but on each person's relationship to the social environment.

_____ 3. Most developmentalists agree that the nature–nurture controversy has been laid to rest.

_____ 4. Few developmental theorists today believe that humans have instincts or abilities that arise from our species' biological heritage.

_____ 5. Of the major developmental theories, cognitive theory gives the most emphasis to the interaction of genes and experience in shaping development.

_____ 6. New research suggests that homosexuality is at least partly genetic.

_____ 7. According to Piaget, a state of cognitive equilibrium must be attained before cognitive growth can occur.

_____ 8. In part, cognitive theory examines how an individual's understandings and expectations affect his or her behavior.

_____ 9. According to Piaget, children begin to think only when they reach preschool age.

_____ 10. Most contemporary researchers have adopted an eclectic perspective on development.

Progress Test 2

Progress Test 2 should be completed during a final chapter review. Answer the following questions after you thoroughly understand the correct answers for the Chapter Review and Progress Test 1.

Multiple-Choice Questions

1. Which developmental theorist has been criticized for suggesting that every child, in every culture, in every nation, passes through certain fixed stages?
   a. Freud   c. Piaget
   b. Erikson   d. all of the above.

2. Of the following terms, the one that does *not* describe a stage of Freud's theory of childhood sexuality is:
   a. phallic.
   b. oral.
   c. anal.
   d. sensorimotor.

3. We are more likely to imitate the behavior of others if we particularly admire and identify with them. This belief finds expression in:
   a. stage theory.
   b. sociocultural theory.
   c. social learning theory.
   d. Pavlov's experiments.

4. How do minitheories differ from grand theories of development?
   a. Unlike the more comprehensive grand theories, minitheories explain only a part of development.
   b. Unlike grand theories, which usually reflect the thinking of many researchers, minitheories tend to stem from one person.
   c. Only the recency of the research on which they are based keeps minitheories from having the sweeping influence of grand theories.
   d. They differ in all the above ways.

5. According to Erikson, an adult who has difficulty establishing a secure, mutual relationship with a life partner might never have resolved the crisis of:
   a. initiative versus guilt.
   b. autonomy versus shame and doubt.
   c. intimacy versus isolation.
   d. trust versus mistrust.

6. Who would be most likely to agree with the statement, "anything can be learned"?
   a. Jean Piaget   c. John Watson
   b. Lev Vygotsky   d. Erik Erikson

7. Classical conditioning is to _____ as operant conditioning is to _____ .
   a. Skinner; Pavlov   c. Pavlov; Skinner
   b. Watson; Vygotsky   d. Vygotsky; Watson

8. Behaviorists have found that they can often solve a person's seemingly complex psychological problem by:
   a. analyzing the patient.
   b. admitting the existence of the unconscious.
   c. altering the environment.
   d. administering well-designed punishments.

9. According to Piaget, an infant first comes to know the world through:
   a. sucking and grasping.
   b. naming and counting.
   c. preoperational thought.
   d. instruction from parents.

10. According to Piaget, the stage of cognitive development that generally characterizes preschool children (2 to 6 years old) is the:
    a. preoperational stage.   c. oral stage.
    b. sensorimotor stage.   d. psychosocial stage.

11. In Piaget's theory, cognitive equilibrium refers to:
    a. a state of mental balance.
    b. a kind of imbalance that leads to cognitive growth.
    c. the ultimate stage of cognitive development.
    d. the first stage in the processing of information.

12. You teach your dog to "speak" by giving her a treat each time she does so. This is an example of:
    a. classical conditioning.   c. reinforcement.
    b. respondent conditioning. d. modeling.

13. A child who must modify an old idea in order to incorporate a new experience is using the process of:
    a. assimilation.
    b. accommodation.
    c. cognitive equilibrium.
    d. guided participation.

14. Which of the following is a common criticism of sociocultural theory?
    a. It places too great an emphasis on unconscious motives and childhood sexuality.
    b. Its mechanistic approach fails to explain many complex human behaviors.
    c. Development is more gradual than its stages imply.
    d. It neglects developmental processes that are not primarily social.

15. A major pioneer of the sociocultural perspective was:
    a. Jean Piaget.   c. Lev Vygotsky.
    b. Albert Bandura.   d. Ivan Pavlov.

Matching Items

Match each theory or term with its corresponding description or definition.

Theories or Terms

__f__   1. psychoanalytic theory
__k__   2. nature
__A__   3. behaviorism
__i__   4. social learning theory
__h__   5. cognitive theory
__d__   6. nurture
__g__   7. sociocultural theory
__e__   8. conditioning
__b__   9. emergent theories
__c__   10. modeling
__j__   11. epigenetic systems theory

Descriptions or Definitions

a. emphasizes the impact of the immediate environment on behavior
b. relatively new, comprehensive theories
c. emphasizes that people learn by observing others
d. environmental influences that affect development
e. a process of learning, as described by Pavlov or Skinner
f. emphasizes the "hidden dramas" that influence behavior
g. emphasizes the cultural context in development
h. emphasizes how our thoughts shape our actions
i. the process whereby a person learns by imitating someone else's behavior
j. emphasizes the interaction of genes and environmental forces
k. traits that are inherited

Thinking Critically About Chapter 2

Answer these questions the day before an exam as a final check on your understanding of the chapter's terms and concepts.

1. Many songbirds inherit a genetically programmed species song that enhances their ability to mate and establish a territory. The evolution of such a trait is an example of:
   a. selective adaptation.
   b. epigenetic development.
   c. accommodation.
   d. assimilation.

2. When a pigeon is rewarded for producing a particular response, and so learns to produce that response to obtain rewards, psychologists describe this chain of events as:
   a. operant conditioning.   c. modeling.
   b. classical conditioning.   d. reflexive actions.

3. Research studies have shown that human handling of rat pups makes them smarter as adults. This is because handling:
   a. increases the mother's grooming of her pup.
   b. indirectly decreases the release of stress hormones.
   c. leads to less brain degeneration in the face of adult stresses.
   d. does all of the above.

4. Dr. Ivey's research focuses on the biological forces that shape each child's characteristic way of reacting to environmental experiences. Evidently, Dr. Ivey is working from a(n) _____ perspective.
   a. psychoanalytic   c. sociocultural
   b. cognitive   d. epigenetic systems

5. Which of the following is the best example of guided participation?
   a. After watching her mother change her baby sister's diaper, 4-year-old Brandy changes her doll's diaper.
   b. To help her son learn to pour liquids, Sandra engages him in a bathtub game involving pouring water from cups of different sizes.
   c. Seeing his father shaving, 3-year-old Kyle pretends to shave by rubbing whipped cream on his face.
   d. After reading a recipe in a magazine, Jack gathers ingredients from the cupboard.

6. A child who calls all furry animals "doggie" will experience cognitive _____ when she encounters a hairless breed for the first time. This may cause her to revamp her concept of "dog" in order to _____ the new experience.
   a. disequilibrium; accommodate
   b. disequilibrium; assimilate
   c. equilibrium; accommodate
   d. equilibrium; assimilate

7. A confirmed neo-Freudian, Dr. Thomas strongly endorses the views of Erik Erikson. She would be most likely to disagree with Freud regarding the importance of:
   a. unconscious forces in development.
   b. irrational forces in personality formation.
   c. early childhood experiences.
   d. sexual urges in development.

8. After watching several older children climbing around a new junglegym, 5-year-old Jennie decides to try it herself. Which of the following best accounts for her behavior?
   a. classical conditioning
   b. modeling
   c. guided participation
   d. reinforcement

9. I am 8 years old, and although I understand some logical principles, I have trouble thinking about hypothetical concepts. According to Piaget, I am in the _____ stage of development.
   a. sensorimotor
   b. preoperational
   c. concrete operational
   d. formal operational

10. Two-year-old Jamail has a simple understanding for "dad," and so each time he encounters a man with a child, he calls him "dad." When he learns that these other men are not "dad," Jamail experiences:
    a. conservation.   c. equilibrium.
    b. cognition.   d. disequilibrium.

11. (In Person) Most adults become physiologically aroused by the sound of an infant's laughter. These interactive reactions, in which caregivers and babies elicit responses in each other:
    a. help ensure the survival of the next generation.
    b. do not occur in all human cultures.
    c. are the result of conditioning very early in life.
    d. are more often found in females than in males.

12. The school psychologist believes that each child's developmental needs can be understood only by taking into consideration the child's broader social and cultural background. Evidently, the school psychologist is working within the _____ perspective.
    a. psychoanalytic   c. social learning
    b. epigenetic systems   d. sociocultural

13. Four-year-old Bjorn takes great pride in successfully undertaking new activities. Erikson would probably say that Bjorn is capably meeting the psychosocial challenge of:
    a. trust vs. mistrust.
    b. initiative vs. guilt.
    c. industry vs. inferiority.
    d. identity vs. role diffusion.

14. Dr. Cleaver's developmental research draws upon insights from several theoretical perspectives. Evidently, Dr. Cleaver is working from a(n) _____ perspective.
    a. cognitive
    b. behaviorist
    c. eclectic
    d. sociocultural

15. Dr. Bazzi believes that development is a lifelong process of gradual and continuous growth. Based on this information, with which of the following theories would Dr. Bazzi most likely agree?
    a. Piaget's cognitive theory
    b. Erikson's psychosocial theory
    c. Freud's psychoanalytic theory
    d. behaviorism

Key Terms

Writing Definitions

Using your own words, write a brief definition or explanation of each of the following terms on a separate piece of paper.

1. developmental theory
2. grand theories
3. minitheories
4. emergent theories
5. psychoanalytic theory
6. behaviorism
7. conditioning
8. classical conditioning
9. operant conditioning
10. reinforcement
11. social learning theory
12. modeling
13. self-efficacy
14. cognitive theory
15. cognitive equilibrium
16. sociocultural theory
17. apprenticeship in thinking
18. guided participation
19. zone of proximal development
20. epigenetic systems theory
21. selective adaptation
22. ethology
23. nature
24. nurture
25. eclectic perspective

Cross-Check

After you have written the definitions of the key terms in this chapter, you should complete the crossword puzzle to ensure that you can reverse the process—recognize the term, given the definition.

ACROSS

2. Behaviorism focuses on the sequences and processes involved in the _____ of behavior.
8. An instinctive or learned behavior that is elicited by a specific stimulus.
11. All the genetic influences on development.
12. Developmental perspective that accepts elements from several theories.
14. Influential theorist who developed a stage theory of cognitive development.
16. Type of theory that brings together information from many disciplines into a comprehensive model of development.
18. All the environmental (non-genetic) influences on development.
19. An early and especially strong proponent of learning theory in America.

DOWN

1. Theory that focuses on some specific area of development.
3. Theory that emphasizes the interaction of genetic and environmental factors in development.
4. The process by which the consequences of a behavior make the behavior more likely to occur.
5. Comprehensive theory of development that has proven to be inadequate in explaining the full range of human development.
6. Theory of personality and development that emphasizes unconscious forces.
7. Learning process that occurs through the association of two stimuli or through the use of reinforcement.
9. Influential theorist who outlined the principles of operant conditioning.
10. The study of behavior as it relates to the evolution and survival of a species.
13. The process of learning by imitating another person's behavior.
14. Russian scientist who outlined the principles of classical conditioning.
15. Psychoanalytic theorist who viewed development as a series of psychosocial crises.
17. The developer of psychoanalytic theory.

ANSWERS
CHAPTER REVIEW

1. developmental theory
2. coherent; hypotheses
3. grand; mini; emergent
4. motives; drives; unconscious; irrational
5. psychoanalytic; psychosexual stages; oral; anal; phallic; conflicts; id; unconscious; superego; ego; rational

Oral stage: The mouth is the focus of pleasurable sensations as the baby becomes emotionally attached to the person who provides the oral gratifications derived from sucking.

Anal stage: Pleasures related to control and self-control, initially in connection with defecation and toilet training, are paramount.

Phallic stage: Pleasure is derived from genital stimulation.

Genital stage: Mature sexual interests that last throughout adulthood emerge.

6. psychosocial; eight; crisis (challenge); span

Age Period	Stage
Birth to 1 yr.	trust vs. **mistrust**
1–3 yrs.	autonomy vs. **shame and doubt**
3–6 yrs.	initiative vs. **guilt**
7–11 yrs.	**industry** vs. inferiority
Adolescence	identity vs. **role diffusion**
Young adulthood	**intimacy** vs. isolation
Middle adulthood	**generativity** vs. stagnation
Older adulthood	**integrity** vs. despair

7. behaviorism; John B. Watson; learning

8. at all ages; conditioning; classical conditioning; operant conditioning

9. Ivan Pavlov; respondent; neutral

10. B. F. Skinner; operant; consequence; instrumental

11. reinforcement; reinforcer

12. Harry Harlow; attachment; contact comfort; psychoanalytic; behaviorism's

13. social learning; modeling

14. uncertain or inexperienced; admired and powerful, nurturing, or similar to the observer; self-understanding; self-efficacy

15. cognitive; Jean Piaget

16. sensorimotor; 2

17. 6; preoperational; symbolically; egocentric

18. 7; concrete operational

19. formal operational; abstract (hypothetical); 12

20. cognitive equilibrium

21. cognitive disequilibrium

22. assimilate; accommodate

23. Freud; Erikson; Piaget; Watson; Pavlov; Skinner

24. less; emotions; actions; thoughts

25. cultural; genes

26. many

27. dynamic interaction; culture

28. Lev Vygotsky; cognitive

29. novices; mentors (or tutors); apprenticeship in thinking

30. guided participation

31. zone of proximal development; assistance

Sociocultural theory has emphasized the need to study development in the specific cultural context in which it occurs. The theory has been criticized for neglecting the importance of developmental process-es that are not primarily social, such as the role of biological maturation in development.

32. epigenetic systems; genes; environment

33. instincts; biological

34. environmental; genetic instructions; stress; facilitating

35. selective adaptation

36. all

37. cause corresponding changes and adjustments in every other part

38. ethology; social contact; infant caregiving

39. a. sociocultural
    b. cognitive
    c. behaviorism
    d. psychoanalytic
    e. epigenetic systems

40. a. behaviorism
    b. cognitive
    c. psychoanalytic
    d. epigenetic systems
    e. sociocultural

41. continuous; discontinuous; stage; do not; do; intervals

42. differences; deficits; raise a child

43. a. In psychoanalytic theory, a deficit would appear when a mother does not spend enough time with the child or is unresponsive

    b. In behaviorism, too much aggression in school would be a deficit resulting from parental modeling and reinforcement

    c. In cognitive theory, a deficit would be evident if children are slow to develop or never curious and talkative.

    d. In sociocultural thoery, a deficit would occur when a child who has been raised by the standards of one culture does not function well in another culture.

    e. In epigenetic systems theory, a deficit would be any environmental condition that does not provide proper nurturance for the developing child.

44. nature–nurture; genes (nature); nurture

45. interaction

46. nurture; nature

47. eclectic

PROGRESS TEST 1

Multiple-Choice Questions

1. **d.** is the answer (pp. 35–36)

2. **a.** is the answer. (p. 36)

   b. Behaviorism emphasizes the influence of the immediate environment on behavior.

   c. Cognitive theory emphasizes the impact of *conscious* thought processes on behavior.

   d. Sociocultural theory emphasizes the influence on development of social interaction in a specific cultural context.

3. **a.** is the answer. (p. 39)

4. **a.** is the answer. (p. 38)

   b. & c. Whereas Freud identified four stages of psychosexual development, Erikson proposed eight psychosocial stages.

   d. Although his theory places greater emphasis on social and cultural forces than Freud's did, Erikson's theory is nevertheless classified as a psychoanalytic theory.

5. **c.** is the answer. Sociocultural theory is an emergent theory. (p. 36)

   a., b., & d. Each of these is an example of a grand theory.

6. **c.** is the answer. (p. 41)

7. **a.** is the answer. In classical conditioning, a neutral stimulus—in this case, the bell—is associated with a meaningful stimulus—in this case, food. (pp. 40–41)

   b. In operant conditioning, the consequences of a voluntary response determine the likelihood of its being repeated. Salivation is an involuntary response.

   c. & d. Positive reinforcement and social learning pertain to voluntary, or operant, responses.

8. **c.** is the answer. (pp. 59–60)

   a. These are both examples of nurture.

   b. Both of these refer to nature.

   d. The impact of changing historical concepts of childhood on development is an example of how environmental forces (nurture) shape development.

9. **d.** is the answer. (p. 43)

   a. & c. These can be true in all types of learning.

   b. This was not discussed as an aspect of developmental theory.

10. **d.** is the answer. (p. 51)

    a. & c. Sociocultural theory and behaviorism focus almost entirely on environmental factors (nurture) in development.

    b. Cognitive theory emphasizes the developing person's own mental activity but ignores genetic differences in individuals.

11. **a.** is the answer. (p. 51)

    b. Vygotsky's theory does not emphasize biological processes.

    c. & d. Vygotsky's theory places considerable emphasis on language and social factors.

12. **a.** is the answer. (p. 45)

13. **c.** is the answer. (p. 45)

    a. This refers to the core of Erikson's psychosocial stages, which deals with people's interactions with the environment.

    b. Equilibrium occurs when existing schemes *do* fit a person's current experiences.

    d. Negative reinforcement is the removal of a stimulus as a consequence of a desired behavior.

14. **b.** is the answer. (p. 60)

    c. This is only true of psychoanalytic theory.

    d. Although the grand theories have emphasized nurture over nature in this matter, no theory suggests that sexual orientation is voluntarily chosen.

15. **c.** is the answer. (p. 50)

    a. This is a stage of Piaget's cognitive theory.

    b. This describes positive reinforcement.

    d. This is an aspect of social learning theory.

True or False Items

1. T (p. 39)

2. T (p. 38)

3. F Although most developmentalists believe that nature and nurture interact in shaping development, the practical implications of whether nature or nurture plays a greater role in certain abilities keep the controversy alive. (pp. 59–61)

4. F This assumption lies at the heart of epigenetic systems theory. (p. 51)

5. F Epigenetic systems theory emphasizes the interaction of genes and experience. (p. 51)

6. T (pp. 60–61)

7. F On the contrary, *dis*equilibrium often fosters greater growth. (p. 45)

8. T (p. 45)

9. F   The hallmark of Piaget's theory is that, at every age, individuals think about the world in unique ways. (p. 44)

10. T (p. 62)

PROGRESS TEST 2

Multiple-Choice Questions

1. **d.** is the answer. (p. 47)

2. **d.** is the answer. This is one of Piaget's stages of cognitive development. (pp. 39, 45)

3. **c.** is the answer. (p. 44)

4. **a.** is the answer. (p. 36)

   b. *Grand* theories, rather than minitheories, usually stem from one person.

   c. This describes emergent theories.

5. **d.** is the answer. (p. 38)

6. **c.** is the answer. (p. 39)

   a. Piaget formulated a cognitive theory of development.

   b. Vygotsky formulated a sociocultural theory of development.

   d. Erikson formulated a psychoanalytic theory of development.

7. **c.** is the answer. (pp. 40, 41)

8. **c.** is the answer. (p. 41)

   a. & b. These are psychoanalytic approaches to treating psychological problems.

   d. Behaviorists generally do not recommend the use of punishment.

9. **a.** is the answer. These behaviors are typical of infants in the sensorimotor stage. (p. 45)

   b., c., & d. These are typical of older children.

10. **a.** is the answer. (p. 45)

    b. The sensorimotor stage describes development from birth until 2 years of age.

    c. This is a psychoanalytic stage described by Freud.

    d. This is not the name of a stage; "psychosocial" refers to Erikson's stage theory.

11. **a.** is the answer. (p. 45)

    b. This describes *dis*equilibrium.

    c. This is formal operational thinking.

    d. Piaget's theory does not propose stages of information processing.

12. **c.** is the answer. (p. 41)

a. & b. Teaching your dog in this way is an example of operant, rather than classical (respondent), conditioning.

d. Modeling involves learning by imitating others.

13. **b.** is the answer. (p. 46)

    a. Assimilation occurs when new experiences do *not* clash with existing ideas.

    c. Cognitive equilibrium is mental balance, which occurs when ideas and experiences do *not* clash.

    d. This is Vygotsky's term for the process by which a mentor engages a child in shared learning activities.

14. **d.** is the answer. (p. 51)

    a. This is a common criticism of psychoanalytic theory.

    b. This is a common criticism of behaviorism.

    c. This is a common criticism of psychoanalytic and cognitive theories that describe development as occurring in a sequence of stages.

15. **c.** is the answer. (p. 49)

Matching Items

1. f (p. 36)	5. h (p. 44)	9. b (p. 36)
2. k (p. 60)	6. d (p. 60)	10. i (p. 43)
3. a (p. 40)	7. g (p. 48)	11. j (p. 51)
4. c (p. 43)	8. e (p. 40)	

THINKING CRITICALLY ABOUT CHAPTER 2

1. **a.** is the answer. (p. 52)

   b. This term was not used to describe development.

   c. & d. These terms describe the processes by which cognitive concepts incorporate (assimilate) new experiences or are revamped (accommodated) by them.

2. **a.** is the answer. This is an example of operant conditioning because a response recurs due to its consequences. (p. 41)

   b. & d. In classical conditioning, the individual learns to associate a neutral stimulus with a meaningful stimulus.

   c. In modeling, learning occurs through the observation of others, rather than through direct exposure to reinforcing consequences, as in this example.

3. **d.** is the answer. (p. 53)

4. d. is the answer. (p. 51)

a. Psychoanalytic theorists focus on the role of unconscious forces in development.

b. Cognitive theorists emphasize how the developing person actively seeks to understand experiences.

c. Sociocultural theorists focus on the social context, as expressed through people, language, and customs.

5. b. is the answer. (p. 49)

a. & c. These are both examples of modeling.

d. Guided participation involves the coaching of a mentor. In this example, Jack is simply following written directions.

6. a. is the answer. (pp. 45–46)

b. Because the dog is not furry, the child's concept of dog cannot incorporate (assimilate) the discrepant experience without being revamped.

c. & d. Equilibrium exists when ideas (such as what a dog is) and experiences (such as seeing a hairless dog) do *not* clash.

7. d. is the answer. (p. 38)

8. b. is the answer. Evidently, Jennie has learned by observing the other children at play. (p. 43)

a. Classical conditioning is concerned with the association of stimuli, not with complex responses, as in this example.

c. Guided participation involves the interaction of a mentor and a child.

d. Reinforcement is a process for getting a response to recur.

9. c. is the answer. (p. 45)

10. d. is the answer. When Jamail experiences something that conflicts with his existing understanding, he experiences disequilibrium. (p. 45)

a. Conservation is the ability to recognize that objects do not change when their appearances change.

b. Cognition refers to all mental activities associated with thinking.

c. If Jamail's thinking were in equilibrium, all men would be "dad"!

11. a. is the answer. (p. 54)

b. & c. Infant social reflexes and adult caregiving impulses occur in all cultures (b), which indicates that they are the product of nature rather than nurture (c).

d. The text does not address the issue of gender differences in infant reflexes or caregiving impulses.

12. d. is the answer. (p. 48)

13. b. is the answer. (p. 38)

a. According to Erikson, this crisis concerns younger children.

c. & d. In Erikson's theory, these crises concern older children.

14. c. is the answer. (p. 62)

a., b., & d. These are three of the many theoretical perspectives upon which someone working from an eclectic perspective might draw.

15. d. is the answer. (p. 56)

a., b., & c. Each of these theories emphasizes that development is a discontinuous process that occurs in stages.

KEY TERMS

Writing Definitions

1. A **developmental theory** is a systematic statement of principles and generalizations that explains behavior and development and provides a framework for future research. (p. 35)

2. **Grand theories** are comprehensive theories of human development that have proven to be inadequate in the face of research evidence that development is more diverse than the theories proposed. Examples of grand theories are psychoanalytic and cognitive theories and behaviorism. (p. 36)

3. **Minitheories** are less general and comprehensive than grand theories, focusing instead on some specific area of development. (p. 36)

4. **Emergent theories**, such as sociocultural theory and epigenetic systems theory, are newer comprehensive theories that bring together information from many disciplines but are not yet a coherent, comprehensive whole. (p. 36)

5. **Psychoanalytic theory**, a grand theory, interprets human development in terms of intrinsic drives and motives, many of which are irrational and unconscious. (p. 36)

6. **Behaviorism,** a grand theory, emphasizes the sequences and processes by which behavior is learned. (p. 40)

7. **Conditioning** is the learning process that occurs either through the association of two stimuli (classical conditioning) or through the use of positive or negative reinforcement or punishment (operant conditioning). (p. 40)

8. **Classical conditioning** is the process by which a neutral stimulus becomes associated with a meaningful one so that both are responded to in the same way. (p. 40)

9. **Operant conditioning** is the process by which a response is gradually learned through reinforcement or punishment. (p. 41)

10. **Reinforcement** is the process by which the consequences of a particular behavior strengthen the behavior, making it more likely that the behavior will be repeated. (p. 41)

11. An application of behaviorism, **social learning theory** emphasizes that people often learn new behaviors through observation and imitation of other people. (p. 43)

12. **Modeling** refers to the process by which we observe other people's behavior and then pattern our own after it. (p. 43)

13. In social learning theory, **self-efficacy** is the belief that one is effective. (p. 44)

14. **Cognitive theory,** a grand theory, emphasizes that the way people think and understand the world shapes their perceptions, attitudes, and actions. (p. 44)

15. In Piaget's theory, **cognitive equilibrium** is a state of mental balance, in which a person's thoughts about the world seem not to clash with each other or with his or her experiences. (p. 45)

16. **Sociocultural theory,** an emergent theory, seeks to explain development as the result of a dynamic interaction between developing persons and their surrounding culture. (p. 48)

17. In sociocultural theory, an **apprenticeship in thinking** is the process by which novices learn by interacting with more skilled parents, teachers, or other mentors. (p. 49)

18. **Guided participation** is a learning process in which the learner is tutored, or mentored, through social interaction with a skilled teacher. (p. 49)

19. According to Vygotsky, developmental growth occurs when mentors draw children into the **zone of proximal development,** which is the range of skills the child can exercise with assistance but cannot perform independently. (p. 50)

20. The **epigenetic systems theory** emphasizes the genetic origins of behavior but also stresses that genes, over time, are directly and systematically affected by environmental forces. (p. 51)

21. **Selective adaptation** is the evolutionary process through which useful genes that enhance survival become more frequent within individuals. (p. 52)

22. **Ethology** is the study of behavior as it relates to the evolution and survival of a species. (p. 54)

23. **Nature** refers to all the traits, capacities, and limitations that a person inherits at the moment of conception. (p. 60)

24. **Nuture** refers to all the environmental influences that affect a person's development following the moment of conception. (p. 60)

25. Developmentalists who work from an **eclectic perspective** accept elements from several theories, instead of adhering to only a single perspective. (p. 62)

Cross-Check

ACROSS
2. learning
8. response
11. nature
12. eclectic
14. Piaget
16. emergent
18. nurture
19. Watson

DOWN
1. minitheory
3. epigenetic systems
4. reinforcement
5. grand
6. psychoanalytic
7. conditioning
9. Skinner
10. ethology
13. modeling
14. Pavlov
15. Erikson
17. Freud

Chapter Three

Heredity and Environment

Chapter Overview

Conception occurs when the male and female reproductive cells—the sperm and ovum, respectively—come together to create a new, one-celled zygote with its own unique combination of genetic material. The genetic material furnishes the instructions for development—not only for obvious physical characteristics, such as sex, coloring, and body shape but also for certain psychological characteristics, such as bashfulness, moodiness, and vocational aptitude.

Every year scientists make new discoveries and reach new understandings about genes and their effects on the development of individuals. This chapter presents some of their findings, including that most human characteristics are polygenic and multifactorial, the result of the interaction of many genetic and environmental influences. Perhaps the most important findings have come from research into the causes of genetic and chromosomal abnormalities. The chapter discusses the most common of these abnormalities and concludes with a section on genetic counseling. Genetic testing before and after conception can help predict whether a couple will have a child with a genetic problem.

Many students find the technical material in this chapter difficult to master, but it *can* be done with a great deal of rehearsal. Working through the Chapter Review several times and mentally reciting terms are both useful techniques for rehearsing this type of material.

NOTE: Answer guidelines for all Chapter 3 questions begin on page 50.

Guided Study

The text chapter should be studied one section at a time. Before you read, preview each section by skimming it, noting headings and boldface items. Then read the appropriate section objectives from the following outline. Keep these objectives in mind and, as you read the chapter section, search for the information that will enable you to meet each objective. Once you have finished a section, write out answers for its objectives.

Genetics: Foundations in Biology and Ethics
(pp. 67–78)

1. Describe the process of conception and the first hours of development of the zygote. Conception begins when the sperm fertilizes the egg to form a zygote (cell that forms when sperm and egg fuse). In the first hrs the zygote forms thru duplication and division first the combined genetic materail duplicates forming 2 complete sets and the zygote divides each cell w/ 1 set of chromosomes. These 2 divide to 4 to we divide to 8 At the eight cell stage when the cells differentiate they begin to specialize taking different forms and reproducing at different rates.

2. Identify the mechanisms of heredity, and explain how sex is determined. The mechanisms of heredity are the genes which is the basic unit for transmition of heredity instructions genes are located on a chromosome which are 1 of 46 molecules of DNA in 23 pairs that each cell of the body together contain all human genes. The sex is determined by the 23rd pair of chromosomes. In females the 23rd pair is XX in males it is XY So the crucial factor in creating sex is which sperm reaches the ovum first.

3. (text and Changing Policy) Discuss age-related changes in the sex ratio and whether there should be a social policy to regulate sex selection of children. If we were to inforce the more women less men as age goes on there will be less nurses + teachers which means as medical advances become greater there will be no one to take care of them and children are not taught and prepared for any type of future.
No I don't think we should be able to regulate sex selection.

4. Discuss genetic continuity and diversity, and distinguish between monozygotic and dizygotic twins. *Monozygotic twins are identical because they originated from the same zygote they share identical genetic instructions. Dizygotic twins or fraternal twins begin life as 2 seperate zygotes created by fertilization of 2 ova at roughly the same time.*

genetic continuity includes common physical structures, behavioral tendencies and reproductive potential. Diversity comes in the 8 trillion genes and 64,000 different genetic combination.

5. (text and In Person) Discuss infertility and several legal and ethical issues raised by assisted reproductive technology. *Infertility – refers to a couple who are unable to have kids after a year of trying. Legal issues – should 3rd party donors have legal parental rights, should ART be available to everyone even single mothers or spite sexual orientation, lifestyle or age.*

Ethical should the children know if the parents are not the biological parents. Does society have a right to ban ART.

From Genotype to Phenotype (pp. 78–84)

6. Differentiate genotype from phenotype, and explain the polygenic and multifactorial nature of human traits. *The Genotype is a persons entire genetic inheritance including the genes that are not expressed. The phenotype is all the genetic traits including physical ones + behavioral tendencies that are expressed in a person. Genes are both polygenic and multifaceted polygenic means that traits are effected by many genes and multifactorial-influenced by many factors including environment. You may be genetically predisposed to become an alcoholic but don't grow up around alcohol you won't become an*

7. Explain the additive and nonadditive patterns of genetic interaction. Give examples of the traits that result from each type of interaction. *An Additive gene happens when the phenotype reflects a contribution of all genes involved (ie. height) A nonadditive gene reflects only 1 of the 2 choices usually the dominant (stronger) of the 2 rather than the recessive.*

8. Discuss X-linked genes in terms of genotype and phenotype, and explain the concept of genetic imprinting. *An X-linked gene is one found on the X chromosome. For males any recessive trait on the X chromosome is going to be expressed in the phenotype b/c they have only one. This is why many males are color blind, have hemophilia b/c these are X linked traits. In genotype it means that the women can be a carrier and pass it on to their sons. Genetic imprinting is the tendency of certain genes to be expressed differently from one parent rather than another.*

9. Explain how scientists distinguish the effects of genes and environment on development, and explain the role of molecular genetics in this process. *The easiest way to do this is studying twins (identical) who were raised in different environments to distinguish between nature and nurture. Molecular genetics brings the nature portion to life.*

Environmental Influences on Emotional Conditions (pp. 84–88)

10. Identify some environmental variables that affect genetic inheritance, and describe how a particular trait, such as shyness (inhibition) or schizophrenia, might be affected. *If children who were shy are gently and not embarrassed in coerced they can learn to become less shy and less inhibited. However if a shy child's parents are shy themselves the child will never learn to come out of shell. The pt. being that the genetic influences do not disappear completely.*

11. Discuss the interaction of genes and environment in the development of alcoholism. *Culture counts in a person with a strong tendency toward alcohol spends a lifetime where alcohol is unavailable the genotype will never be expressed.*

Inherited Abnormalities (pp. 89–99)

12. Describe the most common chromosomal abnormalities, including abnormalities involving the sex chromosomes. *The most common are down syndrome which is caused by an extra chromosome #23 Fragile-x-syndrome where the X chromosome where it is barely attached to the other half and produces MR in males that inherit it.*

13. Explain the major methods of prenatal diagnosis, noting the advantages of each.
1) Chronic villi sampling - can be done earlier but at a price could cause spontaneous abortion.
2) Preimplantation test - before implantation can be tested to find chromosomal abnormalities and the others can be implanted if no defect is found.
3) Amniocentisis - Reveals the sex of the baby.

14. Identify two common genetic disorders, and discuss reasons for their relatively low incidence of occurrence. *Tourette Syndrome?*
Huntingtons dieses
dont have children b/c dont want to RISk passing it on. *?*
exceptions.

15. (Changing Policy) Describe four situations in which couples should seek genetic testing and counseling.
1) Bearing child w/ specific disease
2) Advice how to prevent
3) Discover genotype availible
4)

Chapter Review

When you have finished reading the chapter, work through the material that follows to review it. Complete the sentences and answer the questions. As you proceed, evaluate your performance for each section by consulting the answers on page 50. Do not continue with the next section until you understand each answer. If you need to, review or reread the appropriate section in the textbook before continuing.

1. Genetic influence is _____ , by which is meant genes are influenced by their ongoing interaction with the _____ .

Genetics: Foundations in Biology and Ethics
(pp. 67–78)

2. The human reproductive cells, which are called *gametes* , include the male's *sperm* and the female's *ovum* .

3. When the gametes' genetic material combines, a living cell called a *zygote* is formed.

4. Before the zygote begins the process of cellular division that starts human development, the combined genetic material from both gametes is *duplicated* to form two complete sets of genetic instructions. At about the eight-cell stage, the cells start to *differenciate* , with various cells beginning to specialize and reproduce at different rates.

5. A complete copy of the genetic instructions inherited by the zygote at the moment of conception is found in *every* (every/most/only a few) cell(s) of the body.

6. The basic units of genetic instructions are the *genes* , which are discrete segments of a *chromosome* , which is a molecule of *DNA* .

7. Genetic instructions are "written" in a chemical code, made up of four pairs of bases: *guanine* , *adenine* , *cytosine* , and *thymine* . The precise nature of a gene's instructions is determined by the *base pairing* , that is, by the overall *order* in which base pairs appear along each segment of the DNA molecule.

8. The _Human_ _Genome_ _Project_ is the ongoing international effort to map and interpret the complete genetic code. This task is complicated by the fact that some genes appear in several versions, called _alleles_ , and that most genes have _several different_ (only one/several different) function(s).

9. Genes ensure both genetic _continuity_ across the species and genetic _diversity_ within it.

10. Each normal person inherits _46_ chromosomes, _23_ from each parent.

11. During cell division, the gametes each receive _one_ (one/both) member(s) of each chromosome pair. Thus, in number each gamete has _23_ chromosomes.

12. The developing person's sex is determined by the _23rd_ pair of chromosomes. In the female, this pair is composed of two _X_ -shaped chromosomes and is designated _female_ . In the male, this pair includes one _X_ and one _Y_ chromosome and is therefore designated _male_ .

13. (text and Changing Policy) At birth, the overall sex ratio has always _roughly equal_ (favored males/favored females/been roughly equal); unless wars or other catastrophes occur, it is equal when men and women reach _prime reproductive_ age. However, because _female_ (females/males) have a slightly higher rate of childhood death, a balance occurs when men and women reach age _adolescence_ .

14. (Changing Policy) With advancing age, the sex ratio favors _women_ . In countries such as China, prenatal tests that show the sex of the child have been used to _practice female infanticide_ .

15. (Changing Policy) Today, choosing the sex of children _is_ (is/is not) feasible and _is not_ (is/is not) widespread.

16. The critical factor in the determination of a zygote's sex is which _sperm_ (sperm/ovum) reaches the other gamete first.

17. When the twenty-three chromosome pairs divide up during the formation of gametes, which of the two pair members will end up in a particular gamete is determined by _chance_ .

18. Genetic variability is also affected by the _crossing_ - _over_ of genes, and by the interaction of genetic instructions in ways unique to the individual. This means that any given mother and father can form approximately _64,000_ genetically different offspring.

19. Identical twins, which occur about once in every _270_ births, are called _identical_ twins because they come from one zygote. Such twins _are_ (are/are not) genetically identical.

20. Twins who begin life as two separate zygotes created by the fertilization of two ova are called _dizygotic_ twins. Such twins have approximately _50_ percent of their genes in common.

21. Dizygotic births occur naturally about once in every _60_ births. Women in their _30s_ (what age?) are three times as likely to have dizygotic twins than women in their _20s_ .

22. The number of multiple births has _increased_ (increased/decreased/remained unchanged) in many nations because of the increased use of _fertility drugs._ . Generally, the more embryos that develop together, the _smaller_ , less _mature_ , and more _vulnerable_ each one is.

23. Infertility, which affects _2-3_ % (what percent?) of all couples, is defined as being unable to produce a baby after at least _1 yr._ (how long?) of trying.

24. To help them conceive, many infertile couples turn to _Assisted_ _Reproductive_ _Technology_. In the method of _in_ _vitro_ _fertilization_, ova are surgically removed from a woman and mixed with sperm.

(In Person) Identify several ethical and legal questions that are raised by assisted reproductive techniques.
- Should 3rd party donors have parental rights.
- Should ART be availible to everyone?
- Do children have a right to know if their parents are not their biological parents.

From Genotype to Phenotype (pp. 78–84)

25. Most human characteristics are affected by many genes, and so they are _polygenic_; and by many factors, and so they are _multifactorial_.

26. The sum total of all the genes a person inherits is called the _genotype_. The sum total of all the genetic traits that are actually expressed is called the _phenotype_.

27. A person who has a gene in his or her genotype that is not expressed in the phenotype but that can be passed on to the person's offspring is said to be a _carrier_ of that gene.

28. For any given trait, the phenotype arises from the interaction of the proteins synthesized from the specific _amino acids_ that make up the genotype, and from the interaction between the genotype and the _environment_.

29. A phenotype that reflects the sum of the contributions of all the genes involved in its determination illustrates the _additive_ pattern of genetic interaction. Examples include genes that affect _height_ and _skin color_ _hair curliness_.

30. Less often, genes interact in a _non additive_ fashion. In one example of this pattern, some genes are more influential than others; this is called the _dominant_ – _recessive_ pattern. In this pattern, the more influential gene is called _dominant_, and the weaker gene is called _recessive_. Hundreds of _physical_ characteristics follow this basic pattern. In one variation of this pattern, the phenotype is influenced primarily, but not exclusively, by the dominant gene; this is the _incomplete_ _dominence_ pattern.

31. Some recessive genes are located only on the *X* chromosome and so are called _X_-_linked_. Examples of such genes are the ones that determine _color blindness, many allergies several diseases, LDs_. Because they have only one X chromosome, _males_ (females/males) are more likely to have these characteristics in their phenotype.

32. Complicating inheritance further is the fact that dominant genes sometimes do not completely _penetrate_ the phenotype. This may be caused by _temperature, stress_, or other factors. Furthermore, chromosome pairs sometimes do not split precisely, resulting in a _mosaic_, a person who has a mixture of cells.

33. Whether a gene is inherited from the mother or the father _does_ (does/does not) influence its behavior. This tendency of genes is called _genetic_ _imprinting_, or tagging.

34. The complexity of genetic interaction is particularly apparent in _behavioral_ _genetics_, which is the study of the genetic origins of _psychological_ characteristics. These include _personality_ traits such as _sociability assertiveness, moodiness_ psychological disorders such as _schizophrenia depression A_; and _ADHD_ traits such as _cognitive memory for #s, spatial perception's fluency of expression_.

35. Most behavioral traits are affected by the _interaction_ of large numbers of _genes_ with _environmental_ factors. Traits that are plastic early in life _do not always_ (always/do not always) remain plastic thereafter.

36. To identify genetic influences on development, researchers must distinguish genetic effects from _environmental_ effects. To this end, researchers study _monozygotic_ and _dizygotic_ children.

37. If _monozygotic_ (monozygotic/dizygotic) twins are found to be much more similar on a particular trait than _dizygotic_ (monozygotic/dizygotic) twins are, it is likely that genes play a significant role in the appearance of that trait.

38. Traits that show a strong correlation between adopted children and their _biological_ (adoptive/biological) parents suggest a genetic basis for those characteristics.

39. The best way to try to separate the effects of genes and environments is to study _monozygotic_ twins who have been raised in _different_ (the same/different) environments.

40. Environment affects _every_ (most/every/few) human characteristic(s).

41. The study of the chemical codes that make up a particular molecule of DNA is called _molecular_ _genetics_.

42. Researchers can now directly compare a pattern of genes shared by two individuals with a promising new statistical technique called _quantitative_ _trait_ _loci_.

Briefly explain how shyness (or inhibition), which is influenced by genes, is also affected by the social environment.

43. Other psychological traits that have strong genetic influences but may be affected by environment include _intelligence_, _activity level_, _aggression_, and _religiosity_.

44. If one monozygotic twin develops schizophrenia, about _2/3_ of the time the other twin does, too. Researchers have pinpointed a gene on chromosome _6_, which predisposes schizophrenia.

45. Environmental influences _do_ (do/do not) play an important role in the appearance of schizophrenia. One predisposing factor is birth during _late winter_, probably because a certain _virus_ is more prevalent at this time of year.

46. Another disease that develops from the complex interaction of genes and environmental conditions is _Alzheimer's_ _disease_.

47. Alcoholism _is_ (is/is not) partly genetic; furthermore, its expression _is_ (is/is not) affected by the environment. Certain temperamental traits correlate with abusive drinking, including _violent temper_. A person is most likely to become an active alcoholic between ages _15_ and _25_.

48. Because alcohol is taboo for Mexican women, Mexican-American babies almost never have _fetal_ _alcohol_ _syndrome_ unless the mother was raised in the United States and became _acculturated_.

Inherited Abnormalities (pp. 89–99)

Researchers study genetic and chromosomal abnormalities for three major reasons. They are:

1. Disruptions of normal development provide insight to the complexities of genetic interaction

2. Knowledge of the origens helps to realize how to reduce harmful consequences

3. Misinformation and prejudice compound the problem.

49. Chromosomal abnormalities occur during the formation of the _gamete_ , producing a sperm or ovum that does not have the normal complement of chromosomes.

50. An estimated _1/2_ of all zygotes have too few or too many chromosomes. Most of these _do not_ (do/do not) begin to develop, usually because a _spontaneous abortion_ occurs. Nevertheless, about 1 in every _200_ newborns has one chromosome too few or one too many, leading to a cluster of characteristics called a _syndrome_ .

51. One test for neural-tube defects and Down syndrome analyzes the level of _alpha fetoprotein_ in the mother's blood. An ultrasound, or _sonogram_ , uses high-frequency sound waves to produce an image of the fetus.

52. The "mainstay" of prenatal diagnosis is _Amniocentesis_ , in which a small amount of fluid surrounding the fetus, inside the placenta, is analyzed for chromosomal or genetic abnormalities. A test that provides the same information but can be performed much earlier during the pregnancy is called _Chronic Villi Sampling_ .

53. When conception occurs in a laboratory dish, called _in vitro_ , cells can be analyzed for genetic defects before they are inserted into the uterus. This procedure is called _pre-implantation testing_ .

54. The most common extra-chromosome syndrome is _Down's Syndrome_ , which is also called _trisomy-21_ .

55. People with Down syndrome age _faster_ (faster/more slowly) than other adults. By middle age, people with Down syndrome almost invariably develop _Alzheimer's disease_ , which severely impairs their already limited _communication_ skills.

List several of the physical and psychological characteristics associated with Down syndrome.
3rd chromosome in 21 spot.
Specific facial features including thick tongue, round face, slanted eyes and distinctive hand and foot prints.
psychological characteristics include: Mental retardation, sweet-tempered, don't cry or complain like other children.

56. About 1 in every 500 infants is either missing a _sex_ chromosome or has two or more such chromosomes. One such syndrome is _Klinefelter Syndrome_ , in which a boy inherits the _XXY_ chromosome pattern.

57. In some individuals, part of the X chromosome is attached by such a thin string of molecules that it seems about to break off; this abnormality is called _fragile - X_ syndrome.

58. The variable that most often correlates with chromosomal abnormalities is _maternal age_ .

59. Chromosomal abnormalities such as Down syndrome _almost always_ (rarely/almost always) follow an age-related pattern.

60. It is much _more_ (more/less) likely that a person is a carrier of one or more harmful genes than that he or she has abnormal chromosomes.

61. Most of the known genetic disorders are _dominant_ (dominant/recessive). Genetic disorders usually _are not_ (are/are not) seriously disabling.

62. Two exceptions are the central nervous system disease called _Huntington's Cholera_ and the disorder that causes its victims to exhibit uncontrollable tics and explosive outbursts, called _Tourette's Syndrome_ .

63. Genetic disorders that are _Recessive_____ and _multifactoial_ claim more victims than dominant ones. Three common recessive disorders are _cystic fibrosis_, _fibrosis___ , _thalasemia_ , and _sickle_ - _cell_ _anemia_ .

64. (Changing Policy) Through _Prenatal_____ _Genetic_____ _Counseling___ , couples today can learn more about their genes and about their chances of conceiving a child with chromosomal or other genetic abnormalities.

65. (Changing Policy) List four situations in which genetic counseling is strongly recommended.

    a. _parent, sibling or child with a serious genetic condition._
    b. _history of early spontaneous abortion, still births, and infertility._
    c. _Same ethnic group or subgroup_
    d. _Women 35 or older._

Progress Test 1

Circle your answers to the following questions and check them against the answers on page 52. If your answer is incorrect, read the explanation for why it is incorrect and then consult the appropriate pages of the text (in parentheses following the correct answer).

Multiple-Choice Questions

1. When a sperm and an ovum merge, a one-celled _____ is formed.
   a. zygote
   b. reproductive cell
   c. gamete
   d. monozygote

2. Genes are discrete segments that provide the biochemical instructions that each cell needs to become:
   a. a zygote.
   b. a chromosome.
   c. a specific part of a functioning human body.
   d. deoxyribonucleic acid.

3. In the male, the twenty-third pair of chromosomes is designated _____ ; in the female, this pair is designated _____.
   a. XX; XY
   b. XY; XX
   c. XO; XXY
   d. XXY; XO

4. Since the twenty-third pair of chromosomes in females is XX, each ovum carries an:
   a. XX zygote.
   b. X zygote.
   c. XY zygote.
   d. X chromosome.

5. When a zygote splits, the two identical, independent clusters that develop become:
   a. dizygotic twins.
   b. monozygotic twins.
   c. fraternal twins.
   d. trizygotic twins.

6. In scientific research, the best way to separate the effects of genes and the environment is to study:
   a. dizygotic twins.
   b. adopted children and their biological parents.
   c. adopted children and their adoptive parents.
   d. monozygotic twins raised in different environments.

7. Most of the known genetic disorders are:
   a. dominant.
   b. recessive.
   c. seriously disabling.
   d. sex-linked.

8. When we say that a characteristic is multifactorial, we mean that:
   a. many genes are involved.
   b. many environmental factors are involved.
   c. many genetic and environmental factors are involved.
   d. the characteristic is polygenic.

9. Genes are segments of molecules of:
   a. genotype.
   b. deoxyribonucleic acid (DNA).
   c. karyotype.
   d. phenotype.

10. The potential for genetic diversity in humans is so great because:
    a. there are approximately 8 million possible combinations of chromosomes.
    b. when the sperm and ovum unite, genetic combinations not present in either parent can be formed.
    c. just before a chromosome pair divides during the formation of gametes, genes cross over, producing recombinations.
    d. of all the above reasons.

11. A chromosomal abnormality that affects males only involves a(n):
    a. XO chromosomal pattern.
    b. XXX chromosomal pattern.
    c. YY chromosomal pattern.
    d. XXY chromosomal pattern.

12. Polygenic complexity is most apparent in _____ characteristics.
    a. physical   **c.** recessive gene
    b. psychological   **d.** dominant gene

13. Babies born with trisomy-21 (Down syndrome) are often:
    a. born to older parents.
    b. unusually aggressive.
    c. abnormally tall by adolescence.
    d. blind.

14. To say that a trait is polygenic means that:
    a. many genes make it more likely that the individual will inherit the trait.
    b. several genes must be present in order for the individual to inherit the trait.
    c. the trait is multifactorial.
    d. most people carry genes for the trait.

15. Some genetic diseases are recessive, so the child cannot inherit the condition unless both parents:
    a. have Kleinfelter syndrome.
    b. carry the same recessive gene.
    c. have *XO* chromosomes.
    d. have the disease.

Matching Items

Match each term with its corresponding description or definition.

Terms

___C___ **1.** gametes
___h___ **2.** chromosome
___m___ **3.** genotype
___i___ **4.** phenotype
___b___ **5.** monozygotic
___f___ **6.** dizygotic
___g___ **7.** additive
___j___ **8.** fragile-X syndrome
___e___ **9.** carrier
___d___ **10.** zygote
___k___ **11.** alleles
___a___ **12.** XX
___l___ **13.** XY

Descriptions or Definitions

a. chromosome pair inherited by genetic females
b. identical twins
c. sperm and ovum
d. the first cell of the developing person
e. a person who has a recessive gene in his or her genotype that is not expressed in the phenotype
f. fraternal twins
g. a pattern in which each gene in question makes an active contribution to the final outcome
h. a DNA molecule
i. the behavioral or physical expression of genetic potential
j. a chromosomal abnormality
k. alternate versions of a gene
l. chromosome pair inherited by genetic males
m. a person's entire genetic inheritance

Progress Test 2

Progress Test 2 should be completed during a final chapter review. Answer the following questions after you thoroughly understand the correct answers for the Chapter Review and Progress Test 1.

1. Which of the following provides the best broad description of the relationship between heredity and environment in determining height?
   a. Heredity is the primary influence, with environment affecting development only in severe situations.
   b. Heredity and environment contribute equally to development.
   c. Environment is the major influence on physical characteristics.
   d. Heredity directs the individual's potential and environment determines whether and to what degree the individual reaches that potential.

2. Research studies of monozygotic twins who were raised apart suggest that:
   a. virtually every human trait is affected by both genes and environment.
   b. only a few psychological traits, such as emotional reactivity, are affected by genes.
   c. most traits are determined by environmental influences.
   d. most traits are determined by genes.

3. Males with fragile-X syndrome are:
   a. feminine in appearance.
   b. less severely affected than females.
   c. frequently retarded intellectually.
   d. likely to have fatty deposits around the breasts.

4. Disorders that are _____ are most likely to pass undetected from generation to generation.
   a. dominant
   b. dominant and polygenic
   c. recessive
   d. recessive and multifactorial

5. The effect of a gene on a particular physical characteristic depends on whether the gene comes from the mother or the father. This is called:
   a. the dominant-recessive pattern.
   b. genetic imprinting.
   c. the additive pattern.
   d. molecular genetics.

6. Dizygotic twins result when:
   a. a single egg is fertilized by a sperm and then splits.
   b. a single egg is fertilized by two different sperm.
   c. two eggs are fertilized by two different sperm.
   d. either a single egg is fertilized by one sperm or two eggs are fertilized by two different sperm.

7. Molecules of DNA that in humans are organized into 23 complementary pairs are called:
   a. zygotes.   c. chromosomes.
   b. genes.   d. ova.

8. Shortly after the zygote is formed, it begins the processes of duplication and division. Each resulting new cell has:
   a. the same number of chromosomes as was contained in the zygote.
   b. half the number of chromosomes as was contained in the zygote.
   c. twice, then four times, then eight times the number of chromosomes as was contained in the zygote.
   d. all the chromosomes except those that determine sex.

9. If an ovum is fertilized by a sperm bearing a Y chromosome:
   a. a female will develop.
   b. cell division will result.
   c. a male will develop.
   d. spontaneous abortion will occur.

10. When the male cells in the testes and the female cells in the ovaries divide to produce gametes, the process differs from that in the production of all other cells. As a result of the different process, the gametes have:
    a. one rather than both members of each chromosome pair.
    b. 23 chromosome pairs.
    c. X but not Y chromosomes.
    d. chromosomes from both parents.

11. Most human traits are:
    a. polygenic.
    b. multifactorial.
    c. determined by dominant-recessive patterns.
    d. both a. and b.

12. Genotype is to phenotype as _____ is to _____ .
    a. genetic potential; physical expression
    b. physical expression; genetic potential
    c. sperm; ovum
    d. gamete; zygote

13. The genes that influence height and skin color interact according to the _____ pattern.
    a. dominant-recessive   c. additive
    b. X-linked   d. nonadditive

14. X-linked recessive genes explain why some traits seem to be passed from:
    a. father to son.
    b. father to daughter.
    c. mother to daughter.
    d. mother to son.

15. A 35-year-old woman who is pregnant is most likely to undergo which type of test for the detection of prenatal chromosomal or genetic abnormalities?
    a. pre-implantation testing
    b. ultrasound
    c. amniocentesis
    d. alpha-fetoprotein assay

True or False Items

Write T (*true*) or F (*false*) on the line in front of each statement.

_____ 1. Most human characteristics are multifactorial, caused by the interaction of genetic and environmental factors.

_____ 2. Less than 10 percent of all zygotes have harmful genes or an abnormal chromosomal makeup.

_____ 3. Research suggests that susceptibility to alcoholism is at least partly the result of genetic inheritance.

_____ 4. The human reproductive cells (ova and sperm) are called gametes.

_____ 5. Only a very few human traits are polygenic.

_____ 6. The zygote contains all the biologically inherited information—the genes and chromosomes—that a person will have during his or her life.

_____ 7. A couple should probably seek genetic counseling if several earlier pregnancies ended in spontaneous abortion.

_____ 8. Many genetic conditions are recessive; thus, a child will have the condition even if only the mother carries the gene.

_____ 9. Two people who have the same phenotype may have a different genotype for a trait such as eye color.

_____ 10. When cells divide to produce reproductive cells (gametes), each sperm or ovum receives only 23 chromosomes, half as many as the original cell.

_____ 11. Most genes have only one function.

_____ 12. Couples are said to be infertile when they have been unable to conceive after 6 months of trying.

Thinking Critically About Chapter 3

Answer these questions the day before an exam as a final check on your understanding of the chapter's terms and concepts.

1. The international effort to map the complete human genetic code is complicated by the fact that:
   a. the total number of human genes is far greater than the 100,000 previously estimated.
   b. some genes appear in several different versions.
   c. genes are made up of thousands of DNA particles called alleles.
   d. All of the above have complicated the effort to map the genetic code.

2. Before their first child was born, Jack and Diane decided that they should be karyotyped, which means that:
   a. their chromosomes were photographed.
   b. a genetic counselor filled out a complete history of genetic diseases in their families.
   c. they each took a fertility test.
   d. they selected the sex of their child.

3. Which of the following is an inherited abnormality that quite possibly could develop into a recognizable syndrome?
   a. Just before dividing to form a sperm or ovum, corresponding gene segments of a chromosome pair break off and are exchanged.
   b. Just before conception, a chromosome pair splits imprecisely, resulting in a mixture of cells.
   c. A person inherits an X chromosome in which part of the chromosome is attached to the rest of it by a very slim string of molecules.
   d. A person inherits a recessive gene on his Y chromosome.

4. Some men are color-blind because they inherit a particular recessive gene from their mother. That recessive gene is carried on the:
   a. *X* chromosome.
   b. *XX* chromosome pair.
   c. *Y* chromosome.
   d. *X* or *Y* chromosome.

5. If your mother is much taller than your father, it is most likely that your height will be:
   a. about the same as your mother's, because the X chromosome determines height.
   b. about the same as your father's, because the Y chromosome determines height.
   c. somewhere between your mother's and father's heights because of genetic imprinting.
   d. greater than both your mother's and father's because of your grandfather's dominant gene.

6. If a dizygotic twin develops schizophrenia, the likelihood of the other twin experiencing serious mental illness is much lower than is the case with monozygotic twins. This suggests that:
   a. schizophrenia is caused by genes.
   b. schizophrenia is influenced by genes.
   c. environment is unimportant in the development of schizophrenia.
   d. monozygotic twins are especially vulnerable to schizophrenia.

7. A person's skin turns yellow-orange as a result of a carrot-juice diet regimen. This is an example of:
   a. an environmental influence.
   b. an alteration in genotype.
   c. polygenic inheritance.
   d. incomplete dominance.

8. The personality trait of inhibition (shyness) seems to be partly genetic. A child who inherits the genes for shyness will be shy:
   a. under most circumstances.
   b. only if shyness is the dominant gene.
   c. if the environment does not encourage greater sociability.
   d. if he or she is raised by biological rather than adoptive parents.

9. If a man carries the recessive gene for cystic fibrosis and his wife does not, the chances of their having a child with cystic fibrosis is:
   a. one in four.
   b. fifty-fifty.
   c. zero.
   d. dependent upon the wife's ethnic background.

10. One of the best ways to distinguish the relative influence of genetic and environmental factors on behavior is to compare children who have:
    a. the same genes and environments.
    b. different genes and environments.
    c. similar genes and environments.
    d. the same genes but different environments.

11. In the case of identical twins reared apart, research has confirmed that:
    a. most psychological characteristics and personality traits are genetically influenced.
    b. most psychological characteristics and personality traits are influenced by the environment.
    c. some traits are genetically influenced while others are due to environmental effects.
    d. both a. and b. are true.

12. Laurie and Brad, who both have a history of alcoholism in their families, are concerned that the child they hope to have will inherit a genetic predisposition to alcoholism. Based on information presented in the text, what advice should you offer them?
    a. "Stop worrying, alcoholism is only weakly genetic."
    b. "It is almost certain that your child will become alcoholic."
    c. "Social influences, such as the family and peer environment, play a critical role in determining whether alcoholism is expressed."
    d. "Wait to have children until you are both middle aged, in order to see if the two of you become alcoholic."

13. Sixteen-year-old Joey experiences some mental slowness and hearing and heart problems, yet he is able to care for himself and is unusually sweet-tempered. Joey probably:
    a. is mentally retarded.
    b. has Alzheimer's disease.
    c. has Kleinfelter syndrome.
    d. has Down syndrome.

14. Genetically, Claude's potential height is 6'0. Because he did not receive a balanced diet, however, he grew to only 5'9". Claude's actual height is an example of a:
    a. recessive gene.
    b. dominant gene.
    c. genotype.
    d. phenotype.

15. Winona inherited a gene from her mother that, regardless of her father's contribution to her genotype, will be expressed in her phenotype. Evidently, the gene Winona received from her mother is a(n) _____ gene.

   a. polygenic   **c.** dominant
   b. recessive   **d.** X-linked

Key Terms

Writing Definitions

Using your own words, write on a separate piece of paper a brief definition or explanation of each of the following terms.

1. gamete
2. zygote
3. genes
4. chromosome
5. genetic code
6. Human Genome Project
7. allele
8. twenty-third pair
9. XX
10. XY
11. monozygotic twins
12. dizygotic twins
13. infertile
14. assisted reproductive technology (ART)
15. in vitro fertilization (IVF)
16. polygenic
17. multifactorial
18. genotype
19. phenotype
20. carrier
21. additive gene
22. dominant gene
23. recessive gene
24. X-linked gene
25. genetic imprinting
26. behavioral genetics
27. molecular genetics
28. spontaneous abortion
29. fragile-X syndrome
30. genetic counseling

Cross-Check

After you have written the definitions of the key terms in this chapter, you should complete the crossword puzzle to ensure that you can reverse the process—recognize the term, given the definition.

ACROSS

2. Cluster of distinct characteristics that tend to occur together in a given disorder.
7. A person who has a gene in his or her genotype that is not evident in his or her phenotype.
8. The sum total of all the genes a person inherits.
10. The single cell formed from the fusing of an ovum and a sperm.
13. The stronger gene in an interacting pair of genes.
14. A tool of molecular genetics that pinpoints the chemical codes that make up a particular DNA molecule (abbrev.).
15. All of the genetic traits that are expressed in a person.
17. Genes that are on the X chromosome.
18. The sequence of chemical bases held within DNA molecules that directs development.
19. One of 46 in each normal human cell.
20. A genetic disease that nearly always develops in people with a particular allele of a particular gene.
21. The genes that affect height, hair curliness, and skin color are of this type.

DOWN

1. A genetic disorder in which part of the X chromosome is attached to the rest of it by a very slim string of molecules.
3. Fraternal twins.
4. All the nongenetic factors that can affect development.
5. The growth process in which cells begin to specialize, taking different forms and dividing at different rates.
6. The basic unit of genetic instruction.
7. The genetic process that during the formation of gametes adds greatly to genetic diversity.
9. A spontaneous abortion.
11. The international project that aims to map the complete human genetic code.
12. Type of trait produced by the interaction of many genes (rather than by a single gene).
13. The most common extra-chromosome syndrome (also called trisomy-21).
16. The weaker gene in an interacting pair of genes.

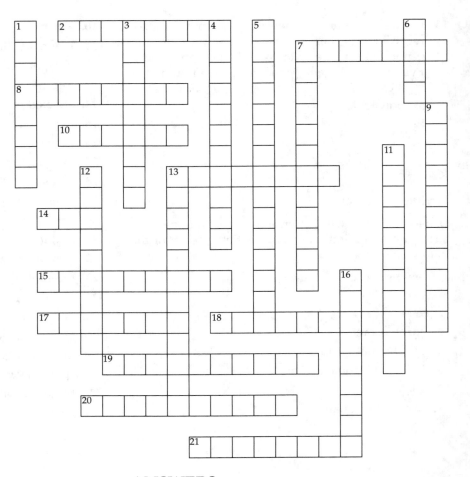

ANSWERS

CHAPTER REVIEW

1. epigenetic; environment
2. gametes; sperm; ovum
3. zygote
4. duplicated; differentiate
5. every
6. genes; chromosome; DNA
7. adenine; guanine; cytosine; thymine; genetic code; sequence
8. Human Genome Project; alleles; several different
9. diversity; continuity
10. 46; 23
11. one; 23
12. twenty-third; *X*; *XX*; *X*; *Y*; *XY*
13. been roughly equal; reproductive; males; 45
14. women; abort female fetuses because couples are permitted only one child and males are preferred
15. is; is not
16. sperm

17. chance

18. crossing-over; 64 trillion

19. 270; monozygotic; are

20. dizygotic (fraternal); 50

21. 60; late 30s; early 20s

22. increased; fertility drugs; smaller; mature; vulnerable

23. 2 to 30 percent; one year

24. assisted reproductive technology (ART); in vitro fertilization (IVF)

Among the questions raised by ART are the following: Should sperm or ova donors have parental rights? Should ART be available to everyone? Do children have the right to know if the persons who raise them are not their biological parents? Does society have the right to forbid any form of ART?

25. polygenic; multifactorial

26. genotype; phenotype

27. carrier

28. genes; environment

29. additive; height; skin color (or hair curliness)

30. nonadditive; dominant–recessive; dominant; recessive; physical; incomplete dominance

31. X-linked; color blindness, many allergies, several diseases, and some learning disabilities; males

32. penetrate; temperature; stress; mosaic

33. does; genetic imprinting

34. behavioral genetics; psychological; personality; sociability, assertiveness, moodiness, and fearfulness; schizophrenia, depression, and attention-deficit/hyperactivity disorder; cognitive; memory for numbers, spatial perception, and fluency of expression

35. interaction; genes; environmental; do not always

36. environmental; twins; adopted

37. monozygotic; dizygotic

38. biological

39. identical (or monozygotic); different

40. every

41. molecular genetics

42. quantitative trait loci (QTL)

A genetically shy child whose parents are outgoing, for example, would have many more contacts with other people and would observe his or her parents socializing more freely than if this same child's parents were also shy. In growing up, the child might learn to relax in social settings and would become less observably shy than he or she would have been with more introverted parents, despite the genetic predis-

position toward shyness. Culture plays a role in the expression of shyness.

43. intelligence; activity level; aggression; religiosity

44. two-thirds; 6

45. do; late winter; virus

46. Alzheimer's disease

47. is; is; a quick temper, a willingness to take risks, and a high level of anxiety; 15; 25

48. fetal alcohol syndrome; acculturated

By studying genetic disruptions of normal development, researchers (a) gain a fuller appreciation of the complexities of genetic interaction, (b) reduce misinformation and prejudice directed toward those afflicted by such disorders, and (c) help individuals understand the likelihood of occurrence and to become better prepared to limit their harmful effects.

49. gametes

50. half; do not; spontaneous abortion; 200; syndrome

51. alpha-fetoprotein; sonogram

52. amniocentesis; chorionic villi sampling

53. in vitro; pre-implantation testing

54. Down syndrome; trisomy-21

55. faster; Alzheimer's disease; communication

Most people with Down syndrome have certain facial characteristics—a thick tongue, round face, slanted eyes—as well as distinctive hands, feet, and fingerprints. Many also have hearing problems, heart abnormalities, muscle weakness, and short stature. Almost all experience some mental slowness.

56. sex; Klinefelter syndrome; XXY

57. fragile-X

58. maternal age

59. almost always

60. more

61. dominant; are not

62. Huntington's chorea; Tourette syndrome

63. recessive; multifactorial; cystic fibrosis, thalassemia, sickle-cell anemia

64. prenatal genetic counseling

65. Genetic counseling is recommended for (a) those who have a parent, sibling, or child with a serious genetic condition; (b) those who have a history of spontaneous abortions, stillbirths, or infertility; (c) couples who are from the same ethnic group or subgroup; and (d) women over age 35.

PROGRESS TEST 1

Multiple-Choice Questions

1. **a.** is the answer. (p. 69)

   b. & c. The reproductive cells (sperm and ova), which are also called gametes, are individual entities.

   d. *Monozygote* refers to one member of a pair of identical twins.

2. **c.** is the answer. (pp. 69–70)

   a. The zygote is the first cell of the developing person.

   b. Chromosomes are molecules of DNA that *carry* genes.

   d. DNA molecules contain genetic information.

3. **b.** is the answer. (p. 72)

4. **d.** is the answer. When the gametes are formed, one member of each chromosome pair splits off; because in females both are *X* chromosomes, each ovum must carry an *X* chromosome. (p. 72)

   a., b., & c. The zygote refers to the merged sperm and ovum that is the first new cell of the developing individual.

5. **b.** is the answer. *Mono* means "one." Thus, monozygotic twins develop from one zygote. (p. 75)

   a. & c. Dizygotic, or fraternal, twins develop from two (*di*) zygotes.

   d. A trizygotic birth would result in triplets (*tri*), rather than twins.

6. **d.** is the answer. In this situation, one factor (genetic similarity) is held constant while the other factor (environment) is varied. Therefore, any similarity in traits is strong evidence of genetic inheritance. (p. 83)

7. **a.** is the answer. (p. 93)

   c. & d. Most dominant disorders are neither seriously disabling nor sex-linked.

8. **c.** is the answer. (p. 78)

   a., b., & d. *Polygenic* means "many genes"; *multifactorial* means "many factors," which are not limited to either genetic or environmental factors.

9. **b.** is the answer. (p. 69)

   a. Genotype is a person's genetic potential.

   c. A karyotype is a picture of a person's chromosomes.

   d. Phenotype is the actual expression of a genotype.

10. **d.** is the answer. (p. 75)

11. **d.** is the answer. (p. 92)

    a. & b. These chromosomal abnormalities affect females.

    c. There is no such abnormality.

12. **b.** is the answer. (p. 81)

    c. & d. The text does not equate polygenic complexity with either recessive or dominant genes.

13. **a.** is the answer. (p. 93)

14. **b.** is the answer. (p. 78)

15. **b.** is the answer. (p. 95)

    a. & c. These abnormalities involve the sex chromosomes, not genes.

    d. In order for an offspring to inherit a recessive condition, the parents need only be carriers of the recessive gene in their genotypes; they need not actually have the disease.

Matching Items

1. c (p. 69)	5. b (p. 75)	9. e (p. 78)
2. h (p. 69)	6. f (p. 76)	10. d (p. 69)
3. m (p. 78)	7. g (p. 79)	11. k (p. 71)
4. i (p. 78)	8. j (p. 92)	12. a (p. 72)
		13. l (p. 72)

PROGRESS TEST 2

Multiple-Choice Questions

1. **d.** is the answer. (p. 82)

2. **a.** is the answer. (p. 83)

3. **c.** is the answer. (p. 93)

   a. Physical appearance is usually normal in this syndrome.

   b. Males are more frequently and more severely affected.

   d. This is true of the *XXY* chromosomal abnormality, but not the fragile-*X* syndrome.

4. **d.** is the answer. (p. 93)

5. **b.** is the answer. (p. 80)

   a. & c. These patterns are based on the interaction of both parents' genes.

   d. Molecular genetics is the study of the chemical codes that make up a particular molecule of DNA.

6. **c.** is the answer. (p. 76)

   a. This would result in monozygotic twins.

   b. Only one sperm can fertilize an ovum.

d. A single egg fertilized by one sperm would produce a single offspring or monozygotic twins.

7. c. is the answer. (p. 69)

a. Zygotes are fertilized ova.

b. Genes are the smaller units of heredity that are organized into sequences on chromosomes.

d. Ova are female reproductive cells.

8. a. is the answer. (p. 69)

9. c. is the answer. The ovum will contain an X chromosome; with the sperm's Y chromosome, it will produce the male XY pattern. (p. 72)

a. Only if the ovum is fertilized by an X chromosome from the sperm will a female develop.

b. Cell division will occur regardless of whether the sperm contributes an X or a Y chromosome.

d. Spontaneous abortions are likely to occur when there are chromosomal or genetic abnormalities; the situation described is perfectly normal.

10. a. is the answer. (p. 72)

b. & d. These are true of all body cells *except* the gametes.

c. Gametes have either X or Y chromosomes.

11. d. is the answer. (p. 78)

12. a. is the answer. Genotype refers to the sum total of all the genes a person inherits; phenotype refers to the actual expression of the individual's characteristics. (p. 78)

13. c. is the answer. (p. 79)

14. d. is the answer. X-linked genes are located only on the X chromosome. Because males inherit only one X chromosome, they are more likely than females to have these characteristics in their phenotype. (pp. 79–80)

15. c. is the answer. (p. 90)

a. Pre-implantation testing is conducted on zygotes grown in vitro.

b. Ultrasound is used to detect visible signs of abnormality.

d. Alpha-fetoprotein assay is used to detect the presences of AFP, an indicator of neural-tube defects.

True or False Items

1. T (p. 78)

2. F   An estimated half of all zygotes have an odd number of chromosomes. (p. 89)

3. T (p. 86)

4. T (p. 69)

5. F   Most traits are polygenic. (p. 78)

6. T (p. 69)

7. T (p. 96)

8. F   A trait from a recessive gene will be part of the phenotype only when the person has two recessive genes for that trait. (p. 98)

9. T (pp. 78)

10. T (p. 72)

11. F   Most genes have several functions. (p. 70)

12. F   A couple is said to be infertile when they have been unable to conceive after at least one year of trying. (p. 76)

THINKING CRITICALLY ABOUT CHAPTER 3

1. b. is the answer. (p. 71)

a. In fact, the total number of human genes is probably *less* than 100,000.

c. Alleles are alternate versions of a specific gene.

2. a. is the answer. (p. 72)

3. c. is the answer. This describes the fragile-X syndrome. (p. 92)

a. This phenomenon, which is called *crossing over*, merely contributes to genetic diversity.

b. This is merely an example of a particular non-additive gene interaction pattern.

d. For a recessive gene to be expressed, both parents must pass it on to the child.

4. a. is the answer. (pp. 79–80)

b. The male genotype is XY, not XX.

c. & d. The mother contributes only an X chromosome.

5. c. is the answer. (pp. 80–81)

a., b., & d. It is unlikely that these factors account for height differences from one generation to the next.

6. b. is the answer. Since monozygotic twins are genetically identical, while dizygotic twins share only 50 percent of their genes, greater similarity of traits between monozygotic twins suggests that genes are an important influence. (p. 86)

a. & c. Even though schizophrenia has a strong genetic component, it is not the case that if one twin has schizophrenia the other also automatically does. Therefore, the environment, too, is an important influence.

d. This does not necessarily follow.

7. a. is the answer. (p. 82)

b. Genotype is a person's genetic potential, established at conception.

c. Polygenic inheritance refers to the influence of many genes on a particular trait.

d. Incomplete dominance refers to the phenotype being influenced primarily, but not exclusively, by the dominant gene.

8. **c.** is the answer. (pp. 84–85)

   a. & b. Research shows that shyness is affected by both genetic inheritance and the social environment. Therefore, if a child's environment promotes socializing outside the immediate family, a genetically shy child might grow up much less timid socially than he or she would have been with less outgoing parents.

   d. Either biological or adoptive parents are capable of nurturing, or not nurturing, shyness in their children.

9. **c.** is the answer. Cystic fibrosis is a recessive gene disorder; therefore, in order for a child to inherit this disease, he or she must receive the recessive gene from both parents. (p. 93)

10. **d.** is the answer. To separate the influences of genes and environment, one of the two must be held constant. (p. 83)

   a., b., & c. These situations would not allow a researcher to separate the contributions of heredity and environment.

11. **d.** is the answer. (p. 83)

12. **c.** is the answer. (pp. 86–87)

   a. Some people's inherited biochemistry makes them highly susceptible to alcoholism.

   b. Despite a strong genetic influence on alcoholism, the environment also plays a critical role.

   d. Not only is this advice unreasonable, but it might increase the likelihood of chromosomal abnormalities in the parents' sperm and ova.

13. **d.** is the answer. (pp. 91–92)

14. **d.** is the answer. (p. 78)

   a. & b. Genes are discrete segments of a chromosome.

   c. Genotype refers to genetic potential.

15. **c.** is the answer. (pp. 78, 79)

   a. There is no such thing as a "polygenic gene." *Polygenic* means "many genes."

   b. A recessive gene paired with a dominant gene will not be expressed in the phenotype.

   d. *X*-linked genes may be dominant or recessive.

KEY TERMS

Writing Definitions

1. **Gametes** are the human reproductive cells. (p. 69)

2. The **zygote** is the one-celled organism formed during conception by the union of sperm and ovum. (p. 69)

3. **Genes** are discrete segments of a chromosome, which is a DNA molecule, that are the basic units of heredity. (p. 70)

4. **Chromosomes** are molecules of DNA that contain the genes organized in precise sequences. (p. 69)

5. The precise nature of a gene's instructions, called the **genetic code**, is determined by the sequence in which pairs of chemical bases appear along each segment of DNA. (p. 70)

6. The **Human Genome Project** is a worldwide effort to map the complete human genetic code. (p. 70)

7. An **allele** is one of the normal versions of a gene that has several possible sequences of base pairs. (p. 71)

8. The **twenty-third pair** of chromosomes determines the individual's sex. (p. 72)

9. **XX** is the twenty-third chromosome pair that, in humans, determines that the developing fetus will be female. (p. 72)

10. **XY** is the twenty-third chromosome pair that, in humans, determines that the developing fetus will be male. (p. 72)

11. **Monozygotic**, or identical, **twins** develop from a single fertilized ovum that splits in two, producing two genetically identical zygotes. (p. 75)

   Memory aid: Mono means "one"; **monozygotic twins** develop from one fertilized ovum.

12. **Dizygotic**, or fraternal, **twins** develop from two separate ova fertilized by different sperm at roughly the same time, and therefore are no more genetically similar than ordinary siblings. (p. 76)

   Memory aid: A fraternity is a group of two (*di*) or more nonidentical individuals.

13. A couple is said to be **infertile** when they have been unable to conceive after at least one year of trying. (p. 76)

14. **Assisted reproductive technology (ART)** is a general term for the various techniques used to help couples conceive. (p. 76)

15. **In vitro fertilization (IVF)** is a technique for helping infertile couples conceive in which ova

are removed from a woman, mixed with sperm to form a viable zygote, and then inserted into the woman's uterus. (p. 76)

16. Most human traits, especially psychological traits, are **polygenic traits**; that is, they are affected by many genes. (p. 78)

17. Most human traits are also **multifactorial traits**—that is, influenced by many factors, including genetic and environmental factors. (p. 78)

    Memory aid: The roots of the words *polygenic* and *multifactorial* give their meaning: *poly* means "many" and *genic* means "of the genes"; *multi* means "several" and *factorial* obviously refers to factors.

18. The total of all the genes a person inherits—his or her genetic potential—is called the **genotype**. (p. 78)

19. The actual physical or behavioral expression of a genotype, the result of the interaction of the genes with each other and with the environment, is called the **phenotype**. (p. 78)

20. A person who has a recessive gene that is not expressed in his or her genotype but that can be passed on to the person's offspring is called a **carrier** of that gene. (p. 78)

21. When a trait is determined by **additive genes**, the phenotype reflects the sum of the contributions of all the genes involved. The genes affecting height, for example, interact in this fashion. (p. 79)

22. A **dominant gene** is the stronger, controlling member of an interacting pair of genes. (p. 79)

23. A **recessive gene** is the weaker member of an interacting pair of genes. (p. 79)

24. **X-linked genes** are genes that are located only on the X chromosome. Since males have only one X chromosome, they are more likely to have the characteristics determined by these genes in their phenotype than are females. (p. 79)

25. **Genetic imprinting** is the tendency of certain genes to be expressed differently depending on whether they are inherited from the mother or from the father. (p. 80)

26. **Behavioral genetics** is the study of the genetic origins of personality, psychological disorders, intellectual abilities, and other psychological characteristics. (p. 81)

27. **Molecular genetics** is the study of the chemical codes that make up a particular molecule of DNA. (p. 83)

28. Also known as a *miscarriage*, a **spontaneous abortion** is the natural termination of a pregnancy before the fetus is fully developed. (p. 89)

29. The **fragile-X syndrome** is a single-gene disorder in which part of the X chromosome is attached by such a thin string of molecules that it seems about to break off. Although the characteristics associated with this syndrome are quite varied, some mental deficiency is relatively common. (p. 92)

30. **Genetic counseling** involves a variety of tests through which couples can learn more about their genes, and can thus make informed decisions about their childbearing and child-rearing future. (p. 96)

Cross-Check

ACROSS

2. syndrome
7. carrier
8. genotype
10. zygote
13. dominant
14. QTL
15. phenotype
17. X-linked
18. genetic code
19. chromosome
20. Alzheimer's
21. additive

DOWN

1. fragile-X
3. dizygotic
4. environment
5. differentiation
6. gene
7. crossing-over
9. miscarriage
11. Human Genome
12. polygenic
13. Down syndrome
16. recessive

Chapter Four

Prenatal Development and Birth

Chapter Overview

Prenatal development is complex and startlingly rapid—more rapid than any other period of the life span. During the prenatal period, the individual develops from a one-celled zygote to a complex human baby. This development is outlined in Chapter 4, along with some of the problems that can occur—among them prenatal exposure to disease, drugs, and other hazards—and the factors that moderate the risks of teratogenic exposure.

For the developing person, birth marks the most radical transition of the entire life span. No longer sheltered from the outside world, the fetus becomes a separate human being who begins life almost completely dependent upon his or her caregivers. Chapter 4 also examines the process of birth and its possible variations and problems.

The chapter concludes with a discussion of the significance of the parent–newborn bond, including factors that affect its development.

NOTE: Answer guidelines for all Chapter 4 questions begin on page 69.

[handwritten:] At 8 weeks the head is more rounded and the facial features have formed.

Guided Study

The text chapter should be studied one section at a time. Before you read, preview each section by skimming it, noting headings and boldface items. Then read the appropriate section objectives from the following outline. Keep these objectives in mind and, as you read the chapter section, search for the information that will enable you to meet each objective. Once you have finished a section, write out answers for its objectives.

From Zygote to Newborn (pp. 103–110)

1. Describe the significant developments of the germinal period.

[handwritten, margin: First 2 weeks]
[handwritten:] Within the germinal period within hrs. of conception the one celled zygote travels down the fallopian tube to begin cell division and growth. At about the 8 cell stage the cells begin to differentiate, it takes on distinct characteristics and gravitates toward specific locations that may foreshadow functions. The multiplying cells separate into 2 distinct masses the outer mass becomes placenta and inner mass becomes the embryo. The first task of the outer cells is to achieve implantation.

2. Describe the significant developments of the embryonic period.

[handwritten, margin: 3rd to 8th week]
[handwritten:] The mass of cells becomes a distinct human being. The developing organism begins to differentiate into 3 distinct layers that will form key body systems. A perceptible sign of body formation appears, a fold in the outer cells that after 22 days will become the neural tube which will later become the CNS (brain & spinal cord). Head takes shape in 4th week and the blood vessel that is the heart begins to pulsate. 5th week buds that will become arms + legs appear and a primative spine forms. Also at 5 weeks upper arms, forearms palms and webbed feet. Legs feet + webbed toes a few da

3. Describe the significant developments of the fetal period, noting the importance of the age of viability.

[handwritten, margin: 9 weeks till Birth]
[handwritten:] The sex organs take a certain shape newly formed organs send hormones to the developed brain. Movement within the womb, easily changes position. In the 4, 5, 6th months the heartbeat is stronger and the digestive and excretory systems develop more fully. Fingernails, toenails and teeth buds form. The Age of viability is the age (about 22 weeks) after conception the fetus can survive outside the womb if medical attention is availible. The final 3 months matures the cardiovascular and respiratory systems including valves of the heart as they final maturation. The infant gains about 4.5 pds or more of body weight

4. (In Person) Describe the fetus's various responses to its immediate environment (the womb). *The fetus will drink amniotic fluid more rapidly if it is sweet thus the lungs digestion + nutrition are related to the mothers'. The smell of amniotic fluid is more soothing than any other cell. Hearing develops in the 28th week of gestation - remember sounds heard before birth. Infants typically stop crying when held toward the mothers heart b/c it is familiar to them.*

Risk Reduction (pp. 111–118)

5. Explain the main goal of teratology, and discuss several factors that determine whether a specific teratogen will be harmful. *The main goal of teratology is to identify anything that may have a negative impact on the growth or prenatal health to the infant. The factors that make a teratogen harmful are the impact of the teratogen, the amount that the baby was exposed to and the time period within the pregnancy that the teratogen was discovered and the genetic vulnerability to the teratogen. In alcohol for example when a woman carrying fraternal twins the BAL are equal but one may be more effected than the other b/c the enzymes effectability.*

6. Identify at least five teratogens, and describe their effects on the developing embryo or fetus, focusing on the effects of psychoactive drugs.
*1) Rubella - blindness, deafness, heart abnormalities and brain damage.
2) HIV - AIDS immune system can no longer fight of infection.
3) Beer, wine, liquor, LSD, marijuana, cocaine slow down fetal growth and increase the risk of premature labor. All effect the brain that is developing
4) Tobacco - Low Birth weight
5) Marijuana affects CNS high pitched cry that denotes brain damage.*

7. (Changing Policy) Discuss several protective steps that may be taken to prevent drug damage.
*1. Abstinance from all drugs even before pregnancy.
2. Abstinance during 1st Month
3. Moderation thru out pregnancy (when abstinance is impossible)
4. Social Support
5. Postnatal Care*

Low Birthweight (pp. 119–122)

8. Distinguish among low-birthweight (LBW), preterm, and small-for-gestational-age (SGA) infants, and identify the causes of low birthweight, focusing on the relationship of poverty to low birthweight. *Low birthweight is less than 5 1/2 pounds. causes malnutrition and poverty. Preterm is birth that occurs 3 or more weeks before full term. Small for gestational age is a term applied to infants who weigh substantially less than they should given how much time has passed since conception.*
Poverty goes to malnutrition b/c they can't afford food therefore have children with low birth weight.

The Normal Birth (pp. 122–126)

9. Describe the normal process of birth, specifying the events of each stage. *Stage 1 Labor Up to 30 yrs for 1st child. 6-8 in others. Regular contractions are 15-22 min apart. Increase in frequency and intensity.
Stage 2 labor and Delivery lasts 10-40 minutes forceful and regular contractions (2-3) min
Crowning
• head appears
• episiotmy (vaginal opening to rectum)
Stage 3 placenta coming virtually painless.*

10. Describe the test used to assess the neonate's condition at birth. *The "Apgar test assigns a score of 0,1,2, to heart rate color breathing and muscle tone and reflexes at 1 min after birth and then again at 5 minutes after birth. A score of 1 at 1 min is usually a warning sign for problems but most people rapidly improve*

11. Discuss the importance of medical attention and the question of how much and what type of medical attention are appropriate. *Medical attention makes delivery faster easier + safer. OBGYN + midwives and hospital visits are the norm now.*

Birth Complications (pp. 126–127)

12. Explain the causes of cerebral palsy, and discuss the special needs of high-risk infants.

Events during and before birth for example anoxia which is a temporary lack of oxygen that can cause brain damage. Similarly low birth weight babies before, during or immediately after birth. High risk infants will first go to intensive care where there environment can be controlled/monitored & then are taken home

Bonding After Birth (pp. 128–130)

13. (text and Thinking Like a Scientist) Explain the concept of parent–newborn bonding and the current view of most developmentalists regarding bonding in humans. The parent new born bond is the strong feelings of attachment that arises between parents & their new born infants.

Chapter Review

When you have finished reading the chapter, work through the material that follows to review it. Complete the sentences and answer the questions. As you proceed, evaluate your performance for each section by consulting the answers on page 69. Do not continue with the next section until you understand each answer. If you need to, review or reread the appropriate section in the textbook before continuing.

From Zygote to Newborn (pp. 103–110)

1. Prenatal development is divided into ___3___ main periods. The first two weeks of development are called the ___germinal___ period; from the ___3rd___ week through the ___8th___ week is known as the ___embryonic___ period; and from this point until birth is the ___fetal___ period.

Some developmentalists prefer to divide pregnancy into 3-month periods called ___trimesters___ .

2. At about the ___8___-cell stage, clusters of cells begin to take on distinct traits. The first clear sign of this process, called ___differentation___ , occurs about ___one___ week(s) after conception, when the multiplying cells separate into outer cells that will become the ___placenta___ and inner cells that will become the ___embryo___ .

3. The next significant event is the burrowing of the outer cells of the organism into the lining of the uterus, a process called ___implantation___. This process ___is not___ (is/is not) automatic.

4. At the beginning of the period of the embryo, a fold in the outer cells of the developing individual forms a structure that will become the ___nueral___ ___tube___ , which will develop into the ___central___ ___nervous___ ___system___ .

Briefly describe the major features of development during the second month.
Head takes shape, Eyes, ears, nose form within days in 4 week the blood vessel that will be the heart begains to pump 5th week buds that will be the legs and arms form and spinal cord. 8th week facial features head rounded.

5. Eight weeks after conception, the embryo weighs about ___1 gram___ and is about ___1 inch___ in length. The organism now becomes known as the ___fetus___ .

6. The first stage of development of the sex organs is the appearance in the ___6___ week of the ___indifferent___ ___gonad.___ , a cluster of cells that can develop into male or female sex organs.

7. If the fetus has a(n) _____Y_____ (X/Y) chromosome, a gene on this chromosome sends a biochemical signal that triggers the development of the ___male___ (male/female) sex organs. Without that gene, no signal is sent, and the fetus begins to develop ___female___ (male/female) sex organs. Not until the ___12th___ week are the external male or female genital organs fully formed. Most functions of the brain are ___gender nuetral___ (sex-linked/gender-neutral), and all sex-related functions are ___epigenetic___, depending on internal and external factors that continue throughout life.

8. By the end of the ___3rd___ month, the fetus is fully formed, weighs approximately ___3 oz.___, and is about ___3 in___ long. These figures ___vary___ (vary/do not vary) from fetus to fetus.

9. The placenta connects the mother's ___umbilical_____cord_____ with that of her growing embryo.

10. During the fourth, fifth, and sixth months the brain increases in size by a factor of ___6___. This neurological maturation is essential to the regulation of such basic body functions as ___breathing___ and ___sucking___. The brain develops new neurons in a process called ___nuerogenesis___ and new connections between them in a process called ___synaptogenesis___. These developments occur during the ___middle___ trimester.

11. The age at which a fetus has at least some chance of surviving outside the uterus is called the ___age_____of_____ ___viability___, which occurs ___22___ weeks after conception.

12. At about ___28___ weeks after conception, brain-wave patterns begin to resemble the ___sleep___-___wake___ cycles of a newborn.

13. A 28-week-old fetus typically weighs about ___3 lbs.___ and has more than a ___95.1'___ percent chance of survival.

14. Two crucial aspects of development in the last months of prenatal life are maturation of the ___cardiovascular___ and ___respiratory___ systems.

15. The average newborn weighs ___7.5 pds.___.

16. An important part of the fetus's weight gain is the formation of body ___fat___, which will provide a layer of insulation to keep the newborn warm.

17. This weight gain also provides the fetus with ___calories___ for use until the mother's breast milk is fully established. Severe ___malnutrition___ in the second or third trimester reduces the child's ability to ___learn___.

18. (In Person) The most remarkable fetal learning involves the sense of ___hearing___, with the first fetal responses evident at the ___28th___ week.

Risk Reduction (pp. 111–118)

19. The scientific study of birth defects is called ___teratology___. Harmful agents that can cause birth defects, called ___teratogens___, include ___drugs, pollutants and conditions like stress___.

20. Substances that impair the child's action and intellect by harming the brain are called ___behavioral_____teratogens___.

Approximately __3.1°__ percent of all fetuses are born with major structural abnormalities, and __10-20__ percent with behavioral difficulties related to prenatal damage.

21. Teratology is a science of __RISK analysis__, which attempts to evaluate the factors that can make prenatal harm more or less likely to occur.

22. Three crucial factors that determine whether a specific teratogen will cause harm, and of what nature, are the __timing__ of exposure, the __amount__ of exposure, and the developing organism's __genetic vulnerability__ to damage from the substance.

23. The time when a particular part of the body is most susceptible to teratogenic damage is called its __critical period__. For physical structure and form, this is the entire period of the __embryo__. However, for __behavioral__ teratogens, which damage the __brain__ and __nervous system__, the entire prenatal period is critical.

24. Two especially critical periods are at the beginning of pregnancy, when __stress__ can impede __implantation__, and during the final weeks, when the fetus is particularly vulnerable to damage that can cause __learning disabilities__.

25. Some teratogens have a __threshold__ effect—that is, the substances are harmless until exposure reaches a certain frequency or amount. However, the __interactions__ of some teratogens when taken together may make them more harmful at lower dosage levels than when taken separately.

26. Genetic susceptibilities to the prenatal effects of alcohol and to certain birth disorders, such as cleft palate, may involve defective __enzymes__.

27. When the mother-to-be's diet is deficient in __folic acid__, neural-tube defects such as __spina bifida__ or __anencephaly__ may result.

28. Genetic vulnerability is also related to the sex of the developing organism. Generally, __male__ (male/female) embryos and fetuses are more vulnerable to teratogens. This sex not only has a higher rate of teratogenic birth defects and later behavioral problems, but also a higher rate of __spontaneous abortions__, and older members of this sex have more __learning Disabilities__. For instance, they are four times as likely as the other sex to be __autistic__.

29. When contracted during the critical period, German measles, also called __Rubella__, is known to cause structural damage to the heart, eyes, ears, and brain.

30. The most devastating viral teratogen is __Human immunedeficiency Virus__, which gradually overwhelms the body's natural immune responses and leads to a host of diseases that together constitute __Acquired immune deficient syndrome__. About __25__ percent of infants born to women with this virus acquire it from the mother either __prenatally__ or during __birth__.

31. Prevention of pediatric AIDS may be possible if a pregnant HIV-positive woman takes __antiretroviral__ drugs and gives birth by __cesarean section__.

32. Some widely used medicinal drugs, including _psychoactive drugs_____, are proven teratogens. Other drugs, such as _antidepressants_____, *may* be teratogenic.

33. Psychoactive drugs such as _Beer, wine_____ _tobacco, heroin, methadone_____ _LSD, marijuana_____ slow fetal _growth_____ and can trigger premature _labor_____. The potential long-term teratogenic effects of such drugs include _LD, impaired self control_____ _poor concentration, irritibility____.

34. (text and Table 4.3) Prenatal exposure to alcohol may lead to _Fetal_____ _Alcohol_____ _Syndrome_____, which includes such symptoms as abnormal facial characteristics, slowed physical growth, behavior problems, and mental retardation. Likely victims of this syndrome are those whose mothers ingest more than _3 or more_____ drinks daily during pregnancy. Even more moderate alcohol consumption can be teratogenic, causing _Fetal_____ _Alcohol_____ _Effects_____.

(Table 4.4) List some of the effects of fetal exposure to tobacco. _malformation of the limbs and urinary tract_

35. (Table 4.4) Infants born to heavy users of marijuana often show impairment to their _Central_____ _Nervous_____ system.

(Table 4.4) List some of the effects of fetal exposure to cocaine. _growth retardation, problems w/placenta, specific learning problems_

Ongoing- language development

36. The specific effects of illicit drugs _are_____ (are/are not) difficult to document because users often use multiple drugs and have other problems, including _malnutrition, stress sickness._ _poor family support_

(Changing Policy) List five protective steps pregnant women should take to prevent drug damage to their offspring.
1. _Abstain from all drugs before pregnancy_
2. _Abstain for 1st month_
3. _Moderate use if no abstain possible_
4. _Social support_
5. _Post natal care._

37. (Changing Policy) Babies born to women who recently emigrated to the United States often weigh _more_____ (more/less) than babies of native-born women of the same ethnicity. One likely reason is that these women are more often _drug_____-_free_____.

38. (Changing Policy) Teratogenic effects of psychoactive drugs _do_____ (do/do not) accumulate throughout pregnancy.

Low Birthweight (pp. 119–122)

39. Newborns who weigh less than _5.5 pds_____ are classified as _Low_____-_Birthweight_ babies. Below 3 pounds, they are called _very_____-_low_____-_birthweight_ babies; at less than 2 pounds they are _extremely_____-_low_____-_birthweight_ babies. Worldwide, rates of this condition _vary_____ (vary/do not vary) from nation to nation.

40. Many factors can cause low birthweight, including _malnutrition_ and _poverty_____.

41. Babies who are born 3 or more weeks early are called PRETERM_____.

State several factors that increase the likelihood of early birth. placenta may be detached from uterine wall, may be unable to accomodate fetal growth. high doses of psychoactive drugs extreme stress or chronic exhaustion.

42. Infants who weigh substantially less than they should, given how much time has passed since conception, are called small_r____ for_____ gestational age_____.

43. About 25 percent of all low-birthweight (LBW) births in the United States are linked to maternal use of tabacco_____, which is responsible for about 50_____ percent of LBW in many European nations.

44. Virtually all the risk factors for low birthweight are related to poverty!____. Mothers of low-birthweight babies are more likely to be ill_____, mainourished teenaged_____, and stressed_____.

45. Poverty is part of the explanation for differences between nations, with developing nations having the most low-birthweight infants.

46. While socioeconomic status is an important factor in low birthweight, other factors, such as cultural values_____ and paternal support_____, have more effect.

The Normal Birth (pp. 122–126)

47. At about the 266th day, the fetal brain signals the release of certain hormone_____ into the mother's bloodstream, which trigger her uterine_____ muscles contractions to contract and relax. The normal birth process

begins when these contractions become regular. The average length of labor is ____8____ for first births and ____3____ for subsequent births.

48. The newborn is usually rated on the apgar_____ scale_____, which assigns a score of 0, 1, or 2 to each of the following five characteristics: heart rate, breathing muscle tone color + reflex. A score below ____4____ indicates that the newborn is in critical condition and requires immediate attention; if the score is ____7____ or better, all is well. This rating is made twice, at ____1____ minute(s) after birth and again at ____5____ minutes.

49. The mother's birth experience is influenced by several factors, including preparation, physical + emotional health position + size of fetus

50. When a normal vaginal delivery is likely to be hazardous, a doctor may recommend a surgical procedure called a c-_____ section_____. Another common procedure, which involves a minor incision of the tissue at the opening of the vagina, is the episotomy__.

51. In many nations, increasing numbers of trained midwives____ preside over uncomplicated births. Many North American mothers today use a professional birth coach, or doula_____, to assist them. Even in hospital births, an increasing number of deliveries occur in the labor_____ room_____. An even more family-oriented environment is the birthing_____ center_____.

Birth Complications (pp. 126–127)

52. The disorder cerebral_____ palsy_____, which affects motor centers in the brain, often results from genetic_____ vulnerability, worsened by exposure to teratogens and episodes of

_anoxia_____, a temporary lack of _oxygen_____ during birth.

53. Because they are often confined to an isolette or hooked up to medical machinery, low-birthweight infants may be deprived of normal kinds of _stimulation_, such as _rocking_.

54. Providing extra soothing stimulation to vulnerable infants in the hospital _does_____ (does/does not) aid weight gain and _does_____ (does/does not) increase overall alertness.

55. Among the minor developmental problems that accompany preterm birth are being late to _smile, hold a bottle communicate_ High-risk infants are often more _distractible_, less _obundant_, and slower to _talk_____.

56. The deficits related to low birthweight usually _can_____ (can/cannot) be overcome.

The Beginning of Bonding (pp. 128–130)

57. The term used to describe the close relationship that begins within the first hours after birth is the _parent_____–_newborn bond_____.

58. (Thinking Like a Scientist) The best evidence for such a relationship comes from studies of various species of _mammals_.

59. Research suggests that a sensitive period for bonding _does not_____ (does/does not) exist in humans, leading some social scientists to conclude that bonding is a _social construction_.

60. Some new mothers experience a profound feeling of sadness called _postpartum depression_.

Progress Test 1

Multiple-Choice Questions

Circle your answers to the following questions and check them with the answers on page 71. If your answer is incorrect, read the explanation for why it is incorrect and then consult the appropriate pages of the text (in parentheses following the correct answer).

1. The third through the eighth week after conception is called the:
   a. embryonic period.
   b. ovum period.
   c. fetal period.
   d. germinal period.

2. The neural tube develops into the:
   a. respiratory system.
   b. umbilical cord.
   c. brain and spinal column.
   d. circulatory system.

3. To say that a teratogen has a "threshold effect" means that it is:
   a. virtually harmless until exposure reaches a certain level.
   b. harmful only to low-birthweight infants.
   c. harmful to certain developing organs during periods when these organs are developing most rapidly.
   d. harmful only if the pregnant woman's weight does not increase by a certain minimum amount during her pregnancy.

4. By the eighth week after conception, the embryo has almost all the basic organs except the:
   a. skeleton.   c. sex organs.
   b. elbows and knees. d. fingers and toes.

5. The most critical factor in attaining the age of viability is development of the:
   a. placenta.   c. brain.
   b. eyes.   d. skeleton.

6. An important nutrient that many women do not get in adequate amounts from the typical diet is:
   a. vitamin A.   c. guanine.
   b. zinc.   d. folic acid.

7. An embryo begins to develop male sex organs if
   _____ , and female sex organs if
   _____ .
   a. genes on the Y chromosome send a biochemi-
      cal signal; no signal is sent from an X chromo-
      some
   b. genes on the Y chromosome send a biochemi-
      cal signal; genes on the X chromosome send a
      signal
   c. genes on the X chromosome send a biochemi-
      cal signal; no signal is sent from an X chromo-
      some
   d. genes on the X chromosome send a biochemi-
      cal signal; genes on the Y chromosome send a
      signal

8. A teratogen:
   a. cannot cross the placenta during the period of
      the embryo.
   b. is usually inherited from the mother.
   c. can be counteracted by good nutrition most of
      the time.
   d. may be a virus, a drug, a chemical, radiation,
      or environmental pollutants.

9. Among the characteristics of babies born with
   fetal alcohol syndrome are:
   a. slowed physical growth and behavior prob-
      lems.
   b. addiction to alcohol and methadone.
   c. deformed arms and legs.
   d. blindness.

10. The birth process begins:
    a. when the fetus moves into the right position.
    b. when the uterus begins to contract at regular
       intervals to push the fetus out.
    c. about 8 hours (in the case of firstborns) after
       the uterus begins to contract at regular inter-
       vals.
    d. when the baby's head appears at the opening
       of the vagina.

11. The Apgar scale is administered:
    a. only if the newborn is in obvious distress.
    b. once, just after birth.
    c. twice, 1 minute and 5 minutes after birth.
    d. repeatedly during the newborn's first hours.

12. Most newborns weigh about:
    a. 5 pounds.   c. 7$\frac{1}{2}$ pounds.
    b. 6 pounds.   d. 8$\frac{1}{2}$ pounds.

13. Low-birthweight babies born near the due date
    but weighing substantially less than they should:
    a. are classified as preterm.
    b. are called small for gestational age.
    c. usually have no sex organs.
    d. show many signs of immaturity.

14. Approximately 1 out of every 4 low-birthweight
    births in the United States is caused by maternal
    use of:
    a. alcohol.
    b. tobacco.
    c. crack cocaine.
    d. household chemicals.

15. (Thinking Like a Scientist) The idea of a
    parent–newborn bond in humans arose from:
    a. observations in the delivery room.
    b. data on adopted infants.
    c. animal studies.
    d. studies of disturbed mother–newborn pairs.

Matching Items

Match each definition or description with its corresponding term.

Terms

  j   **1.** embryonic period
  c   **2.** fetal period
  h   **3.** placenta
  k   **4.** preterm
  b   **5.** teratogens
  e   **6.** rubella
  g   **7.** HIV
  a   **8.** critical period
  d   **9.** neural tube
  f   **10.** fetal alcohol syndrome
  i   **11.** germinal period

Definitions or Descriptions

a. term for the period during which a developing baby's body parts are most susceptible to damage

b. external agents and conditions that can damage the developing organism

c. the age when viability is attained

d. the precursor of the central nervous system

e. also called German measles

f. characterized by abnormal facial characteristics, slowed growth, behavior problems, and mental retardation

g. a virus that gradually overwhelms the body's immune responses

h. the life-giving organ that nourishes the embryo and fetus

i. when implantation occurs

j. the prenatal period when all major body structures begin to form

k. a baby born 3 or more weeks early

Progress Test 2

Progress Test 2 should be completed during a final chapter review. Answer the following questions after you thoroughly understand the correct answers for the Chapter Review and Progress Test 1.

Multiple-Choice Questions

1. During which period does cocaine use affect the fetus and/or newborn?
   a. throughout pregnancy
   b. before birth
   c. after birth
   d. during all of the above periods

2. In order, the correct sequence of prenatal stages of development is:
   a. embryo; germinal; fetus
   b. germinal; fetus; embryo
   c. germinal; embryo; fetus
   d. ovum; fetus; embryo

3. Monika is preparing for the birth of her first child. If all proceeds normally, she can expect that her labor will last about:
   a. three hours.   c. ten hours.
   b. eight hours.   d. twelve hours.

4. Tetracycline, retinoic acid, and most hormones:
   a. can be harmful to the human fetus.
   b. have been proven safe for pregnant women after the embryonic period.
   c. will prevent spontaneous abortions.
   d. are safe when used before the fetal period.

5. One of the first teratogens to be recognized, possibly causing deafness, blindness, and brain damage if the fetus is exposed early during the pregnancy, is:
   a. rubella (German measles).
   b. anoxia.
   c. acquired immune deficiency syndrome (AIDS).
   d. neural-tube defect.

6. (Changing Policy) The most realistic way for pregnant women to reduce the risk of birth defects in their unborn children is to avoid unnecessary drugs and:
   a. have a diagnostic X-ray or sonogram.
   b. improve their genetic predispositions.
   c. seek early and regular prenatal care.
   d. avoid exposure to any suspected pollutant.

7. Among the characteristics rated on the Apgar scale are:
   a. shape of the newborn's head and nose.
   b. presence of body hair.
   c. interactive behaviors.
   d. muscle tone and color.

8. A newborn is classified as low birthweight if he or she weighs less than:
   a. 7 pounds.
   b. 6 pounds.
   c. $5^1/_2$ pounds.
   d. 4 pounds.

9. The most critical problem for preterm babies is:
   a. the immaturity of the sex organs—for example, undescended testicles.
   b. spitting up or hiccupping.
   c. infection from intravenous feeding.
   d. breathing difficulties.

10. (In Person) The most remarkable examples of learning by the developing fetus involve the sense of:
    a. touch.
    b. vision.
    c. hearing.
    d. smell.

11. Many low-birthweight infants experience:
    a. genetic defects.
    b. brain damage.
    c. congenital deformities of their limbs.
    d. all the above.

12. Which Apgar score indicates that a newborn is in normal health?
    a. 4   c. 6
    b. 5   d. 7

13. Infants born with HIV always develop pediatric AIDS because drugs that reverse the course of HIV have not been tested on children and because:
    a. their mothers had to undergo a cesarean delivery.
    b. the virus overwhelms a very young body faster than a fully grown one.
    c. AZT does not pass through the placenta and so cannot immunize the fetus.
    d. prenatal care is not available for low-income women in developed countries.

14. Many of the factors that contribute to low birthweight are related to poverty; for example, women of lower socioeconomic status tend to:
    a. be less well nourished.
    b. have less education.
    c. be subjected to stressful living conditions.
    d. be all of the above.

15. The critical period for preventing physical defects appears to be the:
    a. zygote period.
    b. embryonic period.
    c. fetal period.
    d. entire pregnancy.

True or False Items

Write T (*true*) or F (*false*) on the line in front of each statement.

_____ 1. (In Person) Newborns can recognize some of what they heard while in the womb.

_____ 2. Eight weeks after conception, the embryo has formed almost all the basic organs.

_____ 3. Infants who are HIV-positive do not always develop pediatric AIDS.

_____ 4. In general, behavioral teratogens have the greatest effect during the embryonic period.

_____ 5. The effects of cigarette smoking during pregnancy remain highly controversial.

_____ 6. The Apgar scale is used to measure vital signs such as heart rate, breathing, and reflexes.

_____ 7. Newborns usually cry on their own, moments after birth.

_____ 8. (Thinking Like a Scientist) Research shows that immediate mother–newborn contact at birth is necessary for the normal emotional development of the child.

_____ 9. Low birthweight is often correlated with poverty and malnutrition.

_____ 10. Cesarean sections are rarely performed in the United States today because of the resulting danger to the fetus.

Thinking Critically About Chapter 4

Answer these questions the day before an exam as a final check on your understanding of the chapter's terms and concepts.

1. Babies born to mothers who are powerfully addicted to a psychoactive drug are *most* likely to suffer from:
   a. structural problems.
   b. behavioral problems.
   c. both a. and b.
   d. neither a. nor b.

2. I am about 1 inch long and 1 gram in weight. I have all of the basic organs (except sex organs) and features of a human being. What am I?
   a. a zygote   c. a fetus
   b. an embryo   d. an indifferent gonad

3. Karen and Brad report to their neighbors that, 5 weeks after conception, a sonogram of their child-to-be revealed female sex organs. The neighbors are skeptical of their statement because:
   a. sonograms are never administered before the ninth week.
   b. sonograms only reveal the presence or absence of male sex organs.
   c. the fetus does not begin to develop female sex organs until about the eighth week.
   d. it is impossible to determine that a woman is pregnant until six weeks after conception.

4. Five-year-old Benjamin can't sit quietly and concentrate on a task for more than a minute. Dr. Simmons, who is a teratologist, suspects that Benjamin may have been exposed to _____ during prenatal development.
   a. human immunodeficiency virus
   b. a behavioral teratogen
   c. rubella
   d. lead

5. Sylvia and Stan, who are of British descent, are hoping to have a child. Doctor Caruthers asks for a complete nutritional history and is particularly concerned when she discovers that Sylvia may have a deficiency of folic acid in her diet. Doctor Caruthers is probably worried about the risk of _____ in the couple's offspring.
   a. FAS   c. neural-tube defects
   b. brain damage   d. FAE

6. Three-year-old Kenny was born underweight and premature. Today, he is small for his age. His doctor suspects that:
   a. Kenny is a victim of fetal alcohol syndrome.
   b. Kenny suffers from fetal alcohol effects.
   c. Kenny's mother smoked heavily during her pregnancy.
   d. Kenny's mother used cocaine during her pregnancy.

7. Which of these fetuses is most likely to experience serious prenatal damage?
   a. a male whose 15-year-old mother has an unusually stressful home life
   b. a female whose mother did not begin to receive prenatal care until the second month of her pregnancy
   c. a female whose 30-year-old mother is on welfare
   d. a male whose mother was somewhat undernourished early in the pregnancy

8. Fetal alcohol syndrome is common in newborns whose mothers were heavy drinkers during pregnancy, whereas newborns whose mothers were moderate drinkers may suffer fetal alcohol effects. This finding shows that to assess and understand risk we must know:
   a. the kind of alcoholic beverage (for example, beer, wine, or whiskey).
   b. the level of exposure to the teratogen.
   c. whether the substance really is teratogenic.
   d. the timing of exposure to the teratogen.

9. Your sister and brother-in-law, who are about to adopt a 1-year-old, are worried that the child will never bond with them. What advice should you offer?
   a. Tell them that, unfortunately, this is true; they would be better off waiting for a younger child who has not yet bonded.
   b. Tell them that, although the first year is a biologically determined critical period for attachment, there is a fifty-fifty chance that the child will bond with them.
   c. Tell them that bonding is a long-term process between parent and child that is determined by the nature of interaction throughout infancy, childhood, and beyond.
   d. Tell them that if the child is female, there is a good chance that she will bond with them, even at this late stage.

10. Which of the following newborns would be most likely to have problems in body structure and functioning?
    a. Anton, whose Apgar score is 6
    b. Debora, whose Apgar score is 7
    c. Sheila, whose Apgar score is 3
    d. Simon, whose Apgar score is 5

11. At birth, Clarence was classified as small for gestational age. It is likely that Clarence:
    a. was born in a rural hospital.
    b. suffered several months of prenatal malnutrition.
    c. was born in a large city hospital.
    d. comes from a family with a history of such births.

12. Of the following, who is *most* likely to give birth to a low-birthweight child?
    a. 21-year-old Janice, who was herself a low-birthweight baby.
    b. 25-year-old May Ling, who gained 25 pounds during her pregnancy.
    c. 16-year-old Donna, who diets frequently despite being underweight, and is under a lot of stress.
    d. 30-year-old Maria, who has already given birth to 4 children.

13. An infant born 266 days after conception, weighing 4 pounds, would be designated a _____ infant.
    a. preterm
    b. low-birthweight
    c. small-for-gestational-age
    d. b. & c.

14. An infant who was born at 35 weeks, weighing 6 pounds, would be called a _____ infant.
    a. preterm
    b. low-birthweight
    c. small-for-gestational-age
    d. premature

15. The five characteristics evaluated by the Apgar scale are:
    a. heart rate, length, weight, muscle tone, and color.
    b. orientation, muscle tone, reflexes, interaction, and responses to stress.
    c. reflexes, breathing, muscle tone, heart rate, and color.
    d. pupillary response, heart rate, reflex irritability, alertness, and breathing.

Key Terms

Using your own words, write a brief definition or explanation of each of the following terms on a separate piece of paper.

1. germinal period
2. embryonic period
3. fetal period
4. implantation
5. neural tube
6. placenta
7. age of viability
8. teratogens
9. behavioral teratogens
10. risk analysis
11. critical period
12. threshold effect
13. interaction effect
14. human immunodeficiency virus (HIV)
15. fetal alcohol syndrome (FAS)
16. low-birthweight (LBW) infant
17. preterm birth
18. small for gestational age (SGA)
19. Apgar scale
20. cesarean section
21. cerebral palsy
22. anoxia
23. parent–newborn bond
24. postpartum depression

ANSWERS
CHAPTER REVIEW

1. three; germinal; third; eighth; embryonic; fetal; trimesters
2. eight; differentiation; one; placenta; embryo
3. implantation; is not
4. neural tube; central nervous system

First, the upper arms, then the forearms, palms, and webbed fingers appear. Legs, feet, and webbed toes follow. At eight weeks, the embryo's head is more rounded, and the facial features are fully formed. The fingers and toes are distinct and separate. The "tail" is no longer visible.

5. $1/30$ ounce (1 gram); 1 inch (2.5 centimeters); fetus

6. sixth; indifferent gonad

7. Y; male; female; twelfth; gender-neutral; epigenetic

8. third; 3 ounces (87 grams); 3 inches (7.5 centimeters); vary

9. circulatory system

10. six; breathing; sucking; neurogenesis; synaptogenesis; middle

11. age of viability; 22

12. 28; sleep–wake

13. 3 pounds (1,300 grams); 95

14. respiratory; cardiovascular

15. $7^1/2$ pounds (3,400 grams)

16. fat

17. calories; malnutrition; learn

18. hearing; twenty-eighth

19. teratology; teratogens; viruses, drugs, chemicals, pollutants, stressors, and malnutrition

20. behavioral teratogens; 3; 10 to 20

21. risk analysis

22. timing; amount; genetic vulnerability

23. critical period; embryo; behavioral; brain; nervous system

24. stress; implantation; learning disabilities

25. threshold; interaction

26. enzymes

27. folic acid; spina bifida; anencephaly

28. male; spontaneous abortions; learning disabilities; autistic

29. rubella

30. human immunodeficiency virus (HIV); acquired immune deficiency syndrome (AIDS); 25; prenatally; birth

31. antiretroviral; cesarean section

32. tetracycline, anticoagulants, phenobarbital, bromides, anticonvulsants, retinoic acid, and most hormones; aspirin, antacids, and diet pills

33. beer, wine, liquor, cigarettes, smokeless tobacco, heroin, methadone, LSD, marijuana, cocaine, inhalants, and antidepressant pills; growth; labor; learning difficulties, impaired self-control, poor concentration, and overall irritability

34. fetal alcohol syndrome; three; fetal alcohol effects

Smoking increases the risk of abnormalities and reduces birthweight and size. Babies born to regular smokers tend to have respiratory problems and, in adulthood, increased risk of becoming smokers themselves.

35. central nervous

Cocaine use causes overall growth retardation, increases the risk of problems with the placenta, and often leads to learning problems in the first months of life.

36. are; malnutrition, stress, sickness, poor family support and health care

The five protective steps are:

a. Abstain from drugs altogether, even before pregnancy.

b. Abstain from drugs after the first month.

c. Use drugs in moderation throughout pregnancy (if abstinence is impossible).

d. Seek social support.

e. Keep up with postnatal care.

37. more; drug-free

38. do

39. 2,500 grams ($5^1/2$ pounds); low-birthweight; very-low-birthweight; extremely-low-birthweight; vary

40. malnutrition; poverty

41. preterm

The possible causes of early birth include infections, drugs, extreme stress, exhaustion, a placenta that becomes detached from the uterine wall, and a uterus that cannot accommodate further growth.

42. small for gestational age

43. tobacco; 50

44. poverty; ill, malnourished, teenaged, stressed

45. developing

46. cultural values; paternal support

47. hormones; uterine muscles; eight hours; three hours

48. Apgar scale; heart rate, breathing, muscle tone, color, and reflexes; 4; 7; 1; 5

49. the mother's preparation for birth, the physical and emotional support provided by birth attendants, the position and size of the fetus, the cultural context, the nature and degree of medical attention

50. cesarean section; episiotomy

51. midwives; doula; labor room; birthing center

52. cerebral palsy; genetic; teratogens; anoxia; oxygen

53. stimulation; rocking (or regular handling)

54. does; does

55. smile, hold a bottle, and to communicate; distractible; obedient; talk

56. can

57. parent–newborn bond

58. mammals

59. does not; social construction

60. postpartum depression

PROGRESS TEST 1

Multiple-Choice Questions

1. **a.** is the answer. (p. 103)

    b. This term, which refers to the germinal period, is not used in the text.

    c. The fetal period is from the ninth week until birth.

    d. The germinal period covers the first two weeks.

2. **c.** is the answer. (p. 105)

3. **a.** is the answer. (p. 113)

    b., c., & d. Although low birthweight (b), critical periods of organ development (c), and maternal malnutrition (d) are all hazardous to the developing person during prenatal development, none is an example of a threshold effect.

4. **c.** is the answer. The sex organs do not begin to take shape until the fetal period. (p. 106)

5. **c.** is the answer. (p. 107)

6. **d.** is the answer. (p. 113)

7. **a.** is the answer. (p. 106)

8. **d.** is the answer. (p. 111)

    a. In general, teratogens can cross the placenta at any time.

    b. Teratogens are agents in the environment, not heritable genes (although *susceptibility* to individual teratogens has a genetic component).

    c. Although nutrition is an important factor in healthy prenatal development, the text does not suggest that nutrition alone can usually counteract the harmful effects of teratogens.

9. **a.** is the answer. (p. 115)

10. **b.** is the answer. (p. 122)

11. **c.** is the answer. (pp. 123–124)

12. **c.** is the answer. (pp. 108–109)

13. **b.** is the answer. (p. 121)

14. **b.** is the answer. (p. 121)

15. **c.** is the answer. (p. 128)

Matching Items

1. j (p. 103)
2. c (p. 103)
3. h (p. 107)
4. k (p. 120)
5. b (p. 111)
6. e (p. 114)
7. g (p. 114)
8. a (p. 112)
9. d (p. 105)
10. f (p. 115)
11. i (p. 103)

PROGRESS TEST 2

Multiple-Choice Questions

1. **d.** is the answer. (pp. 115–117)

2. **c.** is the answer. (p. 103)

3. **b.** is the answer. (p. 123)

    a. The average length of labor for subsequent births is three hours.

4. **a.** is the answer. (p. 115)

5. **a.** is the answer. (p. 114)

6. **c.** is the answer. (p. 118)

7. **d.** is the answer. (pp. 123–124)

8. **c.** is the answer. (p. 119)

9. **d.** is the answer. (p. 108)

10. **c.** is the answer. (p. 109)

11. **b.** is the answer. (pp. 119–120)

12. **d.** is the answer. (p. 124)

13. **b.** is the answer. (p. 114)

14. **d.** is the answer. (p. 122)

15. **b.** is the answer. (p. 112)

True or False Items

1. T (p. 109)

2. T (p. 106)

3. F   Sadly, within months or years, infants who are HIV-positive always develop AIDS. (p. 114)

4. F   Behavioral teratogens can affect the fetus at any time during the prenatal period. (p. 113)

5. F   There is no controversy about the damaging effects of smoking during pregnancy. (p. 115)

6. T (pp. 123–124)

7. T (p. 123)

8. F   Though highly desirable, mother–newborn contact at birth is not necessary for the child's normal development or for a good parent–child relationship. Many opportunities for bonding occur throughout childhood. (pp. 128–129)

9. T (pp. 121–122)

10. F   About 22 percent of births in the United States are now cesarean. (p. 125)

THINKING CRITICALLY ABOUT CHAPTER 4

1. **c.** is the answer. (pp. 115–116)

2. **b.** is the answer. (pp. 105–106)

   a. The zygote is the fertilized ovum.

   c. The developing organism is designated a fetus starting at the ninth week.

   d. The indifferent gonad is the mass of cells that will eventually develop into female or male sex organs.

3. **c.** is the answer. (p. 106)

4. **b.** is the answer. (pp. 111, 116)

   a. This is the virus that causes AIDS.

   c. Rubella may cause blindness, deafness, and brain damage.

   d. The text does not discuss the effects of exposure to lead.

5. **c.** is the answer. (p. 113)

   a. FAS is caused in infants by the mother-to-be drinking three or more drinks daily during pregnancy.

   b. Brain damage is caused by the use of social drugs during pregnancy.

   d. FAE is caused in infants by the mother-to-be drinking 1 ounce of alcohol per day.

6. **c.** is the answer. (p. 121)

7. **a.** is the answer. (p. 122)

8. **b.** is the answer. (pp. 115–116)

9. **c.** is the answer. (p. 128)

   a. & b. Bonding in humans is not a biologically determined event limited to a critical period, as it is in many other animal species.

   d. There is no evidence of any gender differences in the formation of the parent–newborn bond.

10. **c.** is the answer. If a neonate's Apgar score is below 4, the infant is in critical condition and needs immediate medical attention. (p. 124)

11. **b.** is the answer. (p. 121)

    a., c., & d. Prenatal malnutrition is the most common cause of a small-for-dates neonate.

12. **c.** is the answer. Donna has three risk factors that are related to having an LBW baby, including being a teenager; underweight, and stressed. (pp. 121–122)

    a. & d. Neither of these has been linked to increased risk of having LBW babies.

    b. In fact, based only on her age and normal weight gain, May Ling's baby would *not* be expected to be LBW.

13. **d.** is the answer. (pp. 119, 121)

    a. & c. At 266 days, this infant is full term.

14. **a.** is the answer. (p. 120)

    b. Low birthweight is defined as weighing less than $5^1/_2$ pounds.

    c. Although an infant can be both preterm and small for gestational age, this baby's weight is within the normal range of healthy babies.

    d. This term is no longer used to describe early births.

15. **c.** is the answer. (pp. 123–124)

KEY TERMS

1. The first two weeks of development after conception, characterized by rapid cell division and the beginning of cell differentiation, are called the **germinal period.** (p. 103)

   Memory aid: A *germ* cell is one from which a new organism can develop. The ***germ**inal period* is the first stage in the development of the new organism.

2. The **embryonic period** is approximately the third through the eighth week of prenatal development, when the rudimentary forms of all anatomical structures develop. (p. 103)

3. From the ninth week until birth is the **fetal period**, when the organs grow in size and complexity. (p. 103)

4. **Implantation** is the process by which the outer cells of the organism burrow into the uterine lining and rupture its blood vessels to obtain nourishment and trigger the bodily changes that signify the beginning of pregnancy. (p. 104)

5. The **neural tube** forms from a fold of outer embryonic cells during the period of the embryo; it is the precursor of the central nervous system. (p. 105)

   Memory aid: Neural means "of the nervous system." The **neural tube** is the precursor of the central nervous system.

6. The **placenta** is the organ that connects the mother's circulatory system with that of her growing embryo, providing nourishment to the developing organism and removing wastes. (p. 107)

7. About 22 weeks after conception, the fetus attains the **age of viability**, at which point it has at least some slight chance of survival outside the uterus if specialized medical care is available. (p. 107)

8. **Teratogens** are external agents and conditions, such as viruses, bacteria, drugs, chemicals, stressors, and malnutrition, that can cause damage to the developing organism. (p. 111)

9. **Behavioral teratogens** tend to damage the brain and nervous system, impairing the future child's intellectual and emotional functioning. (p. 111)

10. The science of teratology is a science of **risk analysis**, meaning that it attempts to evaluate what factors make prenatal harm more or less likely to occur. (p. 111)

11. In prenatal development, a **critical period** is the time when a particular organ or body part is most susceptible to teratogenic damage. (p. 112)

12. A **threshold effect** is the harmful effect of a substance that occurs when exposure to it reaches a certain level. (p. 113)

13. An **interaction effect** occurs when one teratogen intensifies the harmful effects of another. (p. 113)

14. **Human immunodeficiency virus (HIV)** is the most devastating viral teratogen. HIV gradually overwhelms the body's immune system, making the individual vulnerable to the host of diseases and infections that constitute AIDS. (p. 114)

15. Prenatal alcohol exposure may cause **fetal alcohol syndrome (FAS)**, which includes abnormal facial characteristics, slowed physical growth, behavior problems, and mental retardation. Likely victims are those who are genetically vulnerable and whose mothers drink three or more drinks daily during pregnancy. (p. 115)

16. Newborns who weigh less than 2,500 grams ($5^{1}/_{2}$ pounds) are called **low-birthweight (LBW) infants**. Such infants are at risk for many immediate and long-term problems. (p. 119)

17. Infants who are born three or more weeks before the due date are called **preterm**. (p. 120)

18. Infants who weigh substantially less than they should, given how much time has passed since conception, are called **small for gestational age (SGA)**, or small-for-dates. (p. 121)

19. Newborns are rated at one and then at five minutes after birth according to the **Apgar scale**. This scale assigns a score of 0, 1, or 2 to each of five characteristics: heart rate, breathing, muscle tone, color, and reflexes. A score of 7 or better indicates that all is well. (p. 123)

20. In a **cesarean section**, the fetus is removed from the mother surgically. (p. 125)

21. **Cerebral palsy** is a muscular control disorder caused by damage to the brain's motor centers during or before birth. (p. 126)

22. **Anoxia** is a temporary lack of fetal oxygen during the birth process that, if prolonged, can cause brain damage or even death. (p. 126)

23. The term **parent–newborn bond** describes the strong feelings of attachment between parent and child in the early moments of their relationship together. (p. 128)

24. **Postpartum depression** is a profound feeling of sadness and inadequacy sometimes experienced by new mothers. (p. 128)

Chapter Five

The First 2 Years: Biosocial Development

Chapter Overview

Chapter 5 is the first of a three-chapter unit that describes the developing person from birth to age 2 in terms of biosocial, cognitive, and psychosocial development. Physical development is the first to be examined.

The chapter begins with observations on the overall growth and health of infants, including their size and shape. Following is a discussion of brain growth and development and the importance of experience in brain development. The chapter then turns to a discussion of sensory, perceptual, and motor abilities and the ages at which the average infant acquires them. Preventive medicine and the importance of immunizations during the first two years are discussed next, along with a discussion of the possible causes of Sudden Infant Death Syndrome (SIDS). The final section discusses the importance of nutrition during the first two years and the consequences of severe malnutrition and undernutrition.

NOTE: Answer guidelines for all Chapter 5 questions begin on page 86.

Guided Study

The text chapter should be studied one section at a time. Before you read, preview each section by skimming it, noting headings and boldface items. Then read the appropriate section objectives from the following outline. Keep these objectives in mind and, as you read the chapter section, search for the information that will enable you to meet each objective. Once you have finished a section, write out answers for its objectives.

Body Changes (pp. 135–137, 139–140)

1. Describe the size and proportions of an infant's body, including how they change during the first two years and how they compare with those of an adult.

2. Discuss why infants sleep so much, and describe how sleep patterns change through infancy.

Early Brain Development (pp. 140–146)

3. Describe the ways in which the brain changes or matures during infancy.

4. (text and Thinking Like a Scientist) Discuss the role of experience in brain development.

The Senses and Motor Skills (pp. 146–154)

5. Distinguish among sensation, perception, and cognition.

6. Describe the extent and development of an infant's sensory and perceptual abilities in terms of the senses of hearing, vision, taste, touch, and smell.

7. Describe the basic reflexes of the newborn, and distinguish between gross motor skills and fine motor skills.

8. Describe the basic pattern of motor skill development, and discuss variations in the timing of motor skill acquisition.

Preventive Medicine (pp. 154–158)

9. Identify key factors in the worldwide decline in childhood mortality since the middle of the twentieth century, and discuss the importance of childhood immunizations.

10. (text and Changing Policy) Identify risk factors and discuss possible explanations for ethnic group variations in the incidence of sudden infant death syndrome.

Nutrition (pp. 158–163)

11. Describe the nutritional needs of infants.

12. Discuss the causes and effects of malnutrition and undernutrition in the first years, and explain ways of preventing undernutrition.

Chapter Review

When you have finished reading the chapter, work through the material that follows to review it. Complete the sentences and answer the questions. As you proceed, evaluate your performance for each section by consulting the answers on page 86. Do not continue with the next section until you understand each answer. If you need to, review or reread the appropriate section in the textbook before continuing.

Body Changes (pp. 133–135, 139–140)

1. A standard, or average, of physical development that is derived for a specific group or population is a _____ .

2. With the exception of _____ development, infancy is the period of the fastest and most notable increases in _____ and changes in _____ .

3. The average North American newborn measures _____ and weighs a little more than _____ .

4. In the first days of life, most newborns _____ (gain/lose) between 5 and 10 percent of their body weight.

5. The phenomenon in which inadequate nutrition causes the body to stop growing but not the brain is called _____ .

6. By age 1, the typical baby weighs about _____ and measures almost _____ . The typical 2-year-old is almost _____ (what proportion?) of his or her adult weight and _____ (what proportion?) of his or her adult height.

7. A _____ is a statistical index of a child's development represented by a point on a ranking scale of _____ (what number?) to _____ (what number?).

8. (A Case to Study) In the condition called _____ , a child's body weight is at the bottom _____ percent of the norm as a result of _____ _____ . When the child's height is below this percentage, the condition of _____ has occurred.

9. Throughout childhood, regular and ample _____ correlates with _____ maturation, _____ , _____ regulation, and _____ adjustment in school and within the family. Also, more _____ are secreted during sleep than during wakefulness. The average newborn sleeps about _____ hours a day, and the average 1-year-old sleeps about _____ hours a day. Approximately _____ percent of 1-year-olds sleep through the night.

10. Over the first months of life, changes in the _____ of sleep are more notable than changes in the _____ slept. The stage of sleep characterized by flickering eyes behind closed lids and _____ is called _____ _____ . During this stage of sleep brain waves are fairly _____ (slow/rapid). This stage of sleep _____ (increases/decreases) over the first months, as does the dozing stage called _____ _____ . Slow-wave sleep, also called _____ _____ , increases markedly at about _____ months of age. Preterm infants and those who have immature _____ _____ _____ spend _____ (more/less) time in REM sleep than do normal infants.

Early Brain Development (pp. 140–146)

11. At birth, the brain has attained about _____ percent of its adult weight; by age 2 the brain is about _____ percent of its adult weight. In comparison, body weight at age 2 is about _____ percent of what it will be in adulthood.

12. The brain's communication system consists primarily of nerve cells called _____ connected by intricate networks of nerve fibers, called _____ and _____ . The brain's outer layer

called the _____ contains about _____ percent of these cells.

13. Each neuron has many _____ but only a single _____ .

14. Neurons communicate with one another at intersections called _____ . After travelling down the length of the _____ , electrical impulses trigger chemicals called _____ that diffuse across the _____ _____ to the _____ of a "receiving" neuron. Most of the nerve cells _____ (are/are not) present at birth, whereas the fiber networks _____ (are/are not) rudimentary.

15. During the first months of life, brain development is most noticeable in the _____ .

16. From birth until age 2, the density of dendrites in the cortex _____ (increases/ decreases) by a factor of _____ . The phenomenal increase in neural connections over the first two years has been called _____ _____ .

    Following this growth process, neurons in some areas of the brain wither in the process called _____ , because _____ does not activate those brain areas.

17. Brain functions that require basic common experiences to grow are called _____ - _____ brain functions; those that depend on particular, and variable, experiences in order to grow are called _____ - _____ brain functions.

18. (Thinking Like a Scientist) Neuroscientists once believed that brains were entirely formed by _____ and _____ ; today, most believe in _____ , which is the concept that personality, intellect, and emotions change throughout life for _____ (one/a combination of) reason(s). William Greenough

discovered that the brains of rats who were raised in stimulating environments were better developed, with more _____ branching, than the brains of rats raised in barren environments. Orphaned Romanian children who were isolated and deprived of stimulation have been found to be _____ and _____ , have smaller _____ _____ , and show signs of _____ damage. Placed in healthier environments, these children _____ (improved/did not improve); years later, persistent deficits in these children _____ (were/were not) found.

The Senses and Motor Skills (pp. 146–154)

19. The process by which the visual, auditory, and other sensory systems detect stimuli is called _____ ; _____ occurs when the brain becomes activated by a sensation and tries to notice and process it. In the process called _____ , a person thinks about what he or she has perceived. This process _____ (can/cannot) occur without either sensation or perception.

20. Generally speaking, newborns' hearing _____ (is/is not) very acute at birth. Newborns _____ (can/cannot) perceive differences in voices, rhythms, and language.

21. The least mature of the senses at birth is _____ . Newborns' visual focusing is best for objects between _____ and _____ inches away, giving them distance vision of about 20/ _____ .

22. Increasing experience and maturation of the visual cortex accounts for improvements in visual ability, such as the infant's ability to _____ on an object and _____ to its critical areas. The ability to use both eyes together to focus on one object, which is called _____ _____ , develops at about _____ of age.

23. Taste, smell, and touch _____ (function/do not function) at birth. Using their mouths, infants begin to recognize objects by _____ and _____ at _____ month of age.

24. The infant's early sensory abilities seem organized for two goals: _____ _____ and _____ .

25. The most visible and dramatic body changes of infancy involve _____ _____ .

26. An involuntary physical response to a particular stimulus is called a _____ .

27. The involuntary response of breathing, which causes the newborn to take the first breath even before the umbilical cord is cut, is called the _____ _____ . Because breathing is irregular during the first few days, other reflexive behaviors, such as _____ , _____ , and _____ , are common.

28. Shivering, crying, and tucking the legs close to the body are examples of reflexes that help to maintain _____ _____ .

29. A third set of reflexes fosters _____ . One of these is the tendency of the newborn to suck anything that touches the lips; this is the _____ reflex. Another is the tendency of newborns to turn their heads and start to suck when something brushes against their cheek; this is the _____ reflex. Other important reflexes that aid feeding are _____ , _____ , and _____ up.

30. Large movements such as running and climbing are called _____ _____ skills.

31. Most infants are able to crawl on "all fours" (sometimes called *creeping*) between _____ and _____ months of age.

List the major hallmarks in children's mastery of walking.

32. Abilities that require more precise, small movements, such as picking up a coin, are called _____ _____ skills. By _____ of age, most babies can reach for, grab, and hold onto almost any object of the right size. At the same time, most infants can also _____ objects from one hand to the other.

33. Although the _____ in which motor skills are mastered is the same in all healthy infants, the _____ of acquisition of skills varies greatly.

34. The average ages, or _____ , at which most infants master major motor skills are based on a large sample of infants drawn from _____ (a single/many) ethnic group(s).

35. Motor skill norms vary from one _____ group to another.

List several factors that account for the variation in the acquisition of motor skills.

36. Motor skill acquisition in identical twins _____ (is/is not) more similar than in fraternal twins, suggesting that genes _____ (do/do not) play an important role.

Preventive Medicine (pp. 154–158)

37. In 1900, about 1 in _____ (how many?) children died before age 5. This childhood death rate _____ (varied from one nation to another/was the same throughout the world). Today, in the healthiest nations such as _____ , _____ , and _____ , about 1 in _____ (how many?) children who survive birth die before age 5.

38. A key factor in reducing the childhood death rate was the development of _____—a process that stimulates the body's _____ system to defend against attack by contagious diseases.

39. Another reason for lower infant mortality worldwide is a decrease in _____ _____ _____ , in which seemingly healthy infants die unexpectedly in their _____ .

40. (Changing Policy) A key factor in SIDS is _____ background. In ethnically diverse nations, babies of _____ descent are more likely, and babies of _____ descent are less likely, to succumb to SIDS than are babies of _____ descent. In ethnic groups with a low incidence of SIDS, babies are put to sleep _____ (in what position?).

Identify several other practices that may explain why certain ethnic groups have a low incidence of SIDS.

Nutrition (pp. 158–163)

41. The ideal infant food is _____ _____ , beginning with the thick, high-calorie fluid called

_____ . The only situations in which formula may be healthier for the infant than breast milk are when _____ _____ .

State several advantages of breast milk over cow's milk for the developing infant.

42. The most serious nutritional problem of infancy is _____–_____ _____ .

43. Chronically malnourished infants suffer in three ways: Their _____ may not develop normally; they may have no _____ _____ to protect them against disease, and they may develop the diseases _____ or _____ .

44. Severe protein–calorie deficiency in early infancy causes _____ . In toddlers, protein–calorie deficiency is more likely to cause the disease called _____ , which involves swelling or bloating of the face, legs, and abdomen.

45. A more common condition than severe malnutrition is _____ , which is primarily a problem in _____ (developed/developing) nations. In some nations, hospitals have _____ nurses, who encourage mothers to switch too quickly from breast milk to formula.

46. In the United States, _____ (what proportion?) of 6-month-olds are exclusively formula-fed. The reasons are almost all _____ and include _____ _____ .

47. Among bottle-fed babies, _____ deficiency is common, and is caused by

_____ _____ , which
occurs when toddlers are given a bottle of milk
with every nap and meal. Another common consequence of bottle feeding is a deficiency of

_____ .

Progress Test 1

Multiple-Choice Questions

Circle your answers to the following questions and
check them with the answers on page 87. If your
answer is incorrect, read the explanation for why it is
incorrect and then consult the appropriate pages of
the text (in parentheses following the correct answer).

1. The average North American newborn:
   a. weighs approximately 6 pounds.
   b. weighs approximately 7 pounds.
   c. is "overweight" because of the diet of the
      mother.
   d. weighs 10 percent less than what is desirable.

2. Compared to the first year, growth during the
   second year:
   a. proceeds at a slower rate.
   b. continues at about the same rate.
   c. includes more insulating fat.
   d. includes more bone and muscle.

3. The major motor skill most likely to be mastered
   by an infant before the age of 6 months is:
   a. rolling over.
   b. sitting without support.
   c. turning the head in search of a nipple.
   d. coordinating both hands to enclose an object.

4. Norms suggest that the earliest walkers in the
   world are infants from:
   a. Western Europe.   c. Uganda.
   b. the United States. d. Denver.

5. Head-sparing is the phenomenon in which:
   a. the brain continues to grow even though the
      body stops growing as a result of malnutri-
      tion.
   b. The proportions of the infant's body often
      seem "top heavy."
   c. Axons develop more rapidly than dendrites.
   d. Dendrites devlop more rapidly than axons.

6. Dreaming is characteristic of:
   a. slow-wave sleep.
   b. transitional sleep.
   c. REM sleep.
   d. Quiet sleep.

7. The learning of a language is to the learning of a
   specific language as _____ is to _____ .
   a. experience-dependent; experience-expectant
   b. experience-expectant; experience-dependent
   c. experience-independent; experience-dependent
   d. experience-dependent; experience-independent

8. Brain functions that depend on babies' having
   things to see and hear, and people to feed and
   carry them, are called:
   a. experience-dependent.
   b. experience-expectant.
   c. pruning functions.
   d. transient exuberance.

9. Compared with formula-fed infants, breast-fed
   infants tend to have:
   a. greater weight gain.
   b. fewer allergies and digestive upsets.
   c. less frequent feedings during the first few
      months.
   d. more social approval.

10. Marasmus and kwashiorkor are caused by:
    a. bloating.
    b. protein-calorie deficiency.
    c. living in a developing country.
    d. poor family food habits.

11. The infant's first motor skills are:
    a. fine motor skills.   c. reflexes.
    b. gross motor skills.   d. unpredictable.

12. Which of the following is said to have had the
    greatest impact on human mortality reduction
    and population growth?
    a. improvements in infant nutrition
    b. oral rehydration therapy
    c. medical advances in newborn care
    d. childhood immunization

13. Which of the following is true of motor-skill development in healthy infants?
    a. It follows the same basic sequence the world over.
    b. It occurs at different rates from individual to individual.
    c. It follows norms that vary from one ethnic group to another.
    d. All of the above are true.

14. Most of the nerve cells a human brain will ever possess are present:
    a. at conception.
    b. about 1 month following conception.
    c. at birth.
    d. at age 5 or 6.

15. The most common nutritional problem in developing nations is:
    a. marasmus
    b. kwashiorkor
    c. undernutrition
    d. severe malnutrition

Matching Items

Match each definition or description with its corresponding term.

Terms

_____   1. neurons
_____   2. dendrites
_____   3. kwashiorkor
_____   4. marasmus
_____   5. gross motor skill
_____   6. fine motor skill
_____   7. rooting reflex
_____   8. sucking reflex
_____   9. protein–calorie malnutrition
_____ 10. transient exuberance
_____ 11. wasting
_____ 12. stunting
_____ 13. neurotransmitter

Definitions or Descriptions

a. a condition resulting from chronic malnutrition
b. protein deficiency during the first year in which growth stops and body tissues waste away
c. picking up an object
d. the most common serious nutrition problem of infancy
e. protein deficiency during toddlerhood
f. newborns suck anything that touches their lips
g. communication networks among nerve cells
h. running or climbing
i. an involuntary response in which babies turn their head toward anything that brushes their cheeks
j. the phenomenal increase in neural connections over the first 2 years
k. nerve cells
l. a condition resulting from acute malnutrition
m. a brain chemical that carries information across the synaptic gap between two neurons

Progress Test 2

Progress Test 2 should be completed during a final chapter review. Answer the following questions after you thoroughly understand the correct answers for the Chapter Review and Progress Test 1.

Multiple-Choice Questions

1. Dendrite is to axon as neural _____ is to neural _____ .
   a. input; output
   b. output; input
   c. myelin; synapse
   d. synapse; myelin

2. A reflex is best defined as a(n):
   a. fine motor skill.
   b. motor ability mastered at a specific age.
   c. involuntary physical response to a given stimulus.
   d. gross motor skill.

3. A norm is:
   a. a standard, or average, that is derived for a specific group or population.
   b. a point on a ranking scale of 1 to 99.
   c. a milestone of development that all children reach at the same age.
   d. all of the above.

4. Most babies can reach for, grasp, and hold onto an object by about the _____ month.
   a. second
   b. sixth
   c. ninth
   d. fourteenth

5. Activity level, rate of physical maturation, and how fat the infant is affect the age at which an infant walks and acquires other motor skills. They are examples of:
   a. norms.
   b. environmental factors.
   c. inherited factors.
   d. the interaction of environment and heredity.

6. During the first weeks of life, babies seem to focus reasonably well on:
   a. little in their environment.
   b. objects at a distance of 4 to 30 inches.
   c. objects at a distance of 1 to 3 inches.
   d. objects several feet away.

7. Which sleep stage increases markedly at about 3 or 4 months?
   a. REM
   b. transitional
   c. fast-wave
   d. slow-wave

8. An advantage of breast milk over formula is that it:
   a. is always sterile and at body temperature.
   b. contains traces of medications ingested by the mother.
   c. can be given without involving the father.
   d. contains more protein and vitamin D than does formula.

9. The primary cause of malnutrition in developing countries is:
   a. formula feeding.
   b. inadequate food supply.
   c. disease.
   d. early cessation of breast-feeding.

10. Transient exuberance and pruning demonstrate that:
    a. the pace of acquistion of motor skills varies markedly from child to child.
    b. newborns sleep more than older children because their immature nervous systems cannot handle the higher, waking level of sensory stimulation.
    c. the specifics of brain structure and growth depend partly on the infant's experience.
    d. good nutrition is essential to healthy biosocial development.

11. Climbing is to using a crayon as _____ is to _____ .
    a. fine motor skill; gross motor skill
    b. gross motor skill; fine motor skill
    c. reflex; fine motor skill
    d. reflex; gross motor skill

12. Some infant reflexes are critical for survival. Hiccups and sneezes help the infant maintain the _____ and leg tucking maintains _____ .
    a. feeding; oxygen supply
    b. feeding; a constant body temperature
    c. oxygen supply; feeding
    d. oxygen supply; a constant body temperature

13. (Thinking Like a Scientist) Compared to the brains of laboratory rats that were raised in barren cages, those of rats raised in stimulating, toy-filled cages:
    a. were better developed and had more dendrite branching.
    b. had fewer synaptic connections.
    c. showed less transient exuberance.
    d. displayed all of the above characteristics.

14. A common cause of undernutrition in young children is:
    a. ignorance of the infant's nutritional needs.
    b. the absence of socioeconomic policies that reflect the importance of infant nutrition.
    c. problems in the family.
    d. all of the above.

15. Infant sensory and perceptual abilities appear to be especially organized for:
    a. obtaining adequate nutrition and comfort.
    b. comfort and social interaction.
    c. looking.
    d. touching and smelling.

True or False Items

Write T (*true*) or F (*false*) on the line in front of each statement.

_____ 1. By age 2, boys are slightly taller than girls, but girls are slightly heavier.

_____ 2. Putting babies to sleep on their stomachs increases the risk of SIDS.

_____ 3. Reflexive hiccups, sneezes, and thrashing are signs that the infant's reflexes are not functioning properly.

_____ 4. Infants of all ethnic backgrounds develop the same motor skills at approximately the same age.

_____ 5. The typical 2-year-old is 15 to 20 percent of its adult weight and one-half its adult height.

_____ 6. Vision is better developed than hearing in most newborns.

_____ 7. Today, most infants in the United States are breast-fed.

_____ 8. Certain basic sensory experiences seem necessary to ensure full brain development in the human infant.

_____ 9. Severe malnutrition among young children is more common in developing countries than in the United States.

_____ 10. The only motor skills apparent at birth are reflexes.

Thinking Critically About Chapter 5

Answer these questions the day before an exam as a final check on your understanding of the chapter's terms and concepts.

1. Newborns cry, shiver, and tuck their legs close to their bodies. This set of reflexes helps them:
   a. ensure proper muscle tone.
   b. learn how to signal distress.
   c. maintain constant body temperature.
   d. communicate serious hunger pangs.

2. Which of the following demonstrates that the perception of sounds is apparent from birth?
   a. Sudden noises startle newborns.
   b. Rhythmic sounds put infants to sleep.
   c. Newborns distinguish voices, rhythms, and language.
   d. All of the above demonstrate the perception of sounds at birth.

3. Research studies of the more than 100,000 Romanian children orphaned and severely deprived in infancy reported all of the following *except that*:
   a. all of the children were wasted and stunted.
   b. the children had smaller heads.
   c. during early childhood many still showed signs of emotional damage.
   d. most of the children placed in healthy adoptive homes eventually recovered.

4. The Farbers, who are first-time parents, are wondering whether they should be concerned because their 12-month-old daughter, who weighs 22 pounds and measures 30 inches, is not growing quite as fast as she did during her first year. You should tell them that:
   a. any slowdown in growth during the second year is a cause for immediate concern.
   b. their daughter's weight and height are well below average for her age.
   c. growth patterns for a first child are often erratic.
   d. physical growth is somewhat slower in the second year.

5. Regarding body size, a child generally is said to be normal if he or she is:
   a. between the 25th and 75th percentiles.
   b. at the 50th percentile or greater.
   c. between the 40th and 60th percentiles.
   d. between the 45th and 55th percentiles.

6. Which of the following has been offered as an explanation of why REM sleep decreases as a person ages?
   a. Less slow-wave sleep is needed to stimulate the older child's developing brain.
   b. Dreaming allows reorganization and interpretation of daily events, which become more complex as we grow older.
   c. Fast-wave sleep is entirely a product of brain maturation.
   d. All of the above have been offered as explanations.

7. Michael has 20/400 vision and is able to discriminate subtle sound differences. Michael most likely:
   a. is a preterm infant.
   b. has brain damage in the visual processing areas of the cortex.
   c. is a newborn.
   d. is slow-to-mature.

8. A baby turns her head and starts to suck when her receiving blanket is brushed against her cheek. The baby is displaying the:
   a. sucking reflex.
   b. rooting reflex.
   c. thrashing reflex.
   d. tucking reflex.

9. Toddlers whose parents give them a bottle of milk before every nap and with every meal:
   a. may be at increased risk of undernutrition, because the milk reduces the child's appetite for other foods.
   b. are ensured of receiving a sufficient amount of iron in their diets.
   c. are more likely to develop lactose intolerance.
   d. are likely to be overweight throughout life.

10. Sensation is to perception as _____ is to _____ .
    a. hearing; seeing
    b. detecting a stimulus; making sense of a stimulus
    c. making sense of a stimulus; detecting a stimulus
    d. tasting; smelling

11. Sharetta's pediatrician informs her parents that Sharetta's 1-year-old brain is exhibiting transient exuberance. In response to this news, Sharetta's parents:
    a. smile, because they know their daughter's brain is developing new neural connections.
    b. worry, because this may indicate increased vulnerability to a later learning disability.
    c. know that this process, in which neurotransmitters cross the synaptic gap, is normal.
    d. are alarmed, since this news indicates that the frontal area of Sharetta's cortex is immature.

12. To say that most developmentalists are multidisciplinary and believe in plasticity means they believe personality, intellect, and emotions:
    a. change throughout life as a result of biological maturation.
    b. change throughout life for a combination of reasons.
    c. remain very stable throughout life.
    d. more strongly reveal the impact of genes as people get older.

13. Like all newborns, Serena is able to:
    a. differentiate the sound of one consonant from another.
    b. see objects more than 30 inches from her face quite clearly.
    c. use her mouth to recognize objects by taste and touch.
    d. do all of the above.

14. Three-week-old Nathan should have the *least* difficulty focusing on the sight of:
    a. stuffed animals on a bookshelf across the room from his crib.
    b. his mother's face as she holds him in her arms.
    c. the checkerboard pattern in the wallpaper covering the ceiling of his room.
    d. the family dog as it dashes into the nursery.

15. Geneva has been undernourished throughout childhood. It is likely that she will be:
    a. smaller and shorter than her genetic potential would dictate.
    b. slow in intellectual development.
    c. less resistant to disease.
    d. all of the above.

Key Terms

Using your own words, write a brief definition or explanation of each of the following terms on a separate piece of paper.

1. norm
2. head-sparing
3. percentile
4. wasting
5. stunting
6. REM sleep
7. neuron
8. cortex
9. axon
10. dendrites
11. synapses
12. transient exuberance
13. experience-expectant
14. experience-dependent
15. sensation
16. perception
17. binocular vision

18. breathing reflex

19. sucking reflex

20. rooting reflex

21. gross motor skills

22. fine motor skills

23. immunization

24. sudden infant death syndrome (SIDS)

25. protein–calorie malnutrition

26. marasmus

27. kwashiorkor

28. undernutrition

ANSWERS
CHAPTER REVIEW

1. norm

2. prenatal; size; proportion

3. 20 inches (51 centimeters); 7 pounds (3.2 kilograms)

4. lose

5. head-sparing

6. 22 pounds (10 kilograms); 30 inches (75 centimeters); 15 to 20 percent; half

7. percentile; 1; 99

8. wasting; 3; acute malnutrition; stunting

9. sleep; brain; learning, emotional, psychological; growth hormones; 16; 13; 80

10. stages; amount; dreaming; REM sleep; rapid; decreases; transitional sleep; quiet sleep; 3 or 4 months; central nervous systems; more

11. 25; 75; 20

12. neurons; axons; dendrites; cortex; 70

13. dendrites; axon

14. synapses; axon; neurotransmitters; synaptic gap; dendrite; are; are

15. cortex

16. increases; five; transient exuberance; pruning; experience

17. experience-expectant; experience-dependent

18. genes; prenatal influences; plasticity; a combination; dendritic; wasted; stunted; head circumferences; emotional; improved; were

19. sensation; perception; cognition; can

20. is; can

21. vision; 4; 30; 400

22. focus; scan; binocular vision; 14 weeks

23. function; taste; touch; 1

24. social interaction; comfort

25. motor skills

26. reflex

27. breathing reflex; hiccups, sneezes, thrashing

28. body temperature

29. feeding; sucking; rooting; swallowing; crying; spitting

30. gross motor

31. 8; 10

On average, a child can walk while holding a hand at 9 months, can stand alone momentarily at 10 months, and can walk well unassisted at 12 months.

32. fine motor; 6 months; transfer

33. sequence; age

34. norms; many

35. ethnic

Of primary importance in variations in the acquisition of motor skills are inherited factors, such as activity level, rate of physical maturation, and how fat the infant is. Particular patterns of infant care may also be influential.

36. is; do

37. 3; was the same throughout the world; Japan; the Netherlands; France; 200

38. immunization; immune

39. sudden infant death syndrome (SIDS); sleep

40. ethnic; African; Asian; European; on their backs

Chinese parents tend to their babies periodically as they sleep, which makes them less likely to fall into a deep, nonbreathing sleep. Bangladeshi infants are usually surrounded by many family members in a rich sensory environment, making them less likely to sleep deeply for very long.

41. breast milk; colustrum; the mother is HIV-positive, using toxic drugs, or has some other serious condition that makes her milk unhealthy

Breast milk is always sterile and at body temperature; it contains more iron, vitamin C, and vitamin A; it contains antibodies that provide the infant some protection against disease; it is more digestible than any formula; and it decreases the frequency of almost every common infant ailment.

42. protein–calorie malnutrition

43. brains; body reserves; marasmus; kwashiorkor

44. marasmus; kwashiorkor

45. undernutrition; developing; "mothercraft"

46. three-fourths; cultural; fathers' jealousy, employers' restrictions, and mothers' wish for convenience

47. iron; milk anemia; zinc

PROGRESS TEST 1

Multiple-Choice Questions

1. **b.** is the answer. (p. 136)

2. **a.** is the answer. (p. 136)

3. **a.** is the answer. (p. 152)

    b. The age norm for this skill is 7.8 months.

    c. This is a reflex, rather than an acquired motor skill.

    d. This skill is acquired between 11 and 12 months.

4. **c.** is the answer. (p. 152)

5. **a.** is the answer. (p. 136)

6. **c.** is the answer. (p. 139)

7. **b.** is the answer. (p. 143)

    c. & d. Experience-independent is not a developmental term.

8. **b.** is the answer. (p. 143)

    a. Experience-dependent functions depend on particular, and variable, experiences in order to grow.

    c. Pruning refers to the process by which some neurons wither because experience does not activate them.

    d. This refers to the great increase in the number of neurons, dendrites, and synapses that occurs in an infant's brain over the first 2 years of life.

9. **b.** is the answer. This is because breast milk is more digestible than cow's milk or formula. (p. 159)

    a., c., & d. Breast- and bottle-fed babies do not differ in these attributes.

10. **b.** is the answer. (p. 161)

11. **c.** is the answer. (p. 149)

    a. & b. These motor skills do not emerge until somewhat later; reflexes are present at birth.

    d. On the contrary, reflexes are quite predictable.

12. **d.** is the answer. (pp. 154–155)

13. **d.** is the answer. (p. 152)

14. **c.** is the answer. (p. 142)

15. **c.** is the answer. (p. 162)

Matching Items

1. k (p. 141)
2. g (p. 141)
3. e (p. 161)
4. b (p. 161)
5. h (p. 150)
6. c (p. 151)
7. i (p. 150)
8. f (p. 150)
9. d (p. 160)
10. j (p. 142)
11. l (p. 138)
12. a (p. 138)
13. m (p. 142)

PROGRESS TEST 2

Multiple-Choice Questions

1. **a.** is the answer. (pp. 141–142)

2. **c.** is the answer. (p. 149)

    a., b., & d. Each of these refers to voluntary responses that are acquired only after a certain amount of practice; reflexes are involuntary responses that are present at birth and require no practice.

3. **a.** is the answer. (p. 136)

    b. This defines percentile.

4. **b.** is the answer. (p. 151)

5. **c.** is the answer. (p. 152)

    a. Norms are average ages at which certain motor skills are acquired.

6. **b.** is the answer. (p. 148)

    a. Although focusing ability seems to be limited to a certain range, babies do focus on many objects in their environment.

    c. This is not within the range at which babies *can* focus.

    d. Babies have very poor distance vision.

7. **d.** is the answer. (p. 139)

8. **a.** is the answer. (p. 159)

    b. If anything, this is a potential *disadvantage* of breast milk over formula.

    c. So can formula.

    d. Breast milk contains more iron, vitamin C, and vitamin A than cow's milk; it does not contain more protein and vitamin D, however.

9. **b.** is the answer. (p. 160)

10. **c.** is the answer. (pp. 142–143)

11. **b.** is the answer. (pp. 150, 151)

    c. & d. Reflexes are involuntary responses; climbing and using a crayon are both voluntary responses.

12. **d.** is the answer. (p. 149)

13. **a.** is the answer. (p. 145)

14. d. is the answer. (p. 162)

15. b. is the answer. (p. 149)

True or False Items

1. F   Boys are both slightly heavier and taller than girls at 2 years. (p. 136)

2. T   (p. 158)

3. F   Hiccups, sneezes, and thrashing are common during the first few days, and they are entirely normal reflexes. (p. 149)

4. F   Although all healthy infants develop the same motor skills in the same sequence, the age at which these skills are acquired can vary greatly from infant to infant. (p. 152)

5. T (p. 136)

6. F   Vision is relatively poorly developed at birth, whereas hearing is well developed. (pp. 147, 148)

7. F   Three out of every four 6-month-olds are formula fed. (p. 163)

8. T (p. 143)

9. T (p. 160)

10. T (p. 149)

THINKING CRITICALLY ABOUT CHAPTER 5

1. c. is the answer. (p. 149)

2. c. is the answer. (p. 147)

a. & b. These abilities merely demonstrate that hearing (sensation) is present at birth.

3. d. is the answer. Although all of the children improved, persistent deficits remained in many of them. (p. 145)

4. d. is the answer. (p. 136)

a. & b. Although slowdowns in growth during infancy are often a cause for concern, their daughter's weight and height are typical of 1-year-old babies.

c. Growth patterns are no more erratic for first children than for later children.

5. a. is the answer. (p. 136)

6. b. is the answer. (p. 140)

7. c. is the answer. (pp. 147, 148)

8. b. is the answer. (p. 150)

a. This is the reflexive sucking of newborns in response to anything that touches their *lips*.

c. This is the response that infants make to escape something that covers their face.

d. In this response to startling noises, newborns fling their arms outward and then bring them together on their chests as if to hold on to something.

9. a. is the answer. (p. 163)

10. b. is the answer. (p. 146)

a. & d. Sensation and perception operate in all these sensory modalities.

11. a. is the answer. Transient exuberance results in a proliferation of neural connections during infancy, some of which will disappear because they are not used; that is, they are not needed to process information. (p. 142)

b. & d. Transient exuberance is a normal developmental process that occurs in all healthy infants.

c. This describes the normal communication process among neurons.

12. b. is the answer. (p. 144)

13. a. is the answer. (p. 147)

b. Objects at this distance are out of focus for newborns.

c. This ability does not emerge until about 1 month of age.

14. b. is the answer. This is true because, at birth, focusing is best for objects between 4 and 30 inches away. (p. 148)

a., c., & d. Newborns have very poor distance vision; each of these situations involves a distance greater than the optimal focus range.

15. d. is the answer. (p. 162)

KEY TERMS

1. A **norm** is an average age for the acquisition of a particular behavior, developed for a specific group population. (p. 135)

2. **Head-sparing** is the phenomenon by which the brain continues to grow even though the body stops growing in a malnourished child. (p. 136)

3. A **percentile** is any point on a ranking scale of 1 to 99; percentiles are often used to compare a child's development to group norms. (p. 136)

4. **Wasting** is a condition in which a person's body weight is at the bottom 3 percent of the norm as a result of acute malnutrition. (p. 139)

5. **Stunting** is a condition in which a person's height is at the bottom 3 percent of the norm as a result of chronic malnutrition. (p. 139)

6. **REM sleep**, or rapid eye movement sleep, is a stage of sleep characterized by flickering eyes behind closed eyelids, dreaming, and rapid brain waves. (p. 139)

7. A **neuron**, or nerve cell, is the main component of the central nervous system. (p. 141)

8. The **cortex** is the thin outer layer of the brain that is involved in the voluntary, cognitive aspects of the mind. (p. 141)

   Memory aid: Cortex in Latin means "bark." As bark covers a tree, the cortex is the "bark of the brain."

9. An **axon** is the nerve fiber extension that sends impulses from one neuron to the dendrites of other neurons. (p. 141)

10. **Dendrites** are nerve fiber extensions that receive the impulses transmitted from other neurons via their axons. (p. 141)

11. A **synapse** is the point at which the axon of a sending neuron meets the dendrites of a receiving neuron. (p. 142)

12. **Transient exuberance** is the dramatic increase in neural connections that occurs in an infant's brain over the first 2 years of life. (p. 142)

13. **Experience-expectant** brain functions are those that require basic common experiences (such as having things to see and hear) in order to grow. (p. 143)

14. **Experience-dependent** brain functions are those that depend on particular, and variable, experiences (such as experiencing language) in order to grow. (p. 143)

15. **Sensation** is the process by which a sensory system detects a particular stimulus. (p. 146)

16. **Perception** is the process by which the brain tries to make sense of a stimulus such that the individual becomes aware of it. (p. 146)

17. **Binocular vision** is the ability to use both eyes together to focus on a single object. (p. 148)

   Memory aid: Bi- indicates "two"; *ocular* means something pertaining to the eye. **Binocular vision** is vision for "two eyes."

18. The **breathing reflex** is an involuntary physical response that ensures that the infant has an adequate supply of oxygen and discharges carbon dioxide. (p. 149)

19. The **sucking reflex** is the involuntary tendency of newborns to suck anything that touches their lips. This reflex fosters feeding. (p. 150)

20. The **rooting reflex**, which helps babies find a nipple, causes them to turn their heads and start to suck when something brushes against their cheek. (p. 150)

21. **Gross motor skills** are physical abilities that demand large body movements, such as climbing, jumping, or running. (p. 150)

22. **Fine motor skills** are physical abilities that require precise, small movements, such as picking up a coin. (p. 151)

23. **Immunization** is the process through which the body's immune system is stimulated (as by a vaccine) to defend against attack by a particular contagious disease. (p. 155)

24. **Sudden infant death syndrome (SIDS)** is a set of circumstances in which a seemingly healthy infant dies unexpectedly in sleep. (p. 156)

25. **Protein–calorie malnutrition** results when a person does not consume enough nourishment to thrive. (p. 160)

26. **Marasmus** is a disease caused by severe protein–calorie deficiency during the first year of life. Growth stops, body tissues waste away, and the infant dies. (p. 161)

27. **Kwashiorkor** is a disease caused by protein–calorie deficiency during toddlerhood. The child's face, legs, and abdomen swell with water, sometimes making the child appear well fed. Other body parts are degraded, including the hair, which becomes thin, brittle, and colorless. (p. 161)

28. **Undernutrition** refers to inadequate nutrition that doesn't cause visible wasting or stunting, but causes the person to be shorter than the norm for well-fed members of the same ethnic group. (p. 162)

Chapter Six

The First 2 Years: Cognitive Development

Chapter Overview

Chapter 6 explores the ways in which the infant comes to learn about, think about, and adapt to his or her surroundings. It focuses on the various ways in which infant intelligence is revealed: through sensorimotor intelligence, perception, memory, and language development. The chapter begins with a description of Jean Piaget's theory of sensorimotor intelligence, which maintains that infants think exclusively with their senses and motor skills. Piaget's six stages of sensorimotor intelligence are examined.

The second section discusses the information-processing theory, which compares cognition to the ways in which computers analyze data. Eleanor and James Gibson's influential theory is also described. Central to this theory is the idea that infants gain cognitive understanding of their world through the affordances of objects, that is, the activities they can do with them.

The text also discusses the key cognitive elements needed by the infant to structure the environment discovered through his or her newfound perceptual abilities. Using the habituation procedure, researchers have found that the speed with which infants recognize familiarity and seek something novel is related to later cognitive skill. It points out the importance of memory to cognitive development.

Finally, the chapter turns to the most remarkable cognitive achievement of the first two years, the acquisition of language. Beginning with a description of the infant's first attempts at language, the chapter follows the sequence of events that leads to the child's ability to utter two-word sentences. The chapter concludes with an examination of three classic theories of language acquisition and a fourth, hybrid theory that combines aspects of each.

NOTE: Answer guidelines for all Chapter 6 questions begin on page 102.

Guided Study

The text chapter should be studied one section at a time. Before you read, preview each section by skimming it, noting headings and boldface items. Then read the appropriate section objectives from the following outline. Keep these objectives in mind and, as you read the chapter section, search for the information that will enable you to meet each objective. Once you have finished a section, write out answers for its objectives.

Sensorimotor Intelligence (pp. 167–176)

1. Identify and describe Piaget's first two stages of sensorimotor intelligence.

2. Identify and describe stages 3 and 4 of Piaget's theory of sensorimotor intelligence.

3. (Thinking Like A Scientist) Explain what object permanence is, how it is tested in infancy, and what these tests reveal.

4. Identify and describe stages 5 and 6 of Piaget's theory of sensorimotor intelligence.

5. (Changing Policy) Describe some major advances in the scientific investigation of infant cognition.

Information Processing (pp. 176–185)

6. Explain the information-processing theory of cognition.

7. Discuss the Gibsons' contextual view of perception, focusing on the idea of affordances and giving examples of the affordances perceived by infants.

8. Explain what research has revealed about the infant's ability to categorize.

9. Discuss research findings on infant memory and infants' emerging implicit and explicit memories.

Language: What Develops in Two Years? (pp. 185–190)

10. Identify the main features of baby talk, and explain its importance.

11. Describe language development during infancy, and identify its major hallmarks.

Theories of Language Learning (pp. 190–197)

12. Differentiate three theories of language learning, and explain current views on language learning.

Chapter Review

When you have finished reading the chapter, work through the material that follows to review it. Complete the sentences and answer the questions. As you proceed, evaluate your performance for each section by consulting the answers on page 102. Do not continue with the next section until you understand each answer. If you need to, review or reread the appropriate section in the textbook before continuing.

Sensorimotor Intelligence (pp. 167–176)

1. Cogntion involves _____ _____ .

   The first major theorist to realize that infants are active learners was _____ .

2. When infants begin to explore the environment through sensory and motor skills, they are displaying what Piaget called _____ intelligence. In number, Piaget described _____ stages of development of this type of intelligence.

3. The first two stages of sensorimotor intelligence are examples of _____ _____ _____ . Stage one begins with newborns' reflexes, such as _____ , _____ , _____ , and _____ . It lasts from birth to _____ of age.

4. Stage two begins when newborns show signs of _____ of their reflexes to the specifics of the environment. This is revealed in two ways: by _____ of new information into previously developed mental categories, or _____ ; and by _____ of previous mental categories to incorporate new information.

Describe the development of the sucking reflex during stages one and two.

5. In stages three and four, development switches to _____ _____ _____ , involving the baby with an object or with another person. During stage three, which occurs between _____ and _____ months of age, infants repeat a specific action that has just elicited a pleasing response.

Describe a typical stage-three behavior.

6. In stage four, which lasts from _____ to _____ months of age, infants can better _____ events. At this stage, babies also engage in purposeful actions, or _____ - _____ behavior.

7. (text and Thinking Like a Scientist) A major cognitive accomplishment of infancy is the ability to understand that objects exist even when they are _____ . This awareness is called _____ _____ . To test for this awareness, Piaget devised a procedure to observe whether an infant will _____ for a hidden object. Using this test, Piaget concluded that this awareness does not develop until about _____ of age.

8. (Thinking Like a Scientist) Using the _____ and _____ event procedures, one clever experiment demonstrated that infants as young as _____ months have an awareness of object permanence that is concealed by the traditional Piagetian hidden-object tests.

9. During stage five, which lasts from _____ to _____ months, infants begin experimenting in thought and deed. They do so through _____ _____ _____ , which involve taking in experiences and trying to make sense of them.

Explain what Piaget meant when he described the stage-five infant as a "little scientist."

10. Stage six, which lasts from _____ to _____ months, is the stage of achieving new means by using _____ _____ .

11. One sign that children have reached stage six is _____ _____ , which is their emerging ability to imitate others' behaviors.

12. (Changing Policy) Two research tools that have become available since Piaget's time are _____ studies, which capitalize on infant's enjoyment of _____ stimuli, and _____ , which reveals brain activity by showing increases in _____ supply to various parts of the brain as cognition occurs.

Information Processing (pp. 176–185)

13. A perspective on human cognition that is modeled on how computers analyze data is the _____-_____ theory. Three aspects of this theory as applied to human development are _____ , which are analogous to computer input; _____ , which are analogous to programming; and _____ , which involves retrieval of ideas, or output.

14. Much of the current research in perception and cognition has been inspired by the work of the Gibsons, who stress that perception is a(n) _____ (active/passive/automatic) cognitive phenomenon.

15. According to the Gibsons, any object in the environment offers diverse opportunities for interaction; this property of an object is called an _____ .

16. Which of these an individual perceives in an object depends on the individual's

_____ _____ and _____ _____ , on his or her _____ _____ , and on his or her _____ _____ of what the object might be used for.

17. Infants perceive the affordance of _____ long before their manual dexterity has matured. The time it takes infants to grab objects successfully demonstrates that deliberate and thoughtful perception _____ (precedes/does not precede) the action.

18. A firm surface that appears to drop off is called a _____ _____ . Although perception of this drop off was once linked to _____ maturity, later research found that infants as young as _____ are able to perceive the drop off, as evidenced by changes in their _____ _____ and their wide open eyes.

19. Perception that is primed to focus on movement and change is called _____ _____ .

20. From a very early age, infants coordinate and organize their perceptions into _____ .

21. Infants younger than 6 months can categorize objects according to their _____ , _____ , _____ , _____ , _____ , and _____ . By the end of the first year, they can categorize _____ , _____ , and _____ , for example. Although a basic understanding of categories such as these may be biologically based, many researchers believe they are also _____-_____ brain functions.

22. Studies of children from around the world demonstrate that the tendency of young brains to categorize objects _____ (is/is not) universal. Overall, for basic categories and

conceptions, the crucial factor seems to be

_____ _____ ; for

emotional interactions, _____-

_____ factors are most important.

23. According to _____ , no one can
remember anything that happened before the age
of _____ . This hypothesized inability is called _____

_____ .

24. Recent studies demonstrate that babies have great
difficulty storing new memories in their first
_____ (how long?).

25. Research has shown, however, that babies can
show that they remember when three conditions
are met:

(a) _____

(b) _____

(c) _____

26. When these conditions are met, infants as young
as _____ months "remembered"
events from one week earlier or two weeks earlier
if they experienced a _____ prior to
retesting.

27. After about _____ months, infants
become capable of retaining information for
longer periods of time, with less reminding. By
the middle of the second year, toddlers are able to
_____ their memories from particu-
lar details to the general concept.

28. Most researchers believe there _____
(is one type of memory/are many types of memory).

29. Memory of events, objects, and experiences that
can be recognized when certain cues are present
is called _____ memory. Memory
that is available for instant recall, often because it
was deliberately _____ , is called
_____ memory.

Language: What Develops in Two Years?
(pp. 185–190)

30. Children the world over _____
(follow/do not follow) the same sequence of
early language development. The timing of this

sequence _____ (varies/does not
vary).

31. Newborns show a preference for hearing
_____ over other sounds, including
the high-pitched, simplified adult speech called
_____ _____ , which is
sometimes called _____ or
_____ _____ speech.

32. By 4 months of age, most babies' verbal repertoire
consists of _____
_____ .

33. At _____ months of age, babies
begin to repeat certain syllables, a phenomenon
referred to as _____ .

34. Deaf babies begin oral babbling
_____ (earlier/later) than hearing
babies do. Deaf babies may also babble
_____ , with this behavior emerging
_____ (earlier than/at the same
time as/later than) hearing infants begin oral
babbling.

35. The average baby speaks a few words at about
_____ of age. When vocabulary
reaches approximately 50 words, it suddenly
begins to build rapidly, at a rate of
_____ or more words a
month. This language spurt is called the
_____ _____ , because
toddlers learn a disproportionate number of
_____ .

36. Another characteristic is the use of the
_____ , in which a single word
expresses a complete thought.

37. Language acquisition is also shaped by our
_____ , as revealed by the fact that
North American infants learn more
_____ than Chinese or Korean
infants, who learn more _____ .

38. Another characteristic of infant speech is
_____ , or overgeneralization, in
which the infant applies a known word to a variety of objects and contexts. Initially, however,
infants tend toward _____ of word

meanings. Infants also might learn one name for something and refuse to use alternative names; this is called the _____

_____ _____ .

39. Children begin to produce their first two-word sentences at about _____ months, showing a clearly emerging understanding of _____ , which refers to all the methods that languages use to communicate meaning, apart from the words themselves.

Theories of Language Learning (pp. 190–197).

40. Reinforcement and other conditioning processes account for language development, according to the learning theory of _____ .
Support for this theory comes from the fact that there are wide variations in language _____ , especially when children from different cultures are compared. One longitudinal study that followed mother–infant pairs over time found that the frequency of early _____ _____ predicted the child's rate of language acquisition many months later.

41. The theorist who stressed that language is too complex to be mastered so early and easily through conditioning is _____ . This theorist maintained that all children are born with a LAD, or _____

_____ _____ , that enables children to quickly derive the rules of grammar from the speech they hear.

42. Language development is _____ , meaning that it depends on the interaction between genes and other factors.

43. Imbedded in the LAD, the _____ (surface/deep) structure of language is _____-_____ , meaning that words are "expected" by the developing brain. In contrast, the _____ (surface/deep) structure of language, which consists of _____ and _____ , is _____-_____ .

Summarize the research support for Theory Two.

44. A third, _____-_____ theory of language proposes that _____ _____ foster infant language.

45. The original theories of Skinner and Chomsky have been _____ (refuted/supported) by research. A new hybrid theory based on a model called an _____

_____ combines aspects of several theories. A fundamental aspect of this theory is that _____

_____ .

Progress Test 1

Multiple-Choice Questions

Circle your answers to the following questions and check them with the answers on page 103. If your answer is incorrect, read the explanation for why it is incorrect and then consult the appropriate pages of the text (in parentheses following the correct answer).

1. In general terms, the Gibsons' concept of affordances emphasizes the idea that the individual perceives an object in terms of its:
   a. economic importance.
   b. physical qualities.
   c. function or use to the individual.
   d. role in the larger culture or environment.

2. According to Piaget, when a baby repeats an action that has just triggered a pleasing response from his or her caregiver, a stage _____ behavior has occurred.
   a. one   c. three
   b. two   d. six

3. Sensorimotor intelligence begins with a baby's first:
   a. attempt to crawl.
   b. reflex actions.
   c. auditory perception.
   d. adaptation of a reflex.

4. Piaget and the Gibsons would most likely agree that:
   a. perception is largely automatic.
   b. language development is biologically predisposed in children.
   c. learning and perception are active cognitive processes.
   d. it is unwise to "push" children too hard academically.

5. By the end of the first year, infants usually learn how to:
   a. accomplish simple goals.
   b. manipulate various symbols.
   c. solve complex problems.
   d. pretend.

6. When an infant begins to understand that objects exist even when they are out of sight, she or he has begun to understand the concept of object:
   a. displacement.   c. permanence.
   b. importance.   d. location.

7. Today, most cognitive psychologists view language acquisition as:
   a. primarily the result of imitation of adult speech.
   b. a behavior that is determined primarily by biological maturation.
   c. a behavior determined entirely by learning.
   d. determined by both biological maturation and learning.

8. Despite cultural differences, children all over the world attain very similar language skills:
   a. according to ethnically specific timetables.
   b. in the same sequence according to a variable timetable.
   c. according to culturally specific timetables.
   d. according to timetables that vary from child to child.

9. The average baby speaks a few words at about:
   a. 6 months.   c. 12 months.
   b. 9 months.   d. 24 months.

10. A single word used by toddlers to express a complete thought is:
    a. a holophrase.   c. an overextension.
    b. baby talk.   d. an underextension.

11. A distinctive form of language, with a particular pitch, structure, etc., that adults use in talking to infants is called:
    a. a holophrase.   c. baby talk.
    b. the LAD.   d. conversation.

12. At 8 months, infants can categorize objects on the basis of:
    a. angularity.   c. density.
    b. shape.   d. all of the above.

13. (Changing Policy) The imaging technique that reveals brain activity by showing increases in oxygen supply to various parts of the brain is called a(n):
    a. PET scan.
    b. EEG.
    c. fMRI.
    d. CAT scan.

14. A toddler who taps on the computer's keyboard after observing her mother sending e-mail is demonstrating:
    a. assimilation.   c. deferred imitation.
    b. accommodation.   d. dynamic perception.

15. In Piaget's theory of sensorimotor intelligence, reflexes that involve the infant's own body are examples of:
    a. primary circular reactions
    b. secondary circular reactions.
    c. tertiary circular reactions.
    d. none of the above.

Matching Items

Match each definition or description with its corresponding term.

Terms

_____   1. mental combinations
_____   2. affordances
_____   3. object permanence
_____   4. Noam Chomsky
_____   5. B. F. Skinner
_____   6. sensorimotor intelligence
_____   7. babbling
_____   8. holophrase
_____   9. overextension
_____ 10. deferred imitation
_____ 11. dynamic perception

Definitions or Descriptions

a. overgeneralization of a word to inappropriate objects, etc.
b. repetitive utterance of certain syllables
c. perception that focuses on movement and change
d. the ability to witness, remember, and later copy a behavior
e. the realization that something that is out of sight continues to exist
f. trying out actions mentally
g. opportunities for interaction that an object offers
h. theorist who believed that verbal behavior is conditioned
i. a single word used to express a complete thought
j. theorist who believed that language ability is innate
k. thinking through the senses and motor skills

Progress Test 2

Progress Test 2 should be completed during a final chapter review. Answer the following questions after you thoroughly understand the correct answers for the Chapter Review and Progress Test 1.

Multiple-Choice Questions

1. Stage five (12 to 18 months) of sensorimotor intelligence is best described as:
   a. first acquired adaptations.
   b. the period of the "little scientist."
   c. procedures for making interesting sights last.
   d. new means through symbolization.

2. Which of the following is *not* evidence of dynamic perception during infancy?
   a. Babies prefer to look at things in motion.
   b. Babies form simple expectations of the path that a moving object will follow.
   c. Babies use movement cues to discern the boundaries of objects.
   d. Babies quickly grasp that even though objects look different when seen from different viewpoints, they are the same objects.

3. (text and Thinking Like a Scientist) Research suggests that the concept of object permanence:
   a. fades after a few months.
   b. is a skill some children never acquire.
   c. may occur earlier and more gradually than Piaget recognized.
   d. involves pretending as well as mental combinations.

4. According to the Gibsons, graspability is:
   a. an opportunity perceived by a baby.
   b. a quality that resides in toys and other objects.
   c. an ability that emerges at about 6 months.
   d. evidence of manual dexterity in the infant.

5. The eerie phenomenon of *déjà vu*, in which you feel as if you are reliving an earlier experience, is an example of:
   a. implicit memory.
   b. explicit memory.
   c. an experience-dependent brain function.
   d. an experience-reactive brain function.

6. According to Piaget, assimilation and accommodation are two ways in which:
   a. infants adapt their reflexes to the specifics of the environment.
   b. goal-directed behavior occurs.
   c. infants form mental combinations.
   d. language begins to emerge.

7. For Noam Chomsky, the "language acquisition device" refers to:
   a. the human predisposition to acquire language.
   b. the portion of the human brain that processes speech.
   c. the vocabulary of the language the child is exposed to.
   d. all of the above.

8. The first stage of sensorimotor intelligence lasts until:
   a. infants can anticipate events that will fulfill their needs.
   b. infants begin to adapt their reflexes to the environment.
   c. infants interact with objects to produce exciting experiences.
   d. infants are capable of thinking about past and future events.

9. Whether or not an infant perceives certain characteristics of objects, such as "suckability" or "graspability," seems to depend on:
   a. his or her prior experiences.
   b. his or her needs.
   c. his or her sensory awareness.
   d. all of the above.

10. (Thinking Like a Scientist) Piaget was *incorrect* in his belief that infants do not have:
    a. object permanence.
    b. intelligence.
    c. goal-directed behavior.
    d. all of the above.

11. The purposeful actions that begin to develop in sensorimotor stage four are called:
    a. reflexes.
    b. affordances.
    c. goal-directed behaviors.
    d. mental combinations.

12. What is the correct sequence of stages of language development?
    a. crying, babbling, cooing, first word
    b. crying, cooing, babbling, first word
    c. crying, babbling, first word, cooing
    d. crying, cooing, first word, babbling

13. Compared with hearing babies, deaf babies:
    a. are less likely to babble.
    b. are more likely to babble.
    c. begin to babble vocally at about the same age.
    d. begin to babble manually at about the same age as hearing babies begin to babble vocally.

14. According to Skinner, children acquire language:
    a. as a result of an inborn ability to use the basic structure of language.
    b. through reinforcement and other aspects of conditioning.
    c. mostly because of biological maturation.
    d. in a fixed sequence of predictable stages.

15. A fundamental idea of the emergentist coalition model of language acquisition is that:
    a. all humans are born with an innate Language Acquisition Device.
    b. some aspects of language are best learned in one way at one age, others in another way at another age.
    c. language development occurs too rapidly and easily to be entirely the product of conditioning.
    d. imitation and reinforcement are crucial to the development of language.

16. Which of the following is an example of a secondary circular reaction?
    a. a 1-month-old infant staring at a mobile suspended over her crib
    b. a 2-month-old infant sucking a pacifier
    c. realizing that rattles make noise, a 4-month-old infant laughs with delight when his mother puts a rattle in his hand
    d. a 12-month-old toddler licks a bar of soap to learn what it tastes like

Matching Items

Match each definition or description with its corresponding term.

Terms

_____ 1. goal-directed behavior
_____ 2. visual cliff
_____ 3. infantile amnesia
_____ 4. baby talk
_____ 5. assimilation
_____ 6. little scientist
_____ 7. deep structure
_____ 8. underextension
_____ 9. accommodation
_____ 10. LAD
_____ 11. surface structure

Definitions or Descriptions

a. a device for studying depth perception
b. incorporating new information into an existing schema
c. the grammar of a language
d. the inability to access memories from the first years of life
e. a word used more narrowly than its true meaning allows
f. a hypothetical device that facilitates language development
g. also called "Motherese"
h. Piaget's term for the stage-five toddler
i. purposeful actions
j. modifying an existing schema to reflect new information
k. the vocabulary of a language

Thinking Critically About Chapter 6

Answer these questions the day before an exam as a final check on your understanding of the chapter's terms and concepts.

1. A 9-month-old repeatedly reaches for his sister's doll, even though he has been told "no" many times. This is an example of:
   a. primary circular reactions.
   b. an overextension.
   c. delayed imitation.
   d. goal-directed behavior.

2. During her psychology exam, Celine had difficulty recalling key distinctions among the three major theories of language development. Evidently, Celine was experiencing difficulty with her:
   a. implicit memory.
   b. explicit memory.
   c. short-term memory.
   d. epigenetic memory.

3. As an advocate of the social-pragmatic theory, Professor Robinson believes that:
   a. infants communicate in every way they can because they are social beings.
   b. biological maturation is a dominant force in language development.
   c. infants' language abilities mirror those of their primary caregivers.
   d. language develops in many ways for many reasons.

4. According to Skinner's theory, an infant who learns to delight his father by saying "da-da" is probably benefiting from:
   a. social reinforcers, such as smiles and hugs.
   b. modeling.
   c. learning by imitation.
   d. an innate ability to use language.

5. The child's tendency to call every animal "doggie" is an example of:
   a. using a holophrase.   **c.** motherese.
   b. babbling.   **d.** overextension.

6. At about 21 months, the typical child will:
   a. have a vocabulary of between 250 and 350 words.
   b. begin to speak in holophrases.
   c. put words together to form rudimentary sentences.
   d. do all of the above.

7. A 20-month-old girl who is able to try out various actions mentally without having to actually perform them is learning to solve simple problems by using:
   a. dynamic perception.
   b. object permanence.
   c. affordances.
   d. mental combinations.

8. A baby who repeats an action he or she has seen trigger a reaction in someone else is demonstrating an ability that typically occurs in which stage of sensorimotor development?

   a. one   c. three
   b. two   d. four

9. Sixteen-month-old Courtney reserves the word "cat" for her pet feline. Her failure to refer to other felines as cats is an example of:

   a. a holophrase.
   b. an overextension.
   c. babbling.
   d. an underextension.

10. A baby who realizes that a rubber duck that has fallen out of the tub must be somewhere on the floor has achieved:

    a. object permanence.
    b. deferred imitation.
    c. mental combinations.
    d. goal-directed behavior.

11. As soon as her babysitter arrives, 21-month-old Christine holds on to her mother's legs and, in a questioning manner, says "bye-bye." Because Christine clearly is "asking" her mother not to leave, her utterance can be classified as:

    a. babbling.
    b. an overextension.
    c. a holophrase.
    d. subject-predicate order.

12. The 6-month-old infant's continual repetition of sound combinations such as "ba-ba-ba" is called:

    a. cooing.   c. a holophrase.
    b. babbling.   d. an overextension.

13. Which of the following is an example of a linguistic overextension that a 2-year-old might make?

    a. saying "bye-bye" to indicate that he or she wants to go out
    b. pointing to a cat and saying "doggie"
    c. repeating certain syllables, such as "ma-ma"
    d. reversing word order, such as "want it, paper"

14. Many researchers believe that the infant's ability to detect the similarities and differences between shapes and colors marks the beginning of:

    a. mental combinations.
    b. the stage of the little scientist.
    c. category or concept formation.
    d. full object permanence.

15. Like most Korean toddlers, Noriko has acquired a greater number of _____ in her vocabulary than her North American counterparts, who tend to acquire more _____ .

    a. verbs; nouns
    b. nouns; verbs
    c. adjectives; verbs
    d. adjectives; nouns

16. Eighteen-month-old Colin puts a collar on his stuffed dog, then pretends to take it for a walk. Colin's behavior is an example of a:

    a. primary circular reaction.
    b. secondary circular reaction.
    c. tertiary circular reaction.
    d. first acquired adaptation.

Key Terms

Using your own words, write a brief definition or explanation of each of the following terms on a separate piece of paper.

1. sensorimotor intelligence
2. primary circular reactions
3. adaptation
4. assimilation
5. accommodation
6. secondary circular reactions
7. goal-directed behavior
8. object permanence
9. tertiary circular reactions
10. "little scientist"
11. mental combinations
12. deferred imitation
13. habituation
14. fMRI
15. information-processing theory
16. affordance
17. graspability
18. visual cliff
19. dynamic perception
20. infantile amnesia
21. reminder session
22. implicit memory
23. explicit memory
24. baby talk

25. babbling
26. naming explosion
27. holophrase
28. underextension
29. overextension
30. grammar
31. language acquisition device (LAD)

ANSWERS
CHAPTER REVIEW

1. intelligence and learning, memory and language, facts and concepts, beliefs and assumptions, teaching and education; Piaget

2. sensorimotor; 6

3. primary circular reactions; sucking; grasping; staring; listening; 1 month

4. adaptation; assimilation; schemas; accommodation

Stage-one infants suck everything that touches their lips. At about 1 month, they start to adapt their sucking to specific objects. After several months, they have organized the world into objects to be sucked for nourishment, objects to be sucked for pleasure, and objects not to be sucked at all.

5. secondary circular reactions; 4; 8

A stage-three infant may squeeze a duck, hear a quack, and squeeze the duck again.

6. 8; 12; anticipate; goal-directed

7. no longer in sight; object permanence; search; 8 months

8. possible; impossible; $4^1/2$

9. 12; 18; tertiary circular reactions

Having discovered some action or set of actions that is possible with a given object, stage-five "little scientists" seem to ask, "What else can I do with this?"

10. 18; 24; mental combinations

11. deferred imitation

12. habituation; novel; fMRI; oxygen

13. information-processing; affordances; categories; memory

14. active

15. affordance

16. past experiences; developmental level; immediate motivation; sensory awareness

17. graspability; precedes

18. visual cliff; visual; 3 months; heart rate

19. dynamic perception

20. categories

21. angularity; shape; color; density; relative size; number (up to three objects); birds; animals; people; experience-expectant

22. is; brain maturation; experience-dependent

23. Freud; 2 years; infantile amnesia

24. 6 months

25. (a) real-life situations are used; (b) motivation is high; (c) special measures aid memory retrieval

26. 3 months; reminder session

27. 6; generalize

28. are many types of memory

29. implicit; studied; explicit

30. follow; varies

31. speech; baby talk; motherese; child-directed

32. squeals, growls, gurgles, grunts, croons, and yells, as well as some speechlike sounds

33. 6 or 7; babbling

34. later; manually; at the same time as

35. 1 year; 50 to 100; naming explosion; nouns

36. holophrase

37. culture; nouns; verbs

38. overextension; underextension; mutual exclusivity bias

39. 21; grammar

40. B. F. Skinner; fluency; maternal responsiveness

41. Noam Chomsky; language acquisition device

42. epigenetic

43. deep; experience-expectant; surface; pronunciation; vocabulary; experience-dependent

Support for this theory comes from research with deaf and blind babies. Deaf babies have been found to babble manually, then use sign language at the same time and in the same sequence as hearing babies. Blind babies spontaneously use gestures. So, for these babies, language comes from within.

44. social-pragmatic; social impulses

45. refuted; emergentist coalition; some aspects of language are best learned in one way at one age, others in another way at another age

PROGRESS TEST 1

Multiple-Choice Questions

1. **c.** is the answer. (p. 177)

2. **c.** is the answer. (p. 170)

3. **b.** is the answer. This was Piaget's most basic contribution to the study of infant cognition—that intelligence is revealed in behavior at every age. (p. 168)

4. **c.** is the answer. (pp. 167, 177)

   b. This is Chomsky's position.

   d. This issue was not discussed in the text.

5. **a.** is the answer. (p. 171)

   b. & c. These abilities are not acquired until children are much older.

   d. Pretending is associated with stage six (18 to 24 months).

6. **c.** is the answer. (p. 171)

7. **d.** is the answer. (p. 196)

8. **b.** is the answer. (p. 185)

   a., c., & d. Children the world over, and in every Piagetian stage, follow the same sequence, but the timing of their accomplishments may vary considerably.

9. **c.** is the answer. (p. 187)

10. **a.** is the answer. (p. 188)

    b. Baby talk is the speech adults use with infants.

    c. An overextension is a grammatical error in which a word is generalized to an inappropriate context.

    d. An underextension is the use of a word to refer to a narrower category of objects or events than the term signifies.

11. **c.** is the answer. (p. 185)

    a. A holophrase is a single word uttered by a toddler to express a complete thought.

    b. According to Noam Chomsky, the LAD, or language acquisition device, is an innate ability in humans to acquire language.

    d. These characteristic differences in pitch and structure are precisely what distinguish baby talk from regular conversation.

12. **d.** is the answer. (p. 175)

13. **c.** is the answer. (p. 175)

14. **c.** is the answer (pp. 174–175)

    a. & b. In Piaget's theory, these refer to processes by which mental concepts incorporate new experiences (assimilation) or are modified in response to new experiences (accommodation).

    d. Dynamic perception is perception that is primed to focus on movement and change.

15. **a.** is the answer. (p. 168)

    b. Secondary circular reactions involve the baby with an object or with another person.

    c. Tertiary circular reactions involve active exploration and experimentation, rather than mere reflexive action.

Matching Items

1. f (p. 174)   5. h (p. 190)   9. a (p. 189)
2. g (p. 177)   6. k (p. 168)   10. d (pp. 174–175)
3. e (p. 171)   7. b (p. 187)   11. c (p. 179)
4. j (p. 192)   8. i (p. 188)

PROGRESS TEST 2

Multiple-Choice Questions

1. **b.** is the answer. (p. 174)

   a. & c. These are stages two and three.

   d. This is not one of Piaget's stages of sensorimotor intelligence.

2. **d.** is the answer. This is an example of perceptual constancy. (p. 179)

3. **c.** is the answer. (pp. 171–173)

4. **a.** is the answer. (p. 178)

   b. Affordances are perceptual phenomena.

   c. & d. Infants perceive graspability at an earlier age and long before their manual dexterity enables them to actually grasp successfully.

5. **a.** is the answer. (p. 184)

   b. Explicit memory does not depend on the kind of specific retrieval cues that trigger implicit memories such as *déjà vu*.

   c. & d. Experience-dependent brain functions and experience-reactive brain functions are developmental abilities, such as the surface and deep structures of language, respectively.

6. **a.** is the answer. (pp. 168–169)

   b. Assimilation and accommodation are cognitive processes, not behaviors.

   c. Mental combinations are sequences of actions that are carried out mentally.

   d. Assimilation and accommodation do not directly pertain to language use.

7. **a.** is the answer. Chomsky believed that this device is innate. (p. 192)

8. **b.** is the answer. (pp. 168–169)

    a. & c. Both of these occur later than stage one.

    d. This is a hallmark of stage six.

9. **d.** is the answer. (p. 177)

10. **a.** is the answer. (p. 172)

11. **c.** is the answer. (p. 171)

    a. Reflexes are involuntary (and therefore unintentional) responses.

    b. Affordances are perceived opportunities for interaction with objects.

    d. Mental combinations are actions that are carried out mentally, rather than behaviorally. Moreover, mental combinations do not develop until a later age, during sensorimotor stage six.

12. **b.** is the answer. (pp. 185–187)

13. **d.** is the answer. (p. 187)

    a. & b. Hearing and deaf babies do not differ in the overall likelihood that they will babble.

    c. Deaf babies begin to babble vocally several months later than hearing babies do.

14. **b.** is the answer. (p. 190)

    a., c., & d. These views on language acquisition describe the theory offered by Noam Chomsky.

15. **b.** is the answer. (p. 196)

    a. & c. These ideas are consistent with Noam Chomsky's theory.

    d. This is the central idea of B. F. Skinner's theory.

16. **c.** is the answer. (p. 170)

    a. & b. These are examples of primary circular reactions.

    d. This is an example of a tertiary circular reaction.

Matching Items

1. i (p. 171)   5. b (p. 168)   9. j (p. 169)
2. a (p. 178)   6. h (p. 174)   10. f (p. 192)
3. d (p. 182)   7. c (p. 193)   11. k (p. 193)
4. g (p. 185)   8. e (p. 188)

THINKING CRITICALLY ABOUT CHAPTER 6

1. **d.** is the answer. The baby is clearly behaving purposefully, the hallmark of goal-directed behavior. (p. 171)

    a. This is a stage-four behavior, not stages one or two.

    b. An overextension occurs when the infant overgeneralizes the use of a word to an inappropriate object or context.

    c. Delayed imitation is the ability to imitate actions seen in the past.

2. **b.** is the answer. (p. 184)

    a. Implicit memory is memory of events, objects, and experiences that can only be evoked when certain retrieval cues are present.

    c. To enable the type of recall required on a test, information must have been transferred into long-term memory.

    d. There is no such thing as epigenetic memory.

3. **a.** is the answer. (p. 194)

    b. This idea is more consistent with Noam Chomsky's theory.

    c. This idea is more consistent with B. F. Skinner's theory.

    d. This expresses the emergentist coalition theory.

4. **a.** is the answer. The father's expression of delight is clearly a reinforcer in that it has increased the likelihood of the infant's vocalization. (p. 190)

    b. & c. Modeling, or learning by imitation, would be implicated if the father attempted to increase the infant's vocalizations by repeatedly saying "da-da" himself, in the infant's presence.

    d. This is Chomsky's viewpoint; Skinner maintained that language is acquired through learning.

5. **d.** is the answer. The child is clearly overgeneralizing the word "dog" by applying it to other animals. (p. 189)

    a. The holophrase is a single word that is used to express a complete thought.

    b. Babbling is the repetitious uttering of certain syllables, such as "ma-ma," or "da-da."

    c. Motherese, or baby talk, is the characteristic manner in which adults change the structure and pitch of their speech when conversing with infants.

6. **c.** is the answer. (p. 189)

    a. At 21 months of age, most children have much smaller vocabularies.

    b. Speaking in holophrases is typical of younger infants.

7. **d.** is the answer. (p. 174)

    a. Dynamic perception is perception primed to focus on movement and change.

b. Object permanence is the awareness that objects do not cease to exist when they are out of sight.

c. Affordances are the opportunities for perception and interaction that an object or place offers to any individual.

8. **c.** is the answer. (p. 170)

9. **d.** is the answer. (p. 188)

10. **a.** is the answer. Before object permanence is attained, an object that disappears from sight ceases to exist for the infant. (p. 171)

   b. Deferred imitation is the ability to witness, remember, and later copy a particular behavior.

   c. Mental combinations are actions that are carried out mentally.

   d. Goal-directed behavior refers to purposeful actions initiated by infants in anticipation of events that will fulfill their needs and wishes.

11. **c.** is the answer. (p. 188)

   a. Because Christine is expressing a complete thought, her speech is much more than babbling.

   b. An overextension is the application of a word the child knows to an inappropriate context, such as "doggie" to all animals the child sees.

   d. The ability to understand subject-predicate order emerges later, when children begin forming 2-word sentences.

12. **b.** is the answer. (p. 187)

   a. Cooing is the pleasant-sounding utterances of the infant at about 2 months.

   c. The holophrase occurs later and refers to the toddler's use of a single word to express a complete thought.

   d. An overextension, or overgeneralization, is the application of a word to an inappropriate context, such as "doed" for the past tense of "do."

13. **b.** is the answer. In this example, the 2-year-old has overgeneralized the concept "doggie" to all four-legged animals. (p. 189)

14. **c.** is the answer. (p. 180)

   a. Mental combinations—sequences of actions that are carried out mentally—are a hallmark of Piaget's stage four infant.

   b. The stage of the little scientist is Piaget's way of describing the infant as he or she begins to experiment and be creative.

d. Object permanence, or the awareness that objects do not cease to exist simply because they are not in view, is not based on perceiving similarities among objects.

15. **a.** is the answer. (p. 188)

16. **c.** is the answer. (p. 174)

KEY TERMS

1. Piaget's stages of **sensorimotor intelligence** (from birth to about 2 years old) are based on his theory that infants think exclusively with their senses and motor skills. (p. 168)

2. In Piaget's theory, **primary circular reactions** are a type of feedback loop involving the infant's own body, in which infants take in experiences (such as sucking and grasping) and try to make sense of them. (p. 168)

3. A key element of Piaget's theory, **adaptation** is the cognitive process by which information is taken in and responded to. (p. 168)

4. In Piaget's theory, **assimilation** is the adaptation process in which new information is taken into the mind by incorporating it into existing mental schemas. (p. 168)

5. In Piaget's theory, **accommodation** is the adaptation process in which new information is brought into the mind in such a way as to refine or expanding existing mental shemas. (p. 169)

6. **Secondary circular reactions** are a type of feedback loop involving the infant's responses to objects and other people. (p. 170)

7. **Goal-directed behavior** refers to purposeful actions initiated by infants in anticipation of events that will fulfill their needs and wishes. (p. 171)

8. **Object permanence** is the understanding that objects continue to exist even when they cannot be seen, touched, or heard. (p. 171)

9. In Piaget's theory, **tertiary circular reactions** are the most sophisticated type of infant feedback loop, involving active exploration and experimentation. (p. 174)

10. **"Little scientist"** is Piaget's term for the stage-five toddler who learns about the properties of objects in his or her world through active experimentation. (p. 174)

11. In Piaget's theory, **mental combinations** are sequences of actions that are carried out mentally. Mental combinations enable stage-six toddlers to begin to anticipate and solve problems without resorting to trial-and-error experiments. (p. 174)

12. **Deferred imitation** is the ability to witness, remember, and later copy a particular behavior. (pp. 174–175)

13. **Habituation** is the process of becoming so familiar with a stimulus that it no longer triggers the responses it did when it was originally experienced. (p. 175)

14. **Functional magnetic resonance imaging (fMRI)** is a new imaging technique in which the brain's magnetic properties are measured to reveal changes in activity levels in various parts of the brain. (p. 175)

15. **Information-processing theory** is a theory of human cognition that compares thinking to the ways in which a computer analyzes data, through the processes of input, programming, and output. (p. 176)

16. **Affordances** are perceived opportunities for interacting with objects or places in the environment. Infants perceive sucking, grasping, noise-making, and many other affordances of objects at an early age. (p. 177)

17. **Graspability** is the perception of whether or not an object is of the proper size, shape, texture, and distance to afford grasping or grabbing. (p. 178)

18. A **visual cliff** is an apparent (but not actual) drop between one surface and another. (p. 178)

19. **Dynamic perception** is perception that is primed to focus on movement and change. (p. 179)

20. **Infantile amnesia** is the inability, according to Freud, to remember events before age 2. (p. 182)

21. A **reminder session** involves the experiencing of some aspect of an event that triggers the entire memory of the event. (p. 182)

22. **Implicit memory** is memory of events, objects, and experiences that can be recognized only when certain recall cues are present. (p. 184)

23. **Explicit memory** is memory for material that is available for instant recall, often because it was deliberately studied and memorized. (p. 184)

24. **Baby talk** is a form of speech used by adults when talking to infants. It is simplified, it has a higher pitch, and it is repetitive. (p. 185)

25. **Babbling,** which begins at 6 or 7 months, is characterized by the extended repetition of certain syllables (such as "ma-ma"). (p. 187)

26. The **naming explosion** refers to the dramatic increase in the infant's vocabulary that begins at about 18 months of age. (p. 187)

27. Another characteristic of infant speech is the use of the **holophrase,** in which a single word is used to convey a complete thought. (p. 188)

28. An **underextension** of word meaning occurs when a baby applies a word more narrowly than its full meaning allows. (p. 188)

29. **Overextension** is a characteristic of infant speech in which the infant overgeneralizes a known word by applying it to a large variety of objects or contexts. (p. 189)

    Memory aid: In this behavior, the infant *extends* a word or grammatical rule beyond, or *over* and above, its normal boundaries.

30. The **grammar** of a language includes rules of word order, verb forms, and all other methods used to communicate meaning apart from words themselves. (p. 189)

31. According to Chomsky, children possess an innate **language acquisition device (LAD)** that enables them to acquire language, including the basic aspects of grammar. (p. 192)

Chapter Seven

The First 2 Years: Psychosocial Development

Chapter Overview

Chapter 7 describes the emotional and social life of the developing person during the first 2 years. It begins with a description of the infant's emerging emotions and how they reflect mobility and social awareness. Two emotions, contentment and distress, are apparent at birth and are soon joined by anger and fear. Temperament, which affects later personality and is primarily inborn, is influenced by the individual's interactions with the environment.

The second section explores the social context in which emotions develop. By referencing their caregivers' signals, infants learn when and how to express their emotions. As self-awareness develops, many new emotions emerge, including embarrassment, shame, guilt, and pride.

The third section presents the psychoanalytic theories of Freud and Erikson along with behaviorist, cognitive, sociocultural, and epigenetic systems theories, which help us understand how the infant's emotional and behavioral responses begin to take on the various patterns that form personality.

In the next section, emotions and relationships are examined from a different perspective—that of parent–infant interaction. Videotaped studies of parents and infants, combined with laboratory studies of attachment, have greatly expanded our understanding of psychosocial development. The final section explores the impact of day care on infants.

NOTE: Answer guidelines for all Chapter 7 questions begin on page 118.

Guided Study

The text chapter should be studied one section at a time. Before you read, preview each section by skimming it, noting headings and boldface items. Then read the appropriate section objectives from the following outline. Keep these objectives in mind and, as you read the chapter section, search for the informa-

tion that will enable you to meet each objective. Once you have finished a section, write out answers for its objectives.

Emotional Development in Infancy (pp. 201–207)

1. Describe the basic emotions expressed by infants during the first days and months.

2. Describe the main developments in the emotional life of the child between 6 months and 2 years.

3. (text and Thinking Like a Scientist) Discuss the origins and characteristics of different temperaments.

4. (Thinking Like a Scientist) Differentiate the Big Five personality traits.

Emotions in the Social Context (pp. 207–214)

5. Discuss the development of emotional communication between parent and infant and, in particular, the role of play in this process.

6. Discuss the concept of social referencing, noting the difference in how the infant interacts with mother and father.

7. Discuss the links between the infant's emerging self-awareness and his or her continuing emotional development.

Theories About Caregiving (pp. 214–218)

8. Describe Freud's psychosexual stages of infant development.

9. Describe Erikson's psychosocial stages of infant development.

10. Contrast the perspectives of behaviorism, cognitive theory, sociocultural theory, and epigenetic systems theory regarding the importance of caregiver behavior in the first two years of life.

Attachment (pp. 218–224)

11. Describe the synchrony of parent–infant interaction during the first year, and discuss its significance for the developing person.

12. Define attachment, explain how it is measured and how it is influenced by context, and discuss the long-term consequences of secure and insecure attachment.

Infant Day Care (pp. 224–227)

13. Discuss the impact of nonmaternal care on young children, and identify the factors that define high quality day care.

Conclusions in Theory and Practice (pp. 227–229)

14. (Thinking Like a Scientist) Describe four categories of adult attachments and how each affects the child's attachment to the parent.

Chapter Review

When you have finished reading the chapter, work through the material that follows to review it. Complete the sentences and answer the questions. As you proceed, evaluate your performance for each section by consulting the answers on page 118. Do not continue with the next section until you understand each answer. If you need to, review or reread the appropriate section in the textbook before continuing.

Emotional Development in Infancy (pp. 201–207)

1. Before infants _____ they have a smaller range of emotions than later, when more _____ coincides with more emotion.

2. The first emotions that can be reliably discerned in infants are _____ and _____ . Other early infant emotions include _____ , _____ , and _____ .

3. Fully formed fear emerges at about _____ . One expression of this new emotion is _____ _____ ,

which becomes full-blown by _____ months; another is _____ _____ , or fear of abandonment, which peaks at _____ months. During the second year, anger and fear typically _____ (increase/decrease) and become more _____ toward specific things.

4. Toward the end of the second year, the new emotions of _____ , _____ , _____ , and _____ become apparent. These emotions require an awareness of _____ .

5. Emotional development during the first two years follows a timetable set by _____ _____ , yet it is also influenced by the child's _____ context.

6. Infants are born with distinct _____ that are _____ in origin and affect later _____ . These early individual differences in _____ , _____ , and _____ reactivity and self-regulation are _____ (begin in a multitude of genetic instructions) and _____ (can/cannot) change.

7. (Thinking Like a Scientist) The correlations found thus far between neurological measurements and childhood behavior are _____ (large/small). The most famous long-term study of children's temperament is the _____ , begun more than forty years ago. This study found that babies differ in nine characteristics:

_____

_____

_____

8. (Thinking Like a Scientist) By two to three months, infants can be clustered into one of three types: _____ , _____ , and _____ .

Later, researchers identified a list of basic adult traits called the _____ _____ . These include _____ , _____ , _____ , _____ , and _____ .

9. The NYLS trait that is closely related to the adult traits of openness and neuroticism is _____ – _____ . This trait helps classify children as _____ , _____ , or _____ .

10. An important factor in healthy psychosocial development is _____ _____ _____ between the developing child and the caregiving context.

Emotions in the Social Context (pp. 207–214)

11. Infants with _____ , which is caused by indigestion, cry for extended periods of time and sleep less than other infants. An infant's responses in the first three months _____ (are/are not) predictive of later temperament and emotional reactions to stress.

12. Sensitive and familiar caregivers begin to provoke wider grins, cooing, and other reactions that signify special status to the infant at about _____ months of age.

13. The coordinated interaction of response between infant and caregiver is called _____ . Partly through this interaction, infants learn to _____ _____ and to develop some of the basic skills of _____ _____ . Two key factors in this process are the _____ of the interaction and _____ . This process is most evident in _____ interactions.

14. Using the _____ _____ , researchers have discovered that babies become more upset when their parents stop engaging in synchronous behavior than when they leave for a minute or two.

15. Infants often look to trusted adults for emotional cues in uncertain situations; this is called _____ _____ . This process is particularly noticeable in infants at _____ .

16. Early research on psychosocial development focused on _____–_____ relationships. More recently, researchers have found that although fathers provide less _____ _____ than mothers, they play more. Consequently, infants tend to look to fathers for _____ and to mothers for _____ . Compared to mothers' play, fathers' play is more _____ .

17. Researchers speculate that father's teasing may foster an infant's _____ _____ and _____ . Although there is great _____ in the roles parents develop in raising their children, generally speaking, mothers and fathers together _____ (are/are no) better in meeting all their infant's needs than is either parent alone.

18. The emerging sense of "me and mine" is part of what psychologists call _____ .This makes possible many new self-conscious emotions, from pride and confidence to _____ , _____ , and _____ . This awareness of "me" and "mine" emerges between _____ and _____ months.

Briefly describe the nature and findings of the classic rouge-and-mirror experiment on self-awareness in infants.

Theories About Caregiving (pp. 214–218)

19. According to Freud, the experiences of the first _____ years of life and the child's relationship with his or her _____ were decisive in personality formation.

20. In Freud's theory, development begins with the _____ stage, so named because the _____ is the infant's prime source of gratification and pleasure.

21. According to Freud, in the second year the prime focus of gratification comes from stimulation and control of the bowels. Freud referred to this period as the _____ stage.

Describe Freud's ideas on the importance of early oral experiences to later personality development.

22. Research has shown that the parents' overall pattern of _____ is more important to the child's emotional development than the particulars of feeding and weaning or toilet training.

23. The theorist who believed that development occurs through a series of psychosocial crises is _____ . According to his theory, the crisis of infancy is one of _____ , whereas the crisis of toddlerhood is one of _____ .

24. According to early learning theory, personality is molded through the processes of _____ and _____ of the child's various behaviors. A strong proponent of this position was _____ .

25. Later theorists incorporated the role of _____ learning, that is, infants' tendency to observe and _____ the personality traits of their parents. This form of learning is strengthened by _____ .

Briefly explain how, according to behaviorists, the kinds of signals caregivers send to toddlers influence the child's overall emotionality.

26. According to cognitive theory, a person's _____ and _____ determine his or her perspective on the world. More specifically, infants use their early relationships to build a _____ _____ that becomes a frame of reference for organizing perceptions and experiences.

27. The _____ perspective emphasizes the impact of the entire _____ _____ on infant–caregiver relationships. According to _____ _____ theory, each infant is born with a _____ predisposition to develop certain emotional traits; however, change is possible, because genes permit selective _____ to the environment.

Attachment (pp. 218–224)

28. The emotional bond that develops between slightly older infants and their caregivers is called _____ .

29. Approaching, following, and climbing onto the caregiver's lap are signs of _____ -_____ behaviors, while clinging and resisting being put down are signs of _____ -_____ behaviors.

30. An infant who derives comfort and confidence from the secure base provided by the caregiver is displaying _____ _____ . In this type of relationship, the caregiver acts as a secure _____ _____ _____ from which the child is willing to venture forth.

31. By contrast, _____ _____ is characterized by an infant's fear, anger, or seeming indifference to the caregiver. Two extremes of this type of relationship are _____-_____ (type A) and _____-_____ /_____ (type C).

(text and Table 7.2) Briefly describe three types of insecure attachment.

32. The procedure developed by Ainsworth to measure attachment is called the

_____ _____ .

Approximately _____ (what proportion?) of all normal infants tested with this procedure demonstrate secure attachment. When infant–caregiver interactions are inconsistent, infants are classified as _____ .

33. Among the features of caregiving that affect the quality of attachment are the following:

   a. _____

   b. _____

   c. _____

34. Greater _____ in early interactions between a mother and a young infant tends to produce more secure attachment.

Identify several other factors that affect the quality of attachment.

35. Most infants _____ (do/do not) show signs of attachment to other caregivers, such as fathers, siblings, and day-care workers.

36. Experts _____ (agree/disagree) about the nature of attachment and _____ (agree/disagree) about its implications. By itself, a secure or insecure attachment in infancy _____ (determines/does not determine) a child's later social relationships. The most serious problems arise in _____ infants, who often become hostile and aggressive in later childhood.

Infant Day Care (pp. 224–227)

37. According to psychoanalytic theory, continuous maternal care _____ (is/is not) better for young children than being cared for by other people. Proponents of sociocultural theory belive that alternative caregivers _____ (are as good as, and sometimes better/are not as good as) mothers.

38. Regarding the impact of nonmaternal care on young children, recent research studies have generally found that _____

_____ .

List several benefits of good preschool education.

39. Researchers have identified four factors that seem essential to high-quality day care:

   a. _____

   b. _____

   c. _____

   d. _____

40. A large-scale study of day care in the United States found that infants were likely to become insecurely attached only under three circumstances:

    a. _____

    b. _____

    c. _____

Conclusions in Theory and Practice (pp. 227–229)

41. (Figure 7.2 and Thinking Like a Scientist) Mary Main has found that adults can be classified into one of four categories of attachment: _____ adults, who value attachment relationships but can discuss them objectively; _____ adults, who devalue attachment; _____ adults, who dwell on past relationships; and _____ adults, who have not yet reconciled their past experiences with the present.

42. (Figure 7.2 and Thinking Like a Scientist) Autonomous mothers tend to have infants who are _____ attached, dismissing mothers tend to have _____ babies, and preoccupied mothers tend to have _____ infants.

Progress Test 1

Multiple-Choice Questions

Circle your answers to the following questions and check them with the answers on page 119. If your answer is incorrect, read the explanation for why it is incorrect and then consult the appropriate pages of the text (in parentheses following the correct answer).

1. Newborns have two identifiable emotions:
   a. shame and distress.
   b. distress and contentment.
   c. anger and joy.
   d. pride and guilt.

2. Which of the following is customarily used to assess synchrony?
   a. the Strange Situation
   b. the habituation technique
   c. the still face technique
   d. social referencing

3. An infant's fear of being left by the mother or other caregiver, called _____ , peaks at about _____ .
   a. separation anxiety; 14 months
   b. stranger wariness; 8 months
   c. separation anxiety; 8 months
   d. stranger wariness; 14 months

4. Social referencing refers to:
   a. parenting skills that change over time.
   b. changes in community values regarding, for example, the acceptability of using physical punishment with small children.
   c. the support network for new parents provided by extended family members.
   d. the infant response of looking to trusted adults for emotional cues in uncertain situations.

5. The "big five" personality dimensions are:
   a. emotional stability, openness, introversion, sociability, locus of control
   b. neuroticism, extroversion, openness, emotional stability, sensitivity
   c. agreeableness, conscientiousness, neuroticism, openness, extroversion
   d. neuroticism, gregariousness, extroversion, impulsiveness, sensitivity

6. The concept of a working model is most consistent with:
   a. psychoanalytic theory.
   b. behaviorism.
   c. cognitive theory.
   d. sociocultural theory.

7. Freud's oral stage corresponds to Erikson's crisis of:
   a. orality versus anality.
   b. trust versus mistrust.
   c. autonomy versus shame and doubt.
   d. secure versus insecure attachment.

8. Erikson felt that the development of a sense of trust in early infancy depends on the quality of the:
   a. infant's food.
   b. child's genetic inheritance.
   c. maternal relationship.
   d. introduction of toilet training.

9. Keisha is concerned that her 15-month-old daughter, who no longer seems to enjoy face-to-face play, is showing signs of insecure attachment. You tell her:
   a. not to worry; face-to-face play almost disappears toward the end of the first year.
   b. she may be right to worry, because face-to-face play typically increases throughout infancy.
   c. not to worry; attachment behaviors are unreliable until toddlerhood.
   d. that her child is typical of children who spend more than 20 hours in day care each week.

10. (Thinking Like a Scientist) "Easy," "slow to warm up," and "difficult" are descriptions of different:
    a. forms of attachment.
    b. types of temperament.
    c. types of parenting.
    d. toddler responses to the Strange Situation.

11. The more physical play of fathers probably helps the children master motor skills and may contribute to the:
    a. infant's self-awareness.
    b. growth of the infant's social skills and emotional expression.
    c. tendency of the infant to become securely attached.
    d. infant's fear of strangers and separation anxiety.

12. *Synchrony* is a term that describes:
    a. the carefully coordinated interaction between parent and infant.
    b. a mismatch of the temperaments of parent and infant.
    c. a research technique involving videotapes.
    d. the concurrent evolution of different species.

13. The emotional tie that develops between an infant and his or her primary caregiver is called:
    a. self-awareness.   c. affiliation.
    b. synchrony.   d. attachment.

14. Secure attachment is directly correlated with the promotion of:
    a. self-awareness.   c. dependency.
    b. social skills.   d. all of the above.

15. Interest in people, as evidenced by the social smile, appears for the first time when an infant is _____ weeks old.
    a. 3   c. 9
    b. 6   d. 12

True or False Items

Write T (*true*) or F (*false*) on the line in front of each statement.

_____ 1. The major developmental theories all agree that maternal care is better for children than nonmaternal care.

_____ 2. Approximately 25 percent of infants display secure attachment.

_____ 3. A baby at 11 months is likely to display both stranger wariness and separation anxiety.

_____ 4. Emotional development is affected by maturation of motor skills and conscious awareness.

_____ 5. A securely attached toddler is most likely to stay close to his or her mother even in a familiar environment.

_____ 6. Current research shows that the majority of infants in day care are slow to develop cognitive and social skills.

_____ 7. Infants use their fathers for social referencing as much as they use their mothers.

_____ 8. Temperament is genetically determined and is unaffected by environmental factors.

_____ 9. Self-awareness enables toddlers to feel pride as well as guilt.

_____ 10. (Thinking Like a Scientist) Adult attachment classifications tend to parallel those of infancy.

Progress Test 2

Progress Test 2 should be completed during a final chapter review. Answer the following questions after you thoroughly understand the correct answers for the Chapter Review and Progress Test 1.

Multiple-Choice Questions

1. Infant–caregiver interactions that are marked by inconsistency are usually classified as:
   a. disorganized.
   b. insecure-avoidant.
   c. insecure-resistant.
   d. insecure-ambivalant.

2. Freud's anal stage corresponds to Erikson's crisis of:
   a. autonomy versus shame and doubt.
   b. trust versus mistrust.
   c. orality versus anality.
   d. identity versus role confusion.

3. Not until the sense of self begins to emerge do babies realize that they are seeing their own faces in the mirror. This realization usually occurs:
   a. shortly before 3 months.
   b. at about 6 months.
   c. between 15 and 24 months.
   d. after 24 months.

4. Lately, three-month-old Kyle sleeps less at night than other infants and engages in prolonged bouts of fussiness and crying. Kyle's worried mother tells her pediatrician that her son seems to be:
   a. slow to warm up.
   b. a "difficult" baby.
   c. suffering from colic.
   d. low-reactive.

5. Emotions such as shame, guilt, embarrassment, and pride emerge at the same time that:
   a. the social smile appears.
   b. aspects of the infant's temperament can first be discerned.
   c. self-awareness begins to emerge.
   d. parents initiate toilet training.

6. (Thinking Like a Scientist) The NYLS temperamental characteristics are not identical to the Big Five, but there are similarities, indicating that:
   a. temperament is probably innate.
   b. the interaction of parent and child determines later personality.
   c. parents pass their temperaments on to their children through modeling.
   d. self-awareness contributes to the development of temperament.

7. In the second six months, stranger wariness is a:
   a. result of insecure attachment.
   b. result of social isolation.
   c. normal emotional response.
   d. setback in emotional development.

8. The caregiving environment can affect a child's temperament through:
   a. the child's temperamental pattern and the demands of the home environment.
   b. parental expectations.
   c. both a. and b.
   d. neither a. nor b.

9. Compared to children who are insecurely attached, those who are securely attached are:
   a. more independent.   c. more sociable.
   b. more curious.   d. characterized by all of the above.

10. The later consequences of secure attachment and insecure attachment for children are:
    a. balanced by the child's current rearing circumstances.
    b. irreversible, regardless of the child's current rearing circumstances.
    c. more significant in girls than in boys.
    d. more significant in boys than in girls.

11. The attachment pattern marked by anxiety and uncertainty is:
    a. insecure-avoidant.
    b. insecure-resistant/ambivalent.
    c. disorganized.
    d. Type B.

12. Compared with mothers, fathers are more likely to:
    a. engage in noisier, more boisterous play.
    b. encourage intellectual development in their children.
    c. encourage social development in their children.
    d. read to their toddlers.

13. Like Freud, Erikson believed that:
    a. problems arising in early infancy can last a lifetime.
    b. inability to resolve a conflict in infancy may result in a later fixation.
    c. human development can be viewed in terms of psychosexual stages.
    d. all of the above are true.

14. Which of the following most accurately summarizes the relationship between early attachment and later social relationships?
    a. Attachment in infancy determines whether a child will grow to be sociable.
    b. Attachment relationships are sometimes, though rarely, altered as children grow older.
    c. There is, at best, only a weak correlation between early attachment and later social relationships.
    d. Early attachment biases, but does not inevitably determine, later social relationships.

15. (text and Thinking Like a Scientist) Researchers have discovered that:
    a. adult attachment classifications parallel those of infancy.
    b. autonomous mothers tend to have insecurely attached babies.
    c. preoccupied mothers tend to have avoidant babies.
    d. all of the above are true.

Matching Items

Match each theorist, term, or concept with its corresponding description or definition.

Theorists, Terms, or Concepts

_____ 1. temperament
_____ 2. Erikson
_____ 3. the Strange Situation
_____ 4. synchrony
_____ 5. trust versus mistrust
_____ 6. Freud
_____ 7. social referencing
_____ 8. autonomy versus shame and doubt
_____ 9. self-awareness
_____ 10. Ainsworth
_____ 11. proximity-seeking behaviors
_____ 12. contact-maintaining behaviors

Descriptions or Definitions

a. looking to caregivers for emotional cues
b. the crisis of infancy
c. the crisis of toddlerhood
d. approaching, following, and climbing
e. theorist who described psychosexual stages of development
f. researcher who devised a laboratory procedure for studying attachment
g. laboratory procedure for studying attachment
h. the relatively consistent, basic dispositions inherent in a person
i. clinging and resisting being put down
j. coordinated interaction between parent and infant
k. theorist who described psychosocial stages of development
l. a person's sense of being distinct from others

Thinking Critically About Chapter 7

Answer these questions the day before an exam as a final check on your understanding of the chapter's terms and concepts.

1. In laboratory tests of attachment, when the mother returns to the playroom after a short absence, a securely attached infant is most likely to:
   a. cry and protest the mother's return.
   b. climb into the mother's lap, then leave to resume play.
   c. climb into the mother's lap and stay there.
   d. continue playing without acknowledging the mother.

2. After a scary fall, 18-month-old Miguel looks to his mother to see if he should cry or laugh. Miguel's behavior is an example of:
   a. proximity-seeking behavior.
   b. contact-maintaining behavior.
   c. insecure attachment.
   d. the crisis of trust versus mistrust.

3. Which of the following is a clear sign of an infant's attachment to a particular person?
   a. The infant turns to that person when distressed.
   b. The infant protests when that person leaves a room.
   c. The infant may cry when strangers appear.
   d. They are all signs of infant attachment.

4. (Thinking Like a Scientist) If you had to predict a newborn baby's personality "type" solely on the basis of probability, which classification would be the most likely?
   a. easy
   b. slow-to-warm-up
   c. difficult
   d. There is not enough information to make a prediction.

5. (Thinking Like a Scientist) Kenny becomes very emotional when talking about his relationship with his parents; consequently, he is unable to discuss his early attachment experiences objectively. Kenny's attachment classification is probably:
   a. autonomous.   c. preoccupied.
   b. dismissing.   d. unresolved.

6. (text and Thinking Like a Scientist) Which of the following mothers is most likely to have an avoidant son or daughter?
   a. Claudia, who is still coping with the loss of her parents
   b. Kaleen, who idealizes her parents, yet devalues the importance of her own relationships
   c. Pearl, who is able to discuss her own early attachment experiences quite objectively, despite their painful nature
   d. Carmen, who spends a lot of time thinking about her own relationship with her parents

7. Concluding her report on the impact of day care on young children, Deborah notes that infants are likely to become insecurely attached if:
   a. their own mothers are insensitive caregivers.
   b. the quality of day care is poor.
   c. more than 20 hours per week are spent in day care.
   d. all of the above are true.

8. Mashiyat, who advocates epigenetic systems theory in explaining the origins of personality, points to research evidence that:
   a. infants are born with definite and distinct temperaments that can change.
   b. early temperamental traits almost never change.
   c. an infant's temperament does not begin to clearly emerge until 2 years of age.
   d. temperament appears to be almost completely unaffected by the social context.

9. Kalil's mother left him alone in the room for a few minutes. When she returned, Kalil seemed indifferent to her presence. According to Mary Ainsworth's research with children in the Strange Situation, Kalil is probably:
   a. a normal, independent infant.
   b. an abused child.
   c. insecurely attached.
   d. securely attached.

10. (Thinking Like a Scientist) Connie and Lev, who are first-time parents, are concerned because their 1-month-old baby is difficult to care for and hard to soothe. They are worried that they are doing something wrong. You inform them that their child is probably that way because:
    a. they are reinforcing the child's tantrum behaviors.
    b. they are not meeting some biological need of the child's.
    c. of his or her inherited temperament.

d. at 1 month of age all children are difficult to care for and hard to soothe.

11. Two-year-old Anita and her mother visit a day-care center. Seeing an interesting toy, Anita runs a few steps toward it, then stops and looks back to see if her mother is coming. Anita's behavior illustrates:
    a. the crisis of autonomy versus shame and doubt.
    b. synchrony.
    c. dyssynchrony.
    d. social referencing.

12. Felix has a biting, sarcastic manner. Freud would probably say that Felix is:
    a. anally expulsive.
    b. anally retentive.
    c. fixated in the oral stage.
    d. experiencing the crisis of trust versus mistrust.

13. A researcher at the child development center places a dot on an infant's nose and watches to see if the infant reacts to her image in a mirror by touching her nose. Evidently, the researcher is testing the child's:
    a. attachment.   c. self-awareness.
    b. temperament.   d. social referencing.

14. Four-month-old Carl and his 13-month-old sister Carla are left in the care of a babysitter. As their parents are leaving, it is to be expected that:
    a. Carl will become extremely upset, while Carla will calmly accept her parents' departure.
    b. Carla will become more upset over her parents' departure than will Carl.
    c. Carl and Carla will both become quite upset as their parents leave.
    d. Neither Carl nor Carla will become very upset as their parents leave.

15. You have been asked to give a presentation on "Mother–Infant Attachment" to a group of expectant mothers. Basing your presentation on the research of Mary Ainsworth, you conclude your talk by stating that mother–infant attachment depends mostly on:
    a. an infant's innate temperament.
    b. the amount of time mothers spend with their infants.
    c. sensitive and responsive caregiving in the early months.
    d. whether the mother herself was securely attached as an infant.

Key Terms

Using your own words, write a brief definition or explanation of each of the following terms on a separate piece of paper.

1. stranger wariness
2. separation anxiety
3. temperament
4. Big Five
5. approach–withdrawal
6. goodness of fit
7. colic
8. synchrony
9. still face technique
10. social referencing
11. self-awareness
12. oral stage
13. anal stage
14. trust versus mistrust
15. autonomy versus shame and doubt
16. working model
17. attachment
18. proximity-seeking behaviors
19. contact-maintaining behaviors
20. secure attachment
21. secure base for exploration
22. insecure attachment
23. insecure-avoidant
24. insecure-resistant/ambivalent
25. Strange Situation
26. disorganized

ANSWERS

CHAPTER REVIEW

1. walk and talk; mobility
2. distress; contentment; curiosity; pleasure; anger
3. 9 months; stranger wariness; 10 to 14; separation anxiety; 9 to 14; decrease; targeted
4. pride, shame, embarrassment, guilt; what other people might be thinking
5. biological maturation; social

6. temperaments; genetic; personality; emotional, motor, attentional; epigenetic; can
7. small; New York Longitudinal Study (NYLS); activity level, rhythmicity, approach–withdrawal, adaptability, intensity of reaction, threshold of responsiveness, quality of mood, distractibility, attention span
8. easy; difficult; slow to warm up; Big Five; extroversion; agreeableness; conscientiousness; neuroticism; openness
9. approach–withdrawal; fearful, outgoing, low-reactive
10. goodness of fit
11. colic; are not
12. 3
13. synchrony; read other people's emotions; social interaction; timing; imitation; play
14. still face technique
15. social referencing; mealtime
16. mother–infant; basic care; fun; comfort; noisy, emotional, boisterous, physical, and idiosyncratic
17. emotional regulation; social understanding; diversity; are
18. self-awareness; embarrassment; guilt; shame; 15; 18

In the classic self-awareness experiment, babies look in a mirror after a dot of rouge is put on their nose. If the babies react to the mirror image by touching their nose, it is clear they know they are seeing their own face. Most babies demonstrate this self-awareness between 15 and 24 months of age.

19. 4; mother
20. oral; mouth
21. anal

Freud believed that the oral and anal stages are fraught with potential conflict that can have long-term consequences for the infant. If nursing is a hurried or tense event, for example, the child may become fixated at the oral stage, excessively eating, drinking, chewing, biting, or talking in quest of oral satisfaction.

22. warmth and sensitivity or coldness and domination
23. Erikson; trust versus mistrust; autonomy versus shame and doubt
24. reinforcement; punishment; John Watson
25. social; imitate; social referencing

If toddlers receive more signals of interest and encouragement than of fear and prohibition as they explore, they are likely to be friendlier and less aggressive. If an infant or toddler sees few signals of any kind, the child becomes relatively passive and emotionless.

26. thoughts; values; working model

27. sociocultural; social context; epigenetic systems; genetic; adaptation

28. attachment

29. proximity-seeking; contact-maintaining

30. secure attachment; base for exploration

31. insecure attachment; insecure-avoidant; insecure-resistant/ambivalent

Some infants are avoidant: They engage in little interaction with their mother before and after her departure. Others are anxious and resistant: They cling nervously to their mother, are unwilling to explore, cry loudly when she leaves, and refuse to be comforted when she returns. Others are disorganized and/or disoriented: They show an inconsistent mixture of behavior toward the mother.

32. Strange Situation; two-thirds; disorganized

33. a. general sensitivity to the infant's needs

    b. responsiveness to the infant's specific signals

    c. talking and playing with the infant in ways that actively encourage growth and development

34. synchrony

Other factors include the infant's temperament, the father, the marital relationship and overall social context, and changes in family circumstances

35. do

36. agree; disagree; does not determine; disorganized

37. is; are as good as, and sometimes better

38. children are not harmed by, and sometimes benefit from, nonmaternal care

Good preschool education helps children learn more language, think with more perspective, develop better social skills, and achieve more in the long term.

39. (a) adequate attention to each child; (b) encouragement of sensorimotor exploration and language development; (c) attention to health and safety; (d) well-trained and professional caregivers.

40. (a) if their mothers were insensitive; (b) if the day-care quality was poor, (c) if they were in day care more than 20 hours per week

41. autonomous; dismissing; preoccupied; unresolved

42. securely; avoidant; resistant

PROGRESS TEST 1

Multiple-Choice Questions

1. **b.** is the answer. (p. 202)

    a., c., & d. These emotions emerge later in infancy, at about the same time as self-awareness emerges.

2. **c.** is the answer. (p. 210)

    a. The Strange Situation is used to measure attachment.

    b. Habituation, which is not discussed in this chapter, is used to measure an infant's perceptual abilities.

    d. Social referencing is not a research technique; it is the phenomenon in which infants look to trusted caregivers for emotional cues in uncertain situations.

3. **a.** is the answer. (p. 203)

    b. & d. This fear, which is also called fear of strangers, peaks by 10 to 14 months.

4. **d.** is the answer. (p. 210)

5. **c.** is the answer. (p. 205)

6. **c.** is the answer. (p. 217)

7. **b.** is the answer. (p. 215)

    a. Orality and anality refer to personality traits that result from fixation in the oral and anal stages, respectively.

    c. According to Erikson, this is the crisis of toddlerhood, which corresponds to Freud's anal stage.

    d. This is not a developmental crisis in Erikson's theory.

8. **c.** is the answer. (p. 215)

9. **a.** is the answer. (p. 210)

    c. Attachment behaviors are reliably found during infancy.

    d. There is no indication that the child attends day care.

10. **b.** is the answer. (p. 205)

    a. "Secure" and "insecure" are different forms of attachment.

    c. The chapter does not describe different types of parenting.

d. The Strange Situation is a test of attachment rather than of temperament.

11. b. is the answer. (pp. 211–212)

12. a. is the answer. (p. 208)

13. d. is the answer. (p. 218)

a. Self-awareness refers to the infant's developing sense of "me and mine."

b. Synchrony describes the coordinated interaction between infant and caregiver.

c. Affiliation describes the tendency of people at any age to seek the companionship of others.

14. b. is the answer. (p. 223)

a. The text does not link self-awareness to secure attachment.

c. On the contrary, secure attachment promotes *independence* in infants and children.

15. b. is the answer. (p. 203)

True or False Items

1. F Sociocultural theorists contend that alternative caregivers are as good as, and sometimes better than, mothers. (p. 218)
2. F Approximately 50 to 65 percent of infants display secure attachment. (p. 221)
3. T (p. 203)
4. T (p. 203)
5. F A securely attached toddler is most likely to explore the environment, the mother's presence being enough to give him or her the courage to do so. (p. 219)
6. F Researchers believe that high-quality day care is not likely to harm the child. In fact, it is thought to be beneficial to the development of cognitive and social skills. (p. 225)
7. T (p. 211)
8. F Temperament is a product of both nature and nurture. (p. 206)
9. T (p. 213)
10. T (pp. 228–229)

PROGRESS TEST 2

Multiple-Choice Questions

1. **a.** is the answer. (p. 221)
2. **a.** is the answer. (pp. 215, 216)
3. **c.** is the answer. (p. 213)
4. **c.** is the answer. (p. 208)

a., b., & d. These terms relate to temperament; Kyle's condition developed only recently.

5. c. is the answer. (p. 213)

a. & b. The social smile, as well as temperamental characteristics, emerge well before the first signs of self-awareness.

d. Contemporary developmentalists link these emotions to self-consciousness, rather than any specific environmental event such as toilet training.

6. a. is the answer. (pp. 205–206)

b. & c. Although environment, especially parents, affects temperamental tendencies, the similarities point to a genetic component.

d. Self-awareness is not a temperamental characteristic.

7. c. is the answer. (p. 203)

8. c. is the answer. (pp. 206–207)

9. d. is the answer. (pp. 222–223)

10. a. is the answer. (p. 223)

c. & d. The text does not suggest that the consequences of secure and insecure attachment differ in boys and girls.

11. b. is the answer. (p. 219)

a. Insecure-avoidant attachment is marked by behaviors that indicate an infant is uninterested in a caregiver's presence or departure.

c. Disorganized attachment is marked only by the inconsistency of infant–caregiver behaviors.

d. Type B, or secure attachment, is marked by behaviors that indicate an infant is using a caregiver as a secure base from which to explore the environment.

12. a. is the answer. (p. 212)

13. a. is the answer. (pp. 215–216)

b. & c. Freud alone would have agreed with both of these statements.

14. d. is the answer. (p. 223)

15. a. is the answer. (pp. 227, 228)

b. Autonomous mothers tend to have securely attached infants.

c. Preoccupied mothers tend to have resistant infants.

Matching Items

1. h (p. 204)
2. k (p. 215)
3. g (p. 220)
4. j (p. 208)
5. b (p. 215)
6. e (p. 214)
7. a (p. 210)
8. c (p 216)
9. l (p. 213)
10. f (p. 219)
11. d (p. 219)
12. i (p. 219)

THINKING CRITICALLY ABOUT CHAPTER 7

1. **b.** is the answer. (p. 220)

   a., c., & d. These responses are more typical of insecurely attached infants.

2. **b.** is the answer. (p. 219)

3. **d.** is the answer. (pp. 218–219)

4. **a.** is the answer. About 40 percent of young infants can be described as "easy." (p. 205)

   b. About 15 percent of infants are described as "slow to warm up."

   c. About 10 percent of infants are described as "difficult."

5. **c.** is the answer. (p. 228)

   a. Autonomous adults are able to talk objectively about their own early attachments.

   b. Dismissing adults devalue the importance of attachment relationships.

   d. Unresolved adults have not yet reconciled their own early attachments.

6. **b.** is the answer. (pp. 227, 228)

   a. Claudia would be classified as "unresolved."

   c. Autonomous adults, such as Pearl, tend to have securely attached infants.

   d. Preoccupied adults, such as Carmen, tend to have resistant offspring.

7. **d.** is the answer. (p. 226)

8. **a.** is the answer. (p. 218)

   b. Although temperament is genetic in origin, early temperamental traits *can* change.

   c. Temperament is apparent shortly after birth.

   d. As the person develops, the social context exerts a strong effect on temperament.

9. **c.** is the answer. (p. 219)

   a. & d. When their mothers return following an absence, securely attached infants usually reestablish social contact (with a smile or by climbing into their laps) and then resume playing.

   b. There is no evidence in this example that Kalil is an abused child.

10. **c.** is the answer. (p. 205)

    a. & b. There is no evidence in the question that the parents are reinforcing tantrum behavior or failing to meet some biological need of the child's.

    d. On the contrary, about 40 percent of infants are "easy" in temperamental style.

11. **d.** is the answer. (p. 210)

    a. According to Erikson, this is the crisis of toddlerhood.

b. This describes a moment of coordinated and mutually responsive interaction between a parent and an infant.

c. Dyssynchrony occurs when the coordinated pace and timing of a synchronous interaction are temporarily lost.

12. **c.** is the answer. (p. 215)

    a. & b. In Freud's theory, a person who is fixated in the anal stage exhibits messiness and disorganization or compulsive neatness.

    d. Erikson, rather than Freud, proposed crises of development.

13. **c.** is the answer. (pp. 213–214)

14. **b.** is the answer. The fear of being left by a caregiver (separation anxiety) emerges at about 8 or 9 months, and peaks at about 14 months. For this reason, 4-month-old Carl can be expected to become less upset than his older sister. (p. 203)

15. **c.** is the answer. (pp. 221–222)

KEY TERMS

1. A common early fear, **stranger wariness** (also called fear of strangers) is first noticeable at about 6 months. (p. 203)

2. **Separation anxiety**, which is the infant fear of being left by the mother or other caregiver, emerges at about 8 or 9 months, peaks at about 14 months, and then gradually subsides. (p. 203)

3. **Temperament** refers to the set of innate tendencies, or dispositions, that underlie and affect each person's interactions with people, situations, and events. (p. 204)

4. The **Big Five** personality factors that seem to be evident in all people include extroversion, agreeableness, conscientiousness, neuroticism, and openism. (p. 205)

5. **Approach–withdrawal** is a trait whose measurement helps classify children as fearful, outgoing, or low-reactive. (p. 206)

6. **Goodness of fit** is the match between the child's temperamental pattern and the demands of the environment. (p. 206)

7. **Colic** is a condition of infancy in which indigestion triggers prolonged bouts of crying and fussiness. (p. 208)

8. **Synchrony** refers to the coordinated interaction between caregiver and infant that helps infants learn to express and read emotions. (p. 208)

9. The **still face technique** is a method of studying synchony that measures an infant's reaction when his or her caregiver merely stares at the baby for a minute or two. (p. 210)

10. When infants engage in **social referencing,** they are looking to trusted adults for emotional cues on how to interpret uncertain situations. (p. 210)

11. **Self-awareness** refers to a person's sense of himself or herself as being distinct from other people that makes possible many new self-conscious emotions, including shame, guilt, embarrassment, and pride. (p. 213)

12. In Freud's first stage of psychosexual development, the **oral stage,** the mouth is the most important source of gratification for the infant. (p. 215)

13. According to Freud, during the second year infants are in the **anal stage** of psychosexual development and derive sensual pleasure from the stimulation of the bowels and psychological pleasure from their control. (p. 215)

14. In Erikson's theory, the crisis of infancy is one of **trust versus mistrust**, in which the infant learns whether the world is a secure place in which basic needs will be met. (p. 215)

15. In Erikson's theory, the crisis of toddlerhood is one of **autonomy versus shamse and doubt,** in which toddlers strive to rule their own actions and bodies. (p. 216)

16. According to cognitive theory, infants use social relationships to develop a set of assumptions called a **working model** that organizes their perceptions and experiences. (p. 217)

17. **Attachment** is the enduring emotional tie that a person or animal forms with another. (pp. 218–219)

18. Following, approaching, and other **proximity-seeking behaviors** are intended to place an individual close to another person to whom he or she is attached. (p. 219)

19. Clinging, resisting being put down, and other **contact-maintaining behaviors** are intended to keep a person near another person to whom he or she is attached. (p. 219)

20. A **secure attachment** is one in which the infant derives comfort and confidence from the "secure base" provided by a caregiver. (p. 219)

21. Responsive caregivers promote secure attachment by providing a **secure base for exploration** from which their children feel confident in venturing forth. (p. 219)

22. **Insecure attachment** is characterized by the infant's fear, anger, or seeming indifference toward the caregiver. (p. 219)

23. **Insecure-avoidant** is the pattern of attachment in which the infant seems uninterested in the caregiver's presence or departure. (p. 219)

24. **Insecure-resistant/ambivalant** is the pattern of attachment in which an infant resits active exploration, becomes very upset when the caregiver leaves, and both resists and seeks contact when the caregiver returns. (p. 219)

25. The **Strange Situation** is a laboratory procedure developed by Ainsworth for assessing attachment. Infants are observed in a playroom, in several successive episodes, while the caregiver (usually the mother) and a stranger move in and out of the room. (p. 220)

26. **Disorganized** is the pattern of attachment that is neither secure nor insecure, and is marked by inconsistent infant-caregiver interactions. (p. 221)

Chapter Eight

The Play Years: Biosocial Development

Chapter Overview

Chapter 8 introduces the developing person between the ages of 2 and 6. This period is called the play years, emphasizing the central importance of play to the biosocial, cognitive, and psychosocial development of preschoolers.

The chapter begins by outlining the changes in size and shape that occur from ages 2 through 6. This is followed by a look at brain growth and development and its role in the development of physical and cognitive abilities. A description of the acquisition of gross and fine motor skills follows, noting that mastery of such skills develops steadily during the play years along with intellectual growth.

The next section of the chapter addresses the important issues of injury control and accidents, the major cause of childhood death in all but the most disease-ridden or war-torn countries. The chapter concludes with an in-depth exploration of child maltreatment, including its prevalence, contributing factors, consequences for future development, treatment, and prevention.

NOTE: Answer guidelines for all Chapter 8 questions begin on page 134.

Guided Study

The text chapter should be studied one section at a time. Before you read, preview each section by skimming it, noting headings and boldface items. Then read the appropriate section objectives from the following outline. Keep these objectives in mind and, as you read the chapter section, search for the information that will enable you to meet each objective. Once you have finished a section, write out answers for its objectives.

Size and Nourishment (pp. 237–240)

1. Describe normal physical growth during the play years, and account for variations in height and weight.

2. Describe changes in eating habits during the preschool years.

Brain Growth and Development (pp. 240–245)

3. Discuss the processes of myelination and lateralization and their effect on development during the play years.

4. Describe the development of the prefrontal cortex during the play years and its impact on the developing person.

8. Explain what is meant by "injury control," and differentiate three levels of prevention that have significantly reduced accidental death rates for children.

Mastering Motor Skills (pp. 245–248)

5. Distinguish between gross and fine motor skills, and discuss the development of each during the play years.

Child Maltreatment (pp. 252–260)

9. Identify the various categories of child maltreatment, and discuss several factors that contribute to its occurrence.

6. Discuss the significance of artistic expression and drawing during the play years.

10. Describe current efforts to treat child maltreatment, focusing on the concept of differential response.

Injuries and Death (pp. 248–251)

7. Identify several factors that contribute to variation in the risk of accidental injury among children.

11. Discuss the consequences of child maltreatment.

12. Discuss foster care, kinship care, and adoption as intervention options in cases of child maltreatment.

Chapter Review

When you have finished reading the chapter, work through the material that follows to review it. Complete the sentences and answer the questions. As you proceed, evaluate your performance for each section by consulting the answers on page 134. Do not continue with the next section until you understand each answer. If you need to, review or reread the appropriate section in the textbook before continuing.

Size and Nourishment (pp. 237–240)

1. During the preschool years, from age _____ to _____ , children add almost _____ in height and gain about _____ in weight per year. By age 6, the average child in a developed nation weighs about _____ and measures _____ in height.

2. The range of normal physical development is quite _____ (narrow/broad).

3. Of the many factors that influence height and weight, the most influential are the child's _____ , _____ , and _____ .

4. The dramatic differences between physical development in developed and underdeveloped nations are largely due to differences in the average child's _____ .

5. In multiethnic countries, children of _____ descent tend to be tallest, followed by _____ , then _____ , and then _____ . The impact of _____ patterns on physical

development can be seen in families in South Asia and the Indian subcontinent, where _____ (which gender?) are more highly valued and consequently better fed than the other sex when food is scarce.

6. During the preschool years, annual height and weight gain is much _____ (greater/less) than during infancy. This means that children need _____ (fewer/more) calories per pound during this period.

7. The most prevalent nutritional problem in early childhood is an insufficient intake of _____ , _____ , and _____ .

8. An additional problem for American children is that they, like most American adults, consume too much _____ , too much _____ , and too few _____ and _____ . No more than _____ percent of daily calories should come from _____ .

Brain Growth and Development (pp. 240–245)

9. By age 2, most pruning of the brain's _____ has occurred and the brain weighs _____ percent of its adult weight. By age 5, the brain has attained about _____ percent of its adult weight; by age 7 it is _____ percent.

10. Part of the brain's increase in size during childhood is due to the continued proliferation of _____ pathways and the ongoing process of _____ . This process, which is influenced by _____ , is essential for communication that is _____ and _____ . During the play years, this process proceeds most rapidly in brain areas dedicated to _____ and _____ .

11. The band of nerve fibers that connects the right and left sides of the brain, called the

_____ _____ , grows and _____ rapidly during the play years. This helps children better coordinate functions that involve _____

_____ .

12. The two sides of the body and brain _____ (are/are not) identical. The specialization of the two sides of the body and brain, which begins before _____ , is called _____ . Throughout the world, societies are organized to favor _____-handedness.

13. Damage to the left side of the brain, where most _____ functions are located, is more serious in _____ than in _____ . This demonstrates that _____ favors youth.

14. The left hemisphere of the brain controls the _____ side of the body and contains areas dedicated to _____ , _____ , and _____ . The right hemisphere controls the _____ side of the body and contains brains areas dedicated to _____ and _____ impulses.

15. The corpus callosum is thicker in _____ (female/male) brains.

16. The final part of the brain to reach maturity is the _____ _____ , which is sometimes called the _____ area of the brain. Development of this brain area is not completed until _____ . The specific functions of this brain area include

_____

_____ . This brain area also assists in _____ and _____ .

17. Two signs of an undeveloped prefrontal cortex are _____ and _____ , which is the tendency to stick to a thought or action even after it has become inappropriate.

18. Brain development _____ (is/is not) smooth and linear, and brain functions

_____ (improve/do not improve) at the same age for every child. During the school years, many deficiencies in _____ , _____ , _____ , and _____ are directly tied to inadequate lateralization and to _____ and _____ of the frontal cortex.

Mastering Motor Skills (pp. 245–248)

19. Large body movements such as running, climbing, jumping, and throwing are called _____ _____ skills. These skills, which improve dramatically during the preschool years, require guided _____ , as well as a certain level of _____ _____ .

20. Related to both brain maturation and practice of motor skills is _____ _____ , which peaks at age _____ and declines throughout childhood. This factor is measured by _____ . _____ (Boys/Girls) are more active; this gender difference, although initially _____ , is in large part affected by _____ .

21. Most children learn these skills _____ (by themselves/from parents).

List several factors during the play years that correlate with serious criminal behavior in adolescence and adulthood.

22. Skills that involve small body movements, such as pouring liquids and cutting food, are called _____ _____ skills. Preschoolers have greater difficulty with these skills primarily because they have not developed the _____ control, patience, or _____ needed—in part because the _____ of the central nervous system is not complete.

23. Many developmentalists believe that _____ _____ is a form of play that enhances the child's sense of accomplishment. The pictures children draw often reveal their _____ and _____ . Drawing is also a way in which children _____ , and may provide useful insight to psychologists and social workers.

24. The developmental progress in children's drawings of the human figure reveals the gradual maturation of the _____ _____ .

Injuries and Death (pp. 248–251)

25. In all but the most disease-ridden or war-torn countries of the world, the leading cause of childhood death is _____ . Injuries and accidental deaths are _____ (more/less) frequent among boys than girls.

26. Not until age _____ does any disease become a greater cause of mortality.

27. Instead of "accident prevention," many experts speak of _____ _____ , an approach based on the belief that most accidents _____ (are/are not) preventable.

28. Preventive community actions that reduce everyone's chance of injury are called _____ _____ . Preventive actions that avert harm in the immediate situation constitute _____ _____ . Actions aimed at minimizing the impact of an adverse event that has

already occurred constitute _____ _____ .

29. One risk factor in accident rates is _____ _____ , with _____ (high/low)-status children being more likely than other children to die an accidental death.

30. (Changing Policy) The accidental death rate for American children between the ages of 1 and 5 has _____ (increased/decreased) over the past twenty years.

Child Maltreatment (pp. 252–260)

31. Until a few decades ago, the concept of child maltreatment was mostly limited to obvious _____ assault, which was thought to be the outburst of a mentally disturbed person. Today, it is known that most perpetrators of maltreatment _____ (are/are not) mentally ill.

32. Intentional harm to, or avoidable endangerment of, someone under age 18 defines child _____ . Actions that are deliberately harmful to a child's well-being are classified as _____ . A failure to act appropriately to meet a child's basic needs is classified as _____ ; one sign of this form of maltreatment is called _____ _____ _____ , in which an infant or young child gains little or no _____ , despite apparently normal health. Another sign is _____ , in which an older child seems too nervous to concentrate on anything.

33. Since 1993, the ratio of the number of cases of _____ _____ , in which authorities have been officially notified, to cases of _____ _____ , which have been reported and verified, has been about _____ (what ratio?).

34. Laws requiring teachers, social workers, and other professionals to report possible maltreatment _____ (have/have not) resulted in increased reporting. Out of their concern

that reporting does not create enough protection for a maltreated child, some experts advocate a policy of _____
_____ . This policy separates high-risk cases that may require complete investigation and _____ of the child from low-risk cases that may require some sort of _____ measure.

35. Before a particular practice can be considered abusive, _____ and
_____ _____ must be taken into account.

36. Two aspects of the overall context that seem universally conducive to maltreatment are
_____ and _____
_____ . Specifically, physical abuse and all forms of neglect are most likely when there are _____ or more children, an _____ father, a mother who did not complete high school, and homes in a _____ , high-_____ neighborhood.

37. Maltreated children have difficulty learning in part because they may develop abnormal _____ patterns that make learning difficult. The most serious of these is
_____ _____
_____ , which can cause the child's neck to break and damage
_____ _____ and
_____ _____ in the brain.

38. Many maltreated children are _____ and _____ and display other symptoms of _____-
_____ _____
_____ .

Describe other deficits of children who have been maltreated.

39. When maltreatment has been substantiated, the first task is to plan for the long-term care of the child, that is, to engage in _____
_____ . Some children are officially removed from their parents and placed in a _____ _____ arrangement with another adult or family who is paid to nurture them.

40. The phenomenon of maltreated children growing up to become abusive or neglectful themselves is called _____ _____ . A widely held misconception is that this phenomenon _____ (is/is not) avoidable.

41. The average length of stay in foster care in the United States has _____ (increased/decreased), and the number of children needing foster placement has _____ (increased/decreased).

42. In another type of foster care, called _____ _____ , a relative of the maltreated child becomes the approved caregiver. A final option is _____ .

43. Public policy measures and other efforts designed to prevent maltreatment from ever occurring are called _____ _____ .
An approach that focuses on spotting and treating the first symptoms of maltreatment is called _____ _____ . Last ditch measures such as removing a child from an abusive home, jailing the perpetrator, and so forth constitute _____ _____ .

Progress Test 1

Multiple-Choice Questions

Circle your answers to the following questions and check them with the answers on page 135. If your answer is incorrect, read the explanation for why it is incorrect and then consult the appropriate pages of the text (in parentheses following the correct answer).

1. During the preschool years, the most common nutritional problem in developed countries is:
   a. serious malnutrition.
   b. excessive intake of sweets.
   c. insufficient intake of iron, zinc, and calcium.
   d. excessive caloric intake.

2. The brain center for speech is usually located in the:
   a. right brain.
   b. left brain.
   c. corpus callosum.
   d. space just below the right ear.

3. Which of the following is an example of tertiary prevention of child maltreatment?
   a. removing a child from an abusive home
   b. home visitation of families with infants by a social worker
   c. new laws establishing stiff penalties for child maltreatment
   d. public policy measures aimed at creating stable neighborhoods

4. (Changing Policy) Which of the following is not true regarding injury control?
   a. Broad-based television announcements do not have a direct impact on children's risk taking.
   b. Unless parents become involved, classroom safety education has little effect on children's actual behavior.
   c. Safety laws that include penalties are more effective than educational measures.
   d. Accidental deaths of 1- to 5-year-olds have held steady in the United States over the past two decades.

5. Like most Americans, children tend to have too much _____ in their diet.
   a. iron   c. sugar
   b. fat   d. b. and c.

6. Skills that involve large body movements, such as running and jumping, are called:
   a. activity-level skills.
   b. fine motor skills.
   c. gross motor skills.
   d. left-brain skills.

7. The brain's ongoing myelination during childhood helps children:
   a. control their actions more precisely.
   b. react more quickly to stimuli.
   c. control their emotions.
   d. do all of the above.

8. The leading cause of death in childhood is:
   a. accidents.
   b. untreated diabetes.
   c. malnutrition.
   d. iron deficiency anemia.

9. Regarding lateralization, which of the following is not true?
   a. Some cognitive skills require only one side of the brain.
   b. Brain centers for generalized emotional impulses can be found in the right hemisphere.
   c. The left hemisphere contains brain areas dedicated to spatial reasoning.
   d. The right side of the brain controls the left side of the body.

10. Which of the following factors is most responsible for differences in height and weight between children in developed and developing countries?
    a. the child's genetic background
    b. health care
    c. nutrition
    d. age of weaning

11. The so-called executive area of the brain that directs and controls the other areas is the:
    a. corpus callosum.
    b. myelin sheath.
    c. prefrontal cortex.
    d. temporal lobe.

12. The relationship between accident rate and SES can be described as:
    a. a positive correlation.
    b. a negative correlation.
    c. curvilinear.
    d. no correlation.

13. Which of the following is true of the corpus callosum?
    a. It enables short-term memory.
    b. It connects the two halves of the brain.
    c. It must be fully myelinated before gross motor skills can be acquired.
    d. All of the above are correct.

14. The improvements in eye-hand coordination that allow preschoolers to catch and then throw a ball occur, in part, because:
    a. the brain areas associated with this ability become more fully myelinated.
    b. the corpus callosum begins to function.
    c. fine motor skills have matured by age 2.
    d. gross motor skills have matured by age 2.

15. During the school years, inadequate lateralization of the brain and immaturity of the prefrontal cortex may contribute to deficiencies in:
    a. cogntion.
    b. peer relatinoships.
    c. emotional control.
    d. all of the above.

True or False Items

Write T (*true*) or F (*false*) on the line in front of each statement.

_____ 1. Growth between ages 2 and 6 results in body proportions more similar to those of an adult.

_____ 2. During childhood, the legs develop faster than any other part of the body.

_____ 3. For most people, the brain center for speech is located in the left hemisphere.

_____ 4. The health, genes, and nutrition of the preschool child are major influences on growth.

_____ 5. Brain development is not smooth and linear.

_____ 6. Fine motor skills are usually easier for preschoolers to master than are gross motor skills.

_____ 7. Most serious childhood injuries truly are "accidents."

_____ 8. Children often fare as well in kinship care as they do in conventional foster care.

_____ 9. Concern for and protection of the well-being of children vary markedly from culture to culture.

_____ 10. Most child maltreatment does not involve serious physical abuse.

_____ 11. Myelination is essential for basic communication between neurons.

_____ 12. Brain lateralization begins before birth.

Progress Test 2

Progress Test 2 should be completed during a final chapter review. Answer the following questions after you thoroughly understand the correct answers for the Chapter Review and Progress Test 1.

Multiple-Choice Questions

1. Each year from ages 2 to 6, the average child gains and grows, respectively:
   a. 2 pounds and 1 inch.
   b. 3 pounds and 2 inches.
   c. $4^1/_2$ pounds and 3 inches.
   d. 6 pounds and 6 inches.

2. The center for perceiving various types of visual configurations is usually located in the brain's:
   a. right hemisphere.
   b. left hemisphere.
   c. right or left hemisphere.
   d. corpus callosum.

3. Which of the following best describes brain growth during childhood?
   a. It proceeds at a slow, steady, linear rate.
   b. The left hemisphere develops more rapidly than the right.
   c. The right hemisphere develops more rapidly than the left.
   d. It is nonlinear.

4. The text notes that art provides an important opportunity for the child to develop the skill of:
   a. realistic representation of objects.
   b. reading.
   c. perspective.
   d. self-judgment.

5. Seeing her toddler reach for a brightly glowing burner on the stove, Sheila grabs his hand and says, "No, that's very hot." Sheila's behavior is an example of:
   a. primary prevention.
   b. secondary prevention.
   c. tertiary prevention.
   d. none of the above.

6. When parents or caregivers do not provide adequate food, shelter, attention, or supervision, it is referred to as:
   a. abuse.   c. endangering.
   b. neglect.   d. maltreatment.

7. Which of the following is true of a developed nation in which many ethnic groups live together?
   a. Ethnic variations in height and weight disappear.
   b. Ethnic variations in stature persist, but are substantially smaller.
   c. Children of African descent tend to be tallest, followed by Europeans, Asians, and Latinos.
   d. Cultural patterns exert a stronger-than-normal impact on growth patterns.

8. Which of the following is *not* true regarding foster care?
   a. Foster children often have behavioral problems.
   b. The number of foster children in the United States is increasing.
   c. Most foster children become maltreating caregivers.
   d. The average stay in foster care has decreased.

9. Which of the following is an example of a fine motor skill?
   a. kicking a ball
   b. running
   c. drawing with a pencil
   d. jumping

10. Children who have been maltreated often:
    a. regard other children and adults as hostile and exploitative.
    b. are less friendly and more aggresssive.
    c. are more isolated than other children.
    d. are all of the above.

11. The left half of the brain contains areas dedicated to all of the following *except*:
    a. language.
    b. logic.
    c. analysis.
    d. creative impulses.

12. Most gross motor skills can be learned by healthy children by about age:
    a. 2.   c. 5.
    b. 3.   d. 7.

13. Two of the most important factors that affect height during the play years are:
    a. socioeconomic status and health care.
    b. gender and health care.
    c. heredity and nutrition.
    d. heredity and activity level.

14. (Changing Policy) Over the past two decades, the accidental death rate for American children between the ages of 1 and 5 has:
    a. decreased, largely as a result of new safety laws.
    b. decreased, largely because parents are more knowledgeable about safety practices.
    c. increased.
    d. remained unchanged.

15. During the play years, children's appetites seem _____ they were in the first two years of life.
    a. larger than
    b. smaller than
    c. about the same as
    d. erratic, sometimes smaller and sometimes larger than

Matching Items

Match each term or concept with its corresponding description or definition.

Terms or Concepts

_____ 1. corpus callosum
_____ 2. gross motor skills
_____ 3. fine motor skills
_____ 4. kinship care
_____ 5. foster care
_____ 6. injury control
_____ 7. right hemisphere
_____ 8. left hemisphere
_____ 9. child abuse
_____ 10. child neglect
_____ 11. primary prevention
_____ 12. secondary prevention
_____ 13. tertiary prevention

Descriptions or Definitions

a. brain area that is primarily responsible for processing language
b. brain area that is primarily responsible for recognizing visual shapes
c. legal placement of a child in the care of someone other than his or her biological parents
d. a form of care in which a relative of a maltreated child takes over from the biological parents
e. procedures to prevent unwanted events or circumstances from ever occurring
f. running and jumping
g. actions that are deliberately harmful to a child's well-being
h. actions for averting harm in the immediate situation
i. painting a picture or tying shoelaces
j. failure to appropriately meet a child's basic needs
k. an approach emphasizing accident prevention
l. actions aimed at reducing the harm that has occurred
m. band of nerve fibers connecting the right and left hemispheres of the brain

Thinking Critically About Chapter 8

Answer these questions the day before an exam as a final check on your understanding of the chapter's terms and concepts.

1. An editorial in the local paper claims that there is no reason children younger than 6 cannot be taught basic literacy skills. You write to the editor, noting that:
   a. she has an accurate grasp of developmental processes.
   b. before age 6, brain myelination and development are too immature to enable children to form links between spoken and written language.
   c. although the right hemisphere is relatively mature at age 6, the left is not.
   d. although this may be true for girls, boys (who are slower to mature neurologically) would struggle.

2. Two-year-old Carrie is hyperactive, often confused between fantasy and reality, and jumps at any sudden noise. Her pediatrician suspects that she is suffering from:
   a. shaken baby syndrome.
   b. failure to thrive.
   c. post-traumatic stress disorder.
   d. child neglect.

3. Following an automobile accident, Amira developed severe problems with her speech. Her doctor believes that the accident injured the _____ of her brain.
   a. left side
   b. right side
   c. communication pathways
   d. corpus callosum

4. Two-year-old Ali is quite clumsy, falls down frequently, and often bumps into stationary objects. Ali most likely:

   a. has a neuromuscular disorder.

   b. has an underdeveloped right hemisphere of the brain.

   c. is suffering from an iron deficiency.

   d. is a normal 2-year-old whose gross motor skills will improve dramatically during the preschool years.

5. Climbing a fence is an example of a:

   a. fine motor skill.   c. circular reaction.

   b. gross motor skill.   d. launching event.

6. To prevent accidental death in childhood, some experts urge forethought and planning for safety and measures to limit the damage of such accidents as do occur. This approach is called:

   a. protective analysis.   c. injury control.

   b. safety education.   d. childproofing.

7. After his daughter scraped her knee, Ben gently cleansed the wound and bandaged it. Ben's behavior is an example of:

   a. primary prevention.

   b. secondary prevention.

   c. tertiary prevention.

   d. none of the above.

8. Which of the following activities would probably be the most difficult for a 5-year-old child?

   a. climbing a ladder

   b. catching a ball

   c. throwing a ball

   d. pouring juice from a pitcher without spilling it

9. Of the following children, the child with the greatest risk of accidental injury is:

   a. 6-year-old Brandon, whose family lives below the poverty line.

   b. 6-year-old Stacey, whose family lives below the poverty line.

   c. 3-year-old Daniel, who comes from an affluent family.

   d. 3-year-old Bonita, who comes from an affluent family.

10. Most child maltreatment:

    a. does not involve serious physical abuse.

    b. involves a rare outburst from the perpetrator.

    c. involves a mentally ill perpetrator.

    d. can be predicted from the victim's personality characteristics.

11. A mayoral candidate is calling for sweeping policy changes to help ensure the well-being of children by promoting home ownership, high-quality community centers, and more stable neighborhoods. If these measures are effective in reducing child maltreatment, they would be classified as:

    a. primary prevention.

    b. secondary prevention.

    c. tertiary prevention.

    d. differential response.

12. A factor that would figure very little into the development of fine motor skills, such as drawing and writing, is:

    a. strength.   c. judgment.

    b. muscular control.   d. short, fat fingers.

13. Parents who were abused as children:

    a. almost always abuse their children.

    b. are more likely to neglect, but not necessarily abuse, their children.

    c. are no more likely than anyone else to mistreat their children.

    d. do none of the above.

14. Which aspect of brain development during the play years contributes *most* to enhancing communication among the brain's various specialized areas?

    a. increasing brain weight

    b. proliferation of dendrite networks

    c. myelination

    d. increasing specialization of brain areas

15. Three-year-old Kyle's parents are concerned because Kyle, who generally seems healthy, doesn't seem to have the hefty appetite he had as an infant. Should they be worried?

    a. Yes, because appetite normally increases throughout the preschool years.

    b. Yes, because appetite remains as good during the preschool years as it was earlier.

    c. No, because caloric need is less during the preschool years than during infancy.

    d. There is not enough information to determine whether Kyle is developing normally.

Key Terms

Using your own words, write a brief definition or explanation of each of the following terms on a separate piece of paper.

1. myelination
2. corpus callosum
3. lateralization
4. prefrontal cortex
5. perseveration
6. activity level
7. injury control/harm reduction
8. primary prevention
9. secondary prevention
10. tertiary prevention
11. child maltreatment
12. child abuse
13. child neglect
14. failure to thrive
15. reported maltreatment
16. substantiated maltreatment
17. differential response
18. shaken baby syndrome
19. post-traumatic stress disorder
20. permanency planning
21. foster care
22. kinship care
23. adoption

ANSWERS

CHAPTER REVIEW

1. 2; 6; 3 inches (7 centimeters); $4^{1}/_{2}$ pounds (2 kilograms); 46 pounds (21 kilograms); 46 inches (117 centimeters)
2. broad
3. genes; health; nutrition
4. nutrition
5. African; Europeans; Asians; Latinos; cultural; boys
6. less; fewer
7. iron; zinc; calcium
8. sugar; fat; fruits; vegetables; 30; fat
9. dendrites; 75; 90; 100
10. communication; myelination; experience; fast; complex; memory; reflection

11. corpus callosum; myelinates; both sides of the brain and body
12. are not; birth; lateralization; right
13. language; adults; young children; plasticity
14. right; logic; analysis; language; left; emotional; creative
15. female
16. prefrontal cortex; executive; mid-adolescence; planning, analyzing, selecting responses, and coordinating messages throughout the brain; self-control; self-regulation
17. impulsiveness; perseveration
18. is not; do not improve; cognition, peer relationships; emotional control; classroom learning; immaturity; asymmetry
19. gross motor; practice; brain maturation
20. activity level; 2; how much children move parts of their bodies while they remain in one place or by how much their whole bodies move from one spot to another; Boys; biological; experience
21. by themselves

These factors include poor motor control, living in crowded urban areas, and difficulty making friends

22. fine motor; muscular; judgment; myelination
23. artistic expression; perception; cognition; communicate
24. prefrontal cortex
25. accidents; more
26. 40
27. injury control (or harm reduction); are
28. primary prevention; secondary prevention; tertiary prevention
29. socioeconomic status; low
30. decreased
31. physical; are not
32. maltreatment; abuse; neglect; falure to thrive; weight; hypervigilance
33. reported maltreatment; substantiated maltreatment; 3-to-1
34. have; differential response; removal; supportive
35. customs; community standards
36. poverty; social isolation; 3; unemployed; poor; crime
37. brain; shaken baby syndrome; blood vessels; neural connections

38. hyperactive; hypervigilant; post-traumatic stress disorder (PTSD)

Maltreated children tend to regard other people as hostile and exploitative, and hence are less friendly, more aggressive, and more isolated than other children. As adolescents and adults they often use drugs or alcohol, choose unsupportive relationships, become victims or aggressors, sabotage their own careers, eat too much or too little, and generally engage in self-destructive behavior.

39. permanency planning; foster care

40. intergenerational transmission; is not

41. decreased; increased

42. kinship care; adoption

43. primary prevention; secondary prevention; tertiary prevention

PROGRESS TEST 1

Multiple-Choice Questions

1. **c.** is the answer. (p. 238)

    a. Serious malnutrition is much more likely to occur in infancy or in adolescence than in early childhood.

    b. Although an important health problem, eating too much candy or other sweets is not as serious a problem as this.

    d. Since growth is slower during the preschool years, children need fewer calories per pound during this period.

2. **b.** is the answer. (p. 242)

    a. & d. The right brain is the location of areas associated with generalized emotional and creative impulses.

    c. The corpus callosum helps integrate the functioning of the two halves of the brain; it does not contain areas specialized for particular skills.

3. **a.** is the answer. (p. 260)

    b. This is an example of secondary prevention.

    c. & d. These are examples of primary prevention.

4. **d.** is the answer. Accident rates have *decreased* during this time period. (p. 251)

5. **d.** is the answer. (p. 238)

6. **c.** is the answer. (p. 245)

7. **d.** is the answer. (pp. 240, 243)

8. **a.** is the answer. (p. 248)

9. **a.** is the answer. (p. 242)

10. **c.** is the answer. (p. 238)

11. **c.** is the answer. (p. 243)

    a. The corpus callosum is the band of fibers that link the two halves of the brain.

    b. The myelin sheath is the fatty insulation that surrounds some neurons in the brain.

    d. The temporal lobes of the brain contain the primary centers for hearing.

12. **b.** is the answer. Children with *lower* SES have *higher* accident rates. (p. 250)

13. **b.** is the answer. (p. 241)

    a. The corpus callosum is not directly involved in memory.

    c. Myelination of the central nervous system is important to the mastery of *fine* motor skills.

14. **a.** is the answer. (p. 240)

    b. The corpus callosum begins to function long before the play years.

    c. & d. Neither fine nor gross motor skills have fully matured by age 2.

15. **d.** is the answer. (p. 244)

True or False Items

1. T (p. 237)

2. F   During childhood, the brain develops faster than any other part of the body. (p. 240)

3. T (p. 242)

4. T (p. 238)

5. T (p. 244)

6. F   Fine motor skills are more difficult for preschoolers to master than are gross motor skills. (p. 246)

7. F   Most serious accidents involve someone's lack of forethought. (p. 249)

8. T (p. 259)

9. T (p. 255)

10. T (p. 252)

11. F   Although myelination is not essential for basic communication between neurons, it is essential for fast and complex communication (p. 240)

12. T (p. 241)

PROGRESS TEST 2

Multiple-Choice Questions

1. **c.** is the answer. (p. 237)

2. **a.** is the answer. (p. 242)

b. & c. The left hemisphere of the brain contains areas associated with language development.

d. The corpus callosum does not contain areas for specific behaviors.

3. **d.** is the answer. (p. 244)

b. & c. The left and right hemispheres develop at similar rates.

4. **d.** is the answer. (p. 247)

5. **b.** is the answer. (p. 249)

6. **b.** is the answer. (p. 252)

a. Abuse is deliberate, harsh injury to the body.

c. Endangerment was not discussed.

d. Maltreatment is too broad a term.

7. **c.** is the answer. (pp. 237–238)

8. **c.** is the answer. Foster children often become good, nonmaltreating caregivers. (p. 258)

9. **c.** is the answer. (p. 246)

a., b., & d. These are gross motor skills.

10. **d.** is the answer. (p. 257)

11. **d.** is the answer. Brain areas that control generalized creative and emotional impulses are found in the right hemisphere. (p. 242)

12. **c.** is the answer. (p. 245)

13. **c.** is the answer. (p. 238)

14. **a.** is the answer. (p. 251)

b. Although safety education is important, the decrease in accident rate is largely the result of new safety laws.

15. **b.** is the answer. (p. 238)

Matching Items

1. m (p. 241)
2. f (p. 245)
3. i (p. 246)
4. d (p. 258)
5. c (p. 258)
6. k (p. 249)
7. b (p. 241)
8. a (p. 241)
9. g (p. 252)
10. j (p. 252)
11. e (p. 249)
12. h (p. 249)
13. l (p. 249)

THINKING CRITICALLY ABOUT CHAPTER 8

1. **b.** is the answer. (p. 244)

2. **c.** is the answer. (p. 257)

a. Shaken baby syndrome is a consequence of maltreatment associated with memory impairment and delays in logical thinking.

b. Failure to thrive is associated with little or no weight gain, despite apparent good health.

d. Child neglect simply refers to failure to meet a child's basic needs. Carrie's specific symptoms may be caused by neglect or maltreatment, but they are most directly signs of PTSD.

3. **a.** is the answer. In most people, the left hemisphere of the brain contains centers for language, including speech. (p. 242)

4. **d.** is the answer. (p. 245)

5. **b.** is the answer. (p. 245)

a. Fine motor skills involve small body movements, such as the hand movements used in painting.

c. & d. These events were not discussed in this chapter.

6. **c.** is the answer. (p. 249)

7. **c.** is the answer. (p. 249)

8. **d.** is the answer. (p. 246)

a., b., & c. Preschoolers find these gross motor skills easier to perform than fine motor skills such as that described in d.

9. **a.** The strongest risk factor in accidental injuries is low SES. (p. 250)

b. & d. Boys, as a group, suffer more injuries than girls do.

10. **a.** is the answer. (p. 252)

11. **a.** is the answer. (p. 259)

b. Had the candidate called for measures to spot the early warning signs of maltreatment, this answer would be true.

c. Had the candidate called for jailing those who maltreat children or providing greater counseling and health care for victims, this answer would be true.

d. Differential response is not an approach to prevention of maltreatment; rather, it refers to separate reporting procedures for high- and low-risk families.

12. **a.** is the answer. Strength is a more important factor in the development of gross motor skills. (p. 246)

13. **d.** is the answer. Approximately 30 percent of adults who were abused as children themselves become abusive parents. (p. 258)

14. **b.** is the answer. (p. 240)

15. **c.** is the answer. (p. 238)

KEY TERMS

1. **Myelination** is the insulating process that speeds up the transmission of nerve impulses. (p. 240)

2. The **corpus callosum** is a band of nerve fibers that connects the right and left hemispheres of the brain. (p. 241)

3. **Lateralization** refers to the differentiation of the two sides of the brain so that each serves specific, specialized functions. (p. 241)

4. The so-called executive area of the brain, the **prefrontal cortex** specializes in planning, selecting, and coordinating thoughts. (p. 243)

5. **Perseveration** is the tendency to stick to thoughts or actions, even after they have become unhelpful or inappropriate. In young children, perseveration is a normal product of immature brain functions. (p. 244)

   Memory Aid: To persevere is to continue, or persist, at something.

6. A general measure of how much children move around, **activity level** is related to both brain maturation and practice. (p. 245)

7. **Injury control** (also called harm reduction) is the practice of limiting the extent of injuries by planning ahead, controlling the circumstances, preventing certain dangerous activities, and adding safety features to others. (p. 249)

8. **Primary prevention** refers to actions that change overall background conditions to prevent some unwanted event or circumstance. (p. 249)

9. **Secondary prevention** involves actions that avert harm in the immediate situation. (p. 249)

10. **Tertiary prevention** involves actions taken after an adverse event occurs, aimed at reducing the harm or preventing disability. (p. 249)

11. **Child maltreatment** is intentional harm to, or avoidable endangerment of, anyone under age 18. (p. 252)

12. **Child abuse** refers to deliberate actions that are harmful to a child's physical, emotional, or sexual well-being. (p. 252)

13. **Child neglect** refers to failure to appropriately meet a child's basic needs. (p. 252)

14. A sign of possible child neglect, **failure to thrive** occurs when an otherwise healthy child gains little or no weight. (p. 252)

15. Child maltreatment that has been officially reported to the police, or other authority, is called **reported maltreatment**. (p. 253)

16. Child maltreatment that has been officially reported to authorities, investigated, and verified is called **substantiated maltreatment**. (p. 253)

17. **Differential response** refers to separating child maltreatment reports into two categories: high-risk cases that require immediate investigation and possible removal of the child, and low-risk cases that require supportive measures to encourage better parental care. (p. 254)

18. A serious condition caused by sharply shaking an infant to stop his or her crying, **shaken baby syndrome** is associated with severe brain damage that results from internal hemorrhaging. (p. 256)

19. **Post-traumatic stress disorder (PTSD)** is a syndrome triggered by exposure to an extreme traumatic stressor. In maltreated children, symptoms of PTSD include hyperactivity and hypervigilance, sleeplessness, and confusion between fantasy and reality. (p. 257)

20. **Permanency planning** is the process of finding a long-term solution to the care of a child who has been abused. (p. 258)

21. **Foster care** is a legally sanctioned, publicly supported arrangement in which children are removed from their biological parents and temporarily given to another adult to nurture. (p. 258)

22. **Kinship care** is a form of foster care in which a relative of a maltreated child becomes the child's legal caregiver. (p. 258)

23. **Adoption** is the process whereby nonbiological parents are given legal custody and care of a child. (p. 259)

Chapter Nine

The Play Years: Cognitive Development

Chapter Overview

In countless everyday instances, as well as in the findings of numerous research studies, young children reveal themselves to be remarkably thoughtful, insightful, and perceptive thinkers whose grasp of the causes of everyday events, memory of the past, and mastery of language are sometimes astonishing. Chapter 9 begins by comparing Piaget's and Vygotsky's views of cognitive development at this age. According to Piaget, young children's thought is prelogical: between the ages of 2 and 6, they are unable to perform many logical operations and are limited by irreversible, centered, and static thinking. Lev Vygotsky, a contemporary of Piaget's, saw learning as a social activity more than as a matter of individual discovery. Vygotsky focused on the child's "zone of proximal development" and the relationship between language and thought.

The chapter next focuses on what preschoolers can do, including their competence in working with numbers, storing and retrieving memories, and theorizing about the world. This leads into a description of language development during the play years. Although young children demonstrate rapid improvement in vocabulary and grammar, they have difficulty with abstractions, metaphorical speech, analogies, and certain rules of grammar. A discussion of whether bilingualism in young children is useful concludes the section on language. The chapter ends with a discussion of preschool education, including a description of "quality" preschool programs and an evaluation of their lifelong impact on children.

NOTE: Answer guidelines for all Chapter 9 questions begin on page 149.

Guided Study

The text chapter should be studied one section at a time. Before you read, preview each section by skimming it, noting headings and boldface items. Then read the appropriate section objectives from the following outline. Keep these objectives in mind and, as you read the chapter section, search for the information that will enable you to meet each objective. Once you have finished a section, write out answers for its objectives.

How Young Children Think: Piaget and Vygotsky
(pp. 263–270)

1. Describe and discuss the major characteristics of preoperational thought, according to Piaget.

2. Discuss Vygotsky's views on cognitive development, focusing on the concept of guided participation.

3. Explain the significance of the zone of proximal development and scaffolding in promoting cognitive growth.

4. Describe Vygotsky's view of the role of language in cognitive growth.

5. (Thinking Like a Scientist) Compare and contrast the theories of Piaget and Vygotsky, and explain why findings have led to qualification or revision of their descriptions of cognition during the play years.

Information Processing (pp. 270–279)

6. Discuss young children's understanding of the concept of quantity, and identify the factors that contribute to number competence.

7. Discuss young children's memory abilities and limitations, noting the role of meaning in their ability to recall events.

8. Explain the typical young child's theory of mind, noting how it is affected by cultural context, and relate it to the child's developing ability to understand pretense.

Language (pp. 279–284)

9. (text and In Person) Describe the development of vocabulary in children, and explain the role of fast mapping in this process.

10. Describe the development of grammar during the play years, noting limitations in the young child's language abilities, and discuss the value of bilingualism at a young age.

Early-Childhood Education (pp. 284–291)

11. Discuss historical and cultural variations in early-childhood education.

12. Identify the characteristics of a high-quality preschool program, and discuss the long-term benefits of preschool education for the child and his or her family.

Chapter Review

When you have finished reading the chapter, work through the material that follows to review it. Complete the sentences and answer the questions. As you proceed, evaluate your performance for each section by consulting the answers on page 149. Do not continue with the next section until you understand each answer. If you need to, review or reread the appropriate section in the textbook before continuing.

How Young Children Think: Piaget and Vygotsky (pp. 263–270)

1. For many years, researchers maintained that young children's thinking abilities were sorely limited by their _____ .

2. Piaget referred to cognitive development between the ages of 2 and 6 as _____ thought.

3. Young children's tendency to think about one aspect of a situation at a time is called _____ . One particular form of this characteristic is children's tendency to contemplate the world exclusively from their personal perspective, which is referred to as _____ . They also tend to focus on _____ to the exclusion of other attributes of objects and people.

4. Preschoolers' understanding of the world tends to be _____ (static/dynamic), which means that they tend to think of their world as _____ . A closely related characteristic is _____
—the inability to recognize that reversing a process will restore the original conditions from which the process began.

5. The idea that amount is unaffected by changes in shape or configuration is called _____ . In the case of _____ _____ _____ , preschoolers who are shown pairs of checkers in two even rows and who then observe one row being spaced out will say that the spaced-out row has more checkers.

6. The term _____-_____ highlights the idea that children attempt to construct theories to explain everything they see and hear. The idea that children are "apprentices in thinking" emphasizes that children's intellectual growth is stimulated by their _____ _____ in _____ experiences of their environment. The critical element in this process is that the mentor and the child _____ to accomplish a task.

7. Much of the research from the sociocultural perspective on the young child's emerging cognition is inspired by the Russian psychologist _____ .According to this perspective, an adult can most effectively help a child solve a problem by taking three steps:

   a. _____

   b. _____

   c. _____

8. Unlike Piaget, this psychologist believed that cognitive growth is a _____ _____ more than a matter of individual discovery.

9. Vygotsky suggested that for each developing individual there is a _____ _____ _____ _____ , a range of skills that the person can exercise with assistance but is not yet able to perform independently.

10. How and when new skills are developed depends, in part, on the willingness of tutors to _____ the child's participation in learning encounters.

11. Vygotsky believed that language is essential to the advancement of thinking in two crucial ways. The first is through the internal dialogue in which a person talks to himself or herself, called _____ _____ . In preschoolers, this dialogue is likely to be

_____

(expressed silently/uttered aloud).

12. According to Vygotsky, another way language advances thinking is as the _____ of social interaction.

13. (Thinking Like a Scientist) Many contemporary theorists believe that children are less _____ than Piaget believed and less dependent on _____ _____ than Vygotsky believed.

Information Processing (pp. 270–279)

14. Infants _____ (do/do not) have a perceptual awareness of quantity. Nevertheless, it takes time to master basic counting principles such as _____ _____ , _____-_____- _____ _____ , and the _____ principle.

15. The results of the classic study in which young children were asked to count a display of dots demonstrated that by age _____ , most children performed perfectly. Among the factors that contribute to the child's understanding of number are _____ development, maturation of _____ , and the flowering of the child's innate _____ . Another factor is the structure and _____ support provided by parents, other adults, and older children.

16. Preschoolers are notorious for having a poor _____ . This shortcoming is due to the fact that they have not yet acquired skills for deliberate _____ and efficient _____ of information. Memories for _____ experiences tend to be easier for young children.

17. For people of all ages, the most difficult part of memory is called _____ _____ , which is defined as the ability to recall _____ .

18. One way in which preschoolers are quite capable of storing in mind a representation of past events is by retaining _____ of familiar sequences of events.

19. Research studies demonstrate that four factors are especially likely to aid memory in young children: _____ _____ ; _____ _____ in an event; _____ that names the objects and experiences; and _____ _____ asked by a friendly person.

20. As a result of their experiences with others, young children acquire a _____ _____ _____ that reflects their developing concepts about human mental processes.

Describe the theory of mind of children between the ages of 3 and 6.

21. Most 3-year-olds _____ (have/do not have) difficulty realizing that a belief can be false.

22. Research studies reveal that theory-of-mind development depends as much on general _____ ability as it does on _____ _____ . A third helpful factor is having at least one _____ . Finally, _____ may be a factor.

23. Even before children can pass a standard theory of mind test, many create vivid

_____ _____ , which demonstrate that people of all ages have theories about their experiences and observations.

Language (pp. 279–284)

24. Although early childhood does not appear to be a _____ period for langauge development, it does seem to be a _____ period for the learning of vocabulary, grammar, and pronunciation.

25. During the preschool years, a dramatic increase in language occurs, with _____ increasing exponentially.

26. Through the process called _____ _____ preschoolers often learn words after only one or two hearings. A closely related process is _____ _____ , by which children are able to apply newly learned words to other objects in the same category. The importance of the social context in these processes is illustrated by the fact that children who have _____ _____ map out some vocabulary differences more quickly than _____-_____ children do.

27. Abstract nouns, metaphors, and analogies are _____ (more/no more) difficult for preschoolers to understand.

28. Because preschool children tend to think in absolute terms, they have difficulty with words that express _____ , as well as words expressing relativities of _____ and _____ .

29. The structures, techniques, and rules that a language uses to communicate meaning define its _____ . By age _____ , children typically demonstrate extensive understanding of this aspect of language.

30. Preschoolers' tendency to apply rules of grammar when they should not is called

_____ .

Give several examples of this tendency.

31. During the preschool years, children are able to comprehend _____ (more/less) complex grammar and vocabulary than they can produce.

32. Most developentalists agree that bilingualism _____ (is/is not necessarily) an asset to children in today's world. Nevertheless, there is evidence that both _____ and _____ advance cognitive development.

33. Children who speak two languages by age 5 often are less _____ in their understanding of language and more advanced in their _____ _____ _____ . Advocates of monolingualism point out that bilingual proficiency comes at the expense of _____ _____ in the dominant language, slowing down the development of _____ .

Early-Childhood Education (pp. 284–291)

34. Early-childhood programs _____ (vary/do not vary significantly) from one culture to another. Japanese culture places great emphasis on_____ _____ and_____ . Reflecting this emphasis, Japanese preschools provide training in the behavior and attitudes appropriate for _____ _____ . In contrast, preschools in the United States are often designed to foster _____ and _____ .

35. Early-childhood education _____ (has/has not) always been deemed important in most cultures. Today, _____ (about half/most/almost all) 5-year-olds are in some sort of school. One factor in this shift is the dramatic increase in the percentage of mothers who are _____ .

36. The term _____ _____ is generally used to refer to a child whose chances of poor educational achievement are higher than average.

37. In 1965, _____ _____ _____ was inaugurated to give low-income children some form of compensatory education during the preschool years. Longitudinal research found that, as they made their way through elementary school, graduates of this program scored _____ (higher/no higher) on achievement tests and had more positive school report cards than their non–Headstart counterparts.

List several characteristics of high-quality early childhood education.

Progress Test 1

Multiple-Choice Questions

Circle your answers to the following questions and check them with the answers on page 150. If your answer is incorrect, read the explanation for why it is incorrect and then consult the appropriate pages of the text (in parentheses following the correct answer).

1. Piaget believed that children are in the preoperational stage from ages:
   a. 6 months to 1 year.   c. 2 to 6 years.
   b. 1 to 3 years.   d. 5 to 11 years.

2. Which of the following is *not* a characteristic of preoperational thinking?
   a. focus on appearance
   b. static reasoning
   c. lack of imagination
   d. centration

3. Which of the following provides evidence that early childhood is a sensitive period, rather than a critical period, for language learning?
   a. People can and do master their native language after early childhood.
   b. Vocabulary, grammar, and pronunciation are acquired especially easily during early childhood.
   c. Neurological characteristics of the young child's developing brain facilitate language acquistion.
   d. a. and b.
   e. a., b., and c.

4. The typical script of a 4-year-old:
   a. has a beginning and an end.
   b. fails to recognize the causal flow of events.
   c. pertains only to the most familiar routines.
   d. is very difficult to follow for most adults.

5. Preschoolers' poor performance on memory tests is primarily due to:
   a. their tendency to rely too extensively on scripts.
   b. their lack of efficient storage and retrieval skills.
   c. the incomplete myelination of cortical neurons.
   d. their short attention span.

6. The vocabulary of preschool children consists primarily of:
   a. metaphors.
   b. self-created words.
   c. abstract nouns.
   d. verbs and concrete nouns.

7. Preschoolers sometimes apply the rules of grammar even when they shouldn't. This tendency is called:
   a. overregularization.   c. practical usage.
   b. literal language.   d. single-mindedness.

8. The Russian psychologist Vygotsky emphasized that:
   a. language helps children form ideas.
   b. children form concepts first, then find words to express them.
   c. language and other cognitive developments are unrelated at this stage.
   d. preschoolers learn language only for egocentric purposes.

9. Private speech can be described as:
   a. a way of formulating ideas to oneself.
   b. fantasy.
   c. an early learning difficulty.
   d. the beginnings of deception.

10. The child who has not yet grasped the principle of conservation is likely to:
    a. insist that a tall, narrow glass contains more liquid than a short, wide glass, even though both glasses actually contain the same amount.
    b. be incapable of egocentric thought.
    c. be unable to reverse an event.
    d. do all of the above.

11. In later life, Head Start graduates showed:
    a. better report cards, but more behavioral problems.
    b. significantly higher IQ scores.
    c. higher scores on achievement tests.
    d. alienation from their original neighborhoods and families.

12. The best preschool programs are generally those that provide the most:
    a. behavioral control.
    b. positive social interactions among children and teachers.
    c. instruction in conservation and other logical principles.
    d. demonstration of toys by professionals.

13. Compared with their rate of speech development, children's understanding of language develops:
    a. more slowly.
    b. at about the same pace.
    c. more rapidly.
    d. more rapidly in some cultures than in others.

14. Preschoolers can succeed at tests of conservation when:
    a. they are allowed to work cooperatively with other children.
    b. the test is presented as a competition.
    c. they are informed that they are being observed by their parents.
    d. the test is presented in a simple, nonverbal, and gamelike way.

15. Through the process called fast mapping, children:
    a. immediately assimilate new words by connecting them through their assumed meaning to categories of words they have already mastered.
    b. acquire the concept of conservation at an earlier age than Piaget believed.
    c. are able to move beyond egocentric thinking.
    d. become skilled in the practical use of language.

True or False Items

Write T *(true)* or F *(false)* on the line in front of each statement.

_____ 1. Preschoolers who construct imaginary companions are generally considered to be at high risk educationally.

_____ 2. In conservation problems, many preschoolers are unable to understand the transformation because they focus exclusively on appearances.

_____ 3. Preschoolers use private speech more selectively than older children.

_____ 4. Whether or not a preschooler demonstrates conservation in an experiment depends in part on the conditions of the experiment.

_____ 5. Preoperational children tend to focus on one aspect of a situation to the exclusion of all others.

_____ 6. Piaget focused on what children cannot do rather than what they can do.

_____ 7. With the beginning of preoperational thought, most preschoolers can understand abstract words.

_____ 8. A preschooler who says "You comed up and hurted me" is demonstrating a lack of understanding of English grammar.

_____ 9. Successful preschool programs generally have a low teacher-to-child ratio.

_____ 10. Vygotsky believed that cognitive growth is largely a social activity.

_____ 11. "Theory-theory" refers to the tendency of young children to see the world as an unchanging reflection of their current construction of reality.

Progress Test 2

Progress Test 2 should be completed during a final chapter review. Answer the following questions after you thoroughly understand the correct answers for the Chapter Review and Progress Test 1.

Multiple-Choice Questions

1. Three-year-old Megan insists that her brother spilled a glass of milk even though he was nowhere nearby. The fact that the milk _was_ spilled indicates that Megan is:
   a. constructing a theory-theory.
   b. having difficulty with her source memory of the event.
   c. demonstrating centration.
   d. demonstrating static reasoning.

2. Piaget believed that preoperational children fail conservation of liquid tests because of their tendency to:
   a. focus on appearance.
   b. fast map.
   c. overregularize.
   d. do all of the above.

3. A preschooler who focuses his or her attention on only one feature of a situation is demonstrating a characteristic of preoperational thought called:
   a. centration.   c. reversibility.
   b. overregularization.   d. egocentrism.

4. One characteristic of preoperational thought is:
   a. the ability to categorize objects.
   b. the ability to count in multiples of 5.
   c. the inability to perform logical operations.
   d. difficulty adjusting to changes in routine.

5. The zone of proximal development represents the:
   a. skills or knowledge that are within the potential of the learner but are not yet mastered.
   b. influence of a child's peers on cognitive development.
   c. explosive period of language development during the play years.
   d. normal variations in children's language proficiency.

6. According to Vygotsky, language advances thinking through private speech, and by:
   a. helping children to privately review what they know.
   b. helping children explain events to themselves.
   c. serving as a mediator of the social interaction that is a vital part of learning.
   d. facilitating the process of fast mapping.

7. Irreversibility refers to the:
   a. inability to understand that other people view the world from a different perspective than one's own.
   b. inability to think about more than one idea at a time.
   c. failure to understand that changing the arrangement of a group of objects doesn't change their number.
   d. failure to understand that undoing a process will restore the original conditions.

8. According to Piaget:
   a. it is impossible for preoperational children to grasp the concept of conservation, no matter how carefully it is explained.
   b. preschoolers fail to solve conservation problems because they center their attention on the transformation that has occurred and ignore the changed appearances of the objects.
   c. with special training, even preoperational children are able to grasp some aspects of conservation.
   d. preschoolers fail to solve conservation problems because they have no theory of mind.

9. Scaffolding of a child's cognitive skills can be provided by:
   a. a mentor.
   b. the objects or experiences of a culture.
   c. the child's past learning.
   d. all of the above.

10. Which theorist would be most likely to agree with the statement, "Learning is a social activity more than it is a matter of individual discovery"?
    a. Piaget   c. both a. and b.
    b. Vygotsky   d. neither a. nor b.

11. Children first demonstrate some understanding of grammar:
    a. as soon as the first words are produced.
    b. once they begin to use language for practical purposes.
    c. through the process called fast mapping.
    d. in their earliest sentences.

12. Preschoolers' memories may be aided by:

    a. assimilating the experience into a mental script.

    b. conversation with an adult that names the experience.

    c. parents conducting an unstructured, friendly interview about the experience.

    d. all of the above.

13. Most 5-year-olds have difficulty understanding analogies because:

    a. they have not yet begun to develop grammar.

    b. the literal nature of the fast-mapping process allows only one meaning per word.

    c. of their limited vocabulary.

    d. of their tendency to overregularize.

14. Overregularization indicates that a child:

    a. is clearly applying rules of grammar.

    b. persists in egocentric thinking.

    c. has not yet mastered the principle of conservation.

    d. does not yet have a theory of mind.

15. Regarding the value of preschool education, most developmentalists believe that:

    a. most disadvantaged children will not benefit from an early preschool education.

    b. most disadvantaged children will benefit from an early preschool education.

    c. the early benefits of preschool education are likely to disappear by grade 3.

    d. the relatively small benefits of antipoverty measures such as Head Start do not justify their huge costs.

Matching Items

Match each term or concept with its corresponding description or definition.

Terms or Concepts

    _____ **1.** script

    _____ **2.** scaffold

    _____ **3.** theory of mind

    _____ **4.** zone of proximal development

    _____ **5.** overregularization

    _____ **6.** fast mapping

    _____ **7.** irreversibility

    _____ **8.** centration

    _____ **9.** conservation

    _____ **10.** private speech

    _____ **11.** guided participation

    _____ **12.** static reasoning

Descriptions or Definitions

    a. the idea that amount is unaffected by changes in shape or placement

    b. the tendency to see the world as an unchanging place

    c. the cognitive distance between a child's actual and potential levels of development

    d. the tendency to think about one aspect of a situation at a time

    e. the process whereby the child learns through social interaction with a "tutor"

    f. our understanding of mental processes in ourselves and others

    g. the process by which words are learned after only one hearing

    h. an inappropriate application of rules of grammar

    i. the internal use of language to form ideas

    j. the inability to understand that original conditions are restored by the undoing of some process

    k. to structure a child's participation in learning encounters

    l. memory-facilitating outline of past experiences

Thinking Critically About Chapter 9

Answer these questions the day before an exam as a final check on your understanding of the chapter's terms and concepts.

1. An experimenter first shows a child two rows of checkers that each have the same number of checkers. Then, with the child watching, the experimenter elongates one row and asks the child if each of the two rows still has an equal number of checkers. This experiment tests the child's understanding of:
   a. reversibility.
   b. conservation of matter.
   c. conservation of number.
   d. centration.

2. A preschooler believes that a "party" is the one and only attribute of a birthday. She says that Daddy doesn't have a birthday because he never has a party. This thinking demonstrates the tendency Piaget called:
   a. egocentrism.
   b. centration.
   c. conservation of events.
   d. mental representation.

3. A child who understands that 6 + 3 = 9 means that 9 – 6 = 3 has had to master the concept of:
   a. reversibility.
   b. number.
   c. conservation.
   d. egocentrism.

4. A 4-year-old tells the teacher that a clown should not be allowed to visit the class because "Pat is 'fraid of clowns." The 4-year-old thus shows that he can anticipate how another will feel. This is evidence of the beginnings of:
   a. egocentrism.
   b. deception.
   c. a theory of mind.
   d. conservation.

5. A Japanese visitor to an American preschool would probably be struck by its emphasis on fostering _____ in children.
   a. conformity
   b. concern for others
   c. cooperation
   d. self-reliance

6. A nursery school teacher is given the job of selecting holiday entertainment for a group of preschool children. If the teacher agrees with the ideas of Vygotsky, she is most likely to select:
   a. a simple TV show that every child can understand.
   b. a hands-on experience that requires little adult supervision.
   c. brief, action-oriented play activities that the children and teachers will perform together.
   d. holiday puzzles for children to work on individually.

7. When asked to describe her dinner last night, 3-year-old Hilary says, "We sat at the table, mommy served meat and potatoes, we ate, we left the table." Hilary evidently:
   a. is very egocentric in her thinking.
   b. is retrieving from a "dinner script."
   c. failed to retrieve the memory that they ate out last night.
   d. has acquired a sophisticated theory of mind.

8. That a child produces sentences that follow such rules of word order as "the initiator of an action precedes the verb, the receiver of an action follows it" demonstrates a knowledge of:
   a. grammar.
   b. semantics.
   c. pragmatics.
   d. phrase structure.

9. The 2-year-old child who says, "We goed to the store," is making a grammatical:
   a. centration.
   b. overregularization.
   c. extension.
   d. script.

10. An experimenter who makes two balls of clay of equal amount, then rolls one into a long, skinny rope and asks the child if the amounts are still the same, is testing the child's understanding of:
    a. conservation.
    b. reversibility.
    c. perspective-taking.
    d. centration.

11. Dr. Jones, who believes that children's language growth greatly contributes to their cognitive growth, evidently is a proponent of the ideas of:
    a. Piaget.
    b. Chomsky.
    c. Flavell.
    d. Vygotsky.

12. Jack constantly "talks down" to his 3-year-old son's speech level. Jack's speech is:
    a. appropriate, because 3-year-olds have barely begun to comprehend grammatical rules.
    b. commendable, given the importance of scaffolding in promoting cognitive growth.
    c. unnecessary, because preschoolers are able to comprehend more complex grammar and vocabulary than they can produce.
    d. clearly within his son's zone of proximal development.

13. In describing the limited logical reasoning of preschoolers, a developmentalist is *least* likely to emphasize:
    a. irreversibility.   c. its action-bound nature.
    b. centration.   d. its static nature.

14. A preschooler fails to put together a difficult puzzle on her own, so her mother encourages her to try again, this time guiding her by asking questions such as, "For this space do we need a big piece or a little piece?" With Mom's help, the child successfully completes the puzzle. Lev Vygotsky would attribute the child's success to:
    a. additional practice with the puzzle pieces.
    b. imitation of her mother's behavior.
    c. the social interaction with her mother that restructured the task to make its solution more attainable.
    d. modeling and reinforcement.

15. Mark is answering an essay question that asks him to "discuss the positions of major developmental theorists regarding the relationship between language and cognitive development." To help organize his answer, Mark jots down a reminder that _____ contended that language is essential to the advancement of thinking, as private speech, and as a _____ of social interactions.
    a. Piaget; mediator   c. Piaget; theory
    b. Vygotsky; mediator   d. Vygotsky; theory

Key Terms

Using your own words, write a brief definition or explanation of each of the following terms on a separate piece of paper.

1. preoperational thought
2. centration
3. egocentrism
4. focus on appearance

5. static reasoning
6. irreversibility
7. conservation
8. theory-theory
9. apprentice in thinking
10. guided participation
11. zone of proximal development
12. scaffold
13. private speech
14. social mediation
15. source memory
16. scripts
17. theory of mind
18. imaginary companion
19. sensitive period
20. critical period
21. fast mapping
22. overregularization
23. high risk

ANSWERS
CHAPTER REVIEW

1. perspective (or egocentrism)
2. preoperational
3. centration; egocentrism; appearances
4. static; unchanging; irreversibility
5. conservation; conservation of number
6. theory-theory; guided participation; social; interact
7. Lev Vygotsky
   a. structuring the task to make its solution more attainable
   b. focusing attention on the important steps
   c. providing motivation
8. social activity
9. zone of proximal development
10. scaffold
11. private speech; uttered aloud
12. mediator
13. egocentric; parental guidance
14. do; stable order; one-to-one correspondence; cardinal

15. 4; brain; language; curiosity; scaffolding

16. memory; storage; retrieval; emotional

17. source memory; who said or did something or the place where something took place

18. scripts

19. social interaction; personal participation; conversation; specfic questions

20. theory of mind

Between the ages of 3 and 6, young children come to realize that mental phenomena may not reflect reality and that individuals can believe various things and, therefore, can be deliberately deceived or fooled.

21. have

22. language; brain maturation; brother or sister; culture

23. imaginary companions

24. critical; sensitive

25. vocabulary

26. fast mapping; logical extension; older siblings; first-born

27. more

28. comparisons; time; place

29. grammar; 3

30. overregularization

Many preschoolers overapply the rule of adding "s" to form the plural, as well as the rule of adding "ed" to form the past tense. Thus, preschoolers are likely to say "foots" and "snows" and that someone "broked" a toy.

31. more

32. is; monolingualism; bilingualism

33. egocentric; theories of mind; vocabulary development; literacy

34. vary; social consensus; conformity; group activity; self-confidence; self-reliance

35. has not; almost all; employed outside the home

36. high risk

37. Project Head Start; higher

High-quality preschools are characterized by (a) a low teacher-child ratio, (b) a staff with training and credentials in early-childhood education, (c) a curriculum geared toward cognitive development, and (d) an organization of space that facilitates creative and constructive play.

PROGRESS TEST 1

Multiple-Choice Questions

1. **c.** is the answer. (p. 264)

2. **c.** is the answer. In fact, preoperational children have excellent imaginations, as revealed by the creation of imaginary companions and other forms of symbolic play. (pp. 264–265, 278)

3. **e.** is the answer. (p. 279)

4. **a.** is the answer. (p. 274)

   b. & d. Because preschoolers' scripts *do* recognize the causal flow of events, they are not hard to follow.

   c. Preschoolers use scripts not only when recounting familiar routines but also in pretend play.

5. **b.** is the answer. (p. 272)

   a. Scripts tend to *improve* preschoolers' memory.

   c. & d. Although true, neither of these is the *primary* reason for preschoolers' poor memory.

6. **d.** is the answer. (pp. 281–282)

   a. & c. Preschoolers generally have great difficulty understanding, and therefore using, metaphors and abstract nouns.

   b. Other than the grammatical errors of overregularization, the text does not indicate that preschoolers use a significant number of self-created words.

7. **a.** is the answer. (p. 282)

   b. & d. These terms are not identified in the text and do not apply to the use of grammar.

   c. Practical usage, which also is not discussed in the text, refers to communication between one person and another in terms of the overall context in which language is used.

8. **a.** is the answer. (p. 268)

   b. This expresses the views of Piaget.

   c. Because he believed that language facilitates thinking, Vygotsky obviously felt that language and other cognitive developments are intimately related.

   d. Vygotsky did not hold this view.

9. **a.** is the answer. (p. 268)

10. **a.** is the answer. (pp. 265–266)

    b., c., & d. Failure to conserve is the result of thinking that is centered on appearances. Egocentrism and irreversibility are also examples of centered thinking.

11. **c.** is the answer. (p. 289)

b. This is not discussed in the text. However, although there was a slight early IQ advantage in Head Start graduates, the gain seemed to fade as children moved through elementary school.

a. & d. There was no indication of greater behavioral problems or alienation in Head Start graduates.

12. **b.** is the answer. (p. 291)
13. **c.** is the answer. (p. 283)
14. **d.** is the answer. (p. 266)
15. **a.** is the answer. (p. 280)

True or False Items

1. F   Imaginary companions are a normal, healthy sign of cognitive development. (p. 278)
2. T (pp. 265–266)
3. F   In fact, just the opposite is true. (p. 269)
4. T (p. 266)
5. T (p. 264)
6. T (p. 264)
7. F   Preschoolers have difficulty understanding abstract words; their vocabulary consists mainly of concrete nouns and verbs. (p. 281)
8. F   In adding "ed" to form a past tense, the child has indicated an understanding of the grammatical rule for making past tenses in English, even though the construction in these two cases is incorrect. (pp. 282–283)
9. T (p. 291)
10. T (p. 267)
11. F This describes static reasoning; theory-theory is the idea that children attempt to construct a theory to explain all their experiences. (p. 266)

PROGRESS TEST 2

Multiple-Choice Questions

1. **b.** is the answer. (pp. 272–273)

   a., c., & d. Although these are characteristics of preoperational thinking, they have nothing to do with a distorted memory of an actual event.

2. **a.** is the answer. (p. 266)

   b. & c. Fast mapping and overregularization are characteristics of language development during the play years; they have nothing to do with reasoning about volume.

3. **a.** is the answer. (p. 264)

b. Overregularization is the child's tendency to apply grammatical rules even when he or she shouldn't.

c. Reversibility is the concept that reversing an operation, such as addition, will restore the original conditions.

d. This term is used to refer to the young child's belief that people think as he or she does.

4. **c.** is the answer. This is why the stage is called *pre*operational. (p. 264)
5. **a.** is the answer. (p. 268)
6. **c.** is the answer. (p. 269)

   a. & b. These are both advantages of private speech.

   d. Fast mapping is the process by which new words are acquired, often after only one hearing.

7. **d.** is the answer. (p. 265)

   a. This describes egocentrism.

   b. This is the opposite of centration.

   c. This defines conservation of number.

8. **a.** is the answer. (pp. 265–266)

   b. According to Piaget, preschoolers fail to solve conservation problems because they focus on the *appearance* of objects and ignore the transformation that has occurred.

   d. Piaget did not relate conservation to a theory of mind.

9. **d.** is the answer. (p. 268)
10. **b.** is the answer. (p. 267)

    a. Piaget believed that learning is a matter of individual discovery.

11. **d.** is the answer. Preschoolers almost always put subject before verb in their two-word sentences. (p. 282)
12. **b.** is the answer. (pp. 274–275)

    a. Mental scripts do help memory but only for familiar experiences.

    c. Interviews to elicit memories of events should be carefully structured.

13. **b.** is the answer. (p. 282)

    a. By the time children are 3 years old, their grammar is quite impressive.

    c. On the contrary, vocabulary develops so rapidly that, by age 5, children seem to be able to understand and use almost any term they hear.

    d. This tendency to make language more logical by overapplying certain grammatical rules has nothing to do with understanding the *meaning* of analogies.

14. a. is the answer. (pp. 282–283)

b. c., & d. Overregularization is a *linguistic* phenomenon rather than a characteristic type of thinking (b. and d.), or a logical principle (c.).

15. b. is the answer. (p. 290)

Matching Items

1. l (p. 274) **5.** h (p. 282) **9.** a (p. 265)
2. k (p. 268) **6.** g (p. 280) **10.** i (p. 268)
3. f (p. 276) **7.** j (p. 265) **11.** e (p. 267)
4. c (p. 268) **8.** d (p. 264) **12.** b (p. 265)

THINKING CRITICALLY ABOUT CHAPTER 9

1. c. is the answer. (pp. 265–266)

a. A test of reversibility would ask a child to perform an operation, such as adding 4 to 3, and then reverse the process (subtract 3 from 7) to determine whether the child understood that the original condition (the number 4) was restored.

b. A test of conservation of matter would transform the appearance of an object, such as a ball of clay, to determine whether the child understood that the object remained the same.

d. A test of centration would involve the child's ability to see various aspects of a situation.

2. b. is the answer. (p. 264)

a. Egocentrism is thinking that is self-centered.

c. This is not a concept in Piaget's theory.

d. Mental representation is an example of symbolic thought.

3. a. is the answer. (p. 265)

4. c. is the answer. (p. 276)

a. Egocentrism is self-centered thinking.

b. Although deception provides evidence of a theory of mind, the child in this example is not deceiving anyone.

d. Conservation is the understanding that the amount of a substance is unchanged by changes in its shape or placement.

5. d. is the answer. (pp. 285–286)

a., b., & c. Japanese preschools place *more* emphasis on these attitudes and behaviors than do American preschools.

6. c. is the answer. In Vygotsky's view, learning is a social activity more than a matter of individual discovery. Thus, social interaction that provides motivation and focuses attention facilitates learning. (p. 267)

a., b., & d. These situations either provide no opportunity for social interaction (b. & d.) or do not challenge the children (a.).

7. b. is the answer. (p. 274)

a. Egocentrism is thinking that is self-focused.

c. Preschoolers do have poor retrieval strategies, but the question doesn't indicate that she confused the events of the preceding evening.

d. This refers to preschoolers' emerging social understanding of others' perspectives.

8. a. is the answer. (p. 282)

b. & d. The text does not discuss these aspects of language.

c. Pragmatics, which is not mentioned in the text, refers to the practical use of language in varying social contexts.

9. b. is the answer. (p. 282)

10. a. is the answer. (pp. 265–266)

11. d. is the answer. (pp. 268–269)

a. Piaget believed that cognitive growth precedes language development.

b. & c. Chomsky focused on the *acquisition* of language, and Flavell emphasizes cognition.

12. c. is the answer. (p. 283)

13. c. is the answer. This is typical of cognition during the first two years, when infants think exclusively with their senses and motor skills. (pp. 264–265)

14. c. is the answer. (pp. 267–268)

15. b. is the answer. (pp. 268–269)

KEY TERMS

1. According to Piaget, thinking between ages 2 and 6 is characterized by **preoperational thought**, meaning that children cannot yet perform logical operations; that is, they cannot use logical principles. (p. 264)

Memory aid: Operations are mental transformations involving the manipulation of ideas and symbols. *Pre*operational children, who lack the ability to perform transformations, are "before" this developmental milestone.

2. Centration is the tendency of preoperational children to focus only on a single aspect of a situation or object. (p. 264)

3. **Egocentrism** refers to the tendency of preoperational children to view the world exclusively from their own perspective. (p. 264)

4. **Focus on appearance** refers to the preoperational child's tendency to focus only on physical attributes and ignore all others. (p. 264)

5. Preoperational thinking is characterized by **static reasoning,** by which is meant that the young child sees the world as unchanging. (p. 265)

6. **Irreversibility** is the characteristic of preoperational thought in which young children fail to recognize that a process can be reversed to restore the original conditions of a situation. (p. 265)

7. **Conservation** is the understanding that the amount or quantity of a substance or object is unaffected by changes in its shape or configuration. (p. 265)

8. **Theory-theory** is Gopnik's term for the tendency of young children to attempt to construct theories to explain everything they experience. (p. 266)

9. According to Vygotsky, a young child is an **apprentice in thinking,** whose intellectual growth is stimulated by more skilled members of society. (p. 267)

10. According to Vygotsky, **guided participation** is the process by which young children learn to think by having social experiences and by exploring their universe. As guides, parents, teachers, and older children offer assistance with challenging tasks, model problem-solving approaches, provide explicit instructions as needed, and support the child's interest and motivation. (p. 267)

11. According to Vygotsky, for each individual there is a **zone of proximal development (ZPD),** which represents the skills that are within the potential of the learner but cannot be performed independently. (p. 268)

12. Tutors who **scaffold** structure children's learning experiences in order to foster their emerging capabilities. (p. 268)

13. **Private speech** is Vygotsky's term for the internal dialogue in which a person talks to himself or herself. Private speech, which often is uttered aloud, helps preschoolers to think, review what they know, and decide what to do. (p. 268)

14. In Vygotsky's theory, **social mediation** is a function of speech by which a person's cognitive skills are refined and extended. (p. 269)

15. **Source memory,** or the ability to remember who said or did something or the place where an event occurred, is particularly difficult for young children. (p. 272)

16. A **script** is a mental road map of familiar sequences of events, used to facilitate the storage and retrieval of memories. (p. 274)

17. A **theory of mind** is an understanding of human mental processes, that is, of one's own or another's emotions, perceptions, intentions, and thoughts. (p. 276)

18. Many young children construct a make-believe person, animal, or other **imaginary companion** to talk to and play with. (p. 278)

19. A **sensitive period** is a time when a certain type of development, such as language acquisition, occurs most rapidly. (p. 279)

20. A **critical period** is a time when a certain type of development must occur or it will never happen. (p. 279)

21. **Fast mapping** is the not very precise process by which children rapidly learn new words by quickly connecting them to words and categories that are already understood. (p. 280)

22. **Overregularization** occurs when children apply rules of grammar when they should not. It is seen in English, for example, when children add "s" to form the plural even in irregular cases that form the plural in a different way. (p. 282)

23. In the context of early-childhood education, **high-risk children** are those whose chances of poor achievement are much higher than average. (p. 289)

Chapter Ten

The Play Years: Psychosocial Development

Chapter Overview

Chapter 10 explores the ways in which young children begin to relate to others in an ever-widening social environment. The chapter begins where social understanding begins, with emotional development and the emergence of the sense of self. With their increasing social awareness, children become more concerned with how others evaluate them and better able to regulate their emotions.

The next section explores the origins of helpful, prosocial behaviors in young children, as well as antisocial behaviors such as the different forms of aggressive behavior. The child's social skills reflect many influences, including learning from playmates through various types of play as well as from television and parenting patterns.

The chapter concludes with a description of children's emerging awareness of male–female differences and gender identity. Five major theories of gender-role development are considered.

NOTE: Answer guidelines for all Chapter 10 questions begin on page 166.

Guided Study

The text chapter should be studied one section at a time. Before you read, preview each section by skimming it, noting headings and boldface items. Then read the appropriate section objectives from the following outline. Keep these objectives in mind and, as you read the chapter section, search for the information that will enable you to meet each objective. Once you have finished a section, write out answers for its objectives.

Emotional Development (pp. 295–299)

1. Discuss emotional development during early childhood, focusing on emotional regulation, and how it is affected by caregiving practices.

2. Discuss the relationship between the child's developing self-concept and self-esteem.

Theories of Emotions (pp. 299–302)

3. Explain the views of Erik Erikson and Daniel Goleman regarding emotional development in young children.

Prosocial and Antisocial Behavior (pp. 302–309)

4. Differentiate four types of aggression during the play years, and explain why certain types of aggression are more troubling to developmentalists.

5. Differentiate five types of play, and discuss the nature and significance of rough-and-tumble and sociodramatic play during the play years.

6. (text and Changing Policy) Discuss how watching television and playing video games contribute to the development of aggression and other antisocial behaviors.

Parenting Patterns (pp. 309–315)

7. Compare and contrast three classic patterns of parenting and their effect on children.

8. Discuss the pros and cons of punishment, and describe the most effective method for disciplining a child.

Boy or Girl: So What? (pp. 315–323)

9. Describe the developmental progression of gender awareness in young children.

10. Summarize five theories of gender-role development during the play years, noting important contributions of each.

Chapter Review

When you have finished reading the chapter, work through the material that follows to review it. Complete the sentences and answer the questions. As you proceed, evaluate your performance for each section by consulting the answers on page 166. Do not continue with the next section until you understand each answer. If you need to, review or reread the appropriate section in the textbook before continuing.

Emotional Development (pp. 295–299)

1. The ability to direct or modify one's feelings, particularly those of _____ , _____ , and _____ , is called _____ _____ . This ability begins with the control of _____ . Children who have _____ problems and lash out at other people or things are said to be _____ (overcontrolled/undercontrolled). Children who have _____ problems tend to be inhibited, fearful, and withdrawn.

2. Genetic influences _____ (are/are not) a source of variation in emotional regulation in young children. One research study found that fearful children had greater activity in the

_____ _____

_____ of their brains, while those who were less withdrawn had greater activity in their _____ _____

_____ .

3. Repeated exposure to extreme stress can kill _____ and make some young children physiologically unable to regulate their emotions. Extreme stress can also affect the release of stress hormones such as _____ . One study found _____ (higher-than-normal/lower-than-normal) levels of this hormone in abused children.

Give several examples of early stress that can inhibit young children's emotional regulation.

4. Another set of influences on emotional regulation is the child's early and current

_____ _____ .

5. Some young children develop irrational and exaggerated fears called _____ . These strong fears probably have their roots in _____ protection of the human race.

6. Psychologists emphasize the importance of children's developing a positive _____ and feelings of pride that enable _____ . Preschoolers typically form impressions of themselves that are quite _____ . One manifestation of this tendency is that preschoolers regularly _____ (overestimate/underestimate) their own abilities. Most preschoolers think of themselves as competent _____ (in all/only in certain) areas.

Theories of Emotions (pp. 299–302)

7. Between 3 and 6 years of age, according to Erikson, children are in the stage of

_____ _____

_____ . Unlike the earlier stage of _____ , children in this stage want to begin *and* _____ something. Erikson also believed that during this stage children begin to feel _____ when their efforts result in failure or criticism.

8. According to _____ , the ability to direct emotions is crucial to the development of

_____ _____ .

Prosocial and Antisocial Behavior (pp. 302–309)

9. Emotions are ultimately expressed in behavior related to _____ , who are other people of about the same _____ and _____ as the child.

10. Sharing, cooperating, and sympathizing are examples of _____

_____ .

These attitudes are indicative of

_____ _____ and correlate with _____

_____ . As the capacity for self-control increases between 2 and 5 years, there is a decrease in _____

_____

_____ .

11. Conversely, actions that are destructive or deliberately hurtful are called _____

_____ . Such actions are often predicted by a lack of _____

_____ .

12. A child's ability to truly understand the emotions of another, called _____ , usually is not evident until about age _____ .

13. The roots of aggression include inadequate _____ _____ during the early preschool years.

14. Developmentalists distinguish four types of physical aggression: _____ , used to obtain or retain a toy or other object; _____ , used in angry retaliation against an intentional or accidental act committed by a peer; _____ , which takes the form of insults or social rejection; and _____ , used in an unprovoked attack on a peer.

15. The form of aggression that is most likely to increase from age 2 to 6 is _____ _____ . Of greater concern are _____ _____ , because it can indicate a lack of _____ _____ , and _____ _____ , which is most worrisome overall.

16. Relational aggression _____ (is/is not) more hurtful than physical aggression. Victims and perpetrators of this type of aggression are more commonly preschoolers who are

_____ .

17. Mildred Parten described five types of childhood play, including _____ play, in which a child plays alone; _____ play, in which a child watches others play; _____ play, in which children play with similar toys but do not interact; _____ play, in which children share materials and emotions, but don't seem to be playing the same game; and _____ play, in which children play together in the most social manner.

18. The type of physical play that mimics aggression is called _____-_____-_____ play. A distinctive feature of this form of play, which _____ (occurs only in some cultures/is universal), is the positive facial expression that characterizes the "_____ _____ ." Age differences are evident, because this type of play relies on the child's _____ _____ . Gender differences _____ (are/are not) evident in rough-and-tumble play.

19. In _____ play, children act out various roles and themes in stories of their own creation. The increase in this form of play is related to the development of the child's _____ _____ _____ and emotional regulation. _____ (Girls/Boys) tend to engage in this type of play more often than do _____ (girls/boys).

20. A typical 2- to 4-year-old child in the United States watches _____ hours of television per day.

21. One longitudinal study found that teenagers who had watched educational television as young children earned _____ _____ and did more _____ than others, especially if they were _____ (boys/girls). Teenagers who watched violent television programs as young children had _____ _____ than others, especially if they were _____ (boys/girls).

(text and Changing Policy) State several negative effects of watching television and playing video games from a developmental perspective.

Parenting Patterns (pp. 309–315)

22. A significant influence on early psychosocial growth is the style of _____ that characterizes a child's family life.

23. The seminal research on parenting styles, which was conducted by _____ , found that parents varied in their _____ toward offspring, in their strategies for _____ , in how well they _____ , and in their expectations for _____ .

24. Parents who adopt the _____ style demand unquestioning obedience from

their children. In this style of parenting, nurturance tends to be _____ (low/high), maturity demands are _____ (low/high), and parent–child communication tends to be _____ (low/high).

25. Parents who adopt the _____ style make few demands on their children and are lax in discipline. Such parents _____ (are/are not very) nurturant, communicate _____ (well/poorly), and make _____ (few/extensive) maturity demands.

26. Parents who adopt the _____ style democratically set limits and enforce rules. Such parents make _____ (high/low) maturity demands, communicate _____ (well/poorly), and _____ (are/are not) nurturant. Two other styles of parenting that have been identified are _____ parenting, in which parents don't seem to care at all about their children, and _____ parenting, in which parents give in to a child's every whim.

27. Follow-up studies indicate that children raised by _____ parents are likely to be obedient but unhappy and those raised by _____ parents are likely to lack self-control. Those raised by _____ parents are more likely to be successful, happy with themselves, and generous with others; these advantages _____ (grow stronger/weaken) over time.

28. An important factor in the effectiveness of parenting style is the child's _____ . A factor that contributes to nurturance in parenting—particularly by parents who themselves are experiencing unusual stress—is _____ _____ for parenting.

29. To be effective, punishment should be more _____ and _____ than _____ . Japanese mothers tend to use _____ as disciplinary techniques more often than do North American mothers, who are more likely to encourage _____

expressions of all sorts in their children. A disciplinary technique in which a child is required to stop all activity and sit quietly for a few minutes is the _____-_____ . This technique is widely used in _____ _____ .

30. Physical punishment of children is against the law for parents and teachers in _____ . In contrast, in some _____ nations, all parents are expected to physically punish their children.

31. Throughout the world, most parents _____ (believe/do not believe) that spanking is acceptable at times. Although spanking _____ (is/is not) effective, it may teach children to be more _____ .

32. One study investigated the relationship between punishment at home and aggressive behavior at school in the child. Observers scored kindergartners for instances of aggressive behavior. Compared with children who were not spanked, those children who were spanked were more likely to engage in _____ aggression.

Boy or Girl: So What? (pp. 315–323)

33. Social scientists distinguish between biological, or _____ , differences between males and females, and cultural, or _____ , differences in the _____ and behaviors of males and females.

34. True sex differences are _____ (more/less) apparent in childhood than in adulthood; _____ differentiation seems more significant to children than to adults.

35. By age _____ , children can consistently apply gender labels and have a rudimentary understanding of the permanence of their own gender. By age _____ , most children express stereotypic ideas of each sex. Awareness that sex is a fixed biological characteristic does not become solid until about age _____ .

36. Freud called the period from age 3 to 6 the
_____ _____ . According to
his view, boys in this stage develop sexual feelings about their _____
and become jealous of their _____ .
Freud called this phenomenon the

_____ _____ .

37. In Freud's theory, preschool boys resolve their
guilty feelings defensively through
_____ with their father. Boys also
develop, again in self-defense, a powerful con-
science called the _____ .

38. According to Freud, during the phallic stage little
girls may experience the _____
_____ , in which they want to get rid of
their mother and become intimate with their
father. Alternatively, they may become jealous of
boys because they have a penis; this emotion
Freud called _____ _____ .

39. According to behaviorism, preschool children
develop gender-role ideas by being
_____ for behaviors deemed appropriate for their sex and _____
for behaviors deemed inappropriate.

40. Behaviorists also maintain that children learn
gender-appropriate behavior not only through
direct reinforcement but also by _____ .

41. Cognitive theorists focus on children's
_____ of male–female differences.
When their experience is ambiguous, preschoolers search for the simple _____ they
have formed regarding gender roles.

42. Gender education varies by region, socioeconomic status, and historical period, according to the
_____ theory. Gender distinctions are
emphasized in many _____ cultures.
This theory points out that children can maintain
a balance of male and female characteristics, or
_____ , only if their culture promotes
that idea.

43. According to _____
_____ theory, gender attitudes and
roles are the result of interaction between

_____ and _____

_____ .

44. The idea that is supported by recent research is
that some gender differences are
_____ based because of differences
between male and female _____ .

45. These differences probably _____
(are/are not) the result of any single gene. More
likely, they result from the differing

_____ _____

that influence brain development. However, the
theory maintains that the manifestations of biological origins are shaped, enhanced, or halted by

_____ _____ .

Progress Test 1

Multiple-Choice Questions

Circle your answers to the following questions and
check them with the answers on page 167. If your
answer is incorrect, read the explanation for why it is
incorrect and then consult the appropriate pages of
the text (in parentheses following the correct answer).

1. Preschool children have a clear (but not necessarily accurate) concept of self. Typically, the preschooler believes that she or he:
   a. owns all objects in sight.
   b. is great at almost everything.
   c. is much less competent than peers and older
children.
   d. is more powerful than her or his parents.

2. According to Freud, the third stage of psychosexual development, during which the penis is the
focus of psychological concern and pleasure, is
the:
   a. oral stage.   c. phallic stage.
   b. anal stage.   d. latency period.

3. Because it helps children rehearse social roles,
work out fears and fantasies, and learn cooperation, an important form of social play is:
   a. sociodramatic play.
   b. mastery play.
   c. rough-and-tumble play.
   d. sensorimotor play.

4. The three *basic* patterns of parenting described by Diana Baumrind are:
   a. hostile, loving, and harsh.
   b. authoritarian, permissive, and authoritative.
   c. positive, negative, and punishing.
   d. indulgent, neglecting, and traditional.

5. Authoritative parents are receptive and loving, but they also normally:
   a. set limits and enforce rules.
   b. have difficulty communicating.
   c. withhold praise and affection.
   d. encourage aggressive behavior.

6. (text and Changing Policy) Children who watch a lot of violent television:
   a. are more likely to be aggressive.
   b. become desensitized to violence.
   c. tend to have lower grades in school.
   d. have all of the above characteristics.

7. Between 2 and 6 years of age, the form of aggression that is most likely to increase is:
   a. reactive
   b. instrumental
   c. relational
   d. bullying

8. During the play years, a child's self-concept is defined largely by his or her:
   a. expanding range of skills and competencies.
   b. physical appearance.
   c. gender.
   d. relationship with family members.

9. Behaviorists emphasize the importance of _____ in the development of the preschool child.
   a. identification   c. initiative
   b. praise and blame   d. a theory of mind

10. Children apply gender labels and have definite ideas about how boys and girls behave as early as age:
   a. 2.   c. 5.
   b. 4.   d. 7.

11. Psychologist Daniel Goleman believes that emotional regulation is especially crucial to the preschooler's developing:
   a. sense of self.
   b. social awareness.
   c. emotional intelligence.
   d. sense of gender.

12. Six-year-old Leonardo has superior verbal ability rivaling that of most girls his age. Dr. Laurent believes this is due to the fact that although his sex is predisposed to slower language development, Leonardo's upbringing in a linguistically rich home enhanced his biological capabilities. Dr. Laurent is evidently a proponent of:
   a. cognitive theory.
   b. psychoanalytic theory.
   c. sociocultural theory.
   d. epigenetic systems theory.

13. Three-year-old Jake, who lashes out at the family pet in anger, is displaying signs of _____ problems, which suggests that he is emotionally
   a. internalizing; overcontrolled
   b. internalizing; undercontrolled
   c. externalizing; overcontrolled
   d. externalizing; undercontrolled

14. Compared to Japanese mothers, North American mothers are more likely to:
   a. use reasoning to control their preschoolers' social behavior.
   b. use expressions of disappointment to control their preschoolers' social behavior.
   c. encourage emotional expressions of all sorts in their preschoolers.
   d. do all of the above.

15. When her friend hurts her feelings, Maya shouts that she is a "mean old stinker!" Maya's behavior is an example of:
   a. instrumental aggression.
   b. reactive aggression.
   c. bullying aggression.
   d. relational aggression.

True or False Items

Write *T* (*true*) *or F* (*false*) on the line in front of each statement.

_____ 1. According to Diana Baumrind, only authoritarian parents make maturity demands on their children.

_____ 2. Children of authoritative parents tend to be successful, happy with themselves, and generous with others.

_____ 3. True sex differences are more apparent in childhood than in adulthood.

_____ 4. Spanking is associated with higher rates of aggression toward peers.

_____ 5. Some gender differences are genetically based.

_____ 6. Children can be truly androgynous only if their culture promotes such ideas and practices.

_____ 7. Developmentalists do not agree about how children acquire gender roles.

_____ 8. By age 4, most children have definite ideas about what constitutes typical masculine and feminine behavior.

_____ 9. Identification was defined by Freud as a defense mechanism in which people identify with others who may be stronger and more powerful than they.

_____ 10. Sociodramatic play allows children free expression of their emotions.

Progress Test 2

Progress Test 2 should be completed during a final chapter review. Answer the following questions after you thoroughly understand the correct answers for the Chapter Review and Progress Test 1.

Multiple-Choice Questions

1. Children of permissive parents are *most* likely to lack:
   - a. social skills.
   - b. self-control.
   - c. initiative and guilt.
   - d. care and concern.

2. Children learn how to manage conflict through the use of humor most readily from their interaction with:
   - a. their mothers.
   - b. their fathers.
   - c. friends.
   - d. others of the same sex.

3. The initial advantages of parenting style:
   - a. do not persist past middle childhood.
   - b. remain apparent through adolescence.
   - c. are likely to be even stronger over time.
   - d. have an unpredictable impact later in children's lives.

4. When they are given a choice of playmates, 2- to 5-year-old children:
   - a. play with children of their own sex.
   - b. play equally with girls and boys.
   - c. segregate by gender in cultures characterized by traditional gender roles.
   - d. prefer to play alone.

5. Which of the following best summarizes the current view of developmentalists regarding gender differences?
   - a. Some gender differences are biological in origin.
   - b. Gender differences are not biological in origin.
   - c. Nearly all gender differences are cultural in origin.
   - d. All developmentalists are in agreement about the origin of gender differences.

6. According to Freud, a young boy's jealousy of his father's relationship with his mother, and the guilt feelings that result, are part of the:
   - a. Electra complex.
   - b. Oedipus complex.
   - c. phallic complex.
   - d. penis envy complex.

7. The style of parenting in which the parents make few demands on children, the discipline is lax, and the parents are nurturant and accepting is:
   - a. authoritarian.
   - b. authoritative.
   - c. permissive.
   - d. traditional.

8. Cooperating with a playmate is to _____ as insulting a playmate is to _____ .
   - a. antisocial behavior; prosocial behavior
   - b. prosocial behavior; antisocial behavior
   - c. emotional regulation; antisocial behavior
   - d. prosocial behavior; emotional regulation

9. Which of the following children would probably be said to have a phobia?
   - a. Nicky, who has an exaggerated and irrational fear of furry animals
   - b. Nairobi, who is frightened by loud thunder
   - c. Noriko, who doesn't like getting shots
   - d. All of the above have phobias.

10. Which of the following theories advocates the development of gender identification as a means of avoiding guilt over feelings for the opposite-sex parent?
    - a. behaviorism
    - b. sociocultural
    - c. psychoanalytic
    - d. social learning

11. A parent who wishes to use a time-out to discipline her son for behaving aggressively on the playground would be advised to:
    a. have the child sit quietly indoors for a few minutes.
    b. tell her son that he will be punished later at home.
    c. tell the child that he will not be allowed to play outdoors for the rest of the week.
    d. choose a different disciplinary technique since time-outs are ineffective.

12. The preschooler's readiness to learn new tasks and play activities reflects his or her:
    a. emerging competency and self-awareness.
    b. theory of mind.
    c. relationship with parents.
    d. growing identification with others.

13. Emotional regulation is in part related to maturation of a specific part of the brain in the:
    a. prefrontal cortex.
    b. parietal cortex.
    c. temporal lobe.
    d. occipital lobe.

14. In which style of parenting is the parents' word law and misbehavior strictly punished?
    a. permissive
    b. authoritative
    c. authoritarian
    d. traditional

15. Erikson noted that preschoolers eagerly begin many new activities but are vulnerable to criticism and feelings of failure; they experience the crisis of:
    a. identity versus role confusion.
    b. initiative versus guilt.
    c. basic trust versus mistrust.
    d. efficacy versus helplessness.

Matching Items

Match each term or concept with its corresponding description or definition.

Terms or Concepts

_____ 1. rough-and-tumble play
_____ 2. androgyny
_____ 3. sociodramatic play
_____ 4. prosocial behavior
_____ 5. antisocial behavior
_____ 6. Electra complex
_____ 7. Oedipus complex
_____ 8. authoritative
_____ 9. authoritarian
_____ 10. identification
_____ 11. instrumental aggression

Descriptions or Definitions

a. aggressive behavior whose purpose is to obtain an object desired by another
b. Freudian theory that every daughter secretly wishes to replace her mother
c. parenting style associated with high maturity demands and low parent–child communication
d. an action performed for the benefit of another person without the expectation of reward
e. Freudian theory that every son secretly wishes to replace his father
f. parenting style associated with high maturity demands and high parent–child communication
g. two children wrestle without serious hostility
h. an action that is intended to harm someone else
i. two children act out roles in a story of their own creation
j. a defense mechanism through which children cope with their feelings of guilt during the phallic stage
k. a balance of traditional male and female characteristics in an individual

Thinking Critically About Chapter 10

Answer these questions the day before an exam as a final check on your understanding of the chapter's terms and concepts.

1. Bonita eventually copes with the fear and anger she feels over her hatred of her mother and love of her father by:
   a. identifying with her mother.
   b. copying her brother's behavior.
   c. adopting her father's moral code.
   d. competing with her brother for her father's attention.

2. A little girl who says she wants her mother to go on vacation so that she can marry her father is voicing a fantasy consistent with the _____ described by Freud.
   a. Oedipus complex
   b. Electra complex
   c. theory of mind
   d. crisis of initiative versus guilt

3. According to Erikson, before the preschool years children are incapable of feeling guilt because:
   a. guilt depends on a sense of self, which is not sufficiently established in preschoolers.
   b. they do not yet understand that they are male or female for life.
   c. this emotion is unlikely to have been reinforced at such an early age.
   d. guilt is associated with the resolution of the Oedipus complex, which occurs later in life.

4. Parents who are strict and aloof are *most* likely to make their children:
   a. cooperative and trusting.
   b. obedient but unhappy.
   c. violent.
   d. withdrawn and anxious.

5. When 4-year-old Seema grabs for Vincenzo's Beanie Baby, Vincenzo slaps her hand away, displaying an example of:
   a. bullying aggression.
   b. reactive aggression.
   c. instrumental aggression.
   d. relational aggression.

6. The belief that almost all sexual patterns are learned rather than inborn would find its strongest adherents among:
   a. cognitive theorists.
   b. behaviorists.
   c. psychoanalytic theorists.
   d. epigenetic systems theorists.

7. In explaining the origins of gender distinctions, Dr. Christie notes that every society teaches its children its values and attitudes regarding preferred behavior for men and women. Dr. Christie is evidently a proponent of:
   a. behaviorism.
   b. sociocultural theory.
   c. epigenetic systems theory.
   d. psychoanalytic theory.

8. Five-year-old Rodney has a better-developed sense of self and is more confident than Darnell. According to the text, it is likely that Rodney will also be more skilled at:
   a. tasks involving verbal reasoning.
   b. social interaction.
   c. deception.
   d. all of the above.

9. Summarizing her report on neurological aspects of emotional regulation, Alycia notes that young children who have internalizing problems tend to have greater activity in the:
   a. right temporal lobe
   b. left temporal lobe
   c. right prefrontal cortex
   d. left prefrontal cortex

10. Concerning children's concept of gender, which of the following statements is true?
    a. Before the age of 3 or so, children think that boys and girls can change gender as they get older.
    b. Children as young as 1 year have a clear understanding of the physical differences between girls and boys and can consistently apply gender labels.
    c. Not until age 5 or 6 do children show a clear preference for gender-typed toys.
    d. All of the above are true.

11. Which of the following is *not* a feature of parenting used by Baumrind to differentiate authoritarian, permissive, and authoritative parents?
    a. maturity demands for the child's conduct
    b. efforts to control the child's actions
    c. nurturance
    d. adherence to stereotypic gender roles

12. Seeking to discipline her 3-year-old son for snatching a playmate's toy, Cassandra gently says, "How would you feel if Juwan grabbed your car?" Developmentalists would probably say that Cassandra's approach:
    a. is too permissive and would therefore be ineffective in the long run.
    b. would probably be more effective with a girl.
    c. will be effective in increasing prosocial behavior because it promotes empathy.
    d. will backfire and threaten her son's self-confidence.

13. Five-year-old Curtis, who is above average in height and weight, often picks on children who are smaller than he is. Curtis' behavior is an example of:
    a. bullying aggression.
    b. reactive aggression.
    c. instrumental aggression.
    d. relational aggression.

14. Which of the following is true regarding the effects of spanking?
    a. Spanking seems to reduce reactive aggression.
    b. When administered appropriately, spanking promotes psychosocial development.
    c. Spanking is associated with increased aggression toward peers.
    d. None of the above is true.

15. Aldo and Jack are wrestling and hitting each other. Although this rough-and-tumble play mimics negative, aggressive behavior, it serves a useful purpose, which is to:
    a. rehearse social roles.
    b. develop interactive skills.
    c. improve fine motor skills.
    d. do both b. and c.

Key Terms

Writing Definitions

Using your own words, write a brief definition or explanation of each of the following terms on a separate piece of paper.

1. emotional regulation
2. externalizing problems
3. internalizing problems
4. phobia
5. self-concept
6. self-esteem
7. initiative versus guilt
8. emotional intelligence
9. peers
10. prosocial behavior
11. antisocial behavior
12. empathy
13. aggression
14. instrumental aggression
15. reactive aggression
16. relational aggression
17. bullying aggression
18. rough-and-tumble play
19. sociodramatic play
20. authoritarian parenting
21. permissive parenting
22. authoritative parenting
23. neglectful parenting
24. indulgent parenting
25. time-out
26. sex differences
27. gender differences
28. phallic stage
29. Oedipus complex
30. identification
31. superego
32. Electra complex
33. androgyny

Cross-Check

After you have written the definitions of the key terms in this chapter, you should complete the crossword puzzle to ensure that you can reverse the process—recognize the term, given the definition.

ACROSS

1. Physical play that often mimics aggression but involves no intent to harm.
3. A behavior, such as cooperating or sharing, performed to benefit another person without the expectation of a reward.
8. In psychoanalytic theory, the self-critical and judgmental part of personality that internalizes the moral standards set by parents and society.
9. An exaggerated and irrational fear of an object or experience.
13. Behavior that takes the form of insults or social rejection is called _____ aggression.
15. Act intended to obtain or retain an object desired by another is called _____ aggression.
16. Style of parenting in which parents make few demands on their children yet are nurturant and accepting and communicate well with their children.

DOWN

2. Cultural differences in the roles and behaviors of males and females.
4. Defense mechanism through which a person takes on the role and attitudes of a person more powerful than himself or herself.
5. Ability to manage and modify one's feelings, particularly feelings of fear, frustration, and anger.
6. In Freud's phallic stage of psychosexual development, a boy's sexual attraction toward the mother and resentment of the father.
7. Style of child-rearing in which the parents show little affection or nurturance for their children, maturity demands are high, and parent–child communication is low.
10. In Freud's phallic stage of psychosexual development, a girl's sexual attraction toward the father and resentment of the mother.
11. Style of parenting in which the parents set limits and enforce rules but do so more democratically than do authoritarian parents.
12. Form of aggression involving an unprovoked attack on another child.

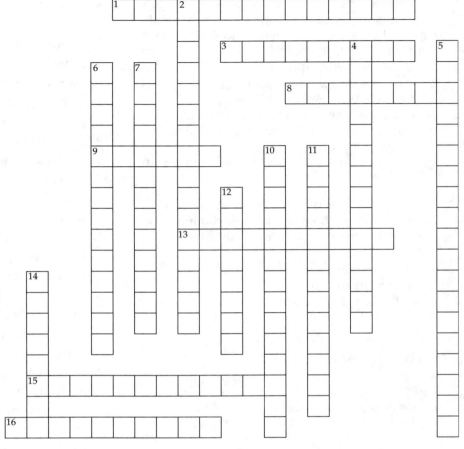

14. Aggressive behavior that is an angry retaliation for some intentional or incidental act by another person.

ANSWERS

CHAPTER REVIEW

1. fear, frustration, anger; emotional regulation; impulses; externalizing; undercontrolled; internalizing
2. are; right prefrontal cortex; left prefrontal cortex
3. neurons; cortisol; lower-than-normal

Prenatal examples of early stress that can inhibit emotional regulation include pregnant women who experience stress, suffer illness, or are heavy drug users. Postnatal examples inlcude if the infant suffered chronic malnourishment, injury, or fear.

4. care experiences
5. phobias; genetic
6. self-concept; self-esteem; favorable; overestimate; in all
7. initiative versus guilt; autonomy; complete; guilt

8. Daniel Goleman; emotional intelligence

9. peers; age; status

10. prosocial behavior; social competence; the making of new friends; violent temper tantrums, uncontrollable crying, and terrifying phobias

11. antisocial behavior; emotional regulation

12. empathy; 4

13. emotional regulation

14. instrumental; reactive; relational; bullying

15. instrumental aggression; reactive aggression; emotional regulation; bullying aggression

16. is; lonely and unwilling to share with others

17. solitary; onlooker; parallel; associative; cooperative

18. rough-and-tumble; is universal; play face; social experience; are

19. sociodramatic; theory of mind; Girls; boys

20. 3

21. higher grades; reading; boys; lower grades; girls
Television takes away from active, interactive, and imaginative play; exposes children to faulty nutritional messages and sexist, racist, and ageist stereotypes; undermines sympathy for emotional pain; and undercuts values that lead to prosocial activity. Video games are worse in that they are more violent, more sexist, and more racist.

22. parenting

23. Baumrind; nurturance; discipline; communicate; maturity

24. authoritarian; low; high; low

25. permissive; are; well; few

26. authoritative; high; well; are; neglectful; indulgent

27. authoritarian; permissive; authoritative; grow stronger

28. temperament; community support

29. proactive; preventive; punitive; reasoning; emotional; time-out; North America

30. Sweden; Caribbean

31. believe; is; aggressive

32. reactive

33. sex; gender; roles

34. less; gender

35. 2; 6; 8

36. phallic stage; mothers; fathers; Oedipus complex

37. identification; superego

38. Electra complex; penis envy

39. reinforced; punished

40. modeling

41. understanding; script

42. sociocultural; traditional; androgyny

43. epigenetic systems; genes; early experience

44. biologically; brains

45. are not; sex hormones; environmental factors

PROGRESS TEST 1

Multiple-Choice Questions

1. **b.** is the answer. (pp. 299–300)

2. **c.** is the answer. (p. 317)

   a. & b. In Freud's theory, the oral and anal stages are associated with infant and early childhood development, respectively.

   d. In Freud's theory, the latency period is associated with development during the school years.

3. **a.** is the answer. (p. 306)

   b. & d. These two types of play are not discussed in this chapter. Mastery play is play that helps children develop new physical and intellectual skills. Sensorimotor play captures the pleasures of using the senses and motor skills.

   c. Rough-and-tumble play is physical play that mimics aggression.

4. **b.** is the answer. (p. 310)

   d. Traditional is a variation of the basic styles uncovered by later research. Indulgent and neglecting are abusive styles and clearly harmful, unlike the styles initially identified by Baumrind.

5. **a.** is the answer. (p. 310)

   b. & c. Authoritative parents communicate very well and are quite affectionate.

   d. This is not typical of authoritative parents.

6. **d.** is the answer. (pp. 308–309)

7. **b.** is the answer. (p. 304)

8. **a.** is the answer. (pp. 299–300)

9. **b.** is the answer. (p. 319)

   a. This is the focus of Freud's phallic stage.

   c. This is the focus of Erikson's psychosocial theory.

   d. This is the focus of cognitive theorists.

10. **a.** is the answer. (p. 316)

11. **c.** is the answer. (p. 301)

12. **d.** is the answer. In accounting for Leonardo's verbal ability, Dr. Laurent alludes to both genetic and environmental factors, a giveaway for epigenetic systems theory. (p. 321)

a., b., & c. These theories do not address biological or genetic influences on development.

13. **d.** is the answer. (p. 296)

    a. & b. Children who display internalizing problems are withdrawn and bottle up their emotions.

    c. Jake is displaying an inability to control his negative emotions.

14. **c.** is the answer. (p. 313)

    a. & b. These strategies are more typical of Japanese mothers.

15. **d.** is the answer. (p. 304)

True or False Items

1. F   All parents make some maturity demands on their children; maturity demands are high in both the authoritarian and authoritative parenting styles. (p. 310)

2. T (p. 311)

3. F   Just the opposite is true. (p. 315)

4. T (p. 314)

5. T (p. 321)

6. T (p. 321)

7. T (pp. 317–321)

8. T (p. 317)

9. T (p. 317)

10. F   The reverse is true; it provides a way for children to learn emotional regulation. (p. 306)

PROGRESS TEST 2

Multiple-Choice Questions

1. **b.** is the answer. (p. 311)

2. **c.** is the answer. (p. 305)

    a. & b. Parents, especially mothers, are more understanding and self-sacrificing than playmates and so less able to teach this lesson.

    d. The text does not indicate that same-sex friends are more important in learning these than friends of the other sex.

3. **c.** is the answer. (pp. 311)

4. **a.** is the answer. (p. 316)

    c. & d. The preference for same-sex playmates is universal.

5. **a.** is the answer. Recent research has found that the sexes are different in part because of subtle differences in brain development. (p. 322)

6. **b.** is the answer. (p. 317)

    a. & d. These are Freud's versions of phallic-stage development in little girls.

    c. There is no such thing as the "phallic complex."

7. **c.** is the answer. (p. 310)

    a. & b. Both authoritarian and authoritative parents make high demands on their children.

    d. This is not one of the three parenting styles. Traditional parents could be any one of these types.

8. **b.** is the answer. (p. 302)

9. **a.** is the answer. Exaggeration and irrationality are two hallmarks of phobias. (pp. 298–299)

    b. & c. Neither of these fears seems exaggerated or irrational.

10. **c.** is the answer. (p. 317)

    a. & d. Behaviorism, which includes social learning theory, emphasizes that children learn about gender by rewards and punishments and by observing others.

    b. Sociocultural theory focuses on the impact of the environment on gender identification.

11. **a.** is the answer. (p. 313)

    b. & c. Time-outs involve removing a child from a situation in which misbehavior has occurred. Moreover, these threats of future punishment would likely be less effective because of the delay between the behavior and the consequence.

    d. Although developmentalists stress the need to prevent misdeeds instead of punishing them, and warn that time-outs may have unintended consequences, they nevertheless can be an effective form of discipline.

12. **a.** is the answer. (pp. 299–300)

    b. This viewpoint is associated only with cognitive theory.

    c. Although parent–child relationships are important to social development, they do not determine readiness.

    d. Identification is a Freudian defense mechanism.

13. **a.** is the answer. (p. 296)

14. **c.** is the answer. (p. 310)

15. **b.** is the answer. (p. 301)

    a. & c. According to Erikson, these are the crises of adolescence and infancy, respectively.

    d. This is not a crisis described by Erikson.

Matching Items

1. g (p. 305)	**5.** h (p. 302)	**9.** c (p. 310)
2. k (p. 321)	**6.** b (p. 318)	**10.** j (p. 317)
3. i (p. 306)	**7.** e (p. 317)	**11.** a (p. 304)
4. d (p. 302)	**8.** f (p. 310)	

THINKING CRITICALLY ABOUT CHAPTER 10

1. **a.** is the answer. (p. 317, 318)

2. **b.** is the answer. (p. 318)

   a. According to Freud, the Oedipus complex refers to the male's sexual feelings toward his mother and resentment toward his father.

   c. & d. These are concepts introduced by cognitive theorists and Erik Erikson, respectively.

3. **a.** is the answer. (p. 301)

   b. Erikson did not equate gender constancy with the emergence of guilt.

   c. & d. These reflect the viewpoints of learning theory and Freud, respectively.

4. **b.** is the answer. (p. 311)

5. **c.** is the answer. The purpose of Vincenzo's action is clearly to retain the Beanie Baby, rather than to retaliate (b) or bully Seema (a). (p. 304)

   d. Relational aggression takes the form of a verbal insult.

6. **b.** is the answer. (p. 319)

7. **b.** is the answer. (pp. 320–321)

8. **b.** is the answer. (p. 299)

   a. & c. The chapter does not link self-understanding with verbal reasoning or deception.

9. **c.** is the answer. (pp. 296–297)

   a. & b. The temporal lobes are involved in speech and hearing rather than emotional regulation.

   d. Children who have externalizing problems tend to have greater activity in this area.

10. **a.** is the answer. (p. 316)

    b. Not until about age 2 can children consistently apply gender labels.

    c. By age 2, children prefer gender-typed toys.

11. **d.** is the answer. (p. 310)

12. **c.** is the answer. (p. 303)

13. **a.** is the answer. (p. 304)

14. **c.** is the answer. (pp. 314)

15. **b.** is the answer. (pp. 305–306)

KEY TERMS

Writing Definitions

1. **Emotional regulation** is the ability to direct or modify one's feelings, particularly feelings of fear, frustration, and anger. (p. 296)

2. Young children who have **externalizing problems** tend to experience emotions outside themselves and lash out at other people or things. (p. 296)

3. Children who have **internalizing problems** tend to be fearful and withdrawn as a consequence of their tendencies to keep their emotions bottled up inside themselves. (p. 296)

4. A **phobia** is an exaggerated and irrational fear of an object or experience. (p. 298)

5. **Self-concept** refers to people's understanding of who they are. (p. 299)

6. **Self-esteem** is pride in oneself. (p. 299)

7. According to Erikson, the crisis of the preschool years is **initiative versus guilt**. In this crisis, young children eagerly take on new tasks and play activities and feel guilty when their efforts result in failure or criticism. (p. 301)

8. **Emotional intelligence** is Goleman's term for a person's understanding of how to interpret and express emotions. (p. 301)

9. **Peers** are people of about the same age and status as oneself. (p. 302)

10. **Prosocial behavior** is an action, such as cooperating or sharing, that is performed to benefit another person without the expectation of reward. (p. 302)

11. **Antisocial behavior** is an action, such as hitting or insulting, that is intended to hurt another person. (p. 302)

12. **Empathy** is a person's ability to understand the emotions of another person. (p. 303)

13. **Aggression** is a form of antisocial behavior characterized by hostile attitudes and hurtful actions stemming from anger or frustration. (p. 303)

14. **Instrumental aggression** is an action whose purpose is to obtain or retain an object desired by another. (p. 304)

15. **Reactive aggression** is aggressive behavior that is an angry retaliation for some intentional or accidental act by another person. (p. 304)

Memory aid: Instrumental aggression is behavior that is *instrumental* in allowing a child to retain a favorite toy. **Reactive aggression** is a *reaction* to another child's behavior.

16. Aggressive behavior that takes the form of verbal insults or social rejection is called **relational aggression**. (p. 304)

17. An unprovoked physical or verbal attack on another child is an example of **bullying aggression**. (p. 304)

18. **Rough-and-tumble play** is physical play that often mimics aggression but involves no intent to harm. (p. 305)

19. In **sociodramatic play**, children act out roles and themes in stories of their own creation, allowing them to examine personal concerns in a non-threatening manner. (p. 306)

20. **Authoritarian parenting** is Baumrind's term for a style of child rearing in which the parents show little affection or nurturance for their children; maturity demands are high and parent–child communication is low. (p. 310)

Memory aid: Someone who is an **authoritarian** demands unquestioning obedience and acts in a dictatorial way.

21. **Permissive parenting** is Baumrind's term for a style of child rearing in which the parents make few demands on their children, yet are nurturant and accepting and communicate well with their children. (p. 310)

22. **Authoritative parenting** is Baumrind's term for a style of child rearing in which the parents set limits and enforce rules but do so more democratically than do authoritarian parents. (p. 310)

Memory aid: **Authoritative parents** act as *authorities* do on a subject—by discussing and explaining why certain family rules are in place.

23. **Neglectful parenting** is an abusive style of parenting in which the parents do not seem to care about their child at all. (p. 311)

24. **Indulgent parenting** is an abusive style of parenting in which parents give in to their child's every whim. (p. 311)

25. A **time-out** is a form of discipline in which a child is required to stop all activity and sit quietly for a few minutes. (p. 313)

26. **Sex differences** are biological differences between females and males. (p. 315)

27. **Gender differences** are cultural differences in the roles and behavior of males and females. (p. 315)

28. In psychoanalytic theory, the **phallic stage** is the third stage of psychosexual development, in which the penis becomes the focus of psychological concerns and physiological pleasure. (p. 317)

29. According to Freud, boys in the phallic stage of psychosexual development develop a collection of feelings, known as the **Oedipus complex**, that center on sexual attraction to the mother and resentment of the father. (p. 317)

30. In Freud's theory, **identification** is the defense mechanism through which a person symbolically takes on the role and attitudes of a person more powerful than himself or herself. (p. 317)

31. In psychoanalytic theory, the **superego** is the self-critical and judgmental part of personality that internalizes the moral standards set by parents and society. (p. 317)

32. According to Freud, girls in the phallic stage may develop a collection of feelings, known as the **Electra complex**, that center on sexual attraction to the father and resentment of the mother. (p. 318)

33. **Androgyny** is a balance of traditionally female and male psychological characteristics in a person. (p. 321)

Cross-Check

ACROSS	DOWN
1. rough-and-tumble	**2.** gender difference
3. prosocial	**4.** identification
8. superego	**5.** emotional regulation
9. phobia	**6.** Oedipus complex
13. relational	**7.** authoritarian
15. instrumental	**10.** Electra complex
16. permissive	**11.** authoritative
	12. bullying
	14. reactivez

Chapter Eleven

The School Years: Biosocial Development

Chapter Overview

This chapter introduces middle childhood, the years from 7 to 11. Changes in physical size and shape are described, and the problem of obesity is addressed. The discussion then turns to the continuing development of motor and intellectual skills during the school years, culminating in an evaluation of intelligence testing. A final section examines the experiences of children with special needs, such as autistic children, children with learning disabilities, and those diagnosed as having attention-deficit hyperactivity disorder. The causes of and treatments for these problems are discussed, with emphasis placed on insights arising from the new developmental psychopathology perspective. This perspective makes it clear that the manifestations of any special childhood problem will change as the child grows older and that treatment must often focus on all three domains of development.

NOTE: Answer guidelines for all Chapter 11 questions begin on page 182.

Guided Study

The text chapter should be studied one section at a time. Before you read, preview each section by skimming it, noting headings and boldface items. Then read the appropriate section objectives from the following outline. Keep these objectives in mind and, as you read the chapter section, search for the information that will enable you to meet each objective. Once you have finished a section, write out answers for its objectives.

A Healthy Time (pp. 331–336)

1. Describe normal physical growth and development during middle childhood, and account for the usual variations among children.

2. Discuss the problems of obese children in middle childhood.

3. Identify the major causes of obesity, and outline the best approaches to treating obesity.

4. Discuss the physical and psychological impact of chronic illness, especially asthma, during middle childhood.

Development of Motor Skills (pp. 336–339)

5. Describe motor-skill development during the school years, focusing on variations due to gender, culture, and genetics.

6. Discuss the role of brain maturation in motor and cognitive development during middle childhood.

Children with Special Needs (pp. 339–355)

7. Explain the new developmental psychopathology perspective, and discuss its value in treating children with special needs.

8. Identify the symptoms of autism, and describe its most effective treatment.

9. Explain how achievement and aptitude tests are used in evaluating individual differences in cognitive growth, and discuss why use of such tests is controversial.

10. (Changing Policy) Describe Sternberg's and Gardner's theories of multiple intelligences, and explain the significance of these theories.

11. Discuss the characteristics of learning disabilities.

12. Describe the symptoms and possible causes of AD/HD (attention-deficit/hyperactivity disorder) and ADD (attention-deficit disorder).

13. Discuss the types of treatment available for children with AD/HD.

14. Describe techniques that have been tried in efforts to educate children with special needs.

Chapter Review

When you have finished reading the chapter, work through the material that follows to review it. Complete the sentences and answer the questions. As you proceed, evaluate your performance for each section by consulting the answers on page 182. Do not continue with the next section until you understand each answer. If you need to, review or reread the appropriate section in the textbook before continuing.

1. Compared with biosocial development during other periods of the life span, biosocial development from 7 to 11, known as

   _____ _____ , is

   _____ (relatively smooth/often

   fraught with problems). For example, disease and death during these years are

   _____ (more common/rarer) than

   during any other period.

A Healthy Time (pp. 331–336)

2. Children grow _____

   (faster/more slowly) during middle childhood than they did earlier or than they will in adolescence. The typical child gains about

   _____ pounds and

   _____ inches per year.

Describe several other features of physical development during the school years.

3. Variations in growth during middle childhood are caused by differences in

   _____ , _____ and

   _____ .

4. Children are said to be overweight when their body weights are _____ (what percent?) above ideal weight for their age and height and obese when when their body weights are

   _____ (what percent?) above their

   ideal weights.

5. Childhood obesity, which is _____ (increasing/decreasing) in the United States, is hazardous to children's health because it reduces

   _____ and increases

   _____ _____ , both of

   which are associated with serious health problems in middle adulthood.

6. Experts estimate that between _____

   and _____ percent of North

   American children are obese.

7. Adopted children are more often overweight when their _____ (adoptive/biological) parents are obese.

Identify several environmental factors that might contribute to childhood obesity.

8. Excessive television watching by children

   _____ (is/is not) directly correlated

   with obesity. When children watch TV, their

   metabolism _____ .

   (slows down/speeds up).

Identify three factors that make television watching fattening.

9. Fasting and/or repeated dieting

   _____ (lowers/raises) the rate of

   metabolism.

10. Strenuous dieting during childhood _____ (is/is not) potentially dangerous.

11. The best way to get children to lose weight is to increase their _____ _____ . Developmentalists agree that treating obesity early in life _____ (is/is not) very important in ensuring the child's overall health later in life.

12. Compared to the past, middle childhood is now a healthier time _____ (in every nation of the world/only in developed nations).

13. During middle childhood, children are _____ (more/less) aware of one another's, or their own, physical imperfections.

14. A chronic inflammatory disorder of the airways is called _____ . It usually disappears by _____ .

15. The causes or triggers of asthma include _____ , _____ , and exposure to _____ such as pet hair.

16. The use of injections, inhalers, and pills to treat asthma is an example of _____ prevention. Less than _____ (how many?) asthmatic children in the United States benefit from this type of treatment. The best approach to treating childhood diseases is _____ _____ , which in the case of asthma includes proper _____ of homes and schools, decreased _____ , eradication of cockroaches, and safe outdoor _____ _____ .

Development of Motor Skills (pp. 336–339)

17. Children become more skilled at controlling their bodies during the school years, in part because they _____ .

18. The length of time it takes a person to respond to a particular stimulus is called _____ _____ . A key factor in this motor skill is _____ _____ .

19. Other important abilities that continue to develop during the school years are _____–_____ _____ , balance, and judgment of _____ .

20. Because during the school years boys have greater _____-_____ strength than girls, they tend to have an advantage in sports such as _____ , whereas girls have an advantage in sports such as _____ .

21. Expertise in athletic skills depends on _____ influences that are rarely the same for boys and girls. Beginning at about age _____ and increasingly until age _____ , gender differences in _____ patterns are dramatic, with boys tending to play in relatively _____ (large/small) groups in organized games that encourage _____ , _____ , and _____ motor skills. In contrast, girls form play groups that are _____ and more _____ , and in which _____ is discouraged and _____ motor skills are emphasized.

22. Many of the sports that adults value _____ (are/are not) well suited for children.

23. Due to _____ differences, some children are simply more gifted in developing specific motor skills.

24. The brain reaches adult size at about age _____ . As the _____ functions of the brain develop, several behaviors that were common in early childhood can be controlled, including _____ _____ . Two other advances in brain function at this time include the ability to _____ , and the _____ of thoughts and actions that are repeated in sequence.

25. Motor habits that rely on coordinating both sides of the body improve because the _____ _____ between the brain's hemispheres continues to mature. Animal research also demonstrates that brain development is stimulated through _____ . In addition, _____ play may help boys overcome their genetic tendencies toward

_____

because it helps with regulation in the _____ _____ of the brain.

Children with Special Needs (pp. 339–355)

26. Among the conditions that give rise to "special needs" are _____

_____ .

27. Down syndrome and other conditions that give rise to "special needs" begin with a _____ anomaly.

28. The process of formally identifying a child with special needs usual begins with a teacher _____ , which may ultimately lead to agreement on an _____ _____ _____ for the child.

29. The field of study that is concerned with childhood psychological disorders is

_____ _____ . This perspective has provided several lessons that apply to all children. Three of these are that _____ is normal; disability _____ (changes/does not change) over time; and adolescence and adulthood may be

_____ .

30. This perspective also has made diagnosticians much more aware of the _____ _____ of childhood problems. This awareness is reflected in the official diagnostic guide of the American Psychiatric Association, which is the _____

_____ .

31. One of the most severe disturbances of early childhood is _____ , a term that Leo

Kanner first used to describe children who are _____ . Autism is an example of a

_____ _____

_____ .

32. Children who have autistic symptoms that are less severe than those in the classic syndrome are sometimes diagnosed with

_____ _____ .

33. Autism is more common in _____ (boys/girls).

34. In early childhood autism, severe deficiencies appear in three areas: _____ ability, _____ _____ , and _____ _____ . The first two deficiencies are usually apparent during

_____ .

35. Some autistic children engage in a type of speech called _____ , in which they repeat, word for word, things they have heard.

36. The unusual play patterns of autistic children are characterized by repetitive _____ and an absence of spontaneous

_____ play.

37. The most devastating problem of autistic children often proves to be the lack of _____ _____ . Autistic children appear to have an inadequate _____

_____ _____ .

38. Unaffected by others' opinions, autistic children also lack _____

_____ .

39. Some children have difficulty in school due to an overall slowness in development; that is, they suffer _____ _____ . If that difficulty _____ (is/is not) attributable to an overall intellectual slowness, a physical handicap, a severely stressful situation, or a lack of basic education, the child is said to have a _____

_____ .

40. The potential to learn a particular skill or body of knowledge is a person's _____ . The

most commonly used tests of this type are
_____ _____ . In the
original version of the most commonly used test
of this type, a person's score was calculated as a
_____ (the child's _____
_____ divided by the child's
_____ _____ and mul-
tiplied by 100 to determine his or her
_____).

41. Tests that are designed to measure what a child
has learned are called _____ tests.
Tests that are designed to measure learning
potential are called _____ tests.

42. Some achievement tests are _____-
_____ , or based on a certain grade
level; others are _____-
_____ , or based on a standard of
performance.

43. Two highly regarded IQ tests are the
_____ _____
_____ _____ and the
_____-_____ .

44. Although IQ tests are quite reliable in predicting
_____ achievement, they are not
designed to identify _____
_____ .

45. (Changing Policy) IQ testing is controversial in
part because no test can measure _____
without also measuring _____ .
Another reason is that a child's test performance
can be affected by nonacademic factors, such as
_____ .

46. (Changing Policy) Robert Sternberg believes that
there are three distinct types of intelligence:
_____ , _____ , and
_____ . Similarly, Howard Gardner
describes _____ (how many?) dis-
tinct intelligences, to which he has recently added
another category, _____ .

47. A disability in reading is called
_____ ; in math, it is called

_____ . Other specific academic
subjects that may show a learning disability are
_____ and _____ .

48. Childhood psychopathology often improves if
the child is carefully taught new patterns of
thought that can become _____ . In
the development of such patterns, the
_____ _____ of the
brain is particularly important.

49. A disability that manifests itself in a difficulty in
concentrating for more than a few moments and a
need to be active, often accompanied by excitability and impulsivity, is called
_____-_____

_____ _____ .
The crucial problem in these conditions seems to
be a neurological difficulty in paying
_____ .

50. About _____ (how many?) of children with learning disabilites also have poor
_____ skills. The presence of more
than one disorder in one person at the same time
is called _____ .

51. Researchers have identified several factors that
may contribute to AD/HD. These include
_____ _____ , prenatal
damage from _____ , and postnatal
damage, such as from
_____
_____ .

52. Children with attention-deficit disorder (ADD)
without hyperactivity appear to be prone to
_____ and _____ .

53. Many children with AD/HD are at increased risk
of developing _____−
_____ and _____
disorders.

54. Developmental and contextual variations in
AD/HD help explain _____ differ-
ences in the frequency of this disorder. For example, children in _____
_____ are less likely to be diag-

nosed as having AD/HD than U.S. children, but they are more likely to be diagnosed with

_____ _____ .

55. In childhood, the most effective forms of treatment for AD/HD are _____ ,

_____ therapy, and changes in the

_____ .

56. Certain drugs that stimulate adults, such as

_____ and _____ ,

have a reverse effect on many hyperactive children.

57. In response to a 1975 Act requiring that children with special needs be taught in the

_____

_____ , the strategy of not separating special-needs children into special classes, called _____ , emerged. More recently, some schools have developed a

_____ _____ , in which such children spend part of each day with a teaching specialist. In the most recent approach, called _____ , learning-disabled children receive targeted help within the setting of a regular classroom.

Progress Test 1

Multiple-Choice Questions

Circle your answers to the following questions and check them with the answers on page 183. If your answer is incorrect, read the explanation for why it is incorrect and then consult the appropriate pages of the text (in parentheses following the correct answer).

1. As children move into middle childhood:
   a. the rate of accidental death increases.
   b. sexual urges intensify.
   c. the rate of weight gain increases.
   d. biological growth slows and steadies.

2. During middle childhood:
   a. girls are usually stronger than boys.
   b. boys have greater physical flexibility than girls.
   c. boys have greater upper-arm strength than girls.
   d. the development of motor skills slows drastically.

3. To help obese children, nutritionists usually recommend:
   a. strenuous dieting to counteract early overfeeding.
   b. the use of amphetamines and other drugs.
   c. more exercise and proper health habits.
   d. no specific actions.

4. A factor that is *not* primary in the development of motor skills during middle childhood is:
   a. practice.   c. brain maturation.
   b. gender.   d. age.

5. Dyslexia is a learning disability that affects the ability to:
   a. do math.   c. write.
   b. read.   d. speak.

6. In relation to weight in later life, childhood obesity is:
   a. not an accurate predictor of adolescent or adult weight.
   b. predictive of adolescent but not adult weight.
   c. predictive of adult but not adolescent weight.
   d. predictive of both adolescent and adult weight.

7. The developmental psychopathology perspective is characterized by its:
   a. contextual approach.
   b. emphasis on the unchanging nature of developmental disorders.
   c. emphasis on the cognitive domain of development.
   d. concern with all of the above.

8. The time—usually measured in fractions of a second—it takes for a person to respond to a particular stimulus is called:
   a. the interstimulus interval.
   b. reaction time.
   c. the stimulus-response interval.
   d. response latency.

9. Researchers have suggested that excessive television watching is a possible cause of childhood obesity because:
   a. children move less while watching TV.
   b. children often snack while watching TV.
   c. body metabolism slows while watching TV.
   d. of all the above reasons.

10. The underlying problem in attention-deficit/hyperactivity disorder appears to be:
    a. low overall intelligence.
    b. a neurological difficulty in paying attention.
    c. a learning disability in a specific academic skill.
    d. the existence of a conduct disorder.

11. Comorbidity refers to:
    a. the presence of more than one disorder in one person at the same time
    b. the teaching of special needs children in a special classroom.
    c. the teaching of special needs children with other children in a regular classroom.
    d. the lifelong struggle in psychological development that special needs children often face.

12. Most of the variation in children's growth can be attributed to:
    a. gender.
    b. nutrition.
    c. genes.
    d. the interaction of the above factors.

13. Autistic children generally have severe deficiencies in all but which of the following?
    a. social skills
    b. imaginative play
    c. echolalia
    d. communication ability

14. Although asthma has genetic origins, several environmental factors contribute to its onset, including:
    a. urbanization.
    b. airtight windows.
    c. dogs and cats living inside the house.
    d. all of the above.

15. Psychoactive drugs are most effective in treating attention-deficit/hyperactivity disorder when they are administered:
    a. before the diagnosis becomes certain.
    b. for several years after the basic problem has abated.
    c. as part of the labeling process.
    d. with psychological support or therapy.

16. Tests that measure a child's potential to learn a new subject are called _____ tests.
    a. aptitude
    b. achievement
    c. vocational
    d. intelligence

17. In the earliest aptitude tests, a child's score was calculated by dividing the child's _____ age by his or her _____ age to find the _____ quotient.
    a. mental; chronological; intelligence
    b. chronological; mental; intelligence
    c. intelligence; chronological; mental
    d. intelligence; mental; chronological

True or False Items

Write *T (true) or F (false)* on the line in front of each statement.

_____ 1. Variations in children's growth are usually caused by diet rather than heredity.

_____ 2. Childhood obesity usually does not correlate with adult obesity.

_____ 3. Research shows a direct correlation between television watching and obesity.

_____ 4. The quick reaction time that is crucial in some sports can be readily achieved with practice.

_____ 5. Despite the efforts of teachers and parents, most children with learning disabilities can expect their disabilities to persist and even worsen as they enter adulthood.

_____ 6. The best way for children to lose weight is through strenuous dieting.

_____ 7. Autistic children have their own, unique theory of mind.

_____ 8. Stressful living conditions is an important consideration in diagnosing a learning disability.

_____ 9. AD/HD is diagnosed more often in Great Britain than in the United States.

_____ 10. The drugs sometimes given to children to reduce hyperactive behaviors have a reverse effect on adults.

Progress Test 2

Progress Test 2 should be completed during a final chapter review. Answer the following questions after you thoroughly understand the correct answers for the Chapter Review and Progress Test 1.

Multiple-Choice Questions

1. During the years from 7 to 11, the average child:
   a. becomes slimmer.
   b. gains about 12 pounds a year.
   c. has decreased lung capacity.
   d. is more likely to become obese than at any other period in the life span.

2. Among the factors that are known to contribute to obesity are activity level, quantity and types of food eaten, and:
   a. a traumatic event.
   b. television watching.
   c. attitudes toward food.
   d. all of the above.

3. A specific learning disability that becomes apparent when a child experiences unusual difficulty in learning to read is:
   a. dyslexia.   c. AD/HD.
   b. dyscalcula.   d. ADD.

4. Problems in learning to write, read, and do math are collectively referred to as:
   a. learning disabilities.
   b. attention-deficit/hyperactivity disorder.
   c. hyperactivity.
   d. dyscalcula.

5. Children are classified as obese if their body weights are _____ percent above the ideal for their ages and heights.
   a. 5   c. 20
   b. 10   d. 30

6. Aptitude and achievement testing are controversial because:
   a. most tests are unreliable with respect to the individual scores they yield.
   b. test performance can be affected by many factors other than the child's intellectual potential or academic achievement.
   c. they often fail to identify serious learning problems.
   d. of all of the above reasons.

7. The most effective form of help for children with AD/HD is:
   a. medication.
   b. psychological therapy.
   c. environmental change.
   d. a combination of some or all of the above.

8. A key factor in reaction time is:
   a. whether the child is male or female.
   b. brain maturation.
   c. whether the stimulus to be reacted to is an auditory or visual one.
   d. all of the above.

9. The first noticeable symptom of autism is usually:
   a. the lack of spoken language.
   b. abnormal social responsiveness.
   c. both a. and b.
   d. unpredictable.

10. Which of the following is true of children with a diagnosed learning disability?
    a. They are, in most cases, average in intelligence.
    b. They often have a specific physical handicap, such as hearing loss.
    c. They often lack basic educational experiences.
    d. All of the above are true.

11. During the school years:
    a. boys are, on average, at least a year ahead of girls in the development of physical abilities.
    b. girls are, on average, at least a year ahead of boys in the development of physical abilities.
    c. boys and girls are about equal in physical abilities.
    d. motor-skill development proceeds at a slower pace, since children grow more rapidly at this age than at any other time.

12. Which approach to education may best meet the needs of learning-disabled children in terms of both skill remediation and social interaction with other children?
    a. mainstreaming
    b. special education
    c. inclusion
    d. resource rooms

13. Asperger syndrome is a disorder in which:
    a. body weight fluctuates dramatically over short periods of time.
    b. verbal skills seem normal, but social perceptions and skills are abnormal.
    c. an autistic child is extremely aggressive.
    d. a child of normal intelligence has difficulty mastering a specific cognitive skill.

14. Which of the following is *not* a contributing factor in most cases of AD/HD?
    a. genetic inheritance
    b. dietary sugar and caffeine
    c. prenatal damage
    d. postnatal damage

15. Tests that measure what a child has already learned are called _____ tests.
    a. aptitude
    b. vocational
    c. achievement
    d. intelligence

16. (Changing Policy) Which of the following is not a type of intelligence identified in Robert Sternberg's theory?
    a. academic   c. achievement
    b. practical   d. creative

Matching Items

Match each term or concept with its corresponding description or definition.

Terms or Concepts

_____ 1. dyslexia
_____ 2. dyscalcula
_____ 3. mental retardation
_____ 4. attention-deficit/hyperactivity disorder
_____ 5. asthma
_____ 6. echolalia
_____ 7. autism
_____ 8. developmental psychopathology
_____ 9. DSM-IV-R
_____ 10. learning disability
_____ 11. mainstreaming
_____ 12. norm-referenced
_____ 13. criterion-referenced

Descriptions or Definitions

a. a test that is assessed relative to a certain group average
b. speech that repeats, word for word, what has just been heard
c. the diagnostic guide of the American Psychiatric Association
d. a pervasive delay in cognitive development
e. system in which learning-disabled children are taught in general education classrooms
f. disorder characterized by the absence of a theory of mind
g. a test that is assessed relative to a certain benchmark or standard
h. chronic inflammation of the airways
i. behavior problem involving difficulty in concentrating, as well as excitability and impulsivity
j. difficulty in math
k. applies insights from studies of normal development to the study of childhood disorders
l. an unexpected difficulty with one or more academic skills
m. difficulty in reading

Thinking Critically About Chapter 11

Answer these questions the day before an exam as a final check on your understanding of the chapter's terms and concepts.

1. According to developmentalists, the best game for a typical group of 8-year-olds would be:
   a. football or baseball.
   b. basketball.
   c. one in which reaction time is not crucial.
   d. a game involving one-on-one competition.

2. Dr. Rutter, who believes that knowledge about normal development can be applied to the study and treatment of psychological disorders, evidently is working from which of the following perspectives?
   a. clinical psychology
   b. developmental psychopathology
   c. behaviorism
   d. psychoanalysis

3. Nine-year-old Jack has difficulty concentrating on his classwork for more than a few moments, repeatedly asks his teacher irrelevant questions, and is constantly disrupting the class with loud noises. If his difficulties persist, Jack is likely to be diagnosed as suffering from:
   a. dyslexia.
   b. dyscalcula.
   c. autism.
   d. attention-deficit/hyperactivity disorder.

4. Angela was born in 1984. In 1992, she scored 125 on an intelligence test. Using the original formula, what was Angela's mental age when she took the test?
   a. 6   c. 10
   b. 8   d. 12

5. Ten-year-old Clarence is quick-tempered, easily frustrated, and is often disruptive in the classroom. Clarence may be suffering from:
   a. dyslexia.
   b. dyscalcula.
   c. attention-deficit disorder.
   d. attention-deficit/hyperactivity disorder.

6. Because 11-year-old Wayne is obese, he runs a greater risk of developing:
   a. heart problems.
   b. diabetes.
   c. psychological problems.
   d. all of the above.

7. Of the following individuals, who is likely to have the fastest reaction time?
   a. a 7-year-old   c. an 11-year-old
   b. a 9-year-old   d. an adult

8. Harold weighs about 20 pounds more than his friend Jay. During school recess, Jay can usually be found playing soccer with his classmates, while Harold sits on the sidelines by himself. Harold's rejection is likely due to his:
   a. being physically different.
   b. being dyslexic.
   c. intimidation of his schoolmates.
   d. being hyperactive.

9. In determining whether an 8-year-old has a learning disability, a teacher looks primarily for:
   a. significantly below normal performance in a subject area.
   b. the exclusion of other explanations.
   c. a family history of the learning disability.
   d. both a. and b.

10. When she moved her practice to England, Dr. Williams was struck by the fact that British doctors seemingly applied the criteria she used to diagnose AD/HD to diagnose:
    a. dyslexia.
    b. dyscalcula.
    c. conduct disorder.
    d. antisocial personality.

11. If you were to ask an autistic child with echolalia, "what's your name?" the child would probably respond by saying:
    a. nothing.
    b. "what's your name?"
    c. "your name what's?"
    d. something that was unintelligible.

12. Although 12-year-old Brenda is quite intelligent, she has low self-esteem and few friends, and is often teased. Knowing nothing else about Brenda, you conclude that she may be:
    a. unusually aggressive.   c. arrogant.
    b. obese.   d. socially inept.

13. Danny has been diagnosed as having attention-deficit/hyperactivity disorder. Every day his parents make sure that he takes the proper dose of Ritalin. His parents should:
    a. continue this behavior until Danny is an adult.
    b. try different medications when Danny seems to be reverting to his normal overactive behavior.
    c. make sure that Danny also has psychotherapy.
    d. not worry about Danny's condition; he will outgrow it.

14. In concluding her presentation entitled "Facts and falsehoods regarding childhood obesity," Cheryl states that, contrary to popular belief, _____ is *not* a common cause of childhood obesity.
    a. television watching
    b. lack of exercise
    c. overeating of high-fat foods
    d. a prenatal teratogen

15. Raymond's score on a standardized test indicated that his ability equals that of a typical fifth-grade student. The test Raymond took evidently was:
    a. criterion-referenced.
    b. norm-referenced.
    c. an aptitude test.
    d. all of the above.

16. (Changing Policy) Howard Gardner and Robert Sternberg would probably be most critical of traditional aptitude and achievement tests because they:
    a. inadvertently reflect certain nonacademic competencies.
    b. do not reflect knowledge of cultural ideas.
    c. measure only a limited set of abilities.
    d. underestimate the intellectual potential of disadvantaged children.

Key Terms

Using your own words, write a brief definition or explanation of each of the following terms on a separate piece of paper.

1. middle childhood
2. overweight
3. obesity
4. asthma
5. reaction time
6. automatization
7. child with special needs
8. individual education plan (IEP)
9. developmental psychopathology
10. DSM-IV
11. pervasive developmental disorders
12. autism
13. Asperger syndrome
14. mental retardation
15. learning disability
16. aptitude test
17. IQ test
18. achievement test
19. norm-refernced
20. criterion-referenced
21. Wechsler Intelligence Scale for Children (WISC)
22. dyslexia
23. dyscalcula
24. comorbidity
25. AD/HD (attention-deficit hyperactivity disorder)
26. attention-deficit disorder (ADD)
27. mainstreaming
28. least restrive environment (LRE)
29. resource room
30. inclusion

ANSWERS
CHAPTER REVIEW

1. middle childhood; relatively smooth; rarer
2. more slowly; 5 to 7; 2

During the school years, children generally become slimmer, muscles become stronger, and lung capacity increases.

3. genes; gender; nutrition
4. 20; 30
5. increasing; exercise; blood pressure
6. 20; 30
7. biological

Factors that contribute to childhood obesity include lack of exercise, poor-quality food, too many hours watching television, and the unhealthy foods served during major holiday celebrations.

8. is; slows down

While watching television, children (a) consume many snacks, (b) move less, and (c) burn fewer calories than they would if they were actively playing.

9. lowers

10. is

11. physical activity; is

12. in every nation of the world

13. more

14. asthma; late adolescence

15. genes; infections; allergens

16. tertiary; half; primary prevention; ventilation; pollution; play spaces

17. grow more slowly

18. reaction time; brain maturation

19. hand–eye coordination; movement

20. upper-arm; baseball; gymnastics

21. cultural; 4; 12; play; large; conflict; rivalry; gross; smaller; intimate; competition; fine

22. are not

23. hereditary

24. 7; executive; emotional outbursts, perseverance, inattention, and the insistence on routines; attend to information from many areas of the brain at once; automatization

25. corpus callosum; play; rough-and-tumble; hyperactivity and learning disabilities; frontal lobes

26. aggression, anxiety, autism, conduct disorder, depression, developmental delay, learning disabilities, Down syndrome, atttachment disorder, attention-deficit disorder, bipolar disorder, and Asperger syndome

27. biological

28. referral; individual education plan (IEP)

29. developmental psychopathology; abnormality; changes; better or worse

30. social context; *Diagnostic and Statistical Manual of Mental Disorders* (DSM-IV-R)

31. autism; self-absorbed; pervasive developmental disorder

32. Asperger syndrome

33. boys

34. communication; social skills; imaginative play; infancy

35. echolalia

36. movements; rough-and-tumble or sociodramatic

37. social understanding; theory of mind

38. emotional regulation

39. mental retardation; is not; learning disability

40. aptitude; IQ tests; quotient; mental age; chronological age; IQ

41. achievement; aptitude

42. norm-referenced; criterion-referenced

43. Wechsler Intelligence Scale for Children (WISC); Stanford-Binet

44. school; particular learning or behavioral problems

45. aptitude; achievement; the ability to pay attention and concentrate, to express thoughts verbally, and to ask questions of a stranger if instructions are unclear

46. academic; creative; practical; seven; naturalistic

47. dyslexia; dyscalcula; spelling; handwriting

48. automatic; prefrontal cortex

49. attention-deficit/hyperactivity disorder; attention

50. half; social; comorbidity

51. genetic vulnerability; teratogens; lead poisoning

52. anxiety; depression

53. oppositional–defiant; conduct

54. cultural; Great Britain; conduct disorder

55. medication; psychological; family and school environment

56. amphetamines; methylphenidate (Ritalin)

57. least restrictive environment (LRE); mainstreaming; resource room; inclusion

PROGRESS TEST 1

Multiple-Choice Questions

1. **d.** is the answer. (p. 331)

2. **c.** is the answer. (p. 337)

   a. Especially in forearm strength, boys are usually stronger than girls during middle childhood.

   b. During middle childhood, girls usually have greater overall flexibility than boys.

   d. Motor-skill development improves greatly during middle childhood.

3. **c.** is the answer. (p. 334)

   a. Strenuous dieting can be physically harmful and often makes children irritable, listless, and even sick—adding to the psychological problems of the obese child.

   b. Although not specifically mentioned in the text, the use of amphetamines to control weight is not recommended at any age.

4. **b.** Boys and girls are just about equal in physical abilities during the school years. (p. 337)

5. **b.** is the answer. (p. 349)

   a. This is dyscalcula.

   c. & d. The text does not give labels for learning disabilities in writing or speaking.

6. **d.** is the answer. (p. 334)

7. **a.** is the answer. (p. 342)

   b. & c. Because of its contextual approach, developmental psychopathology emphasizes *all* domains of development. Also, it points out that behaviors change over time.

8. **b.** is the answer. (p. 336)

9. **d.** is the answer. (p. 333)

10. **b.** is the answer. (pp. 351)

11. **a.** is the answer. (p. 351)

12. **d.** is the answer. (p. 332)

    a. The amount of daily exercise a child receives is an important factor in his or her tendency toward obesity; exercise, however, does not explain most of the variation in childhood physique.

    b. In some parts of the world malnutrition accounts for most of the variation in physique; this is not true of developed countries, where most children get enough food to grow as tall as their genes allow.

13. **c.** is the answer. Echolalia *is* a type of communication difficulty, a characteristic form of speech of many autistic children. (p. 344)

14. **d.** is the answer. (p. 335)

15. **d.** is the answer. (pp. 352–353)

16. **a.** is the answer. (p. 346)

    b. Achievement tests measure what has already been learned.

    c. Vocational tests, which, as their name implies, measure what a person has learned about a particular trade, are achievement tests.

    d. Intelligence tests measure general aptitude, rather than aptitude for a specific subject.

17. **a.** is the answer. (p. 346)

True or False Items

1. F Variations in children's growth are caused by heredity and gender as well as nutrition. (p. 332)

2. F If obesity is established in middle childhood, it tends to continue into adulthood. (p. 334)

3. T (p. 333)

4. F Reaction time depends on brain maturation and is not readily affected by practice. (p. 336)

5. F With the proper assistance, many learning-disabled children develop into adults who are virtually indistinguishable from other adults in their educational and occupational achievements. (pp. 343)

6. F Strenuous dieting during childhood can be dangerous. The best way to get children to lose weight is by increasing their activity level. (p. 333)

7. F Autistic children seem to lack a theory of mind. (p. 344)

8. F Stressful living conditions must be excluded before diagnosing a learning disability. (p. 346)

9. F AD/HD is more often diagnosed in the United States than in Great Britain. (p. 352)

10. T (p. 352)

PROGRESS TEST 2

Multiple-Choice Questions

1. **a.** is the answer. (p. 332)

   b. & c. During this period children gain about 5 pounds per year and experience increased lung capacity.

   d. Although childhood obesity is a common problem, the text does not indicate that a person is more likely to become obese at this age than at any other.

2. **b.** is the answer. (p. 333)

3. **a.** is the answer. (p. 349)

   b. This learning disability involves math rather than reading.

   c. & d. These disorders do not manifest themselves in a particular academic skill but instead appear in psychological processes that affect learning in general.

4. **a.** is the answer. (p. 346)

   b. & c. AD/HD is a general learning disability that usually does not manifest itself in specific subject areas. Hyperactivity is a facet of this disorder.

   d. Dyscalcula is a learning disability in math only.

5. **d.** is the answer. (p. 332)

   a. & b. These children would be considered to be of normal body weight.

   c. These children would be considered overweight.

6. **b.** is the answer. (pp. 346–347)

7. **d.** is the answer. (p. 352)

8. **b.** is the answer. (p. 336)

9. **c.** is the answer. (p. 344)

10. **a.** is the answer. (p. 346)

11. **c.** is the answer. (p. 337)

12. c. is the answer. (p. 354)

a. Many general education teachers are unable to cope with the special needs of some children.

b. & d. These approaches undermined the social integration of children with special needs.

13. b. is the answer. (p. 343)

14. b. is the answer. (p. 351)

15. c. is the answer. (p. 346)

16. c. is the answer. (p. 348)

Matching Items

1. m (p. 349)	**6.** b (p. 344)	**11.** e (p. 353)
2. j (p. 349)	**7.** f (p. 343)	**12.** a (p. 346)
3. d (p. 346)	**8.** k (p. 342)	**13.** g (p. 346)
4. i (p. 351)	**9.** c (p. 343)	
5. h (p. 335)	**10.** l (p. 346)	

THINKING CRITICALLY ABOUT CHAPTER 11

1. c. is the answer. (p. 336)

a. & b. Each of these games involves skills that are hardest for schoolchildren to master.

d. Because one-on-one sports are likely to accentuate individual differences in ability, they may be especially discouraging to some children.

2. b. is the answer. (p. 342)

3. d. is the answer. (p. 351)

a. & b. Jack's difficulty is in concentrating, not in reading (dyslexia) or math (dyscalcula).

c. Autism is characterized by a lack of communication skills.

4. c. is the answer. At the time she took the test, Angela's chronological age was 8. Knowing that her IQ was 125, we can solve the equation to yield a mental age value of 10. (p. 346)

5. d. is the answer. (p. 351)

6. d. is the answer. (p. 332)

7. d. is the answer. (p. 336)

8. a. is the answer. (p. 334)

b., c., & d. Obese children are no more likely to be dyslexic, physically intimidating, or hyperactive than other children.

9. d. is the answer. (p. 346)

10. c. is the answer. (p. 352)

11. b. is the answer. (p. 344)

12. b. is the answer. (p. 334)

13. c. is the answer. Medication alone cannot ameliorate all the problems of AD/HD. (pp. 352–353)

14. d. is the answer. There is no evidence that teratogens have anything to do with obesity. (p. 333)

15. b. is the answer.(p. 346)

a. Criterion-referenced tests specify a certain standard of performance rather than comparing a child's performance to that of others.

c. Aptitude tests measure the potential to learn rather than how much material has already been mastered.

16. c. is the answer. Both Sternberg and Gardner believe that there are multiple intelligences rather than the narrowly defined abilities measured by traditional aptitude and achievement tests. (p. 348)

a., b., & d. Although these criticisms are certainly valid, they are not specifically associated with Sternberg or Gardner.

KEY TERMS

1. **Middle childhood** is the period from age 7 to 11. (p. 331)

2. Children whose body weights are 20–29 percent above those considered ideal for their ages and heights are designated as **overweight**. (p. 332)

3. Children whose body weights are 30 percent or more above those that are ideal for their ages and heights are designated as **obese**. (p. 332)

4. **Asthma** is a disorder in which the airways are chronically inflamed. (p. 335)

5. **Reaction time** is the length of time it takes a person to respond to a particular stimulus. (p. 336)

6. **Automatization** is the process by which thoughts and actions that are repeated often enough to become routine no longer require much conscious thought. (p. 338)

7. A **child with special needs** requires particular physical, intellectual, or social accommodations in order to learn. (p. 340)

8. An **individual education plan (IEP)** is a legal document that specifies a set of educational goals for a child with special needs. (p. 342)

9. **Developmental psychopathology** is a new field that applies the insights from studies of normal development to the study and treatment of childhood disorders, and vice versa. (p. 342)

10. The fourth edition of the *Diagnostic and Statistical Manual of Mental Disorders* (DSM-IV-R), developed by the American Psychiatric Association, is the leading means of distinguishing various emotional and behavioral disorders. (p. 343)

11. A **pervasive developmental disorder,** such as autism, is one that affects numerous aspects of the psychological growth of a child under age 3. (p. 343)

12. **Autism** is a severe disturbance of early childhood characterized by an inability to communicate with others in an ordinary way, by extreme self-absorption, and by an inability to learn normal speech. (p. 343)

13. **Asperger syndrome** is a disorder in which a person has many symptoms of autism, despite having near normal speech and intelligence. (p. 343)

14. **Mental retardation** is a pervasive delay in cognitive development. (p. 346)

15. A **learning disability** is a difficulty in a particular cognitive skill that is not attributable to overall intellectual slowness, a physical handicap, a severely stressful living condition, or a lack of basic education. (p. 346)

16. **Aptitude** is the potential to learn a particular skill or body of knowledge. (p. 346)

17. **IQ tests** are aptitude tests, which were originally designed to yield a measure of intelligence and calculated as mental age divided by chronological age, multiplied by 100. (p. 346)

18. **Achievement tests** are tests that measure what a child has already learned in a particular academic subject or subjects. (p. 346)

19. An achievement test that is **norm-referenced** is based on a certain level of achivement that is usual, such as grade level.(p. 346)

20. An achievement test that is **criterion-referenced** is based on a specific standard of performance, such as how well a child reads. (p. 346)

21. The **Wechsler Intelligence Scale for Children (WISC)** is a widely used IQ test that assesses vocabulary, general knowledge, memory, and spatial comprehension. (p. 347)

22. **Dyslexia** is a learning disability in reading. (p. 349)

23. **Dyscalcula** is a learning disability in math. (p. 349)

24. **Comorbidity** refers to the presence of more than one disorder in a person at the same time. (p. 351)

25. **AD/HD (attention-deficit/hyperactivity disorder)** is a behavior problem in which the individual has great difficulty concentrating and is often excessively excitable, impulsive, and overactive. (p. 351)

26. **ADD (attention-deficit disorder)** is a condition in which a child has great difficulty concentrating but is not impulsive or overactive. (p. 351)

27. **Mainstreaming** is an educational approach in which children with special needs are included in regular classrooms. (p. 353)

28. A **least restrictive environment (LRE)** is a school setting that offers special-needs children as much freedom as possible to benefit from the instruction available to other children, often in a mainstreamed classroom. (p. 353)

29. A **resource room** is a classroom equipped with special material, in which children with special needs spend part of their day working with a trained specialist in order to learn basic skills. (p. 354)

30. **Inclusion** is an educational approach in which children with special needs receive individualized instruction within a regular classroom setting. (p. 354)

Chapter Twelve

Chapter Overview

Chapter 12 examines the development of cognitive abilities in children from age 7 to 11. The first section discusses the views of Piaget and Vygotsky regarding the child's cognitive development, which involves a growing ability to use logic and reasoning (as emphasized by Piaget) and to benefit from social interactions with skilled mentors (as emphasized by Vygotsky). The second section focuses on changes in the child's processing speed and capacity, control processes, knowledge base, and metacognition.

The third section looks at language development during middle childhood. During this time, children develop a more analytic understanding of words and show a marked improvement in their language skills, such as changing from one form of speech to another when the situation so demands.

Because the school years are also a time of expanding moral reasoning, the next section examines Kohlberg's stage theory of moral development as well as current reevaluations of his theory. The last section covers educational and environmental conditions that are conducive to learning by schoolchildren, including fluency in a second language. The chapter concludes by examining variations in school policies and structures.

NOTE: Answer guidelines for all Chapter 12 questions begin on page 198.

Guided Study

The text chapter should be studied one section at a time. Before you read, preview each section by skimming it, noting headings and boldface items. Then read the appropriate section objectives from the following outline. Keep these objectives in mind and, as you read the chapter section, search for the information that will enable you to meet each objective. Once you have finished a section, write out answers for its objectives.

Building on Piaget and Vygotsky (pp. 359–363)

1. Identify and discuss the logical operations of concrete operational thought, and give examples of how these operations are demonstrated by schoolchildren.

2. Discuss Vygotsky's views regarding the influence of the sociocultural context on learning during middle childhood.

Information Processing (pp. 363–367)

3. Describe the components of the information-processing system, noting how they interact.

4. Explain how processing speed increases in middle childhood as the result of advances in automatization and a larger knowledge base.

5. Discuss advances in the control processes, especially metacognition, during middle childhood.

Language (pp. 367–372)

6. Describe the development of language during the school years, noting changing abilities in vocabulary and code switching.

Moral Development (pp. 373–379)

7. Outline Kohlberg's stage theory of moral development.

8. Identify and evaluate several criticisms of Kohlberg's theory, and discuss sociocultural effects on moral development.

Schools, Values, and Research (pp. 380–389)

9. Differentiate several approaches to teaching reading and math, and discuss evidence regarding the effectiveness of these methods.

10. Identify several conditions that foster the learning of a second language, and describe the best approaches to bilingual education.

11. Discuss the concept of a hidden curriculum and the merits of smaller class size, educational standards, and testing.

Chapter Review

When you have finished reading the chapter, work through the material that follows to review it. Complete the sentences and answer the questions. As you proceed, evaluate your performance for each section by consulting the answers on page 198. Do not continue with the next section until you understand each answer. If you need to, review or reread the appropriate section in the textbook before continuing.

Building on Piaget and Vygotsky (pp. 359–363)

1. According to Piaget, between ages 7 and 11, children are in the stage of _____

   _____ _____ .

   Vygotsky was critical of Piaget's view of the child as a _____ isolated learner.

2. The concept that objects can be organized into categories according to some common property is

   _____ .

   The concept that a particular object or person may belong to more than one class is

   _____ _____ .

3. Younger children have particular difficulty with the relations between _____ and

   _____ . Eventually, however, they come to understand that categories or subcategories can be _____ ,

   _____ , and _____ .

4. The logical principle that certain characteristics of an object remain the same even when other characteristics change is _____ . The idea that a transformation process can be reversed to restore the original condition is

   _____ .

5. Many concrete operations underlie the basic ideas of elementary-school _____ and

   _____ ; they are also relevant to everyday _____ encounters.

6. Cross-cultural studies of classification and other logical processes demonstrate that these principles _____ (apply/do not apply) throughout the world.

7. Contemporary developmentalists believe that Piaget underestimated the influence of

   _____ , _____ , and

   _____ on cognitive development. In doing so, he also underestimated the

   _____ in development from one child to another.

Information Processing (pp. 363–367)

8. The idea that the advances in thinking that accompany middle childhood occur because of basic changes in how children take in, store, and process data is central to the _____-

   _____ theory.

9. Incoming stimulus information is held for a split second in the _____

   _____ , after which most of it is lost.

10. Meaningful material is transferred into

    _____ _____ , which is

    sometimes called _____-

    _____ _____ . This part of memory handles mental activity that is

    _____ .

11. The part of memory that stores information for days, months, or years is _____-_____ _____ . Crucial in this component of the system is not only storage of the material but also its _____ .

12. Children in the school years are better learners and problem solvers than younger children are, because they have faster _____ _____ , and they have a larger _____ _____ .

13. One reason for the cognitive advances of middle childhood is _____ maturation, especially the _____ of nerve pathways and the development of the _____ _____ .

14. Processing capacity also becomes more efficient through _____ , as familiar mental activities become routine.

15. Memory ability improves during middle childhood in part because of the child's expanded _____ _____ .

16. Research suggests that high-IQ children _____ (are/are not) always more cognitively competent than low-IQ children, and that a larger _____ _____ may be sufficient to overcome slower thinking.

17. The mechanisms of the information-processing system that regulate the analysis and flow of information are the _____ _____ .

18. The ability to use _____ _____—to screen out distractors and concentrate on relevant information—improves steadily during the school years and beyond.

19. The ability to evaluate a cognitive task to determine what to do—and to monitor one's performance—is called _____ .

Language (pp. 367–372)

20. During middle childhood, some children learn as many as _____ new words a day. There is a powerful linkage between early exposure to _____ _____ and later vocabulary performance in school.

21. Schoolchildren's love of words is evident in their _____ , secret _____ , and _____ that they create.

22. Changing from one form of speech to another is called _____-_____ . The _____ _____ , which children use in situations such as the classroom, is characterized by extensive _____ , complex _____ , and lengthy _____ . With their friends, children tend to use the _____ _____ , which has a more limited use of vocabulary and syntax and relies more on _____ and _____ to convey meaning.

23. Compared with the formal code, which is context-_____ (free/bound), the informal code is context-_____ (free/bound). While adults often stress the importance of mastery of the formal code, the informal code is also evidence of the child's _____ .

Moral Development (pp. 373–379)

24. The theorist who has extensively studied moral development by presenting subjects with stories that pose ethical dilemmas is _____ . According to his theory, the three levels of moral reasoning are _____ , _____ , and _____ .

25. (Table 12.3) In preconventional reasoning, emphasis is on getting _____ and avoiding _____ . "Might makes right" describes stage _____ (1/2),

whereas "look out for number one" describes stage _____ (1/2).

26. (Table 12.3) In conventional reasoning, emphasis is on _____ _____ , such as being a dutiful citizen, in stage _____ (3/4), or winning approval from others, in stage _____ (3/4).

27. (Table 12.3) In postconventional reasoning, emphasis is on _____ _____ , such as _____ _____ (stage 5) and _____ _____ _____ (stage 6).

28. During middle childhood, children's moral reasoning generally falls at the _____ and _____ levels.

29. Kohlberg's basic ideas—that moral reasoning advances in _____ and is influenced by _____ _____— have been _____ (confirmed/refuted).

30. One criticism of Kohlberg's theory was that his research methods were _____ . A second is that the later stages reflect values associated with _____ _____ . A third is that Kohlberg ignored the moral development of _____ .

31. To avoid the methodological limitations of moral dilemmas, James Rest developed a questionnaire called the _____ _____ _____ .

32. It is now well established that different cultures _____ (have/do not have) distinctive morals and values.

33. Carol Gilligan believes that females develop a _____ _____ _____ , based on concern for the well-being of others, more than a _____ _____

_____ , based on depersonalized standards of right and wrong.

34. Most researchers believe that abstract reasoning about hypothetical moral dilemmas _____ (is/is not) the only way to measure moral judgment. What children _____ (do/say) is more reflective of moral thinking than what they might _____ (do/say).

Schools, Values, and Research (pp. 380–389)

35. There _____ (is/is not) universal agreement on how best to educate schoolchildren. Internationally and historically, there has been agreement that schools should teach _____ , _____ , and _____ .

36. Two distinct approaches to teaching reading are the _____ approach, in which children learn the sounds of letters first, and the _____-_____ approach, in which children are encouraged to develop all their language skills at the same time.

37. In the United States, math was traditionally taught through _____ _____ . A more recent approach replaces this type of learning by emphasizing _____ .

38. Most of the world's children _____ (learn/do not learn) a second language. The best time to learn a second language by listening and talking is during _____ , and the best time to teach a second language is during _____ _____ .

39. The approach to bilingual education in which the child's instruction occurs entirely in the second language is called _____ _____ . In _____ _____ programs, the child is taught first in his or her native language, until the second language is taught as a "foreign" language.

40. (Table 12.4) In ESL, or _____ _____ programs, children must master the basics of English before joining regular classes with other children. In contrast, _____ _____ requires that teachers instruct children in both their native language as well as in English. An approach to teaching a second language that recognizes the importance of nonnative cultural strategies in learning is called _____– _____ _____ .

41. Immersion programs were successful in _____ , when English-speaking children were initially placed in French-only classrooms. In Guatemala, however, _____ _____ (which strategy?) seems to work best in teaching children a second language. Immersion tends to fail if the child feels _____ , _____ , or _____ _____ .

42. The crucial difference between success and failure in second-language learning rests with _____ _____ , who indicate to the children whether learning a second language is really valued. When both languges are valued, _____ _____ is likely to occur.

43. Middle childhood is a prime time for teaching children _____ as well as specific academic subjects.

44. Every culture creates its own _____ _____ , the unofficial priorities that influence every aspect of school learning.

45. The evidence supporting the popular assumption that smaller class size results in better learning is _____ (strong/weak).

46. Experts _____ (agree/disagree) about what educational standards should be and how they should be measured.

Progress Test 1

Multiple-Choice Questions

Circle your answers to the following questions and check them with the answers on page 199. If your answer is incorrect, read the explanation for why it is incorrect and then consult the appropriate pages of the text (in parentheses following the correct answer).

1. According to Piaget, the stage of cognitive development in which a person understands specific logical ideas and can apply them to concrete problems is called:
   a. preoperational thought.
   b. operational thought.
   c. concrete operational thought.
   d. formal operational thought.

2. Which of the following is the *most* direct reason that thinking speed continues to increase throughout adolescence?
   a. the increasing myelination of neural axons
   b. the continuing development of the frontal cortex
   c. learning from experience
   d. neurological maturation

3. The idea that an object that has been transformed in some way can be restored to its original form by undoing the process is:
   a. identity.   c. total immersion.
   b. reversibility.   d. automatization.

4. Information-processing theorists contend that major advances in cognitive development occur during the school years because:
   a. the child's mind becomes more like a computer as he or she matures.
   b. children become better able to process and analyze information.
   c. most mental activities become automatic by the time a child is about 13 years old.
   d. the major improvements in reasoning that occur during the school years involve increased long-term memory capacity.

5. The ability to filter out distractions and concentrate on relevant details is called:
   a. metacognition.
   b. information processing.
   c. selective attention.
   d. decentering.

6. Concrete operational thought is Piaget's term for the school-age child's ability to:
   a. reason logically about things and events he or she perceives.
   b. think about thinking.
   c. understand that certain characteristics of an object remain the same when other characteristics are changed.
   d. understand that moral principles may supercede the standards of society.

7. The term for the ability to monitor one's cognitive performance—to think about thinking—is:
   a. pragmatics.
   b. information processing.
   c. selective attention.
   d. metacognition.

8. Long-term memory is _____ permanent and _____ limited than working memory.
   a. more; less
   b. less; more
   c. more; more
   d. less; less

9. In making moral choices, according to Gilligan, females are more likely than males to:
   a. score at a higher level in Kohlberg's system.
   b. emphasize the needs of others.
   c. judge right and wrong in absolute terms.
   d. formulate abstract principles.

10. Compared to more advantaged children, children from low-income families show deficits in their development of:
    a. vocabulary.
    b. syntax.
    c. sentence length.
    d. all the above.

11. The formal code that children use in the classroom is characterized by:
    a. limited use of vocabulary and syntax.
    b. context-bound grammar.
    c. extensive use of gestures and intonation to convey meaning.
    d. extensive vocabulary, complex syntax, and lengthy sentences.

12. Which of the following is *not* an approach used in the United States to avoid the shock of complete immersion in the teaching of English?
    a. reverse immersion
    b. English as a second language
    c. bilingual education
    d. bilingual–bicultural education

13. Code-switching occurs most often among:
    a. low-income children.
    b. affluent children.
    c. ethnic minority children.
    d. Children of all backgrounds and ethnicities code-switch.

14. Between 9 and 11 years of age, children are most likely to demonstrate moral reasoning at which of Kohlberg's stages?
    a. preconventional
    b. conventional
    c. postconventional
    d. It is impossible to predict based only on a child's age.

15. Of the following, which was not identified as an important factor in the difference between success and failure in second-language learning?
    a. the age of the child
    b. the attitudes of the parents
    c. community values regarding second language learning
    d. the difficulty of the language

True or False Items

Write T (*true*) or F (*false*) on the line in front of each statement.

_____ 1. A major objection to Piaget's theory is that he underestimated the influence of context, instruction, and culture.

_____ 2. Learning a second language fosters children's overall linguistic and cognitive development.

_____ 3. During middle childhood, children are passionately concerned with issues of right and wrong.

_____ 4. As a group, Japanese, Chinese, and Korean children outscore children in the United States and Canada in math and science.

_____ 5. The process of telling a joke involves remembering the right words and their sequence, a skill usually not mastered before age 6 or 7.

_____ 6. Code switching, especially the occasional use of slang, is a behavior characteristic primarily of children in the lower social strata.

_____ 7. The best time to learn a second language by listening and talking is during middle childhood.

_____ 8. Most information that comes into the sensory register is lost or discarded.

_____ 9. Information-processing theorists believe that advances in the thinking of school-age children occur primarily because of changes in long-term memory.

_____ 10. New standards of math education in many nations emphasize problem-solving skills rather than simple memorization of formulas.

Progress Test 2

Progress Test 2 should be completed during a final chapter review. Answer the following questions after you thoroughly understand the correct answers for the Chapter Review and Progress Test 1.

Multiple-Choice Questions

1. According to Piaget, 8- and 9-year-olds can reason only about concrete things in their lives. "Concrete" means:
   a. logical.
   b. abstract.
   c. tangible or specific.
   d. mathematical or classifiable.

2. Research regarding Piaget's theory has found that:
   a. cognitive development seems to be considerably less affected by sociocultural factors than Piaget's descriptions imply.
   b. the movement to a new level of thinking is much more erratic than Piaget predicted.
   c. there is no dramatc shift in the thinking of children when they reach the age of 5.
   d. all of the above are true.

3. The increase in processing speed that occurs during middle childhood is partly the result of:
   a. ongoing myelination of axons.
   b. neurological development in the limbic system.
   c. the streamlining of the knowledge base.
   d. all of the above.

4. When psychologists look at the ability of children to receive, store, and organize information, they are examining cognitive development from a view based on:
   a. the observations of Piaget.
   b. information processing.
   c. behaviorism.
   d. the idea that the key to thinking is the sensory register.

5. Kohlberg's stage theory of moral development is based on his research on a group of boys and on:
   a. psychoanalytic ideas.
   b. Piaget's theory of cognitive development.
   c. Carol Gilligan's research on moral dilemmas.
   d. questionnaires distributed to a nationwide sample of high school seniors.

6. The logical operations of concrete operational thought are particularly important to an understanding of the elementary-school subject(s) of:
   a. spelling.   c. math and science.
   b. reading.   d. social studies.

7. Although older school-age children are generally at the conventional level of moral reasoning, *when* they reach a particular level depends on:
   a. the specific context and the child's opportunity to discuss moral issues.
   b. the level of moral reasoning reached by their parents.
   c. how strongly their peers influence their thinking.
   d. whether they are male or female.

8. Which of the following Piagetian ideas is *not* widely accepted by developmentalists today?
   a. The thinking of school-age children is characterized by a more comprehensive logic than that of preschoolers.
   b. Children are active learners.
   c. How children think is as important as what they know.
   d. Context, instruction, and culture are less important in a child's developing cognitive ability than his or her active exploration and hypothesis testing.

9. Processing capacity refers to:
   a. the ability to selectively attend to more than one thought.
   b. the ability to simultaneously consider several issues and monitor one's thinking about them.
   c. the size of the child's knowledge base.
   d. all of the above.

10. The retention of new information is called:
    a. retrieval.   c. automatization.
    b. storage.   d. metacognition.

11. According to Kohlberg, a person who is a dutiful citizen and obeys the laws set down by society would be at which level of moral reasoning?
    a. preconventional stage one
    b. preconventional stage two
    c. conventional
    d. postconventional

12. Which aspect of the information-processing system assumes an executive role in regulating the analysis and transfer of information?
    a. sensory register
    b. working memory
    c. long-term memory
    d. control processes

13. An example of schoolchildren's growth in metacognition is their understanding that:
    a. transformed objects can be returned to their original state.
    b. rehearsal is a good strategy for memorizing, but outlining is better for understanding.
    c. easy and hard questions require equal amounts of concentration to solve.
    d. they can use different language styles in different situations.

14. Which of the following most accurately states the relative merits of the phonics approach and the whole-language approach to teaching reading?
    a. The phonics approach is more effective.
    b. The whole-language approach is the more effective approach.

c. Both approaches have merit.
d. Both approaches have been discarded in favor of newer, more interactive methods of instruction.

15. Regarding bilingual education, many contemporary developmentalists believe that:
    a. the attempted learning of two languages is confusing to children and delays proficiency in either one or both languages.
    b. bilingual education is linguistically, culturally, and cognitively advantageous to children.
    c. second-language education is most effective when the child has not yet mastered the native language.
    d. bilingual education programs are too expensive to justify the few developmental advantages they confer.

Matching Items
Match each term or concept with its corresponding description or definition.

Terms or Concepts

_____ 1. automatization
_____ 2. reversibility
_____ 3. conventional
_____ 4. identity
_____ 5. information processing
_____ 6. selective attention
_____ 7. retrieval
_____ 8. storage
_____ 9. metacognition
_____ 10. total immersion
_____ 11. postconventional
_____ 12. preconventional

Descriptions or Definitions

a. the ability to screen out distractions and concentrate on relevant information
b. the idea that a transformation process can be undone to restore the original conditions
c. the idea that certain characteristics of an object remain the same even when other characteristics change
d. developmental perspective that conceives of cognitive development as the result of changes in the processing and analysis of information
e. moral reasoning in which the individual focuses on his or her own welfare
f. moral reasoning in which the individual follows principles that supersede the standards of society
g. an educational technique in which instruction occurs entirely in the second language
h. accessing previously learned information
i. holding information in memory
j. moral reasoning in which the individual considers social standards and laws to be primary
k. process by which familiar mental activities become routine
l. the ability to evaluate a cognitive task and to monitor one's performance on it

Thinking Critically About Chapter 12

Answer these questions the day before an exam as a final check on your understanding of the chapter's terms and concepts.

1. Of the following statements made by children, which best exemplifies the logical principle of identity?
   a. "You can't leave first base until the ball is hit!"
   b. "See how the jello springs back into shape after I poke my finger into it?"
   c. "I know it's still a banana, even though it's mashed down in my sandwich."
   d. "You're my friend, so I don't have to use polite speech like I do with adults."

2. Which of the following statements is the clearest indication that the child has grasped the principle of reversibility?
   a. "See, the lemonade is the same in both our glasses; even though your glass is taller than mine, it's narrower."
   b. "Even though your dog looks funny, I know it's still a dog."
   c. "I have one sister and no brothers. My parents have two children."
   d. "I don't cheat because I don't want to be punished."

3. A psychologist who wishes to study moral reasoning using a more objective methodology than that used by Kohlberg would do well to consult the:
   a. sensory register.   c. knowledge base.
   b. Defining Issues Test.   d. formal code.

4. Dr. Larsen believes that the cognitive advances of middle childhood occur because of basic changes in children's thinking speed, knowledge base, and memory retrieval skills. Dr. Larsen evidently is working from the _____ perspective.
   a. Piagetian
   b. Vygotskian
   c. information-processing
   d. psychoanalytic

5. Some researchers believe that cognitive processing speed and capacity increase during middle childhood because of:
   a. the myelination of nerve pathways.
   b. the maturation of the frontal cortex.
   c. better use of cognitive resources.
   d. all of the above.

6. A child's ability to tell a joke that will amuse his or her audience always depends on:
   a. the child's mastery of reciprocity and reversibility.
   b. code switching.
   c. the child's ability to consider another's perspective.
   d. an expansion of the child's processing capacity.

7. For a 10-year-old, some mental activities have become so familiar or routine as to require little mental work. This development is called:
   a. selective attention.   c. metacognition.
   b. identity.   d. automatization.

8. Lana is 4 years old and her brother Roger is 7. The fact that Roger remembers what their mother just told them about playing in the street while Lana is more interested in the children playing across the street is due to improvements in Roger's:
   a. selective attention.   c. control processes.
   b. automatization.   d. long-term memory.

9. Which of the following statements is the best example of Kohlberg's concept of stage 1 preconventional moral reasoning?
   a. "Might makes right."
   b. "Law and order."
   c. "Nice boys do what is expected of them."
   d. "Look out for number one."

10. According to Carol Gilligan, a girl responding to the hypothetical question of whether an impoverished child should steal food to feed her starving dog is most likely to:
    a. respond according to a depersonalized standard of right and wrong.
    b. hesitate to take a definitive position based on the abstract moral premise of "right and wrong.""
    c. immediately respond that the child was justified in stealing the food.
    d. respond unpredictably, based on her own personal experiences.

11. Four-year-old Tasha, who is learning to read by sounding out the letters of words, evidently is being taught using which approach?
    a. phonics
    b. whole-word
    c. total immersion
    d. reverse immersion

12. As compared with her 5-year-old brother, 7-year-old Althea has learned to adjust her vocabulary to her audience. This is known as:
    a. selective attention.   c. code-switching.
    b. retrieval.   d. reversibility.

13. During the school board meeting a knowledgeable parent proclaimed that the board's position on achievement testing and class size was an example of the district's "hidden curriculum." The parent was referring to the:
    a. unofficial and unstated educational priorities of the school district.
    b. Political agendas of individual members of the school board.
    c. Legal mandates for testing and class size established by the state board of education.
    d. None of the above.

14. Critics of Kohlberg's theory of moral development argue that it:
    a. places too much emphasis on sociocultural factors.
    b. places too much emphasis on traditional, religious beliefs.
    c. is biased toward liberal, Western cultural beliefs.
    d. can't be tested.

15. The study of fourth-graders' memory of a written passage about soccer revealed that:
    a. high-IQ children always did better than low-IQ children.
    b. expert soccer players outperformed novices, even when their IQ was lower.
    c. the size of a child's knowledge base was less important as a factor in his or her memory than IQ was.
    d. novice soccer players performed poorly, regardless of their IQ.

Key Terms

Writing Definitions

Using your own words, write a brief definition or explanation of each of the following terms on a separate piece of paper.

1. concrete operational thought
2. classification
3. identity
4. reversibility
5. sensory register
6. working memory
7. long-term memory
8. knowledge base
9. control processes
10. selective attention
11. metacognition
12. code-switching
13. formal code
14. informal code
15. preconventional moral reasoning
16. conventional moral reasoning
17. postconventional moral reasoning
18. Defining Issues Test (DIT)
19. morality of care
20. morality of justice
21. phonics approach
22. whole-language approach
23. total immersion
24. hidden curriculum

Cross-Check

After you have written the definitions of the key terms in this chapter, you should complete the crossword puzzle to ensure that you can reverse the process—recognize the term, given the definition.

ACROSS

2. Processes that regulate the analysis and flow of information in memory.
6. According to Gilligan, men develop a morality of _____ .
10. The part of memory that stores unlimited amounts of information for days, months, or years.
11. English as a second language.
12. Psychologist who developed an influential theory of cognitive development.
13. According to the theorist in 12 across, cognitive development occurs in _____ .
14. Speech code used by children in school and with adults.
16. Speech code used by children in casual situations.
17. One of Kohlberg's harshest critics.
18. According to Piaget, the type of cognitive operations that occur during middle childhood.
19. Moral reasoning in which the individual considers social standards and laws to be primary.

DOWN

1. The part of memory that handles current, conscious mental activity.
2. According to Gilligan, females develop a morality of
_____ .
3. The ability to evaluate a cognitive task in order to determine what to do.
4. Process by which familiar mental activities become routine.
5. Ongoing neural process that speeds up neural processing.
7. Changing from one form of speech to another.
8. An approach to teaching a second language in which the teacher instructs the children in school subjects using their native language as well as the second language.
9. The body of knowledge that has been learned about a particular area.
15. Neurological development in the _____ cortex during middle childhood helps speed neural processing.

ANSWERS

CHAPTER REVIEW

1. concrete operational thought; socially
2. classification; class inclusion
3. categories; subcategories; hierarchical; overlapping; separate
4. identity; reversibility
5. math; science; social
6. apply
7. context; instruction; culture; variability
8. information-processing
9. sensory register
10. working memory; short-term memory; conscious
11. long-term memory; retrieval
12. processing speed; processing capacity
13. neurological; myelination; frontal cortex
14. automatization
15. knowledge base
16. are not; knowledge base
17. control processes
18. selective attention
19. metacognition
20. 20; sophisticated vocabulary
21. poems; languages; jokes

22. code-switching; formal code; vocabulary; syntax; sentences; informal code; gestures; intonation
23. free; bound; ability
24. Kohlberg; preconventional; conventional; post-conventional
25. rewards; punishments; 1; 2
26. social rules; 4; 3
27. moral principles; social contracts; universal ethical principles
28. preconventional; conventional
29. stages; cognitive maturation; confirmed
30. flawed; Western elites; women
31. Defining Issues Test (DIT)
32. have
33. morality of care; morality of justice
34. is not; do; say
35. is not; reading; writing; arithmetic
36. phonics; whole-language
37. rote learning; concepts and problem solving
38. learn; early childhood; middle childhood
39. total immersion; reverse immersion
40. English as a second language; bilingual education; bilingual–bicultural education
41. Canada; reverse immersion; shy; stupid; socially isolated
42. the attitudes of parents, teachers, and the community; additive bilingualism
43. values
44. hidden curriculum
45. weak
46. disagree

PROGRESS TEST 1

Multiple-Choice Questions

1. **c.** is the answer. (p. 359)
   a. Preoperational thought is "pre-logical" thinking.
   b. There is no such stage in Piaget's theory.
   d. Formal operational thought extends logical reasoning to abstract problems.

2. **c.** is the answer. (p. 364)
   a., b., & d. Although myelination and the development of the frontal cortex, which are both examples of neurological maturation, partly account for increasing speed of processing, learning is a more direct cause.

3. **b.** is the answer. (p. 361)
   a. This is the concept that certain characteristics of an object remain the same even when other characteristics change.
   c. This is a form of bilingual education in which the child is taught totally in his or her nonnative language.

d. This is the process by which familiar mental activities become routine and automatic.

4. **b.** is the answer. (p. 363)
   a. Information-processing theorists use the mind–computer metaphor at every age.
   c. Although increasing automatization is an important aspect of development, the information-processing perspective does not suggest that most mental activities become automatic by age 13.
   d. Most of the important changes in reasoning that occur during the school years are due to the improved processing capacity of the person's *working memory*.

5. **c.** is the answer. (p. 365)
   a. This is the ability to evaluate a cognitive task and to monitor one's performance on it.
   b. Information processing is a perspective on cognitive development that focuses on how the mind analyzes, stores, retrieves, and reasons about information.
   d. Decentering, which refers to the school-age child's ability to consider more than one aspect of a problem simultaneously, is not discussed in this chapter.

6. **a.** is the answer. (p. 359)
   b. This refers to metacognition.
   c. This refers to Piaget's concept of identity.
   d. This is characteristic of Kohlberg's postconventional moral reasoning.

7. **d.** is the answer. (p. 366)
   a. Pragmatics refers to the practical use of language to communicate with others.
   b. The information-processing perspective views the mind as being like a computer.
   c. This is the ability to screen out distractions in order to focus on important information.

8. **a.** is the answer. (pp. 363–364)
9. **b.** is the answer. (pp. 375–376)
10. **d.** is the answer. (p. 367)
11. **d.** is the answer. (pp. 371–372)
   a., b., & c. These are characteristic of the informal code that children use with friends in other settings.

12. **a.** is the answer. (p. 384)
13. **d.** is the answer. (p. 372)
14. **b.** is the answer. (p. 374)
15. **d.** is the answer. (p. 385)

True or False Items

1. T (p. 363)
2. T (p. 383)
3. T (p. 374)
4. T (p. 380)
5. T (p. 370)
6. F   Code switching (including occasional use of slang) is a behavior demonstrated by all children. (p. 372)
7. F   The best time to learn a second language by listening and talking is during *early* childhood. (p. 383)
8. T (p. 363)
9. F   They believe that the changes are due to basic changes in control processes. (p. 365)
10. T (p. 383)

PROGRESS TEST 2

Multiple-Choice Questions

1. **c.** is the answer. (pp. 359–360)
2. **b.** is the answer. (p. 363)
3. **a.** is the answer. (p. 364)
   b. Neurological development in the frontal cortex facilitates processing speed during middle childhood.   The limbic system, which was not discussed in this chapter, is concerned with emotions.
   c. Processing speed is facilitated by *growth*, rather than streamlining, of the knowledge base.
4. **b.** is the answer. (p. 363)
5. **b.** is the answer. (p. 373)
6. **c.** is the answer. (p. 361)
7. **a.** is the answer. (p. 377)
   b., c., & d. Although these may be factors, they don't necessarily determine the child's level of moral reasoning.
8. **d.** is the answer. (p. 363)
9. **b.** is the answer. (p. 364)
10. **b.** is the answer. (p. 364)
    a. This is the *accessing* of already learned information.
    c. Automatization is the process by which well-learned activities become routine and automatic.
    d. This is the ability to evaluate a task and to monitor one's performance on it.
11. **c.** is the answer. (p. 374)
12. **d.** is the answer. (p. 365)

   a. The sensory register stores incoming information for a split second.
   b. Working memory is the part of memory that handles current, conscious mental activity.
   c. Long-term memory stores information for days, months, or years.
13. **b.** is the answer. (pp. 366–367)
14. **c.** is the answer. (p. 381)
15. **b.** is the answer. (pp. 384–385)

Matching Items

1. k (p. 364)
2. b (p. 361)
3. j (p. 373)
4. c (p. 361)
5. d (p. 363)
6. a (p. 366)
7. h (p. 364)
8. i (p. 364)
9. l (p. 366)
10. g (p. 384)
11. f (p. 373)
12. e (p. 373)

THINKING CRITICALLY ABOUT CHAPTER 12

1. **c.** is the answer. (p. 361)
   a., b., & d. Identity is the logical principle that certain characteristics of an object (such as the shape of a banana) remain the same even when other characteristics change.
2. **a.** is the answer. (p. 361)
   b., c., & d. Reversibility is the logical principle that something that has been changed (such as the height of lemonade poured from one glass into another) can be returned to its original shape by reversing the process of change (pouring the liquid back into the other glass).
3. **b.** is the answer. (p. 375)
4. **c.** is the answer. (p. 363)
   a. This perspective emphasizes the logical, active nature of thinking during middle childhood.
   b. This perspective emphasizes the importance of social interaction in learning.
   d. This perspective does not address the development of cognitive skills.
5. **d.** is the answer. (p. 364)
6. **c.** is the answer. Joke telling is one of the clearest demonstrations of schoolchildren's improved ability to know what someone else will think is funny. (p. 370)
7. **d.** is the answer. (p. 364)
   a. Selective attention is the ability to focus on important information and screen out distractions.
   b. Identity is the logical principle that certain characteristics of an object remain the same even when other characteristics change.

c. Metacognition is the ability to evaluate a task and to monitor one's performance on it.

8. **c.** is the answer. (p. 365)

   a. Selective attention *is* a control process, but c. is more specific and thus more correct.

   b. Automatization refers to the tendency of well-rehearsed mental activities to become routine and automatic.

   d. Long-term memory is the part of memory that stores information for days, months, or years.

9. **a.** is the answer. (p. 374)

   b. & c. These exemplify conventional moral reasoning.

   d. This exemplifies stage two preconventional moral reasoning.

10. **b.** is the answer. Gilligan contends that females' morality of care makes them reluctant to judge right and wrong in absolute terms because they are socialized to be nurturant and caring. (pp. 375–376)

11. **a.** is the answer. (p. 381)

    b. This approach encourages children to develop all their language skills at the same time.

    c. & d. These are approaches to bilingual instruction, not reading instruction.

12. **c.** is the answer. (p. 371)

13. **a.** is the answer. (p. 386)

14. **c.** is the answer. (p. 374)

15. **b.** is the answer. (p. 365)

KEY TERMS

Writing Definitions

1. During Piaget's stage of **concrete operational thought,** lasting from ages 7 to 11, children can think logically about concrete events and objects but are not able to reason abstractly. (p. 359)

2. **Classification** is the ability to sort things into groups according to some common property. (p. 360)

3. In Piaget's theory, **identity** is the logical principle that certain characteristics of an object remain the same even when other characteristics change. (p. 361)

4. **Reversibility** is the logical principle that a transformation process can be reversed to restore the original conditions. (p. 361)

5. **Sensory register** is the first component of the information-processing system that stores incoming stimuli for a split second, after which it is passed into working memory, or discarded as unimportant. (p. 363)

6. **Working memory** is the component of the information-processing system that handles current, conscious mental activity; also called short-term memory. (p. 363)

7. **Long-term memory** is the component of the information-processing system that stores unlimited amounts of information for days, months, or years. (p. 364)

8. The **knowledge base** is a broad body of knowledge in a particular subject area that has been learned and on which additional learning can be based. (p. 364)

9. **Control processes** (such as selective attention and metacognition) regulate the analysis and flow of information within the information-processing system. (p. 365)

10. **Selective attention** is the ability to screen out distractions and concentrate on relevant information. (p. 366)

11. **Metacognition** is the ability to evaluate a cognitive task to determine what to do and to monitor one's performance on that task. (p. 366)

12. **Code-switching** is a communication skill that involves changing one's speech and tone from one form to another. (p. 371)

13. The **formal code** is a form of speech used by children in school and other formal situations, characterized by extensive vocabulary, complex syntax, and lengthy sentences. (p. 371)

14. The **informal code** is a form of speech used by children in casual situations, characterized by limited vocabulary and simpler syntax and the use of gestures and intonation to convey meaning. (p. 372)

15. Kohlberg's first level of moral reasoning, **preconventional moral reasoning,** emphasizes obedience to authority in order to avoid punishment (stage 1) and being nice to other people so they will be nice to you (stage 2). (pp. 373, 374)

16. Kohlberg's second level of moral reasoning, **conventional moral reasoning,** emphasizes winning the approval of others (stage 3) and obeying the laws set down by those in power (stage 4). (pp. 373, 374)

17. Kohlberg's third level, **postconventional moral reasoning,** emphasizes the social and contractual nature of moral principles (stage 5) and the existence of universal ethical principles (stage 6). (pp. 373, 374)

18. The **Defining Issues Test (DIT)** is a questionnaire that measures moral reasoning by asking people to rank various possible resolutions to moral dilemmas. (p. 375)

19. According to Carol Gilligan, compared with boys and men, girls and women are more likely to develop a **morality of care** that is based on comparison, nurturance, and concern for the well-being of others. (p. 375)

20. According to Carol Gilligan, compared with girls and women, boys and men are more likely to develop a **morality of justice** based on depersonalized and absolute standards of right and wrong. (p. 375)

21. The **phonics approach** is a method of teaching reading by having children learn the sounds of letters before they begin to learn words. (p. 381)

22. The **whole-language approach** is a method of teaching reading by encouraging children to develop all their langauge skills simultaneously. (p. 381)

23. **Total immersion** is an approach to bilingual education in which the child's instruction occurs entirely in the new language. (p. 384)

24. The **hidden curriculum** is the unofficial, unstated, or implicit rules and priorities that influence the academic curriculum and every other aspect of school learning. (p. 386)

Cross-Check

ACROSS

2. control
6. justice
10. long-term
11. ESL
12. Piaget
13. stages
14. formal
16. informal
17. Gilligan
18. concrete
19. conventional

DOWN

1. working
2. care
3. metacognition
4. automatization
5. myelination
7. code-switching
8. bilingual
9. knowledge base
15. frontal

Chapter Thirteen

The School Years: Psychosocial Development

Chapter Overview

This chapter brings to a close the unit on the school years. We have seen that from ages 7 to 11, the child becomes stronger and more competent, mastering the biosocial and cognitive abilities that are important in his or her culture. Psychosocial accomplishments are equally impressive.

The first section of the chapter begins by exploring the growing social competence of children, as described by Freud and Erikson and behaviorist, cognitive, sociocultural, and epigenetic systems theorists. The section continues with a discussion of the growth of social cognition and self-understanding.

Children's interaction with peers and others in their ever-widening social world is the subject of the next section. Although the peer group often is a supportive, positive influence on children, some children are rejected by their peers or become the victims of bullying.

The next section explores the problems and challenges often experienced by school-age children in our society, including the experience of parental divorce and remarriage and living in single-parent and blended families. The chapter closes with a discussion of the ways in which children cope with stressful situations.

NOTE: Answer guidelines for all Chapter 13 questions begin on page 215.

Guided Study

The text chapter should be studied one section at a time. Before you read, preview each section by skimming it, noting headings and boldface items. Then read the appropriate section objectives from the following outline. Keep these objectives in mind and, as you read the chapter section, search for the information that will enable you to meet each objective. Once you have finished a section, write out answers for its objectives.

Theories of School-Age Development (pp. 393–395)

1. Identify the themes or emphases of different theoretical views of the psychosocial development of school-age children.

Understanding Self and Others (pp. 395–397)

2. Define social cognition, and explain how children's theory of mind and emotional understanding evolve during middle childhood.

3. Describe the development of self-understanding during middle childhood and its implications for children's self-esteem.

The Peer Group (pp. 397-406)

4. Discuss the importance of peer groups, providing examples of how school-age children develop their own subculture and explaining the importance of this development.

5. Discuss how friendship circles change during the school years.

6. Discuss the plight of two types of rejected children.

7. (text and Thinking Like a Scientist) Discuss the special problems of bullies and their victims, and describe possible ways of helping such children.

Family Functions (pp. 407–419)

8. Identify five essential ways in which functional families nurture school-age children, and discuss how they relate to Baumrind's styles of parenting.

9. Differentiate seven basic family structures.

10. Describe how American family structures have changed in recent decades, and discuss the benefits and some disadvantages of children living with both biological parents.

11. (text and Changing Policy) Discuss the impact of divorce and single-parent households on the psychosocial development of the school-age child.

12. Discuss the impact of blended families and other family structures on the psychosocial development of the school-age child.

Coping with Problems (pp. 419–424)

13. Identify the variables that influence the impact of stresses on schoolchildren.

14. Discuss several factors that seem especially important in helping children to cope with stress.

Chapter Review

When you have finished reading the chapter, work through the material that follows to review it. Complete the sentences and answer the questions. As you proceed, evaluate your performance for each section by consulting the answers on page 215. Do not continue with the next section until you understand each answer. If you need to, review or reread the appropriate section in the textbook before continuing.

Theories of School-Age Development (pp. 393–395)

1. Freud describes middle childhood as the period of _____ , when emotional drives are _____ , psychosexual needs are _____ , and unconscious conflicts are _____ .

2. According to Erikson, the crisis of middle childhood is _____

_____ _____ .

3. Developmentalists influenced by behaviorism are more concerned with children's _____ of new cognitive abilities; those influenced by the cognitive perspective focus on _____ . One offshoot of the grand theories, _____ _____ theory, stresses the combination of _____ and _____ that allows children to understand themselves and to be effective and competent. In addition to comparing children from different parts of the world, _____ theory examines various _____ within one nation.

Briefly describe the epigenetic systems perspective on the school-age child's new independence.

Understanding Self and Others (pp. 395–397)

4. Social scientists once categorized societies and individuals into two opposite groups: _____ and _____ . Today, most agree that both _____ forces and _____ forces are at work in every society.

5. School-age children advance in their understanding of other people and groups; that is, they advance in _____ _____ . At this time, the preschooler's one-step theory of mind begins to evolve into a complex, _____ view of others.

6. In the beginning of the school years, children often explain their actions by focusing on the immediate _____ ; a few years later, they more readily relate their actions to their _____ and _____

_____ .

7. In experiments on children's social cognition, older children are more likely to understand the _____ and origin of various behaviors.

8. Another example of children's advancing social cognition is that, as compared with younger children, older children are more likely to focus on _____ (physical characteristics/personality traits) when asked to describe other children.

9. During the school years, children are able to mentally _____ themselves to keep from getting bored, and they can mask or _____ inborn tendencies. As a result of their new social cognition, children can better manage their own _____ .

10. As their self-understanding sharpens, children gradually become _____ (more/less) self-critical, and their self-esteem _____ (rises/dips). One reason is that they more often evaluate themselves through _____ _____ . As they mature, children are also _____ (more/less) likely to feel personally to blame for their shortcomings.

The Peer Group (pp. 397–406)

11. A peer group is defined as _____
_____ .

12. Although working parents tend to worry about their children's after-school supervision, children tend to be more concerned about breakdowns in their _____ _____ and their parents' _____
_____ .

13. Some social scientists call the peer group's subculture the _____
_____ _____ , highlighting the distinctions between children's groups and the general culture.

Identify several distinguishing features of this subculture.

14. Having a personal friend is _____ (more/less) important to children than acceptance by the peer group.

15. Friendships during middle childhood become more _____ and _____ . As a result, older children_____ (change/do not change) friends as often and find it _____ (easier/harder) to make new friends.

16. Middle schoolers tend to choose best friends whose _____ , _____ , and _____ are similar to their own. Generally, having a best friend who is not the same _____ or _____ correlates with being _____ by one's classmates.

17. Friendship groups typically become _____ (larger/smaller) during the school years. This trend _____ (is/is not) followed by both sexes.

18. In their friendship networks, boys tend to emphasize group _____ and _____ , while girls form _____ and more _____ networks.

19. Children who are actively rejected tend to be either _____-_____ or _____-_____ .

Give an example of the immaturity of rejected children.

20. Efforts to teach social skills to rejected children have _____ (been highly successful/met with mixed success). One reason is that social responses are usually learned from _____ and are difficult to _____ . Another reason is that _____ attitudes and actions resist

change. A third reason is that children sometimes say one thing and_____

_____ .

21. Boys who are bullies are often above average in _____ , whereas girls who are bullies are often above average in _____

_____ .

22. One factor in bullying is _____ norms that allow boys to see nothing wrong with acting tough or girls gossiping maliciously. Fewer _____ (boys/girls) become bullies, except in _____ , where _____ aggression is a potent bullying weapon for _____ (boys/girls).

Describe the effects of bullying on children.

23. A key aspect in the definition of bullying is that harmful attacks are _____ .

24. Contrary to the public perception, in middle childhood bullies usually _____ (have/do not have) friends who admire them. Children who regularly victimize other children often become _____ later on.

25. Bullying is _____ (fairly easy/difficult) to change. The origins of bullying and other kinds of _____ behavior may lie in _____ _____ that are present at birth and then strengthened by _____ _____ , poor _____ _____ , and other deficits.

26. (Thinking Like a Scientist) An effective intervention in controlling bullying is to change the _____ _____ within the school so that bully–victim cycles are not allowed to persist.

Family Influences (pp. 407–419)

27. There is an ongoing debate between those who believe that _____ and

_____ are more important influences on children's psychosocial development and those who believe that a child's _____ are much more powerful. Even so, all researchers agree that both _____ and _____ are important.

28. Family function refers to how well the family

_____

_____ .

29. A functional family nurtures school-age children by meeting their basic _____ , encouraging _____ , fostering the development of _____ , nurturing peer _____ , and providing _____ and _____ .

30. Parents who actively promote _____ , _____ , and _____ have children who are more likely to achieve in school and to have solid friendships. Familes with an _____ style generally raise more successful and self-confident children. Many immigrant families have an _____ style, which may assist children by helping the family preserve its _____ .

31. Poverty _____ (always/does not always) interfere with effective family functioning.

32. Family structure is defined as the _____ _____ .

Identify each of the following family structures:

a. _____ A family that includes three or more biologically related generations, including parents and children.

b. _____ A family that consists of the father, the mother, and their biological children.

c. _____ A family that consists of one parent with his or her biological children.

d. _____ A family consisting of two parents, at least one with biological children from another union.

e. _____ A family that consists of children living with their grandparents.

f. _____ A family that consists of one or more nonbiological children whom adults have legally taken to raise as their own.

g. _____ A family that consists of one or more orphaned, neglected, abused, or delinquent children who are temporarily cared for by an adult to whom they are not biologically related.

33. Longitudinal research studies demonstrate that children can thrive _____ (only in certain family structures/in almost any family structure).

34. The "traditional" family structure that dominated most of America's history is becoming _____ (more/less) common.

35. If current trends continue, about _____ percent of American children born in the twenty-first century will live with both biological parents from birth to age 18.

36. Children who have fewer physical, emotional, or learning difficulties are those who are raised in _____ _____ . As adults, they are more likely to _____ _____ .

37. Give four reasons for the benefits of this family structure.

a. _____

b. _____

c. _____

d. _____

38. People who marry and stay married are generally _____ , _____ , better _____ , and less likely to be _____ .

39. In acknowledging that two-parent homes are generally best, the author notes two important qualifications.

a. _____
_____

b. _____
_____

40. An important factor in the ability of a single parent to be patient and responsive is _____ , which tends to increase with age. Single parents tend to be _____ (older/younger) than married parents.

41. The number of _____-_____ households has increased markedly over the past two decades in virtually every major industrialized nation. Two reasons for this trend are

a. _____

b. _____

42. Whether or not the parents are married, were never married, or were married and divorced has _____ (more/less) impact on a child than the family's financial status.

43. (Changing Policy) The disruption surrounding divorce almost always adversely affects children for at least _____ .

44. (Changing Policy) Divorce jeopardizes both the _____ and _____ of a well-functioning family.

(Changing Policy) Identify several circumstances under which divorce may not harm the children.

45. (Changing Policy) Custody means having _____ responsibility for children.

Although _____ _____
is theoretically the best decision following a
divorce, in practice this often is not the case.
Developmental research reveals that
_____ (mothers/fathers/neither
parent) tend(s) to function better as the custodial
parent.

(Changing Policy) Give several reasons that children
whose fathers have custody may fare better than children whose mothers have custody.

46. Most divorced parents _____
(do/do not) remarry within a few years. The
divorce rate for second marriages is
_____ (higher than/lower than/the
same as) that for first marriages.

47. Children in grandparent families are _____
(more/less) likely to benefit than to be harmed.

48. On the whole, being adopted does not produce
either _____ or _____ .
Foster children have a higher than average rate of
_____ and _____
problems when compared to biological children
raised by families of the same economic level and
structure.

49. Children growing up in gay, lesbian, and other
nontraditional families generally develop
_____ (poorly/quite well), depending on the particulars of
_____ . As
nontraditional families become more
_____ acceptable, the negative
effects of nonnuclear families on children have
_____ (increased/decreased).

50. In the United States children of
_____ (which ethnicities?) are more
likely to live in extended families.

Coping with Problems (pp. 419–424)

51. Between ages 7 and 11 the overall frequency of
various psychological problems
_____ (increases/decreases), while
the number of evident competencies
_____ (increases/decreases).

52. Two factors that combine to buffer school-age
children against the stresses they encounter are
the development of _____
_____
and an expanding _____
_____ . Some children are better
able to adapt within the context of adversity, that
is, they seem to be more _____ .

53. The impact of a given stress on a child (such as
divorce) depends on three factors:

   a. _____

   b. _____

   c. _____

54. One reason that competence can compensate for
life stresses is that if children feel confident, their
_____ benefits, and they are better
able to put the rest of their life in perspective.
This explains why older children tend to be
_____ (more/less) vulnerable to
life stresses than are children who are just beginning middle childhood.

55. Another element that helps children deal with
problems is the _____
_____ they receive.

56. A child who is at risk because of poor parenting,
difficult temperament, or poverty _____
(probably will/probably won't) still be at risk as
an adolescent.

57. During middle childhood, there are typically
_____ (fewer/more) sources of
social support. This can be obtained from grandparents or siblings, for example, or from
_____ and _____ .
In addition, _____ can also be psychologically protective for children in difficult circumstances.

58. Most children _____ (do/do not) have an idyllic childhood. Such a childhood _____ (is/is not) necessary for healthy development.

Progress Test 1

Multiple-Choice Questions

Circle your answers to the following questions and check them with the answers on page 216. If your answer is incorrect, read the explanation for why it is incorrect and then consult the appropriate pages of the text (in parentheses following the correct answer).

1. Social cognition is defined as:
   a. a person's awareness and understanding of human personality, motives, emotions, and interactions.
   b. the ability to form friendships easily.
   c. a person's skill in persuading others to go along with his or her wishes.
   d. the ability to learn by watching another person.

2. A common thread running through the five major developmental theories is that cultures throughout history have selected ages 7 to 11 as the time for:
   a. a period of latency.
   b. the emergence of a theory of mind.
   c. more independence and responsibility.
   d. intellectual curiosity.

3. The best strategy for helping children who are at risk of developing serious psychological problems because of multiple stresses would be to:
   a. obtain assistance from a psychiatrist.
   b. increase the child's competencies or social supports.
   c. change the household situation.
   d. reduce the peer group's influence.

4. In explaining psychosocial development during the school years, Professor Wilson stresses the combination of maturation and experience that allows children to understand themselves and to be effective and competent. Professor Wilson is evidently working from the perspective of:
   a. behaviorism.
   b. Erik Erikson's theory of development.
   c. social cognitive theory.
   d. psychoanalysis.

5. Girls who are bullies are often above average in _____ , whereas boys who are bullies are often above average in _____ .
   a. size; verbal assertiveness
   b. verbal assertiveness; size
   c. intelligence; aggressiveness
   d. aggressiveness; intelligence

6. As rejected children get older, their:
   a. problems often get worse.
   b. problems usually decrease.
   c. friendship circles typically become smaller.
   d. their peer group becomes less important to their self-esteem.

7. Compared with average or popular children, rejected children tend to be:
   a. brighter and more competitive.
   b. affluent and "stuck-up."
   c. economically disadvantaged.
   d. socially immature.

8. Compared to middle school girls, middle school boys are more likely to emphasize _____ in their friendship networks.
   a. fewer but closer friends
   b. group identity and loyalty
   c. having one, and only one, best friend on whom they depend
   d. friendships with others who are not the same age or sex

9. (text and Changing Policy) Divorce may not be harmful to the child if the:
   a. family income remains stable.
   b. mother has custody of the children.
   c. father does not interfere with the mother's caregiving.
   d. the parents of the child's friends are also divorced.

10. Older schoolchildren tend to be _____ vulnerable to the stresses of life than children who are just beginning middle childhood because they _____ .
    a. more; tend to overpersonalize their problems
    b. less; have developed better coping skills
    c. more; are more likely to compare their well-being with that of their peers
    d. less; are less egocentric

11. Between the ages of 7 and 11, the overall frequency of various psychological problems:
    a. increases in both boys and girls.
    b. decreases in both boys and girls.
    c. increases in boys and decreases in girls.
    d. decreases in boys and increases in girls.

12. Bullying during middle childhood:
   a. occurs only in certain cultures.
   b. is more common in rural schools than in urban schools.
   c. seems to be universal.
   d. is rarely a major problem, since other children usually intervene to prevent it from getting out of hand.

13. During the school years, children become _____ selective about their friends, and their friendship groups become _____ .
   a. less; larger
   b. less; smaller
   c. more; larger
   d. more; smaller

14. Which of the following was *not* identified as a pivotal issue in determining whether divorce or some other problem will adversely affect a child during the school years?
   a. how many other stresses the child is already experiencing
   b. how the child interprets the stress
   c. how much the stress affects the child's daily life
   d. the specific structure of the child's family

15. Erikson's crisis of the school years is that of:
   a. industry versus inferiority.
   b. acceptance versus rejection.
   c. initiative versus guilt.
   d. male versus female.

True or False Items

Write T (*true*) or F (*false*) on the line in front of each statement.

_____ 1. As they evaluate themselves according to increasingly complex self-theories, school-age children typically experience a rise in self-esteem.

_____ 2. During middle childhood, acceptance by the peer group is valued more than having a close friend.

_____ 3. Children from low-income homes often have lower self-esteem.

_____ 4. In the majority of divorce cases in which the father is the custodial parent, the children do not maintain a close relationship with their mother.

_____ 5. Divorce almost always adversely affects the children for at least a year or two.

_____ 6. The quality of family interaction seems to be a more powerful predictor of children's development than the actual structure of the family.

_____ 7. Withdrawn-rejected and aggressive-rejected children both have problems regulating their emotions.

_____ 8. Most successful people and cultures emphasize individualism, the ability to be independent and other-oriented.

_____ 9. Most aggressive-rejected children are unaware of their social isolation.

_____ 10. School-age children are less able than younger children to cope with chronic stresses.

_____ 11. Gender norms, especially for girls, do not condone bullying.

_____ 12. Friendships become more selective and exclusive as children grow older.

Progress Test 2

Progress Test 2 should be completed during a final chapter review. Answer the following questions after you thoroughly understand the correct answers for the Chapter Review and Progress Test 1.

Multiple-Choice Questions

1. Children who are categorized as _____ are particularly vulnerable to bullying.
   a. aggressive-rejected
   b. passive-aggressive
   c. withdrawn-rejected
   d. passive-rejected

2. The main reason for the special vocabulary, dress codes, and behaviors that flourish within the society of children is that they:
   a. lead to clubs and gang behavior.
   b. are unknown to or unapproved by adults.
   c. imitate adult-organized society.
   d. provide an alternative to useful work in society.

3. In the area of social cognition, developmentalists are impressed by the school-age child's increasing ability to:
   a. identify and take into account other people's viewpoints.
   b. develop an increasingly wide network of friends.
   c. relate to the opposite sex.
   d. resist social models.

4. The school-age child's greater understanding of emotions is best illustrated by:
   a. an increased tendency to take everything personally.
   b. more widespread generosity and sharing.
   c. the ability to see through the insincere behavior of others.
   d. a refusal to express unfelt emotions.

5. Typically, children in middle childhood experience a decrease in self-esteem as a result of:
   a. a wavering self-theory.
   b. increased awareness of personal shortcomings and failures.
   c. rejection by peers.
   d. difficulties with members of the opposite sex.

6. A 10-year-old's sense of self-esteem is most strongly influenced by his or her:
   a. peers.   c. mother.
   b. siblings.   d. father.

7. Which of the following most accurately describes how friendships change during the school years?
   a. Friendships become more casual and less intense.
   b. Older children demand less of their friends.
   c. Older children change friends more often.
   d. Close friendships increasingly involve members of the same sex, ethnicity, and socioeconomic status.

8. Which of the following is an accurate statement about school-age bullies?
   a. They are unapologetic about their aggressive behavior.
   b. They usually have friends who abet, fear, and admire them.
   c. Their popularity fades over the years.
   d. All of the above are accurate statements.

9. The most effective intervention to prevent bullying in the school is to:
   a. change the social climate through community-wide and classroom education.
   b. target one victimized child at a time.
   c. target each bully as an individual.
   d. focus on improving the academic skills of all children in the school.

10. When 4- to 10-year-old children were shown pictures and asked how a mother might respond to a child who curses while playing with blocks, the 4-year-olds tended to focus on:
    a. the child's underlying emotions.
    b. the immediate, observable behavior.
    c. the social consequences of the mother's response.
    d. all of the above.

11. Two factors that most often help the child cope well with multiple stresses are social support and:
    a. social comparison.
    b. competence in a specific area.
    c. remedial education.
    d. referral to mental health professionals.

12. An 8-year-old child who measures her achievements by comparing them to those of her friends is engaging in social:
    a. cognition.   c. reinforcement.
    b. comparison.   d. modeling.

13. Family _____ is more crucial to children's well-being than family _____ is.
    a. structure; SES
    b. SES; stability
    c. stability; SES
    d. functioning; structure

14. According to Freud, the period between ages 7 and 11 when a child's sexual drives are relatively quiet is the:
    a. phallic stage.
    b. genital stage.
    c. period of latency.
    d. period of industry versus inferiority.

15. Research studies have found that, as compared to children without major stress, children who are forced to cope with one serious ongoing stress (for example, poverty or large family size) are:
    a. more likely to develop serious psychiatric problems.
    b. no more likely to develop problems.
    c. more likely to develop intense, destructive friendships.
    d. less likely to be accepted by their peer group.

Matching Items

Match each term or concept with its corresponding description or definition.

Terms or Concepts

_____ 1. behaviorism
_____ 2. social cognition
_____ 3. social comparison
_____ 4. cognitive theory
_____ 5. society of children
_____ 6. aggressive-rejected
_____ 7. withdrawn-rejected
_____ 8. sociocultural theory
_____ 9. epigenetic systems theory
_____ 10. blended family
_____ 11. extended family

Descriptions or Definitions

a. focused on the acquisition of new skills
b. adults living with their children from previous marriages as well as their own biological children
c. an awareness and understanding of others' motives and emotions
d. focused on the development of social awareness
e. children who are disliked because of their confrontational nature
f. evaluating one's abilities by measuring them against those of other children
g. three or more generations of biologically related individuals living together
h. children who are disliked because of timid, anxious behavior
i. views middle schoolers' independence as the result of a species need
j. the games, vocabulary, dress codes, and culture of children
k. focused on the development of self-understanding

Thinking Critically About Chapter 13

Answer these questions the day before an exam as a final check on your understanding of the chapter's terms and concepts.

1. As an advocate of the epigenetic systems perspective, Dr. Wayans is most likely to explain a 10-year-old child's new independence as the result of:
    a. the repression of psychosexual needs.
    b. the acquisition of new skills.
    c. greater self-understanding.
    d. the child's need to join the wider community and the parents' need to focus on younger children.

2. Dr. Ferris believes that skill mastery is particularly important because children develop views of themselves as either competent or incompetent in skills valued by their culture. Dr. Ferris is evidently working from the perspective of:
    a. behaviorism.
    b. social learning theory.
    c. Erik Erikson's theory of development.
    d. Freud's theory of development.

3. Bonnie, who is low achieving, shy, and withdrawn, is rejected by most of her peers. Her teacher, who wants to help Bonnie increase her self-esteem and social acceptance, encourages her parents to:
    a. transfer Bonnie to a different school.
    b. help their daughter improve her motor skills.
    c. help their daughter learn to accept more responsibility for her academic failures.
    d. help their daughter improve her skills in relating to peers.

4. Jorge, who has no children of his own, is worried about his 12-year-old niece because she wears unusual clothes and uses vocabulary unknown to him. What should Jorge do?
    a. Tell his niece's parents that they need to discipline their daughter more strictly.
    b. Convince his niece to find a new group of friends.
    c. Recommend that his niece's parents seek professional counseling for their daughter, because such behaviors often are the first signs of a lifelong pattern of antisocial behavior.
    d. Jorge need not necessarily be worried because children typically develop their own subculture of speech, dress, and behavior.

5. Compared with her 7-year-old brother Walter, 10-year-old Felicity is more likely to describe their cousin:
   a. in terms of physical attributes.
   b. as feeling exactly the same way she does when they are in the same social situation.
   c. in terms of personality traits.
   d. in terms of their cousin's outward behavior.

6. Seven-year-old Chantal fumes after a friend compliments her new dress, thinking that the comment was intended to be sarcastic. Chantal's reaction is an example of:
   a. egocentrism.
   b. feelings of inferiority.
   c. the distorted thought processes of an emotionally disturbed child.
   d. immature social cognition.

7. In discussing friendship, 9-year-old children, in contrast to younger children, will:
   a. deny that friends are important.
   b. state that they prefer same-sex playmates.
   c. stress the importance of help and emotional support in friendship.
   d. be less choosy about who they call a friend.

8. Children who have serious difficulties in peer relationships during elementary school:
   a. are at a greater risk of having emotional problems later in life.
   b. usually overcome their difficulties in a year or two.
   c. later are more likely to form an intense friendship with one person than children who did not have difficulties earlier on.
   d. do both b. and c.

9. (Changing Policy) After years of an unhappy marriage, Brad and Diane file for divorce and move 500 miles apart. In ruling on custody for their 7-year-old daughter, the wise judge decides:
   a. joint custody should be awarded, because this arrangement is nearly always the most beneficial for children.
   b. the mother should have custody, because this arrangement is nearly always the most beneficial for children in single-parent homes.
   c. the father should have custody, because this arrangement is nearly always the most beneficial for children in single-parent homes.
   d. to investigate the competency of each parent, because whoever was the more competent and more involved parent before the divorce should continue to be the primary caregiver.

10. Of the following children, who is likely to have the lowest overall self-esteem?
    a. Karen, age 5
    b. David, age 7
    c. Carl, age 9
    d. Cindy, age 10

11. Ten-year-old Benjamin is less optimistic and self-confident than his 5-year-old sister. This may be explained in part by the tendency of older children to:
    a. evaluate their abilities by comparing them with their own competencies a year or two earlier.
    b. evaluate their competencies by comparing them with those of others.
    c. be less realistic about their own abilities.
    d. do both b. and c.

12. Which of the following was *not* listed as a reason that children living with both biological parents tend to fare best?
    a. Two adults can provide more complete caregiving than one.
    b. Married, biological parents are usually better able to provide financially for their children.
    c. Biological parents are generally more emotionally mature than other parents.
    d. All mammals, including humans, have a genetic impulse to protect and nurture their own children.

13. Of the following children, who is most likely to become a bully?
    a. Karen, who is taller than average
    b. David, who is above average in verbal assertiveness
    c. Carl, who is insecure and lonely
    d. Cindy, who is frequently subjected to physical punishment and verbal criticism at home

14. I am an 8-year-old who frequently is bullied at school. If I am like most victims of bullies, I am probably:
    a. obese.
    b. unattractive.
    c. a child who speaks with an accent.
    d. anxious and insecure.

15. Of the following children, who is most likely to have one, and only one, "best friend"?
    a. 10-year-old Juan
    b. 7-year-old Marcy
    c. 10-year-old Christina
    d. 7-year-old Andrew

Key Terms

Using your own words, write a brief definition or explanation of each of the following terms on a separate piece of paper.

1. latency
2. industry versus inferiority
3. social cognitive theory
4. social cognition
5. social comparison
6. peer group
7. society of children
8. aggressive-rejected children
9. withdrawn-rejected children
10. bullying
11. family function
12. family structure
13. nuclear family
14. extended family
15. single-parent family
16. blended family
17. grandparent family
18. adoptive family
19. foster family

ANSWERS

CHAPTER REVIEW

1. latency; quieter; repressed; submerged
2. industry versus inferiority
3. acquisition; self-understanding; social cognitive; maturation; experience; sociocultural; subcultures

From an epigenetic systems perspective, the school-age child's independence is the result of the species' need to free parental efforts so that they may be focused on younger children and to accustom school-age children to their peers and the adults in the community.

4. individualistic; collective (or independent/dependent; self-oriented/other-oriented; introverted/extroverted); autonomous; social
5. social cognition; multifaceted
6. behavior; implications; possible consequences
7. motivation
8. personality traits

9. distract; alter; emotions
10. more; dips; social comparison; more
11. a group of individuals of similar age and social status who play, work, or learn together
12. peer relationships; fights or alcohol and cigarette use
13. society of children

The society of children typically has special norms, vocabulary, rituals, dress codes, and rules of behavior.

14. more
15. intense; intimate; do not change; harder
16. interests; values; backgrounds; age; sex; rejected
17. smaller; is
18. identity; loyalty; smaller; intimate
19. aggressive-rejected; withdrawn-rejected

Rejected children often misinterpret social situations—considering a compliment to be sarcastic, for example.

20. met with mixed success; parents; unlearn; peer; do another
21. size; verbal assertiveness
22. gender; girls; Japan; relational; girls

Bullied children are anxious, depressed, and under-achieving and have lower self-esteem and painful memories.

23. repeated
24. have; more hostile (or criminals)
25. difficult; antisocial; brain abnormalities; insecure attachment; emotional regulation
26. social climate
27. genes; peers; parents; nature; nuture
28. nurtures its children to develop their full potential
29. needs; learning; self-esteem; friendships; harmony; stability
30. education; self-esteem; social skills; authoritative; authoritarian; cultural identity and values
31. does not always
32. genetic and legal relationships among the members of a family
    a. extended family
    b. nuclear family
    c. single-parent family
    d. blended family
    e. grandparent family
    f. adoptive family
    g. foster family

33. in almost any family structure

34. less

35. 37

36. nuclear families; have successful careers, satisfying home lives, and good mental health

37. **a.** Two adults generally provide more complete caregiving than one.
    b. All mammals have a genetic impulse to protect and nurture their own offspring.
    c. Parents who have a close marriage relationship tend to be psychologically healthier than those who never marry or who get divorced.
    d. Two-parent homes usually have a financial advantage over other forms.

38. richer; healthier; educated; abusive or addicted

39. **a.** Not every biological parent is a fit parent.
    b. Not every marriage creates a nurturant household.

40. maturity; younger

41. single-parent
    a. Births to unmarried mothers are increasing.
    b. Divorce is increasing

42. less

43. a year or two

44. harmony; stability

Divorce may not harm children if the family income remains stable, if fights between the parents are few, and if caregiving by both parents is as good as or better than it was before the divorce.

45. caregiving; joint custody; neither parent

Children, particularly sons, sometimes respond better to a man's authority than to a woman's. In addition, fathers who choose custody are those who are likely to be suited for it, whereas mothers typically have custody whether they prefer it or not. Father-only homes are, on average, more financially secure. Custodial fathers also are more willing to accept caregiving help from relatives of the other sex, including the children's mother.

46. do; higher than

47. more

48. advantages; disadvantages; learning; behavior

49. quite well; how the family functions; socially; decreased

50. Latino and Asian-American

51. decreases; increases

52. social cognition; social world; resilient

53. **a.** how many other stresses the child is experiencing

b. how the stress affects the child's daily life
c. how the child interprets the stress

54. self-esteem; less

55. social support

56. probably will

57. more; peers; pets; religion

58. do not; is not

PROGRESS TEST 1

Multiple-Choice Questions

1. **a.** is the answer. (p. 396)

2. **b.** is the answer. (p. 395)

3. **b.** is the answer. (pp. 422–423)

4. **c.** is the answer. (p. 394)

5. **b.** is the answer. (p. 403)

6. **a.** is the answer. (p. 402)

7. **d.** is the answer. (p. 401)

8. **b.** is the answer. (p. 400)

9. **a.** is the answer. (pp. 413–414, 415)

10. **b.** is the answer. (p. 420)

11. **b.** is the answer. (p. 420)

12. **c.** is the answer. (p. 403)
    d. In fact, children rarely intervene, unless a best friend is involved.

13. **d.** is the answer. (p. 399)

14. **d.** is the answer. (p. 420)

15. **a.** is the answer. (p. 393)

True or False Items

1. F In fact, just the opposite is true. (p. 397)

2. F In fact, just the opposite is true. (p. 399)

3. T (p. 409)

4. F Just the opposite is true. (p. 415)

5. T (p. 414)

6. T (p. 410)

7. T (p. 400)

8. F Most developmentalists agree that successful people and cultures find a balance between autonomy and interdependence. (p. 395)

9. T (p. 402)

10. F Because of the coping strategies that school-age children develop, they are better able than younger children to cope with stress. (p. 420)

11. F   Gender norms that require children to suffer in silence tend to condone bullying. (p. 403)

12. T (p. 399)

PROGRESS TEST 2

Multiple-Choice Questions

1. **c.** is the answer. (p. 402)

   a. These are usually bullies.

   b. & d. These are not subcategories of rejected children.

2. **b.** is the answer. (p. 398)

3. **a.** is the answer. (p. 396)

   b. Friendship circles typically become smaller during middle childhood, as children become more choosy about their friends.

   c. & d. These issues are not discussed in the chapter.

4. **c.** is the answer. (p. 396)

5. **b.** is the answer. (p. 397)

   a. This tends to promote, rather than reduce, self-esteem.

   c. Only 10 percent of schoolchildren experience this.

   d. This issue becomes more important during adolescence.

6. **a.** is the answer. (pp. 397–398)

7. **d.** is the answer. (p. 399)

   a., b., & c. In fact, just the opposite is true of friendship during the school years.

8. **d.** is the answer. (p. 404)

9. **a.** is the answer. (p. 405)

10. **b.** is the answer. (p. 396)

   a. & c. Only older children, with their developing social cognition, were able to focus on the more complex issues.

11. **b.** is the answer. (p. 422)

12. **b.** is the answer. (p. 397)

13. **d.** is the answer. (p. 410)

14. **c.** is the answer. (p. 393)

15. **b.** is the answer. (p. 420)

   c. & d. The text did not discuss how stress influences friendship or peer acceptance.

Matching Items

1. a (p. 394)   **5.** j (p. 394)   **9.** i (p. 398)

2. c (p. 396)   **6.** e (p. 400)   **10.** b (p. 410)

3. f (p. 397)   **7.** h (p. 400)   **11.** g (p. 410)

4. k (p. 394)   **8.** d (p. 394)

THINKING CRITICALLY ABOUT CHAPTER 13

1. **d.** is the answer. (p. 394)

   a. This describes an advocate of Freud's theory of development.

   b. This is the viewpoint of a behaviorist.

   c. This is the viewpoint of a cognitive theorist.

2. **c.** is the answer. The question describes what is, for Erikson, the crisis of middle childhood: industry versus inferiority. (p. 393)

3. **d.** is the answer. (pp. 401–402)

   a. Because it would seem to involve "running away" from her problems, this approach would likely be more harmful than helpful.

   b. Improving motor skills is not a factor considered in the text and probably has little value in raising self-esteem in such situations.

   c. If Bonnie is like most school-age children, she is quite self-critical and already accepts responsibility for her failures.

4. **d.** is the answer. (p. 398)

5. **c.** is the answer. (p. 396)

   a., b., & d. These are more typical of preschoolers.

6. **d.** is the answer. (p. 396)

   a. Egocentrism is self-centered thinking. In this example, Chantal is misinterpreting her friend's comment.

   b. & c. There is no reason to believe that Chantal is suffering from an emotional disturbance or that she is feeling inferior.

7. **c.** is the answer. (pp. 399–400)

8. **a.** is the answer. (p. 402)

9. **d.** is the answer. (p. 415)

10. **d.** is the answer. Self-esteem decreases throughout middle childhood. (p. 397)

11. **b.** is the answer. (p. 397)

   a. & c. These are more typical of preschoolers than school-age children.

12. **c.** is the answer. Although emotional maturity is an important factor in family functioning, the text does not suggest that biological parents are more mature than other parents. (p. 412)

13. **d.** is the answer. (p. 404)

   a. & b. It is taller-than-average *boys* and verbally assertive *girls* who are more likely to bully others.

   c. This is a common myth.

14. **d.** is the answer. (p. 402)

    a., b., & c. Contrary to popular belief, victims are no more likely to be fat or homely or to speak with an accent than nonvictims are.

15. **c.** is the answer. (p. 400)

    a. & d. The trend toward fewer but closer friends is more apparent among girls.

    b. At the end of middle childhood, children become more choosy and have fewer friends.

KEY TERMS

1. In Freud's theory, middle childhood is a period of **latency,** during which emotional drives are quieter, psychosexual needs are repressed, and unconscious conflicts are submerged. (p. 393)

2. According to Erikson, the crisis of middle childhood is that of **industry versus inferiority**, in which children try to master many skills and develop views of themselves as either competent or incompetent and inferior. (p. 393)

3. **Social cognitive theory** stresses the importance of maturation and experience in stimulating learning, cognition, and cultural advances in children. (p. 394)

4. **Social cognition** refers to a person's awareness and understanding of the personalities, motives, emotions, intentions, and interactions of other people and groups. (p. 396)

5. **Social comparison** is the tendency to assess one's abilities, achievements, social status, and other attributes by measuring them against those of others, especially those of one's peers. (p. 397)

6. A **peer group** is a group of individuals of roughly the same age and social status who play, work, or learn together. (p. 397)

7. Children in middle childhood develop and transmit their own subculture, called the **society of children**, which has its own games, vocabulary, dress codes, and rules of behavior. (p. 398)

8. The peer group shuns **aggressive-rejected children** because they are overly confrontational. (p. 400)

9. **Withdrawn-rejected children** are shunned by the peer group because of their withdrawn, anxious behavior. (p. 400)

10. **Bullying** is the repeated, systematic effort to inflict harm on a child through physical, verbal, or social attack. (p. 402)

11. **Family function** refers to the ways families work to foster the development of children by meeting their physical needs, encouraging them to learn, and providing harmony and stability. (p. 408)

12. **Family structure** refers to the legal and genetic relationships among the members of a particular family. (p. 408)

13. A **nuclear family** consists of two parents and their mutual biological offspring. (p. 410)

14. An **extended family** consists of three or more generations of biologically related individuals. (p. 410)

15. A **single-parent family** consists of one parent and his or her (biological) children. (p. 410)

16. A **blended family** consists of two parents, at least one with biological children from another union. (p. 410)

17. A **grandparent family** consists of children living with their grandparents instead of with their parents. (p. 410)

18. An **adoptive family** consists of one or more non-biological children whom adults have legally taken as their own. (p. 410)

19. A **foster family** consists of one or more orphaned, neglected, abused, or delinquent children who are temporarily being cared for by an unrelated adult. (p. 410)

Chapter Fourteen

Adolescence: Biosocial Development

Chapter Overview

Between the ages of 10 and 20, young people cross the great divide between childhood and adulthood. This crossing encompasses all three domains of development—biosocial, cognitive, and psychosocial. Chapter 14 focuses on the dramatic changes that occur in the biosocial domain, beginning with puberty and the growth spurt. The biosocial metamorphosis of the adolescent is discussed in detail, with emphasis on sexual maturation, nutrition, and the possible problems arising from dissatisfaction with one's appearance.

Although adolescence is, in many ways, a healthy time of life, the text addresses two health hazards that too often affect adolescence: sexual abuse and the use of alcohol, tobacco, and other drugs.

NOTE: Answer guidelines for all Chapter 14 questions begin on page 232.

Guided Study

The text chapter should be studied one section at a time. Before you read, preview each section by skimming it, noting headings and boldface items. Then read the appropriate section objectives from the following outline. Keep these objectives in mind and, as you read the chapter section, search for the information that will enable you to meet each objective. Once you have finished a section, write out answers for its objectives.

Puberty Begins (pp. 432–436)

1. Outline the biological events of puberty.

2. Discuss the emotional and psychological impact of pubertal hormones.

3. Identify several factors that influence the onset of puberty.

The Biological Changes (pp. 436–440)

4. Describe the growth spurt in both the male and the female adolescent, focusing on changes in body weight and height.

5. Describe the changes in the body's internal organ systems that accompany the growth spurt.

6. Discuss the development of the primary sex characteristics in males and females during puberty.

11. Discuss sexual abuse, noting its prevalence and consequences for development.

7. Discuss the development of the secondary sex characteristics in males and females during puberty.

Health and Hazards (pp. 449–462)

12. Discuss the nutritional needs and problems of adolescents.

Emotional Responses to Physical Growth (pp. 440–449)

8. Discuss the concurrent roles of hormones and the social context in adolescent emotional responses.

13. Compare and contrast the explanations of eating disorders offered by the major theories of development.

9. Discuss the adolescent's preoccupation with body image and the adjustment problems of boys and girls who develop earlier or later than their peers do.

14. (text and Changing Policy) Discuss drug use and abuse among adolescents today, including its prevalence, its significance for development, and the best methods of prevention.

10. Discuss how adolescents respond to the sexual changes of puberty and the consequences of adolescent immature behavior.

Chapter Review

When you have finished reading the chapter, work through the material that follows to review it. Complete the sentences and answer the questions. As you proceed, evaluate your performance for each section by consulting the answers on page 232. Do not continue with the next section until you understand each answer. If you need to, review or reread the appropriate section in the textbook before continuing.

Puberty Begins (pp. 432–436)

1. The biolological transition to adolescence occurs mostly before age _____ . The social and cognitive transition lasts at least until age _____ . The period of rapid physical growth and sexual maturation that ends childhood and brings the young person to adult size, shape, and sexual potential is called

   _____ .

2. Puberty begins when a hormonal signal from the _____ triggers hormone production in the _____

   _____ , which in turn triggers increased hormone production by the

   _____ _____

   and by the _____ , which include the _____ in males and the _____ in females. This route, called the _____ _____ , also triggers the development of the _____ and _____ sexual characteristics.

3. The hormone _____ causes the gonads to dramatically increase their production of sex hormones, especially _____ in girls and _____ in boys. This, in turn, triggers the hypothalamus and pituitary to increase production of _____ .

4. The increase in the hormone _____ is dramatic in boys and slight in girls, whereas the increase in the hormone _____ is marked in girls and slight in boys.

5. The age of puberty is _____ (highly variable/quite consistent from child to child).

6. Normal children begin to notice pubertal changes between the ages of _____ and

   _____ .

7. The average American girl experiences her first menstrual period, called _____ , between ages _____ and _____ , with age _____ the average.

8. Genes are an important factor in the timing of menarche, as demonstrated by the fact that _____ _____ and _____ and _____ reach menarche at very similar ages.

9. The average age of puberty _____ (varies/does not vary) from nation to nation and from ethnic group to ethnic group.

10. Stocky individuals tend to experience puberty _____ (earlier/later) than those with taller, thinner builds.

11. Menarche seems to be related to the accumulation of a certain amount of body _____ . Consequently, serious athletes and those who are chronically _____ menstruate _____ (earlier/later) than the average girl, whereas females who are relatively inactive menstruate _____ (earlier/later).

12. Another influence on the age of puberty is _____ . Abused children have abnormally high or low levels of the hormone _____ , and those under extreme stress grow more _____ (rapidly/slowly), a condition called _____ _____ . This condition may be due to the fact that _____ _____ levels may be disrupted due to disturbances in

    _____ .

13. Research suggests that family emotional distance and stress may _____ (accelerate/delay) the onset of puberty.

14. Stress may cause production of the hormones that cause _____ . Support for this

hypothesis comes from a study showing that early puberty was associated with

_____ and

_____ .

15. An evolutionary explanation of the stress-puberty hypothesis is that ancestral females growing up in stressful environments may have increased their _____ _____ by accelerating physical maturation.

The Biological Changes (pp. 436–440)

16. Although puberty begins at various ages, the _____ is almost always the same.

List, in order, the major physical changes of puberty in

Girls: _____

_____

Boys: _____

_____

17. The first sign of the growth spurt is increased bone _____ , beginning at the tips of the extremities and working toward the center of the body. At the same time, children begin to _____ (gain/lose) weight at a relatively rapid rate.

18. The change in weight that typically occurs between 10 and 12 years of age is due primarily to the accumulation of body _____ . The amount of weight gain an individual experiences depends on several factors, including

_____ , _____ , _____ , and _____ .

19. During the growth spurt, a greater percentage of fat is retained by _____ (males/females), who naturally have a higher proportion of body fat in adulthood.

20. About a year after these height and weight changes occur, a period of _____ increase occurs, causing the pudginess and clumsiness of an earlier age to disappear. In boys, this increase is particularly notable in the _____ body.

21. Overall, between the ages of 10 and 14, the typical girl gains about _____ in weight and _____ in height; between the ages of 12 and 16, the typical boy gains about _____ in height and about _____ in weight.

22. The chronological age for the growth spurt _____ (varies/does not vary) from child to child.

23. One of the last parts of the body to grow into final form is the _____ .

24. The two halves of the body _____ (always/do not always) grow at the same rate.

25. Internal organs also grow during puberty. The _____ increase in size and capacity, the _____ doubles in size, heart rate _____ (increases/decreases), and blood volume _____ (increases/decreases). These changes increase the adolescent's physical _____ .

Explain why the physical demands placed on a teenager, as in athletic training, should not be the same as those for a young adult of similar height and weight.

26. During puberty, one organ system, the _____ system, decreases in size, making teenagers _____ (more/less) susceptible to respiratory ailments.

27. The hormones of puberty also cause many relatively minor physical changes that can have significant emotional impact. These include increased activity in _____ , _____ , and _____ glands.

28. Changes in _____

_____ _____ involve the sex organs that are directly involved in reproduction. By the end of puberty, reproduction _____ (is/is still not) possible.

Describe the major changes in primary sex characteristics that occur in both sexes during puberty.

29. In girls, the event that is usually taken to indicate sexual maturity is _____ . In boys, the indicator of reproductive potential is the first ejaculation of seminal fluid containing sperm, which is called _____ . In both sexes, full reproductive maturity occurs _____ (at this time/several years later).

30. Attitudes toward menarche, menstruation, and spermarche _____ (have/have not) changed over the past two decades, so that most young people _____ (do/do not) face these events with anxiety, embarrassment, or guilt.

31. Sexual features other than those associated with reproduction are referred to as _____ _____ .

Describe the major pubertal changes in the secondary sex characteristics of both sexes.

32. Two secondary sex characteristics that are mistakenly considered signs of womanhood and manliness, respectively, are _____ _____ and _____ .

Emotional Responses to Physical Growth
(pp. 440–449)

33. The founder of American research on adolescence, _____ , described puberty as inevitably a time of _____ .

34. Conflict, moodiness, and sexual urges _____ (usually do/do not usually) increase during adolescence. This is due in part to the increasingly high levels of hormones such as _____ .

35. During puberty, hormonal levels have their greatest emotional impact _____ (directly/indirectly), via the _____ of _____ . Thinking about sex, which is directly linked to _____ , is also powerfully affected by _____ .

36. Adolescents' mental conception of, and attitude toward, their physical appearance is referred to as their _____ _____ .

Identify some common behaviors related to adolescents' preoccupation with their body image.

37. Concern with body image is especially likely to reach extremes for _____ , because norms of _____ are very narrow for their gender. Boys more often are _____ (thrilled/upset) when the first signs of reproductive possibility appear.

38. Young people who experience puberty at the same time as their friends tend to view the experience more _____ (positively/ negatively) than those who experience it early or late.

39. For girls, _____ (early/late) maturation may be especially troublesome.

Describe several common problems and developmental hazards experienced by early-maturing girls.

40. For boys, _____ (early/late) maturation is usually more difficult.

Describe several characteristics and/or problems of late-maturing boys.

41. Although the average age of first marriage in the United States is about _____ , most boys and girls experience sexual intercourse _____ .

42. Sexually active teenagers have higher rates of _____ _____ _____ such as _____ , _____ _____ , _____ , and _____ .

43. Risk of exposure to HIV increases if a person:

   a. _____

   b. _____

   c. _____

44. A second developmental risk for sexually active adolescent girls is _____ . If this happens within a year or two of menarche, girls are at increased risk of many complications, including _____ _____ . Teenage motherhod slows _____ and _____ achievement and restricts _____ and _____ growth. Babies of young teenagers have a higher risk of _____ and _____ complications, including _____ _____ and _____ _____ .

45. Any activity in which an adult uses an unconsenting person child for his or her own sexual stimulation or pleasure is considered _____ _____ . When such activity involves a young person it is called _____ _____ _____ .

46. The damage done by sexual abuse depends on many factors, including how often it is _____ , how much it distorts _____–_____ , and if it impairs normal _____ .

47. Sexual victimization often begins in _____ , and typically is committed by _____ . Blatant sexual abuse typically begins at _____ , particularly if _____ .

48. Currently in North America the age of consent is between _____ and _____ . Intercourse with a younger person constitutes _____ _____ .

49. Adolescents may react to maltreatment in ways that younger children rarely do, with _____ or by _____ .

50. Adolescent problems, such as pregnancy, often are tied to past _____ _____ .

Health and Hazards (pp. 449–462)

51. The major diseases of adulthood, including _____ and _____ _____ , are _____ (also common/rare) during adolescence. Death rates caused by _____ _____ increase markedly from ages 10 to 25.

52. Due to rapid physical growth, the adolescent needs a higher daily intake of _____ , _____ , and _____ . Specifically, the typical adolescent needs about 50 percent more of the minerals _____ , _____ , and _____ during the growth spurt. Inadequate consumption of _____ is particularly troubling because it is a good souce of the _____ needed for bone growth.

53. One measure of body weight is the _____ _____ _____ , which is a person's weight in _____ divided by the square of his or her _____ in meters. A healthy weight falls between a BMI of _____ and _____ . Every person has a natural weight, called a _____ .

54. One cause of poor eating habits is that adolescents rarely think rationally about the _____ . Most teenagers eat _____ (few/most) meals at home. As a result, they are likely to consume too much _____ , _____ , _____ , and _____ .

55. Because of menstruation, adolescent females need additional _____ in their diets and are more likely to suffer _____-_____ _____ than any other subgroup of the population.

56. The most hazardous periods for eating disorders are at about age _____ , and again at about age _____ .

57. The eating disorder in which a person undereats to the point of emaciation is _____ _____ . The four symptoms of this disorder are

   a. _____
   b. _____
   c. _____
   d. _____

58. Anorexia is suspected when a person's BMI is _____ or lower and he or she loses more than _____ percent of body weight within _____ . This disorder was virtually unknown before _____ . Approximately _____ percent of adolescent and young adult females suffer from this disorder at

some point during their lives, with rates much higher among _____ .

59. A _____ (rarer/more common) eating disorder that is characterized by binge–purge behavior is called _____ _____ . A clinical diagnosis of this disorder is made when the person

   a. _____
   b. _____
   c. _____

60. Those who suffer from bulima usually _____ (are/are not) close to normal weight and may experience a range of serious health problems, including damage to the _____ system and even _____ failure.

61. Which major developmental theory explains eating disorders as the result of

   a. cultural pressure to be "slim and trim"?

   _____

   b. unresolved conflict with one's mother?

   _____

   c. the desire to project a strong, self-controlled, masculine image? _____

   d. low self-esteem and depression (stimulus) that precipitate extreme dieting (response)?

   _____

   e. the impact of genes on the evolutionary mandate to reproduce?

   _____

62. Drug _____ always harms physical and psychological development, whether or not the drug becomes _____ . Drug _____ may or may not be harmful, depending in part on the _____ of the person and the reason for and consequences of the drug's use.

63. Tobacco, alcohol, and marijuana may act as _____ _____ , opening the door not only to regular use of multiple drugs but also to other destructive behaviors, such as

risky _____ , school

_____ , and

_____ .

64. By decreasing food consumption and the absorption of nutrients, tobacco can limit the adolescent

_____ _____ .

65. Because alcohol loosens _____ and impairs _____ , even moderate use can be destructive in adolescence. Alcohol also impairs _____ and _____ by damaging the brain's _____ and

_____ _____ .

66. Marijuana _____ (slows/accelerates) thinking processes, particularly those related to _____ and _____ reasoning.

67. More than _____ (how many?) high school seniors admit to using at least one drug in the last month, with _____ being the most common.

68. Antidrug attitudes _____ (have/have not) softened among adolescent Americans, perhaps because each cohort goes through _____ _____ .

69. Whether a particular teenager uses drugs, and what drugs he or she uses, depends largely on his or her _____ , the _____ , and the national

_____ .

70. (Changing Policy) Students who participate in Project D.A.R.E. are _____ (more/no more) likely to abstain from drugs over the high school years than those who do not.

(Changing Policy) Why do developmentalists urge teens to delay drug experimentation as long as possible?

71. (Changing Policy) Three factors that protect against drug use are

a. _____

b. _____

c. _____

Progress Test 1

Multiple-Choice Questions

Circle your answers to the following questions and check them with the answers on page 234. If your answer is incorrect, read the explanation for why it is incorrect and then consult the appropriate pages of the text (in parentheses following the correct answer).

1. Which of the following most accurately describes the sequence of pubertal development in girls?
   a. breasts and pubic hair; growth spurt in which fat is deposited on hips and buttocks; first menstrual period; ovulation
   b. growth spurt; breasts and pubic hair; first menstrual period; ovulation
   c. first menstrual period; breasts and pubic hair; growth spurt; ovulation
   d. breasts and pubic hair; growth spurt; ovulation; first menstrual period

2. Although both sexes grow rapidly during adolescence, boys typically gain more than girls in their:
   a. muscle strength.
   b. body fat.
   c. internal organ growth.
   d. lymphoid system.

3. The first readily observable sign of the onset of puberty is:
   a. the growth spurt.
   b. the appearance of facial, body, and pubic hair.
   c. a change in the shape of the eyes.
   d. a lengthening of the torso.

4. More than any other group in the population, adolescent girls are likely to have:
   a. asthma.
   b. acne.
   c. iron-deficiency anemia.
   d. testosterone deficiency.

5. The HPA axis is the:
   a. route followed by many hormones to regulate stress, growth, sleep, and appetite.
   b. pair of sex glands in humans.
   c. cascade of sex hormones in females and males.
   d. area of the brain that regulates the pituitary gland.

6. For males, the secondary sex characteristic that usually occurs last is:
   a. breast enlargement.
   b. the appearance of facial hair.
   c. growth of the testes.
   d. the appearance of pubic hair.

7. For girls, the specific event that is taken to indicate fertility is _____ ; for boys, it is _____ .
   a. the growth of breast buds; voice deepening
   b. menarche; spermarche
   c. anovulation; the testosterone surge
   d. the growth spurt; pubic hair

8. The most significant hormonal changes of puberty include an increase of _____ in _____ and an increase of _____ in _____ .
   a. progesterone; boys; estrogen; girls
   b. estrogen; boys; testosterone; girls
   c. progesterone; girls; estrogen; boys
   d. estrogen; girls; testosterone; boys

9. In general, most adolescents are:
   a. overweight.
   b. satisfied with their appearance.
   c. dissatisfied with their appearance.
   d. unaffected by cultural attitudes about beauty.

10. Of the following, who is most likely to suffer from anorexia nervosa?
    a. Bill, a 23-year-old professional football player
    b. Florence, a 30-year-old account executive
    c. Lynn, an 18-year-old college student
    d. Carl, a professional dancer

11. The damage caused by sexual abuse depends on all of the following factors *except*:
    a. repeated incidence.
    b. the gender of the perpetrator.
    c. distorted adult–child relationships.
    d. impairment of the child's ability to develop normally.

12. Early physical growth and sexual maturation:
    a. tend to be equally difficult for girls and boys.
    b. tend to be more difficult for boys than for girls.
    c. tend to be more difficult for girls than for boys.
    d. are easier for both girls and boys than late maturation.

13. Epinephrine and norepinephrine are _____ that are released by the _____ gland(s).
    a. neurotransmitters; pituitary
    b. hormones; pituitary
    c. neurotransmitters; adrenal
    d. hormones; adrenal

14. Body mass index (BMI) is calculated by dividing:
    a. height in meters by weight in kilograms.
    b. weight in kilograms by height in meters.
    c. height in meters squared by weight in kilograms.
    d. weight in kilograms by height in meters squared.

15. Professor Wilson, who believes that the roots of eating disorders are in the gene pool of our species and the evolutionary mandate to reproduce, is evidently a proponent of which theory?
    a. psychoanalytic
    b. behaviorism
    c. epigenetic systems
    d. sociocultural

True or False Items

Write T (*true*) or F (*false*) on the line in front of each statement.

_____ 1. More calories are necessary during adolescence than at any other period during the life span.

_____ 2. Anorexia is suspected if a person's BMI is 18 or lower.

_____ 3. The first indicator of reproductive potential in males is menarche.

_____ 4. Lung capacity, heart size, and total volume of blood increase significantly during adolescence.

_____ 5. Puberty generally begins sometime between ages 8 and 14.

_____ 6. Girls who mature late and are thinner than average tend to be satisfied with their weight.

_____ 7. The strong emphasis on physical appearance is unique to adolescents and finds little support from teachers, parents, and the larger culture.

_____ 8. Childhood habits of overeating and underexercising usually lessen during adolescence.

_____ 9. The problems of the early-maturing girl tend to be temporary.

_____ 10. Both the sequence and timing of pubertal events vary greatly from one young person to another.

Progress Test 2

Progress Test 2 should be completed during a final chapter review. Answer the following questions after you thoroughly understand the correct answers for the Chapter Review and Progress Test 1.

Multiple-Choice Questions

1. Which of the following is the correct sequence of pubertal events in boys?
   a. growth spurt, pubic hair, facial hair, first ejaculation, lowering of voice
   b. facial hair, pubic hair, first ejaculation, growth spurt; lowering of voice, facial hair
   c. lowering of voice, pubic hair, growth spurt, facial hair, first ejaculation
   d. growth spurt, facial hair, lowering of voice, pubic hair, first ejaculation

2. Which of the following statements about adolescent physical development is *not* true?
   a. Hands and feet generally lengthen before arms and legs.
   b. Facial features usually grow before the head itself reaches adult size and shape.
   c. Oil, sweat, and odor glands become more active.
   d. The lymphoid system increases slightly in size, and the heart increases by nearly half.

3. In puberty, a hormone that increases markedly in girls (and only somewhat in boys) is:
   a. estrogen.   c. androgen.
   b. testosterone.   d. menarche.

4. Nutritional deficiencies in adolescence are frequently the result of:
   a. eating red meat.
   b. poor eating habits.
   c. anovulatory menstruation.
   d. excessive exercise.

5. In females, puberty is typically marked by a(n):
   a. significant widening of the shoulders.
   b. significant widening of the hips.
   c. enlargement of the torso and upper chest.
   d. decrease in the size of the eyes and nose.

6. Nonreproductive sexual characteristics, such as the deepening of the voice and the development of breasts, are called:
   a. gender-typed traits.
   b. primary sex characteristics.
   c. secondary sex characteristics.
   d. pubertal prototypes.

7. Puberty is initiated when hormones are released from the _____ , then from the _____ gland, and then from the adrenal glands and the _____ .
   a. hypothalamus; pituitary; gonads
   b. pituitary; gonads; hypothalamus
   c. gonads; pituitary; hypothalamus
   d. pituitary; hypothalamus; gonads

8. The typical bulimic patient is a:
   a. college-age woman.
   b. teenage girl who starves herself to the point of emaciation.
   c. woman in her late forties.
   d. teenager who suffers from life-threatening obesity.

9. With regard to appearance, adolescent girls are *most* commonly dissatisfied with:
   a. timing of maturation.   c. weight.
   b. eyes and other facial features.   d. legs.

10. Statistically speaking, to predict the age at which a girl first has sexual intercourse, it would be *most* useful to know her:
    a. socioeconomic level.
    b. race or ethnic group.
    c. religion.
    d. age at menarche.

11. Individuals who experiment with drugs early are:
    a. typically affluent teenagers who are experiencing an identity crisis.
    b. more likely to have multiple drug-abuse problems later on.
    c. less likely to have alcohol-abuse problems later on.
    d. usually able to resist later peer pressure leading to long-term addiction.

12. Compounding the problem of sexual abuse of boys, abused boys:

    a. feel shame at the idea of being weak.

    b. have fewer sources of emotional support.

    c. are more likely to be abused by fathers.

    d. have all of the above problems.

13. Puberty is *most accurately* defined as the period:

    a. of rapid physical growth that occurs during adolescence.

    b. during which sexual maturation is attained.

    c. of rapid physical growth and sexual maturation that ends childhood.

    d. during which adolescents establish identities separate from their parents.

14. Which of the following does *not* typically occur during puberty?

    a. The lungs increase in size and capacity.

    b. The heart's size and rate of beating increase.

    c. Blood volume increases.

    d. The lymphoid system decreases in size.

15. Teenagers' susceptibility to respiratory ailments typically _____ during adolescence, due to a(n) _____ in the size of the lymphoid system.

    a. increases; increase

    b. increases; decrease

    c. decreases; increase

    d. decreases; decrease

Matching Items

Match each term or concept with its corresponding description or definition.

Terms or Concepts

_____ **1.** puberty

_____ **2.** GH

_____ **3.** testosterone

_____ **4.** estrogen

_____ **5.** growth spurt

_____ **6.** primary sex characteristics

_____ **7.** menarche

_____ **8.** spermarche

_____ **9.** secondary sex characteristics

_____ **10.** body image

_____ **11.** anorexia nervosa

_____ **12.** bulimia nervosa

Descriptions or Definitions

    a. onset of menstruation

    b. period of rapid physical growth and sexual maturation that ends childhood

    c. hormone that increases dramatically in boys during puberty

    d. hormone that increases steadily during puberty in both sexes

    e. an affliction characterized by binge–purge eating

    f. hormone that increases dramatically in girls during puberty

    g. first sign is increased bone length

    h. attitude toward one's physical appearance

    i. an affliction characterized by self-starvation

    j. physical characteristics not involved in reproduction

    k. the sex organs involved in reproduction

    l. first ejaculation containing sperm

Thinking Critically About Chapter 14

Answer these questions the day before an exam as a final check on your understanding of the chapter's terms and concepts.

1. Fifteen-year-old Latoya is preoccupied with her "disgusting appearance" and seems depressed most of the time. The best thing her parents could do to help her through this difficult time would be to:
   a. ignore her self-preoccupation because their attention would only reinforce it.
   b. encourage her to "shape up" and not give in to self-pity.
   c. kid her about her appearance in the hope that she will see how silly she is acting.
   d. offer practical advice, such as clothing suggestions, to improve her body image.

2. Thirteen-year-old Rosa, an avid runner and dancer, is worried because most of her friends have begun to menstruate regularly. Her doctor tells her:
   a. that she should have a complete physical exam, because female athletes usually menstruate earlier than average.
   b. not to worry, because female athletes usually menstruate later than average.
   c. that she must stop running immediately, because the absence of menstruation is a sign of a serious health problem.
   d. that the likely cause of her delayed menarche is an inadequate diet.

3. Twelve-year-old Kwan is worried because his twin sister has suddenly grown taller and more physically mature than he. His parents should:
   a. reassure him that the average boy is one or two years behind the average girl in the onset of the growth spurt.
   b. tell him that within a year or less he will grow taller than his sister.
   c. tell him that one member of each fraternal twin pair is always shorter.
   d. encourage him to exercise more to accelerate the onset of his growth spurt.

4. Calvin, the class braggart, boasts that because his beard has begun to grow, he is more virile than his male classmates. Jacob informs him that:
   a. the tendency to grow facial and body hair has nothing to do with virility.
   b. beard growth is determined by heredity.
   c. girls also develop some facial hair and more noticeable hair on their arms and legs, so it is clearly not a sign of masculinity.
   d. all of the above are true.

5. The most likely source of status for a late-maturing, middle-SES boy would be:
   a. academic achievement or vocational goal.
   b. physical build.
   c. athletic prowess.
   d. success with the opposite sex.

6. Which of the following students is likely to be the most popular in a sixth-grade class?
   a. Vicki, the most sexually mature girl in the class
   b. Sandra, the tallest girl in the class
   c. Brad, who is at the top of the class scholastically
   d. Dan, the tallest boy in the class

7. Regarding the effects of early and late maturation on boys and girls, which of the following is *not* true?
   a. Early maturation is usually easier for boys to manage than it is for girls.
   b. Late maturation is usually easier for girls to manage than it is for boys.
   c. Late-maturing girls may be drawn into involvement with older boys.
   d. Late-maturing boys may not "catch up" physically, or in terms of their self-images, for many years.

8. Allan is 2.0 meters tall and weighs 91 kilograms. His body mass index is such that he would be considered:
   a. anorexic.
   b. of normal body weight.
   c. overweight.
   d. obese.

9. Twenty-four-year-old Connie, who has a distorted view of sexuality, has gone from one abusive relationship with a man to another. It is likely that Connie:
   a. has been abusing drugs all her life.
   b. was sexually abused as a child.
   c. will eventually become a normal, nurturing mother.
   d. had attention-deficit disorder as a child.

10. As a psychoanalyst, Dr. Mendoza is most likely to believe that eating disorders are caused by:
    a. contemporary pressure to be "slim and trim."
    b. low self-esteem and depression, which act as a stimulus for destructive patterns of eating.
    c. unresolved conflicts with parents.
    d. the desire of working women to project a strong, self-controlled image.

11. Which of the following adolescents is likely to begin puberty at the earliest age?
    a. Aretha, an African American teenager who hates exercise
    b. Todd, a football player of European ancestry
    c. Kyu, an Asian American honors student
    d. There is too little information to make a prediction.

12. Of the following teenagers, those most likely to be distressed about their physical development are:
    a. late-maturing girls.
    b. late-maturing boys.
    c. early-maturing boys.
    d. girls or boys who masturbate.

13. Thirteen-year-old Kristin seems apathetic and lazy to her parents. You tell them:
    a. that Kristin is showing signs of chronic depression.
    b. that Kristin may be experiencing psychosocial difficulties.
    c. that Kristin has a poor attitude and needs more discipline.
    d. to have Kristin's iron level checked.

14. I am a hormone that rises steadily during puberty in both males and females. What am I?
    a. estrogen   c. GH
    b. testosterone d. menarche

15. Eleven-year-old Linda, who has just begun to experience the first signs of puberty, laments, "When will the agony of puberty be over?" You tell her that the major events of puberty typically end about _____ after the first visible signs appear.
    a. 6 years   c. 2 years
    b. 3 or 4 years d. 1 year

Key Terms

Writing Definitions

Using your own words, write a brief definition or explanation of each of the following terms on a separate piece of paper.

1. adolescence
2. puberty
3. hypothalamus
4. pituitary gland
5. adrenal glands
6. HPA axis
7. gonads
8. estrogen
9. testosterone
10. menarche
11. spermarche
12. growth spurt
13. primary sex characteristics
14. secondary sex characteristics
15. body image
16. sexually transmitted diseases (STDs)
17. sexual abuse
18. child sexual abuse
19. body mass index (BMI)
20. anorexia nervosa
21. bulimia nervosa
22. drug use
23. drug abuse
24. drug addiction
25. gateway drugs
26. generational forgetting

Cross-Check

After you have written the definitions of the key terms in this chapter, you should complete the crossword puzzle to ensure that you can reverse the process—recognize the term, given the definition.

ACROSS

1. Glands near the kidneys that are stimulated by the pituitary at the beginning of puberty.
7. The first ejaculation of seminal fluid containing sperm.
12. The first menstrual period.
15. The ovaries in girls and the testes or testicles in boys.
17. Gland that stimulates the adrenal glands and the sex glands in response to a signal from the hypothalamus.
18. Event, which begins with an increase in bone length and includes rapid weight gain and organ growth, that is one of the many observable signs of puberty.
19. Ingestion of a drug, regardless of the amount or affect of ingestion.

DOWN

1. The period of biological, cognitive, and psychosocial transition from childhood to adulthood.
2. Organ system, which includes the tonsils and adenoids, that decreases in size at adolescence.
3. Area of the brain that sends the hormonal signal that triggers the biological events of puberty.
4. Widely abused gateway drug that loosens inhibitions and impairs judgment.
5. Dependence on a drug or a behavior in order to feel physically or psychologically at ease.
6. Drugs—usually tobacco, alcohol, and marijuana—whose use increases the risk that a person will later use harder drugs.
8. Ingestion of a drug to the extent that it impairs the user's well-being.
9. Body characteristics that are not directly involved in reproduction but that signify sexual development.
10. Main sex hormone in males.
11. Gateway drug that decreases food consumption, the absorption of nutrients, and fertility.
13. Main sex hormone in females.
14. Period of rapid physical growth and sexual maturation that ends childhood and brings the young person to adult size.
16. Sex organs that are directly involved in reproduction.

ANSWERS

CHAPTER REVIEW

1. 15; 18; puberty
2. hypothalamus; pituitary gland; adrenal glands; gonads (sex glands); testes; ovaries; HPA axis; primary; secondary
3. GnRH (gonad releasing hormone); estrogen; testosterone; GH (growth hormone)
4. testosterone; estrogen
5. highly variable
6. 8; 14
7. menarche; 9; 15; 12
8. monozygotic twins; mothers; daughters
9. varies
10. earlier
11. fat; malnourished; later; earlier
12. stress; cortisol; slowly; deprivation dwarfism; growth hormone; sleep
13. accelerate
14. puberty; conflicted relationships within the family; an unrelated man living in the home
15. reproductive success
16. sequence

Girls: onset of breast growth, initial pubic hair, peak growth spurt, widening of the hips, first menstrual period, completion of pubic-hair growth, and final breast development

Boys: initial pubic hair, growth of the testes, growth of the penis, first ejaculation, peak growth spurt, voice changes, beard development, and completion of pubic-hair growth

17. length; gain

18. fat; sex; heredity; diet; exercise

19. females

20. muscle; upper

21. 38 pounds (17 kilograms); 9 5/8 inches (24 centimeters); 10 inches (25 centimeters); 42 pounds (19 kilograms)

22. varies

23. head

24. do not always

25. lungs; heart; decreases; increases; endurance

The fact that the more visible spurts of weight and height precede the less visible ones of the muscles and organs means that athletic training and weight lifting should match the young person's size of a year or so earlier.

26. lymphoid; less

27. oil; sweat; odor

28. primary sex characteristics; is

Girls: growth of uterus and thickening of the vaginal lining

Boys: growth of testes and lengthening of penis; also scrotum enlarges and becomes pendulous

29. menarche; spermarche; several years later

30. have; do not

31. secondary sex characteristics

Males grow taller than females and become wider at the shoulders than at the hips. Females take on more fat all over and become wider at the hips, and their breasts begin to develop. About 65 percent of boys experience some temporary breast enlargement. As the larynx grows, the adolescent's voice (especially in boys) becomes lower. Head and body hair become coarser and darker in both sexes. Facial hair (especially in boys) begins to grow.

32. breast development; facial and body hair

33. G. Stanley Hall; storm and stress

34. usually do; testosterone

35. indirectly; visible signs; sexual maturation; hormones; culture

36. body image

Many adolescents spend hours examining themselves in front of the mirror; some exercise or diet with obsessive intensity.

37. girls; attractiveness; thrilled

38. positively

39. early

Early-maturing girls may be teased about their big feet or developing breasts. Those who date early may begin "adult" activities at an earlier age, may be pressured by their dates to be sexually active, and may suffer a decrease in self-esteem.

40. late

Late-maturing boys who are short and skinny and who are not athletic are likely to be shunned by girls. They tend to be talkative and restless.

41. 24; before they graduate from high school

42. sexually transmitted diseases; gonorrhea; genital herpes; syphilis; chlamydia

43. **a.** is already infected with other STDs

    b. has more than one sexual partner within a year

    c. does not use condoms during intercourse

44. pregnancy; spontaneous abortion, eclampsia, stillbirth, cesarean section, and a low-birthweight baby; educational; vocational; social; personal; prenatal; birth; low birthweight; brain damage

45. sexual abuse; child sexual abuse

46. repeated; adult–child relationships; development

47. childhood; fathers or stepfathers; puberty; the mother is away, the biological father is absent, and an unrelated male is in the household

48. 14; 18; statutory rape

49. self-destruction; counterattacking

50. sexual abuse

51. cancer; heart disease; rare; accidental injury

52. calories; vitamins; minerals; calcium; iron; zinc; milk; calcium

53. body mass index (BMI); kilograms; height; 19; 24; set point

54. future; few; salt; sugar; fat; preservatives

55. iron; iron-deficiency anemia

56. 12 or 13; 18

57. anorexia nervosa

    a. refusal to maintain body weight at least 85 percent of normal for age and height

    b. intense fear of gaining weight

    c. disturbed body perception and denial of the problem

    d. lack of menstruation

58. 18; 10; a month or two; 1950; 1; runners, gymnasts, and dancers

59. more common; bulimia nervosa

  a. binges and purges at least once a week for three months

  b. has uncontrollable urges to overeat

  c. has a distorted self-judgment based on misperceived body size

60. are; gastrointestinal; heart

61. **a.** sociocultural theory

  b. psychoanalytic theory

  c. cognitive theory

  d. behaviorism

  e. epigenetic systems theory

62. abuse; addictive; use; maturation

63. gateway drugs; sex; failure; violence

64. growth rate

65. inhibitions; judgment; memory; self-control; hippocampus; prefrontal cortex

66. slows; memory; abstract

67. half; alcohol

68. have not; generational forgetting

69. peers; community; culture

70. no more

Delaying experimentation increases the adolescent's chances of becoming realistically informed about the risks of drug use and of developing the reasoning ability to limit or avoid the use of destructive drugs in dangerous circumstances.

71. **a.** active, problem-solving style of coping

  b. competence and well-being

  c. cognitive maturity

PROGRESS TEST 1

Multiple-Choice Questions

1. **a.** is the answer. (p. 436)

2. **a.** is the answer. (p. 437)

  b. Girls gain more body fat than boys do.

  c. & d. The text does not indicate that these are different for boys and girls.

3. **a.** is the answer. (p. 436)

4. **c.** is the answer. This is because each menstrual period depletes some iron from the body. (p. 451)

5. **a.** is the answer. (p. 433)

  b. This describes the gonads.

  c. These include estrogen and testosterone.

  d. This is the hypothalamus.

6. **b.** is the answer. (p. 436)

7. **b.** is the answer. (p. 439)

8. **d.** is the answer. (p. 433)

9. **c.** is the answer. (pp. 443–444)

  a. Although some adolescents become overweight, many diet and lose weight in an effort to attain a desired body image.

  d. On the contrary, cultural attitudes about beauty are an extremely influential factor in the formation of a teenager's body image.

10. **c.** is the answer. (pp. 452–453)

  a. & d. Eating disorders are more common in women than in men.

  b. Eating disorders are more common in younger women.

11. **b.** is the answer. (pp. 448–449)

12. **c.** is the answer. (p. 444)

13. **d.** is the answer. Also known as adrenaline and noradrenaline, epinephrine and norepinephrine are hormones released by the adrenal glands. (p. 432)

14. **d.** is the answer. (p. 450)

15. **c.** is the answer. (p. 455)

  a. Psychoanalytic theorists believe that women develop eating disorders because of conflicts with their mothers.

  b. Behaviorists see fasting, bingeing, and purging as powerful reinforcers.

  d. Sociocultural theorists point to restrictive cultural norms of attractiveness as the roots of eating disorders.

True or False Items

1. T (p. 450)

2. T (p. 452)

3. F The first indicator of reproductive potential in males is ejaculation of seminal fluid containing sperm (spermarche). Menarche (the first menstrual period) is the first indication of reproductive potential in females. (p. 434)

4. T (p. 438)

5. T (p. 433)

6. F Studies show that the majority of adolescent girls, even those in the thinnest group, want to lose weight. (p. 432)

7. F The strong emphasis on appearance is reflected in the culture as a whole; for example, teachers (and, no doubt, prospective employers) tend to judge people who are physically attractive as being more competent than those who are less attractive. (p. 452)

8. F These habits generally *worsen* during adolescence. (pp. 450–451)

9. T (p. 445)

10. F Although there is great variation in the timing of pubertal events, the sequence is very similar for all young people. (p. 436)

PROGRESS TEST 2

Multiple-Choice Questions

1. **b.** is the answer. (pp. 436)

2. **d.** is the answer. During adolescence, the lymphoid system *decreases* in size and the heart *doubles* in size. (p. 438)

3. **a.** is the answer. (p. 433)

   b. Testosterone increases markedly in boys.

   c. Androgen is another name for testosterone.

   d. Menarche is the first menstrual period.

4. **b.** is the answer. (p. 451)

5. **b.** is the answer. (p. 437)

   a. The shoulders of males tend to widen during puberty.

   c. The torso typically lengthens during puberty.

   d. The eyes and nose *increase* in size during puberty.

6. **c.** is the answer. (p. 439)

   a. Although not a term used in the textbook, a gender-typed trait is one that is typical of one sex but not of the other.

   b. Primary sex characteristics are those involving the reproductive organs.

   d. This is not a term used by developmental psychologists.

7. **a.** is the answer. (p. 432)

8. **a.** is the answer. (p. 454)

   b. This describes an individual suffering from anorexia nervosa.

   c. Eating disorders are much more common in younger women.

   d. Most individuals with bulimia nervosa are usually close to normal in weight.

9. **c.** is the answer. (p. 443)

a. If the timing of maturation differs substantially from that of the peer group, dissatisfaction is likely; however, this is not the most common source of dissatisfaction in teenage girls.

b. & d. Although teenage girls are more likely than boys to be dissatisfied with certain features, which body parts are troubling varies from girl to girl.

10. **d.** is the answer. (p. 444)

11. **b.** is the answer. (p. 456)

12. **a.** is the answer. (p. 449)

    b. This was not discussed in the text.

    c. This is true of girls.

13. **c.** is the answer. (p. 432)

14. **b.** is the answer. Although the size of the heart increases during puberty, heart rate *decreases*. (p. 438)

15. **d.** is the answer. (p. 438)

Matching Items

1. b (p. 432)	5. g (p. 436)	9. j (p. 439)
2. d (p. 433)	6. k (p. 439)	10. h (p. 443)
3. c (p. 433)	7. a (p. 434)	11. i (p. 452)
4. f (p. 433)	8. l (p. 434)	12. e (p. 454)

THINKING CRITICALLY ABOUT CHAPTER 14

1. **d.** is the answer. (p. 443)

   a., b., & c. These would likely make matters worse.

2. **b.** is the answer. (p. 435)

   a. Because they typically have little body fat, female dancers and athletes menstruate *later* than average.

   c. Delayed maturation in a young dancer or athlete is usually quite normal.

   d. The text does not indicate that the age of menarche varies with diet.

3. **a.** is the answer. (p. 437)

   b. It usually takes longer than one year for a prepubescent male to catch up with a female who has begun puberty.

   c. This is not true.

   d. The text does not suggest that exercise has an effect on the timing of the growth spurt.

4. **d.** is the answer. (p. 440)

5. **a.** is the answer. (p. 445)

   b., c., & d. These are more typically sources of status for early-maturing boys.

6. **d.** is the answer. (pp. 444–445)

    a. & b. Early-maturing girls are often teased and criticized by their friends.

    c. During adolescence, physical stature is typically a more prized attribute among peers than is scholastic achievement.

7. **c.** is the answer. It is *early*-maturing girls who are often drawn into involvement with older boys. (p. 444)

8. **b.** is the answer. Allan's BMI of 22.75 (91 kilograms divided by 2.0 meters squared) falls between 19 and 24, the normal range. (p. 450)

9. **b.** is the answer. (p. 449)

10. **c.** is the answer. (p. 455)

    a. Those who emphasize sociocultural theory would more likely offer this explanation.

    b. Those who emphasize behaviorism would more likely offer this explanation.

    d. Those who emphasize cognitive theory would more likely offer this explanation.

11. **a.** is the answer. African Americans often begin puberty earlier than Asian Americans or Americans of European ancestry. Furthermore, females who are inactive menstruate earlier than those who are more active. (p. 435)

12. **b.** is the answer. (pp. 444–445)

    a. Late maturation is typically more difficult for boys than for girls.

    c. Early maturation is generally a positive experience for boys.

    d. Adolescent masturbation is no longer the source of guilt or shame that it once was.

13. **d.** Kristin's symptoms are typical of iron-deficiency anemia, which is more common in teenage girls than in any other age group. (p. 451)

14. **c.** is the answer. (p. 433)

    a. Only in girls do estrogen levels rise markedly during puberty.

    b. Only in boys do testosterone levels rise markedly during puberty.

    d. Menarche is the first menstrual period.

15. **b.** is the answer. (p. 436)

KEY TERMS

1. **Adolescence** is the period of biological, cognitive, and psychosocial transition from childhood to adulthood. (p. 431)

2. **Puberty** is the period of rapid physical growth and sexual maturation that ends childhood and brings the young person to adult size, shape, and sexual potential. (p. 432)

3. The **hypothalamus** is the part of the brain that regulates eating, drinking, body temperature, and the production of hormones by the pituitary gland. (p. 432)

4. The **pituitary gland,** under the influence of the hypothalamus, produces hormones that regulate growth and control other glands. (p. 432)

5. The **adrenal glands** secrete epinephrine and norephinephrine, hormones that prepare the body to deal with emergencies or stress. (p. 432)

6. The **HPA axis** (hypothalamus/pituitary/adrenal axis) is the route followed by many hormones to trigger puberty and to regulate stress, growth, and other bodily changes. (p. 433)

7. The **gonads** are the pair of sex glands in humans—the ovaries in females and the testes or testicles in males. (p. 433)

8. **Estrogen** is a sex hormone that is secreted in greater amounts by females than by males. (p. 433)

9. **Testosterone** is a sex hormone that is secreted more by males than by females. (p. 433)

10. **Menarche,** which refers to the first menstrual period, is the specific event that is taken to indicate fertility in adolescent girls. (p. 434)

11. **Spermarche,** which refers to the first ejaculation of sperm, is the specific event that is taken to indicate fertility in adolescent boys. (p. 434)

12. The **growth spurt,** which is a period of relatively sudden and rapid physical growth of every part of the body, is one of the many observable signs of puberty. (p. 436)

13. During puberty, changes in the **primary sex characteristics** involve those sex organs that are directly involved in reproduction. (p. 439)

14. During puberty, changes in the **secondary sex characteristics** involve parts of the body that are not directly involved in reproduction but that signify sexual development. (p. 439)

15. **Body image** refers to adolescents' mental conception of, and attitude toward, their physical appearance. (p. 443)

16. **Sexually transmitted diseases (STDs)** such as syphilis, gonorrhea, herpes, and AIDS, are those that are spread by sexual contact. (p. 445

17. **Sexual abuse** is the use of an unconsenting person for one's own sexual pleasure. (p. 448)

18. **Child sexual abuse** is any activity in which an adult uses a child for his or her own sexual stimulation or pleasure—even if the use does not involve physical contact. (p. 448)

19. A measure of obesity, **body mass index (BMI)** is calculated by dividing a person's weight in kilograms by his or her height in meters squared. (p. 450)

20. **Anorexia nervosa** is a serious eating disorder in which a person restricts eating to the point of emaciation and possible starvation. (p. 452)

21. **Bulimia nervosa** is an eating disorder in which the person engages repeatedly in episodes of binge eating followed by purging through induced vomiting or the abuse of laxatives. (p. 454)

22. **Drug use** is the ingestion of a drug, regardless of the amount or effect of ingestion. (p. 456)

23. **Drug abuse** is the ingestion of a drug to the extent that it impairs the user's well-being. (p. 456)

24. **Drug addiction** is a person's dependence on a drug or a behavior in order to feel physically or psychologically at ease. (p. 456)

25. **Gateway drugs** are drugs—usually tobacco, alcohol, and marijuana—whose use increases the risk that a person will later use harder drugs. (p. 456)

26. **Generational forgetting** is the tendency of each new generation to ignore lessons (such as the hazards of drug use) learned by the previous cohort. (p. 458)

Cross-Check

ACROSS

1. adrenal
7. spermarche
12. menarche
15. gonads
17. pituitary
18. growth spurt
19. drug use

DOWN

1. adolescence
2. lymphoid
3. hypothalamus
4. alcohol
5. drug addiction
6. gateway drugs
8. drug abuse
9. secondary
10. testosterone
11. tobacco
13. estrogen
14. puberty
16. primary

Chapter Fifteen

Adolescence: Cognitive Development

Chapter Overview

Chapter 15 begins by describing the cognitive advances of adolescence. With the attainment of formal operational thought, the developing person becomes able to think in an adult way, that is, to be logical, to think in terms of possibilities, to reason scientifically and abstractly.

Not everyone reaches the stage of formal operational thought, however, and even those who do so spend much of their time thinking at less advanced levels. The discussion of adolescent egocentrism supports this generalization in showing that adolescents have difficulty thinking rationally about themselves and their immediate experiences. Adolescent egocentrism makes them see themselves as psychologically unique and more socially significant than they really are.

The second section addresses the question, "What kind of school best fosters adolescent intellectual growth?" Many adolescents enter secondary school feeling less motivated and more vulnerable to self-doubt than they did in elementary school. The rigid behavioral demands and intensified competition of most secondary schools do not, unfortunately, provide a supportive learning environment for adolescents.

The chapter concludes with a discussion of the adolescent decision-making process in relation to employment, sex, and risk taking in general. The discussion relates choices made by adolescents to their cognitive abilities and typical shortcomings.

NOTE: Answer guidelines for all Chapter 15 questions begin on page 249.

Guided Study

The text chapter should be studied one section at a time. Before you read, preview each section by skimming it, noting headings and boldface items. Then read the appropriate section objectives from the following outline. Keep these objectives in mind and, as you read the chapter section, search for the information that will enable you to meet each objective. Once you have finished a section, write out answers for its objectives.

Intellectual Advances (pp. 465–478)

1. Describe advances in thinking during adolescence.

2. Describe evidence of formal operational thinking during adolescence, and provide examples of adolescents' emerging ability to reason deductively and inductively.

3. Discuss the increasing importance of intuitive thinking in adolescence, particularly as manifested in adolescent egocentrism.

4. Explain adolescents' use of illogical, intuitive thought even when they are capable of logical thought.

8. Discuss whether part-time employment is advisable for adolescents.

9. Discuss sex education and global trends in teen pregnancies and births.

Schools, Learning, and the Adolescent Mind (pp. 478–486)

5. Evaluate the typical secondary school's ability to meet the cognitive needs of the typical adolescent.

10. Discuss the influence of education, national policies, and cultural norms on adolescent risk taking.

6. Discuss three controversial issues in education.

Chapter Review

When you have finished reading the chapter, work through the material that follows to review it. Complete the sentences and answer the questions. As you proceed, evaluate your performance for each section by consulting the answers on page 249. Do not continue with the next section until you understand each answer. If you need to, review or reread the appropriate section in the textbook before continuing.

Adolescent Decision Making (pp. 486–493)

7. Briefly discuss the typical adolescent's inability to make major life decisions.

Intellectual Advances (pp. 465–478)

1. Adolescent thinking advances in three ways:
   basic _____ _____

   continue to develop, _____

emerges, and _____ thinking becomes quicker and more compelling. The basic skills of thinking, learning, and remembering that advance during the school-age years _____ (continue to progress/stabilize) during adolescence.

2. Advances in _____ _____ improve concentration, while a growing _____ _____ and memory skills allow teens to connect new ideas to old ones, and strengthened _____ and _____ help them become better students. Brain maturation _____ (is complete/continues).

3. Reaction time _____ (improves/slows) as a result of ongoing _____ , and the brain's _____ _____ becomes more densely packed. This latter development results in significant advances in the _____ _____ of the brain.

4. Improvements in language include a larger _____ of technical words and _____ words, which makes _____-_____ more sophisticated.

5. The most prominent feature of adolescent thought is the capacity to think in terms of _____ . One specific example of this type of thinking is the development of _____ thought.

6. Compared with younger individuals, adolescents have _____ (more/less) difficulty arguing against their personal beliefs and self-interest.

7. During the school years, children make great strides in _____ (inductive/deductive) reasoning.

8. During adolescence, they become more capable of _____ reasoning—that is, they can begin with a general _____ or

_____ and draw logical _____ from it. This type of reasoning is a hallmark of formal operational thought.

9. Piaget's term for the fourth stage of cognitive development is _____ _____ thought. Other theorists may explain adolescent advances differently, but virtually all theorists agree that adolescent thought _____ (is/is not) qualitatively different from children's thought. Theorists disagree about whether this changes occurs suddenly, as _____ thought; gradually, as emphasized by _____-_____ theory; as the result of context, as emphasized by _____ theory; or biology, as emphasized by _____ _____ theory.

10. The kind of thinking in which adolescents consider unproven possibilities that are logical but not necessarily real is called _____-_____ thinking. This type of thinking is indicative of the stage following formal operational thought, which has been called _____ _____ . It involves a struggle to reconcile _____ and _____ .

11. (Thinking Like a Scientist) Piaget devised a number of famous tasks involving _____ principles to study how children of various ages reasoned hypothetically and deductively.

(Thinking Like a Scientist) Briefly describe how children reason differently about the "balance-beam" problem at ages 7, 10, and 13.

12. More recent research has shown that the growth of formal reasoning abilities _____ (always occurs/does not always occur) during

adolescence and may be _____ (more/less) complete than Piaget and others believed it to be. Each individual's intellect, experiences, talents, and interests _____ (do/do not) affect his or her thinking as much as the ability to reason formally. In addition, past _____ and _____ conditions also have an effect. A study of 13- to 15-year-olds in France found about _____ (what proportion?) at the concrete level, _____ at an intermediate level, and _____ at a formal level. Ten years later, these proportions _____ (had/had not) changed for another group of French students.

13. The strongest criticisms of Piaget's theory come from _____ theorists, who suggest that tests of formal thought may be biased in favor of _____ students who are taught by _____ educators.

14. In addition to advances in the formal, logical, _____-_____ thinking described by Piaget, adolescents advance in their _____ cognition.

15. The adolescent's belief that he or she is uniquely significant and that the social world revolves around him or her is a psychological phenomenon called _____ _____.

16. An adolescent's tendency to feel that he or she is somehow immune to the consequences of dangerous or illegal behavior is expressed in the _____ _____.

17. An adolescent's tendency to imagine that her or his own life is unique, heroic, or even legendary, and that she or he is destined for great accomplishments, is expressed in the _____ _____.

18. Adolescents, who believe that they are under constant scrutiny from nearly everyone, create for themselves an _____

_____ .

Schools, Learning, and the Adolescent Mind
(pp. 478–486)

19. The best setting for personal growth, called the optimum _____–_____ _____ , depends on several factors, including _____ _____ .

20. Instead of there being a good fit between adolescents' needs and the schools, there is often a _____ _____ .

21. (Changing Policy) Elementary school, high school, and college are also referred to as _____ , _____ , and _____ , respectively.

(Changing Policy) Cite several ways in which high school graduates differ from those who do not graduate.

Cite several ways in which educational settings tend *not* to be supportive of adolescents' self-confidence.

22. A large percentage of high school teachers consider _____ _____ their most serious problem. To prevent this problem, adolescents need challenging activities that require _____ _____

within a _____ _____ .

23. One outcome of the relatively common mismatch between student needs and the school environment is a widespread dip in academic _____ as young people enter middle school. In response to poor grades, adolescents may try to preserve their self-esteem by studying less in a process called _____ .

24. Virtually every state has mandated the use of standardized _____-_____ _____ to determine school promotion. One fear is that such tests increase _____ and decrease _____ .

25. A third educational controversy concerns _____ in schools.

Adolescent Decision Making (pp. 486–493)

26. The most likely age group to drive drunk, use heroin, or carry a gun is _____ .

27. Adults try to protect teenagers from poor judgment for three reasons:

    a. _____
       _____

    b. _____
       _____

    c. _____
       _____

28. Unrealistic career expectations _____ (persist/diminish) during high school.

29. In general, teenagers in the United States work _____ (more/less) and learn _____ (more/less) than teenagers elsewhere. Attitudes regarding after-school jobs _____ (vary/do not vary) from country to country.

30. In some nations, such as _____ , almost no adolescent is employed or even does significant chores at home. In many _____ countries, many older adolescents have jobs as part of their school curriculum.

Most parents in the United States _____ (approve/do not approve) of youth employment.

31. Perhaps because many of today's jobs for adolescents are not _____ , research finds that when adolescents are employed more than _____ hours a week, their grades suffer. As adults, those who were employed extensively as teenagers are more likely to use _____ and to feel _____ (more/less) connected to their families.

32. The teen birth rate has _____ (increased/decreased) significantly since 1990. In the United States, this trend has occurred in _____ (every/most) ethnic and age group, but most dramatically among _____-_____ . At the same time, condom use has _____ (increased/decreased).

33. Sexual activity among adolescents _____ (is/is not) more diverse than it was ten years ago.

34. Most secondary schools _____ (provide/do not provide) sex education.

Progress Test 1

Multiple-Choice Questions

Circle your answers to the following questions and check them with the answers on page 249. If your answer is incorrect, read the explanation for why it is incorrect and then consult the appropriate pages of the text (in parentheses following the correct answer).

1. Many psychologists consider the distinguishing feature of adolescent thought to be the ability to think in terms of:
   a. moral issues.
   b. concrete operations.
   c. possibility, not just reality.
   d. logical principles.

2. Piaget's last stage of cognitive development is:
   a. formal operational thought.
   b. concrete operational thought.
   c. universal ethical principles.
   d. symbolic thought.

3. Advances in metamemory and metacognition deepen adolescents' abilities in:
   a. studying.
   b. the invincibility fable.
   c. the personal fable.
   d. adolescent egocentrism.

4. The adolescent who takes risks and feels immune to the laws of mortality is showing evidence of the:
   a. invincibility fable.   c. imaginary audience.
   b. personal fable.   d. death instinct.

5. Imaginary audiences, invincibility fables, and personal fables are expressions of adolescent:
   a. morality.   c. decision making.
   b. thinking games.   d. egocentrism.

6. The typical adolescent is:
   a. tough-minded.
   b. indifferent to public opinion.
   c. self-absorbed and hypersensitive to criticism.
   d. all of the above.

7. When adolescents enter secondary school, many:
   a. experience a drop in their academic self-confidence.
   b. are less motivated than they were in elementary school.
   c. are less conscientious than they were in elementary school.
   d. experience all of the above.

8. During adolescence, which area of the brain becomes more densely packed and efficient, enabling adolescents to analyze possibilities and to pursue goals more effectively?
   a. hypothalamus
   b. brain stem
   c. adrenal glands
   d. prefrontal cortex

9. Thinking that begins with a general premise and then draws logical conclusions from it is called:
   a. inductive reasoning.
   b. deductive reasoning.
   c. "the game of thinking."
   d. hypothetical reasoning.

10. Serious reflection on important issues is a wrenching process for many adolescents because of their newfound ability to reason:
    a. inductively.   c. hypothetically.
    b. deductively.   d. symbolically.

11. Hypothetical-deductive thinking is to heuristic thinking as:
    a. rational analysis is to intuitive thought.
    b. intuitive thought is to rational analysis.
    c. experiential thinking is to inuitive reasoning.
    d. intuitive thinking is to analytical reasoning.

12. Many adolescents seem to believe that *their* love-making will not lead to pregnancy. This belief is an expression of the:
    a. personal fable.   c. imaginary audience.
    b. invincibility fable.   d. "game of thinking."

13. A parent in which of the following countries is *least* likely to approve of her daughter's request to take a part-time job after school?
    a. the United States   c. Great Britain
    b. Germany   d. Japan

14. Sex education classes today tend to:
    a. focus on practice with emotional expression and social interaction.
    b. be based on scare tactics designed to discourage sexual activity.
    c. be more dependent upon bringing the parents and other authoritative caregivers into the education process.
    d. have changed in all of the above ways.

15. To estimate the risk of a behavior, such as unprotected sexual intercourse, it is most important that the adolescent be able to think clearly about:
    a. universal ethical principles.
    b. personal beliefs and self-interest.
    c. probability.
    d. peer pressure.

True or False Items

Write T (*true*) or F (*false*) on the line in front of each statement.

_____ 1. Statistically, adolescents are safer in schools than in their neighborhoods.

_____ 2. Adolescents are generally better able than 8-year-olds to recognize the validity of arguments that clash with their own beliefs.

_____ 3. Everyone attains the stage of formal operational thought by adulthood.

_____ 4. Most adolescents who engage in risky behavior are unaware of the consequences of their actions.

_____ 5. Adolescents often create an imaginary audience as they envision how others will react to their appearance and behavior.

_____ 6. Many states are banning high-stakes tests because of their negative influence on adolescents.

_____ 7. The teen birth rate continues to rise throughout the world.

_____ 8. Inductive reasoning is a hallmark of formal operational thought.

_____ 9. Adolescents are the group with the highest rates of drug abuse.

_____ 10. (Changing Policy) Tertiary education is the informal learning that occurs outside the school system.

Progress Test 2

Progress Test 2 should be completed during a final chapter review. Answer the following questions after you thoroughly understand the correct answers for the Chapter Review and Progress Test 1.

Multiple-Choice Questions

1. Adolescents who fall prey to the invincibility fable may be more likely to:
   a. engage in risky behaviors.
   b. suffer from depression.
   c. have low self-esteem.
   d. drop out of school.

2. Thinking that extrapolates from a specific experience to form a general premise is called:
   a. inductive reasoning.
   b. deductive reasoning.
   c. "the game of thinking."
   d. hypothetical reasoning.

3. Regarding formal operational thought:
   a. it is not always accomplished during adolescence.
   b. it is more likely to be demonstrated in certain domains than in others.
   c. whether it is demonstrated depends in part on an individual's experiences, talents, and interests.
   d. all of the above are true.

4. When young people overestimate their significance to others, they are displaying:
   a. concrete operational thought.
   b. adolescent egocentrism.
   c. a lack of cognitive growth.
   d. immoral development.

5. The personal fable refers to adolescents imagining that:
   a. they are immune to the dangers of risky behaviors.
   b. they are always being scrutinized by others.
   c. their own lives are unique, heroic, or even legendary.
   d. the world revolves around their actions.

6. The typical secondary school environment:
   a. has more rigid behavioral demands than the average elementary school.
   b. does not meet the cognitive needs of the typical adolescent.
   c. emphasizes competition.
   d. is described by all of the above.

7. As compared to elementary schools, most secondary schools exhibit all of the following *except*:
   a. a more flexible approach to education.
   b. intensified competition.
   c. more punitive grading practices.
   d. less individualized attention.

8. A study of 13- to 15-year-old French school children found that:
   a. the proportion of children testing at the formal operational level remained constant over a 10-year period.
   b. the proportion of children testing at the formal operational level changed substantially over a 10-year period.
   c. adolescent girls were more likely than boys to have achieved formal operational thinking.
   d. adolescent boys were more likely than girls to have achieved formal operational thinking.

9. Research has shown that adolescents who work at after-school jobs more than 20 hours per week:
   a. are more likely to use drugs as adults.
   b. have lower grades.
   c. tend to feel less connected to their families.
   d. have all of the above characteristics.

10. Educational settings in which teachers have high expectations:
    a. may be destructive to adolescent development.
    b. tend to increase student interest and aspirations.
    c. are more effective in large schools than in small schools.
    d. have proven very effective in educating minority students.

11. One of the hallmarks of formal operational thought is:
    a. egocentrism.   c. symbolic thinking.
    b. deductive reasoning. d. all of the above.

12. In explaining adolescent advances in thinking, sociocultural theorists emphasize:
    a. the accumulated improvement in specific skills.
    b. mental advances resulting from the transition from primary school to secondary school.
    c. the completion of the myelination process in cortical neurons.
    d. advances in metacognition.

13. After failing his first chemistry test, 15-year-old Louis begins studying less and says he "never wanted to be a doctor anyway." Louis' behavior is an example of:
    a. the personal fable.
    b. the invincibility fable.
    c. self-handicapping.
    d. postformal thinking.

14. Evidence that revised sex education programs are working comes from the fact that _____ is (are) declining.
    a. the birth rate among teenagers
    b. the percentage of sexually active teenagers
    c. the use of condoms among teenagers
    d. all of the above

15. To avoid a volatile mismatch, a school should:
    a. focus on cooperative rather than competitive learning.
    b. base grading on individual test performance.
    c. establish the same goals for every student.
    d. vary its settings and approach according to children's developmental stages and cognition.

Matching Items

Match each term or concept with its corresponding description or definition.

Terms or Concepts

_____ 1. invincibility fable
_____ 2. imaginary audience
_____ 3. person–environment fit
_____ 4. hypothetical thought
_____ 5. deductive reasoning
_____ 6. inductive reasoning
_____ 7. formal operational thought
_____ 8. personal fable
_____ 9. postformal thought
_____ 10. volatile mismatch
_____ 11. adolescent egocentrism

Descriptions or Definitions

a. the tendency of adolescents to focus on themselves to the exclusion of others
b. adolescents feel immune to the consequences of dangerous behavior
c. adolescents feel destined for fame and fortune
d. the idea held by many adolescents that others are intensely interested in them, especially in their appearance and behavior
e. the match or mismatch between an adolescent's needs and the educational setting
f. thinking that struggles to reconcile logic and experience
g. reasoning about propositions that may or may not reflect reality
h. the last stage of cognitive development, according to Piaget
i. thinking that moves from premise to conclusion
j. thinking that moves from a specific experience to a general premise
k. a clash between a teenager's needs and the structure and functioning of his or her school

Thinking Critically About Chapter 15

Answer these questions the day before an exam as a final check on your understanding of the chapter's terms and concepts.

1. A 13-year-old can create and solve logical problems on the computer but is not usually reasonable, mature, or consistent in his or her thinking when it comes to people and social relationships. This supports the finding that:
   a. some children reach the stage of formal operational thought earlier than others.
   b. the stage of formal operational thought is not attained by age 13.
   c. formal operational thinking may be demonstrated in certain domains and not in other domains.
   d. older adolescents and adults often do poorly on standard tests of formal operational thought.

2. An experimenter hides a ball in her hand and says, "Either the ball in my hand is red or it is not red." Most preadolescent children say:
   a. the statement is true.
   b. the statement is false.
   c. they cannot tell if the statement is true or false.
   d. they do not understand what the experimenter means.

3. Fourteen-year-old Monica is very idealistic and often develops crushes on people she doesn't even know. This reflects her newly developed cognitive ability to:
   a. deal simultaneously with two sides of an issue.
   b. take another person's viewpoint.
   c. imagine possible worlds and people.
   d. see herself as others see her.

4. Which of the following is the *best* example of a personal fable?
   a. Adriana imagines that she is destined for a life of fame and fortune.
   b. Ben makes up stories about his experiences to impress his friends.
   c. Kalil questions his religious beliefs when they seem to offer little help for a problem he faces.
   d. Julio believes that every girl he meets is attracted to him.

5. Which of the following is the *best* example of the adolescent's ability to think hypothetically?
   a. Twelve-year-old Stanley feels that people are always watching him.
   b. Fourteen-year-old Mindy engages in many risky behaviors, reasoning that "nothing bad will happen to me."
   c. Fifteen-year-old Philip feels that no one understands his problems.
   d. Thirteen-year-old Josh delights in finding logical flaws in virtually everything his teachers and parents say.

6. Frustrated because of the dating curfew her parents have set, Melinda exclaims, "You just don't know how it feels to be in love!" Melinda's thinking demonstrates:
   a. the invincibility fable.
   b. the personal fable.
   c. the imaginary audience.
   d. adolescent egocentrism.

7. Compared to her 13-year-old brother, 17-year-old Yolanda is likely to:
   a. be more critical about herself.
   b. be more egocentric.
   c. have less confidence in her abilities.
   d. be more capable of reasoning hypothetically.

8. Nathan's fear that his friends will ridicule him because of a pimple that has appeared on his nose reflects a preoccupation with:
   a. his personal fable.
   b. the invincibility fable.
   c. an imaginary audience.
   d. preconventional reasoning.

9. Thirteen-year-old Malcolm, who lately is very sensitive to the criticism of others, feels significantly less motivated and capable than when he was in elementary school. Malcolm is probably:
   a. experiencing a sense of vulnerability that is common in adolescents.
   b. a lower-track student.
   c. a student in a school that emphasizes cooperation.
   d. all of the above.

10. A high school principal who wished to increase the interest level and achievement of students would be well advised to:
    a. create classroom environments in which teachers have high expectations of students.
    b. encourage greater use of standardized testing in the elementary schools that feed students to the high school.
    c. separate students into academic tracks based on achievement.
    d. do all of the above.

11. Seventy-year-old Artemis can't understand why his daughter doesn't want her teenage son to work after school. "In my day," he says, "we learned responsibility and a useful trade by working throughout high school." You wisely point out that:
    a. most after-school jobs for teens today are not very meaningful.
    b. after-school employment tends to have a more negative impact on boys than girls.
    c. attitudes are changing; today, most American parents see adolescent employment as a waste of time.
    d. teens in most European countries almost never work after school.

12. Who is the *least* likely to display mature decision making?
    a. Brenda, an outgoing 17-year-old art student
    b. Fifteen-year-old Kenny, who has few adults in whom he confides
    c. Monique, a well-educated 15-year-old
    d. Damon, an 18-year-old high school graduate who lives alone

13. After hearing that an unusually aggressive child has been in full-time day care since he was 1 year old, 16-year-old Keenan concludes that non-parental care leads to behavior problems. Keenan's conclusion is an example of:
    a. inductive reasoning.
    b. deductive reasoning.
    c. hypothetical thinking.
    d. adolescent egocentrism.

14. On a test of moral reasoning, 16-year-old Carol decides that a person who steals an expensive medicine to save a friend's life is guilty of a crime, but should not be punished because of the circumstances. Carol's reasoning is an example of:
    a. inductive reasoning.
    b. preconventional moral reasoning.
    c. postformal thinking.
    d. self-handicapping.

15. Dr. Malone, who wants to improve the effectiveness of her adolescent sex-education class, would be well advised to:
    a. focus on the biological facts of reproduction and disease, because teenage misinformation is largely responsible for the high rates of unwanted pregnancy and STDs.
    b. personalize the instruction, in order to make the possible consequences of sexual activity more immediate to students.
    c. teach boys and girls in separate classes, so that discussion can be more frank and open.
    d. use all of the above strategies.

Key Terms

Using your own words, write a brief definition or explanation of each of the following terms on a separate piece of paper.

1. hypothetical thought
2. inductive reasoning
3. deductive reasoning
4. formal operational thought
5. postformal thought
6. adolescent egocentrism
7. invincibility fable
8. personal fable
9. imaginary audience
10. person–environment fit
11. volatile mismatch
12. self-handicapping
13. high-stakes tests
14. sexually active

ANSWERS
CHAPTER REVIEW

1. cognitive skills; logic; intuitive; continue to progress

2. selective attention; knowledge base; metamemory; metacognition; continues

3. improves; myelination; prefrontal cortex; executive functions

4. vocabulary; derivative; code-switching

5. possibilities; hypothetical

6. less

7. inductive

8. deductive; premise; theory; conclusions

9. formal operational; is; Piaget; information-processing; sociocultural; epigenetic systems

10. hypothetical-deductive; postformal thought; logic; experience

11. scientific

Preschoolers have no understanding of how to solve the problem. By age 7, children understand balancing the weights but don't know that distance from the center is also a factor. By age 10, they understand the concepts but are unable to coordinate them. By ages 13 or 14, they are able to solve the problem.

12. does not always occur; less; do; education; historical; one-third; one-third; one-third; had

13. sociocultural; elite; Western

14. hypothetical-deductive; intuitive

15. adolescent egocentrism

16. invincibility fable

17. personal fable

18. imaginary audience

19. person–environment fit; the individual's developmental stage and cognition as well as on social traditions and educational objectives

20. volatile mismatch

21. primary; secondary; tertiary

High school graduates stay healthier, live longer, are richer, and are more likely to marry, vote, and buy homes than their less educated contemporaries.

Compared to elementary schools, most secondary schools have more rigid behavioral demands, intensified competition, norm-referenced rather than criterion-referenced tests, more punitive grading practices, as well as less individualized attention and procedures.

22. student apathy; social interaction; supportive context

23. self-confidence; self-handicapping

24. high-stakes tests; ethnic, economic, and sexual inequality; student effort and motivation

25. violence

26. young adults

27. a. The consequences of risk taking are more serious the younger a person is
    b. Adolescent choices are long-lasting
    c. Adolescents overrate the joys of the moment and ignore future costs

28. perisist

29. more; less; vary

30. Japan; European; approve

31. meaningful; 20; drugs; less

32. decreased; every; African-Americans; increased

33. is

34. provide

PROGRESS TEST 1

Multiple-Choice Questions

1. c. is the answer. (p. 468)
   a. Although moral reasoning becomes much deeper during adolescence, it is not limited to this stage of development.
   b. & d. Concrete operational thought, which *is* logical, is the distinguishing feature of childhood thinking.

2. a. is the answer. (pp. 467–468)
   b. In Piaget's theory, this stage precedes formal operational thought.
   c. & d. These are not stages in Piaget's theory.

3. a. is the answer. (p. 465)
   b., c., & d. These are examples of limited reasoning ability during adolescence.

4. a. is the answer. (pp. 472–473)
   b. This refers to adolescents' tendency to imagine their own lives as unique, heroic, or even legendary.
   c. This refers to adolescents' tendency to fantasize about how others will react to their appearance and behavior.
   d. This is a concept in Freud's theory.

5. d. is the answer. These thought processes are manifestations of adolescents' tendency to see themselves as being much more central and important to the social scene than they really are. (p. 472)

6. c. is the answer. (p. 465)

7. **d.** is the answer. (pp. 482–483)

8. **d.** is the answer. (p. 466)

   a., b., & c. These "lower" brain centers, which are not involved in conscious reasoning, control hunger and thirst (hypothalamus); sleep and arousal (brain stem); and the production of stress hormones (adrenal glands).

9. **b.** is the answer. (p. 467)

   a. Inductive reasoning moves from specific facts to a general conclusion.

   c. & d. The "game of thinking," which is an example of hypothetical reasoning, involves the ability to think creatively about possibilities.

10. **c.** is the answer. (pp. 468–469)

11. **a.** is the answer. (p. 472)

    c. Heuristic thinking is both experiential *and* intuitive.

12. **b.** is the answer. (pp. 472–473)

    a. This refers to adolescents' tendency to imagine their own lives as unique, heroic, or even mythical.

    c. This refers to adolescents' tendency to fantasize about how others will react to their appearance and behavior.

    d. This is the adolescent ability to suspend knowledge of reality in order to think playfully about possibilities.

13. **d.** is the answer. Japanese adolescents almost never work after school. (p. 488)

    a. American parents generally approve of adolescent employment.

    b. & c. Jobs are an important part of the school curriculum in many European countries.

14. **a.** is the answer. (p. 491)

    b. Scare tactics were often a central feature of earlier sex education classes.

    c. Generally speaking, parents are not effective sex educators.

15. **c.** is the answer. (p. 487)

True or False Items

1. T (p. 485)

2. T (p. 469)

3. F Some people never reach the stage of formal operational thought. (p. 471)

4. F Adolescents are aware of the fact, but they fail to think through the possible consequences. (pp. 486–487)

5. T (p. 473)

6. F High-stakes testing is mandated by virtually every state legislature in the United States. (p. 484)

7. F The teen birth rate worldwide has dropped significantly since 1990. (p. 490)

8. F Deductive reasoning is a hallmark of formal operational thought. (p. 467)

9. F Young adults are the most likely age group to abuse drugs. (p. 486)

10. F Also called higher education, tertiary education includes colleges and universities. (p. 479)

PROGRESS TEST 2

Multiple-Choice Questions

1. **a.** is the answer. (pp. 472–473)

   b., c., & d. The invincibility fable leads some teens to believe that they are immune to the dangers of risky behaviors; it is not necessarily linked to depression, low self-esteem, or the likelihood that an individual will drop out of school.

2. **a.** is the answer. (p. 467)

   b. Deductive reasoning begins with a general premise and then draws logical conclusions from it.

   c. & d. The "game of thinking," which is an example of hypothetical reasoning, involves the ability to think creatively about possibilities.

3. **d.** is the answer. (p. 471)

4. **b.** is the answer. (p. 472)

5. **c.** is the answer. (p. 473)

   a. This describes the invincibility fable.

   b. This describes the imaginary audience.

   d. This describes adolescent egocentrism in general.

6. **d.** is the answer. (p. 481)

7. **a.** is the answer. (p. 481)

8. **b.** is the answer. (p. 471)

   c. & d. This study did not report a gender difference in the proportion of children who attained formal thinking.

9. **d.** is the answer. (p. 489)

10. **b.** is the answer. (p. 484)

11. **b.** is the answer. (p. 467)

12. **b.** is the answer. (p. 468)

    a. & d. These are more likely to be emphasized by information-processing theorists.

c. This reflects the biological perspective on development.

13. **c.** is the answer. (p. 483)

a. & b. These refer to the egocentric tendency of adolescents to believe their lives are heroic (personal fable) and immune to the laws of mortality (invincibility fable).

d. Postformal thinking is a type of reasoning that is well-suited to solving practical problems because it moves beyond pure logic to benefit from the wisdom of experience.

14. **a.** is the answer. (pp. 490–491)

b. & c. These are on the rise.

15. **d.** is the answer. (pp. 478–479)

Matching Items

1. b (pp. 472–473)   5. i (p. 467)   9. f (p. 469)
2. d (p. 473)   6. j (p. 467)   10. k (p. 479)
3. e (p. 478)   7. h (p. 468)   11. a (p. 472)
4. g (p. 466)   8. c (p. 473)

THINKING CRITICALLY ABOUT CHAPTER 15

1. **c.** is the answer. (p. 471)

2. **c.** is the answer. Although this statement is logically verifiable, preadolescents who lack formal operational thought cannot prove or disprove it. (pp. 467–468)

3. **c.** is the answer. (p. 466)

4. **a.** is the answer. (p. 473)

b. & d. These behaviors are more indicative of a preoccupation with the imaginary audience.

c. Kalil's questioning attitude is a normal adolescent tendency that helps foster moral reasoning.

5. **d.** is the answer. (pp. 466–467)

a. This is an example of the imaginary audience.

b. This is an example of the invincibility fable.

c. This is an example of adolescent egocentrism.

6. **d.** is the answer. (p. 472)

7. **d.** is the answer. (p. 467)

8. **c.** is the answer. (p. 473)

a. In this fable, adolescents see themselves destined for fame and fortune.

b. In this fable, young people feel that they are somehow immune to the consequences of common dangers.

d. This is a stage of moral reasoning in Kohlberg's theory, as discussed in Chapter 12.

9. **a.** is the answer. (pp. 482–483)

10. **a.** is the answer. (p. 484)

11. **a.** is the answer. (p. 489)

b. There is no evidence of a gender difference in the impact of employment on adolescents.

c. & d. In fact, just the opposite are true.

12. **b.** is the answer. Mature decision making is least likely to be displayed by adolescents who are under age 16, who have less education, and who have few adults to talk with. (p. 487)

13. **a.** is the answer. (p. 467)

b. Keenan is reasoning from the specific to the general, rather than vice versa.

c. Keenan is thinking about an actual observation, rather than a hypothetical possibility.

d. Keenan's reasoning is focused outside himself, rather than being self-centered.

14. **c.** is the answer. Postformal thinking is capable of combining contradictory elements (such as the possibility that someone who steals should not be punished) into a comprehensive whole. (p. 469)

a. Inductive reasoning is more typical of logical, formal operational thought.

b. preconventional moral reasoning, which is not discussed in this chapter, is a morality based on avoiding punishment.

d. Self-handicapping refers to choices people make to preserve their self-esteem, at the cost of impeding their chances for success.

15. **b.** is the answer. (pp. 466, 491)

KEY TERMS

1. **Hypothetical thought** involves reasoning about propositions and possibilities that may or may not reflect reality. (p. 466)

2. **Inductive reasoning** is thinking that moves from one or more specific experiences or facts to a general conclusion. (p. 467)

3. **Deductive reasoning** is thinking that moves from the general to the specific, or from a premise to a logical conclusion. (p. 467)

4. In Piaget's theory, the last stage of cognitive development, which arises from a combination of maturation and experience, is called **formal operational thought**. A hallmark of formal operational thinking is the capacity for hypothetical, logical, and abstract thought. (p. 468)

5. **Postformal thought** is reasoning beyond formal thought that struggles to reconcile logic and experience and is well suited to solving real-world problems. (p. 469)

6. **Adolescent egocentrism** refers to the tendency of adolescents to see themselves as much more socially significant than they actually are. (p. 472)

7. Adolescents who experience the **invincibility fable** feel that they are immune to the dangers of risky behaviors. (pp. 472–473)

8. Another example of adolescent egocentrism is the **personal fable,** through which adolescents imagine their own lives as unique, heroic, or even legendary. (p. 473)

9. Adolescents often create an **imaginary audience** for themselves, as they assume that others are as intensely interested in them as they themselves are. (p. 473)

10. The term **person–environment fit** refers to the best setting for personal growth, as in the optimum educational setting. (p. 478)

11. When teenagers' individual needs do not match the size, routine, and structure of their schools, a **volatile mismatch** may occur. (p. 479)

12. **Self-handicapping** involves making deliberate choices that will impede a person's chances of success, often to preserve self-esteem. (p. 483)

13. **High-stakes tests** are tests that have serious consequences for those who take them, including determining whether they will be promoted to the next grade in school or allowed to graduate. (p. 484)

14. Traditionally, **sexually active** teenagers were those who have had intercourse. (p. 490)

Chapter Sixteen

Adolescence: Psychosocial Development

Chapter Overview

Chapter 16 focuses on the adolescent's psychosocial development, particularly the formation of identity, which is required for the attainment of adult status and maturity. Depression, self-destruction, and suicide—the most perplexing problems of adolescence—are then explored. The special problems posed by adolescent lawbreaking are discussed, and suggestions for alleviating or treating these problems are given. The final section examines the influences of family, friends, and society on adolescent psychosocial development. This includes adolescent decision making in the area of sexual behavior, noting the concurrent influences of parents and peers. The chapter concludes with the message that although no other period of life is characterized by so many changes in the three domains of development, for most young people the teenage years are happy ones. Furthermore, serious problems in adolescence do not necessarily lead to lifelong problems.

NOTE: Answer guidelines for all Chapter 16 questions begin on page 264.

Guided Study

The text chapter should be studied one section at a time. Before you read, preview each section by skimming it, noting headings and boldface items. Then read the appropriate section objectives from the following outline. Keep these objectives in mind and, as you read the chapter section, search for the information that will enable you to meet each objective. Once you have finished a section, write out answers for its objectives.

The Self and Identity (pp. 497–507)

1. Describe the development of identity during adolescence.

2. Describe the four major identity statuses, and give an example of each.

3. Discuss the problems encountered in the formation of gender and ethnic identities, and describe cohort and cultural effects on identity formation.

Depression and Self-Destruction (pp. 507–511)

4. Discuss adolescent suicide, noting its incidence and prevalence, contributing factors, warning signs, and gender and national variations.

Rebellion and Destructiveness (pp. 512–516)

5. Discuss delinquency among adolescents today, noting its prevalence, significance for later development, and best approaches for prevention or treatment.

Family and Friends (pp. 516–527)

6. Discuss parental influence on identity formation, including the effect of parent–adolescent conflict and other aspects of family functioning.

7. Discuss the constructive functions of peer relationships and close friendships during adolescence and the unique challenges faced by immigrants.

8. Discuss the the development of male–female relationships during adolescence, including the challenges faced by gay and lesbian adolescents.

9. Discuss the influence of parents and peers on adolescent sexual behavior.

Conclusion (p. 528)

10. Discuss the theme of this text as demonstrated by adolescent development.

Chapter Review

When you have finished reading the chapter, work through the material that follows to review it. Complete the sentences and answer the questions. As you proceed, evaluate your performance for each section by consulting the answers on page 264. Do not continue with the next section until you understand each answer. If you need to, review or reread the appropriate section in the textbook before continuing.

The Self and Identity (pp. 497–507)

1. The momentous changes that occur during the teen years challenge adolescents to find their own _____ . In this process, many adolescents experience _____ _____ , or various fantasies about

what their futures might be if one or another course of action is followed.

2. Adolescents may take on a _____ _____ ; that is, they act in ways they know to be contrary to their true nature. Three variations on this identity status are the

_____ _____

_____ , the _____

_____ _____ , and the

_____ _____

_____ .

3. According to Erikson, the challenge of adolescence is _____ _____

_____ _____ .

4. The ultimate goal of adolescence is to establish a new identity that involves both repudiation and assimilation of childhood values; this is called

_____ _____ .

5. The young person who prematurely accepts earlier roles and parental values without exploring alternatives or truly forging a unique identity is experiencing identity _____ .

6. An adolescent who adopts an identity that is the opposite of the one he or she is expected to adopt has taken on a _____

_____ .

7. The young person who has few commitments to goals or values and is apathetic about defining his or her identity is experiencing

_____ _____ .

8. A time-out period during which a young person experiments with different identities, postponing important choices, is called an identity _____ . An obvious institutional example of this in the United States is attending

_____ .

9. Adolescents who have _____

_____ and those who have prematurely _____ tend to have a strong sense of ethnic identification. Those who have _____ tend to be high in prejudice, while those who are _____

_____ tend to be relatively low in prejudice.

10. The process of identity formation can take _____ or longer.

11. People _____ (can/generally cannot) achieve identity in one domain and still be searching for their identity in another. Identity is formed both from _____ , as when a person recognizes his or her true nature, and from _____ , in response to _____ forces.

12. A person's identification as either male or female is called _____ _____ . This includes accepting all the _____ and _____ that society assigns to that sex.

13. Gender identity and _____ _____ are much more varied than a simple _____ – _____ division.

14. Today, more _____ (boys/girls) graduate from high school and go on to college. As a result, some boys assert their male idenity by rejecting "female" subjects such as _____ , causing developmentalists to worry that they are in a state of identity _____ .

15. For members of minority ethnic groups, identity achievement is often _____ (more/ less) difficult than it is for other adolescents. This may cause them to embrace a _____ identity or, as is more often the case, to _____ on identity prematurely. In general, ethnic identity becomes more important when adolescents see their background as

_____ .

Today, about _____ percent of all teenagers are not European-American.

16. The surrounding culture can aid identity formation in two ways: by providing _____ and by providing _____ _____ and _____ that ease the transition from childhood to adulthood. Some societies and cul-

tures mark the transition from childhood to adulthood with a dramatic ceremony called a

_____ _____

_____ .

17. In a culture where most people hold the same moral, political, religious, and sexual values, identity is _____ (easier/more difficult) to achieve. In modern industrial and postindustrial socieities, cultural consensus is _____ (the norm/rare).

18. Developmentalists who have studied teenagers in European countries marked by extreme social change have generally found that identity formation _____ (was/was not) markedly more difficult. Longitudinal studies of teens whose families were experiencing severe economic stress have found that _____ , _____ , and _____ influences were a successful buffer against the decline in material wealth.

Depression and Self-Destruction (pp. 507–511)

19. Cross-sequential research studies show that, from ages 6 to 18, people generally feel _____ (more/less) competent in most areas of their lives.

20. Two disorders that include high energy and grandiosity are _____ and _____ _____ . These disorders become more common in

_____ .

21. Depression _____ (increases/decreases) at puberty, especially among _____ (males/females).

22. Thinking about committing suicide, called _____ _____ , is _____ (common/relatively rare) among high school students. Explanations for the increase in depression among adolescents include _____ changes, _____ , _____ , and _____ pressures.

23. Adolescents under age 20 are _____ (more/less) likely to kill themselves than adults are.

24. Most suicide attempts in adolescence _____ (do/do not) result in death. A deliberate act of self-destruction that does not result in death is called a _____ .

25. List five factors that affect whether thinking about suicide leads to a self-destructive act or to death.

a. _____

b. _____

c. _____

d. _____

e. _____

26. The rate of suicide is higher for adolescent _____ (males/females). The rate of parasuicide is higher for _____ (males/females).

27. Around the world, cultural differences in the rates of suicidal ideation and completion _____ (are/are not) apparent.

28. When a town or school sentimentalizes the "tragic end" of a teen suicide, the publicity can trigger

_____ _____ .

List several factors that correlate with suicide ideation and completion at any age.

(Table 16.4) Briefly describe ethnic differences in suicide rates in the United States.

Rebellion and Destructiveness (pp. 512–516)

29. Psychologists categorize emotional problems in two ways: _____ problems, which are directed inward and include

    _____ ;

    and _____ problems, which include

    _____ .

    Both types of problems _____ (increase gradually/increase suddenly/decrease gradually/decrease suddenly) at adolescence.

30. According to the _____ perspective, adolescents who act contrary to adult wishes to confirm their _____ are behaving

    _____ .

State three ways in which externalizing behaviors may signify trouble.

31. Arrests are far more likely to occur during the

    _____ _____ of life than during any other time period. Although statistics indicate that the _____ (incidence/prevalence) of arrests is highest among this age group, they do not reveal how widespread, or _____ , lawbreaking is among this age group.

32. If all acts of "juvenile delinquency" are included, the prevalence of adolescent crime is

    _____ (less/greater) than official records report.

Briefly describe data on gender and ethnic differences in adolescent arrests.

33. Research from several nations has shown that a major risk factor for becoming a violent criminal is _____ . The victims of adolescent crime tend to be _____ (teenagers/adults).

34. Experts find it useful to distinguish

    _____-_____ offenders, whose criminal activity stops by age 21, from

    _____-_____-

    _____ offenders, who become career criminals.

35. Developmentalists have found that it _____ (is/is not) currently possible to distinguish children who actually will become career criminals.

36. Adolescents who later become career criminals are among the first of their cohort to

    _____ .

    They also are among the least involved in

    _____ activities and tend to be

    _____ in preschool and elementary school. At an even earlier age, they show signs of

    _____ _____ , such as being slow in _____ development, being _____ , or having poor _____ control.

37. For most delinquents, residential incarceration in a prison or reform school usually

    _____ (is/is not) the best solution.

List several background factors that increase a child's risk of later becoming a career criminal.

Family and Friends (pp. 516–527)

38. People who focus on differences between the younger and older generations speak of a

    _____ _____ . An exception occurs when the parents grow up in a very different _____ and

    _____ .

39. The idea that family members in different developmental stages have a natural tendency to see the family in different ways is called the _____ _____ .

40. Parent–adolescent conflict is most common in _____ (early/late) adolescence and is particularly notable with _____ (mothers/fathers) and their _____ (early/late)-maturing _____ (sons/daughters). This conflict often involves _____ , which refers to repeated, petty arguments about daily habits.

41. Among Chinese-, Korean-, and Mexican-American teens, conflict tends to arise in _____ (early/late) adolescence, possibly because these cultures encourage _____ in their children and emphasize family _____ .

42. Four other elements of family functioning that have been heavily researched include _____ , _____ , _____ , and _____ .

43. In terms of family control, a powerful deterrent to delinquency, risky sex, and drug abuse is _____ _____ . Too much interference, however, may contribute to adolescent _____ .

44. Overall, parent–teen relations in all family types and nations, and among children of both sexes, are typically _____ . If there is conflict, it is more likely to center on details like the adolescent's _____ _____ rather than on _____ _____ .

45. The largely constructive role of peers runs counter to the notion of _____ _____ . Social pressure to conform _____ (falls/rises) dramatically in early adolescence, until about age _____ , when it begins to _____ (fall/rise).

46. For many immigrant families, the normal strain between the generations extends over a _____ (shorter/longer) period of time, because adolescents' physical and cognitive drives mature _____ (before/after) they would in traditional societies. This creates a severe _____ _____ in many minority families.

Outline the course of ethnic identity achievement in young Asian-Americans.

(Thinking Like a Scientist) Briefly outline the four-stage progression of heterosexual involvement.

47. (Thinking Like a Scientist) Cultural patterns _____ (affect/do not affect) the _____ of these stages, but the basic _____ seems to be based on _____ factors.

48. (Thinking Like a Scientist) For gay and lesbian adolescents, added complications usually _____ (slow down/speed up) romantic attachments. In cultures that are _____ , many young men and women with homosexual or lesbian feelings may _____ their feelings or try to _____ or _____ them.

49. Most parents _____ (are/are not) adequate sex educators for their children. One reason is that many parents are too _____ in beginning to discuss sexual issues.

50. One study found that mothers who were more religious, and more disapproving of teen sex, were _____ (more/less) likely to know when their children were sexually active.

51. In terms of postponing sex and using contraception, it's best to have a partner who is

_____ .

52. Cultural attitudes about _____ are considered the prime reason AIDS is spreading faster in Africa among _____ than any other group. Two examples are the tendency of boys to mistakenly believe

   a. _____

   b. _____

Identify several reasons that adolecent peers are not the best sex eduators.

Conclusion (p. 528)

53. For most young people, the teenage years overall are _____ (happy/unhappy) ones.

54. Adolescents who have one serious problem _____ (often have/do not usually have) others.

55. In most cases, adolescent problems stem from earlier developmental events such as

_____ .

Progress Test 1

Multiple-Choice Questions

Circle your answers to the following questions and check them with the answers on page 265. If your answer is incorrect, read the explanation for why it is incorrect and then consult the appropriate pages of the text (in parentheses following the correct answer).

1. According to Erikson, the primary task of adolescence is that of establishing:
   a. basic trust.   c. intimacy.
   b. an identity.   d. integrity.

2. According to developmentalists who study identity formation, foreclosure involves:
   a. accepting an identity prematurely, without exploration.
   b. taking time off from school, work, and other commitments.
   c. opposing parental values.
   d. failing to commit oneself to a vocational goal.

3. When adolescents adopt an identity that is the opposite of the one they are expected to adopt, they are considered to be taking on a:
   a. foreclosed identity.
   b. diffused identity.
   c. negative identity.
   d. reverse identity.

4. The main sources of emotional support for most young people who are establishing independence from their parents are:
   a. older adolescents of the opposite sex.
   b. older siblings.
   c. teachers.
   d. peer groups.

5. For members of minority ethnic groups, identity achievement may be particularly complicated because:
   a. their cultural ideal clashes with the Western emphasis on adolescent self-determination.
   b. peers, themselves torn by similar conflicts, can be very critical.
   c. parents and other relatives tend to emphasize ethnicity and expect teens to honor their roots.
   d. of all of the above reasons.

6. In a crime-ridden neighborhood, parents can protect their adolescents by keeping close watch over activities, friends, and so on. This practice is called:
   a. generational stake.   c. peer screening.
   b. foreclosure.   d. parental monitoring.

7. Conflict between adolescent girls and their mothers is most likely to involve:
   a. bickering over hair, neatness, and other daily habits.
   b. political, religious, and moral issues.
   c. peer relationships and friendships.
   d. relationships with boys.

8. If there is a "generation gap," it is likely to occur in _____ adolescence and to center on issues of _____ .
   a. early; morality
   c. early; self-control
   b. late; self-discipline
   d. late; politics

9. Because of the conflict between their ethnic background and the larger culture, minority adolescents will *most often*:
   a. reject the traditional values of both their ethnic culture and the majority culture.
   b. foreclose on identity prematurely.
   c. declare a moratorium.
   d. experience identity diffusion.

10. Fifteen-year-old Cindy, who has strong self-esteem and is trying out a new, artistic identity "just to see how it feels," is apparently exploring:
    a. an acceptable false self.
    b. a pleasing false self.
    c. an experimental false self.
    d. none of the above.

11. If the vast majority of cases of a certain crime are committed by a small number of repeat offenders, this would indicate that the crime's:
    a. incidence is less than its prevalence.
    b. incidence is greater than its prevalence.
    c. incidence and prevalence are about equal.
    d. incidence and prevalence are impossible to calculate.

12. Compared with normal adolescents, suicidal adolescents are:
    a. more concerned about the future.
    b. academically average students.
    c. rejected by their peers.
    d. less likely to have attempted suicide.

13. The early signs of life-course-persistent offenders include all of the following *except*:
    a. signs of brain damage early in life.
    b. antisocial school behavior.
    c. delayed sexual intimacy.
    d. use of alcohol and tobacco at an early age.

14. Regarding gender differences in self-destructive acts, the rate of parasuicide is _____ and the rate of suicide is _____ .
    a. higher in males; higher in females
    b. higher in females; higher in males
    c. the same in males and females; higher in males
    d. the same in males and females; higher in females

15. Conflict between parents and adolescent offspring is:
    a. most likely to involve fathers and their early-maturing offspring.
    b. more frequent in single-parent homes.
    c. more likely between early-maturing daughters and their mothers.
    d. likely in all of the above situations.

True or False Items

Write T (*true*) or F (*false*) on the line in front of each statement.

_____ 1. In cultures where everyone's values are similar and social change is slight, identity is relatively easy to achieve.

_____ 2. Most adolescents have political views and educational values that are markedly different from those of their parents.

_____ 3. Peer pressure is inherently destructive to the adolescent seeking an identity.

_____ 4. (Thinking Like a Scientist) For most adolescents, group socializing and dating precede the establishment of true intimacy with one member of the opposite sex.

_____ 5. Worldwide, arrests are more likely to occur during the second decade of life than at any other time.

_____ 6. Most adolescent self-destructive acts are a response to an immediate and specific psychological blow.

_____ 7. The majority of adolescents report that they have at some time engaged in law-breaking that might have led to arrest.

_____ 8. In finding themselves, teens try to find an identity that is stable, consistent, and mature.

_____ 9. Adolescents who have foreclosed their identities generally have a weak sense of ethnic identification.

_____ 10. Increased accessibility of guns is a factor in the increased rate of youth suicide in the United States.

Progress Test 2

Progress Test 2 should be completed during a final chapter review. Answer the following questions after you thoroughly understand the correct answers for the Chapter Review and Progress Test 1.

Multiple-Choice Questions

1. Recent studies of adolescents in European nations experiencing massive social change have generally found that:
   a. their lives were seriously disrupted.
   b. a disproportionate number of adolescents experienced severe identity crises.
   c. their search for identity was not adversely affected.
   d. boys experienced more difficulty forming their identities than did girls.

2. Which of the following was *not* identified as a factor in adolescent suicide and ideation?
   a. chronic depression
   b. loneliness
   c. homosexuality
   d. minor law-breaking

3. Parent–teen conflict among Chinese-, Korean-, and Mexican-American families often surfaces late in adolescence because these cultures:
   a. emphasize family closeness.
   b. value authoritarian parenting.
   c. encourage autonomy in children.
   d. do all of the above.

4. If the various cases of a certain crime are committed by many different offenders, this would indicate that the crime's:
   a. incidence is less than its prevalence.
   b. incidence is greater than its prevalence.
   c. incidence and prevalence are about equal.
   d. incidence and prevalence are impossible to calculate.

5. Thinking about committing suicide is called:
   a. cluster suicide.
   b. parasuicide.
   c. suicidal ideation.
   d. fratracide.

6. Which of the following is *not* true regarding peer relationships among gay and lesbian adolescents?
   a. Romantic attachments are usually slower to develop.
   b. In homophobic cultures, many gay teens try to conceal their homosexual feelings by becoming heterosexually involved.
   c. Many girls who will later identify themselves as lesbians are oblivious to these sexual urges as teens.
   d. In many cases, a lesbian girl's best friend is a boy, who is more at ease with her sexuality than another girl might be.

7. The adolescent experiencing identity diffusion is typically:
   a. very apathetic.
   b. experimenting with alternative identities without trying to settle on any one.
   c. willing to accept parental values wholesale, without exploring alternatives.
   d. one who rebels against all forms of authority.

8. Cross-sequential studies of individuals from ages 6 to 18 show that:
   a. children feel less competent each year in most areas of their lives.
   b. feelings of competence become more similar in males and females as time goes on.
   c. boys' self-esteem decreases more than girls' does.
   d. all of the above are true.

9. Crime statistics show that during adolescence:
   a. males and females are equally likely to be arrested.
   b. males are more likely to be arrested than females.
   c. females are more likely to be arrested than males.
   d. males commit more crimes than females but are less likely to be arrested.

10. Which of the following is the most common problem behavior among adolescents?
    a. pregnancy
    b. daily use of illegal drugs
    c. minor lawbreaking
    d. attempts at suicide

11. A time-out period during which a young person experiments with different identities, postponing important choices, is called a(n):
    a. identity foreclosure.   c. identity diffusion.
    b. negative identity.   d. identity moratorium.

12. When adolescents' political, religious, educational, and vocational opinions are compared with their parents', the so-called generation gap is:

   a. much smaller than when the younger and older generations are compared overall.
   b. much wider than when the younger and older generations are compared overall.
   c. wider between parents and sons than between parents and daughters.
   d. wider between parents and daughters than between parents and sons.

13. Identity achievement is easiest in a culture in which:

   a. diversity in moral and political beliefs is appreciated and encouraged.
   b. social change is rapid.
   c. both a. and b. are true.
   d. everyone holds the same values and social change is slow.

14. Parent–teen conflict tends to center on issues related to:

   a. politics and religion.
   b. education.
   c. vacations.
   d. daily details, such as musical tastes.

15. According to a review of studies from various nations, suicidal ideation is:

   a. not as common among high school students as is popularly believed.
   b. more common among males than females.
   c. more common among females than among males.
   d. so common among high school students that it might be considered normal.

Matching Items

Match each term or concept with its corresponding description or definition.

Terms or Concepts

_____ 1. identity
_____ 2. identity achievement
_____ 3. foreclosure
_____ 4. negative identity
_____ 5. identity diffusion
_____ 6. identity moratorium
_____ 7. generation gap
_____ 8. generational stake
_____ 9. parental monitoring
_____ 10. parasuicide
_____ 11. cluster suicide

Descriptions or Definitions

a. premature identity formation
b. a group of suicides that occur in the same community, school, or time period
c. the adolescent has few commitments to goals or values
d. differences between the younger and older generations
e. self-destructive act that does not result in death
f. awareness of where children are and what they are doing
g. an individual's self-definition
h. a time-out period during which adolescents experiment with alternative identities
i. the adolescent establishes his or her own goals and values
j. family members in different developmental stages see the family in different ways
k. an identity opposite of the one an adolescent is expected to adopt

Thinking Critically About Chapter 16

Answer these questions the day before an exam as a final check on your understanding of the chapter's terms and concepts.

1. From childhood, Sharon thought she wanted to follow in her mother's footsteps and be a home-maker. Now, at age 40 with a home and family, she admits to herself that what she really wanted to be was a medical researcher. Erik Erikson would probably say that Sharon:
   a. adopted a negative identity when she was a child.
   b. experienced identity foreclosure at an early age.
   c. never progressed beyond the obvious identity diffusion she experienced as a child.
   d. took a moratorium from identity formation.

2. Fifteen-year-old David is rebelling against his devoutly religious parents by taking drugs, stealing, and engaging in other antisocial behaviors. Evidently, David has:
   a. foreclosed on his identity.
   b. declared an identity moratorium.
   c. adopted a negative identity.
   d. experienced identity diffusion.

3. Fourteen-year-old Sean, who is fiercely proud of his Irish heritage, is prejudiced against members of several other ethnic groups. It is likely that, in forming his identity, Sean:
   a. attained identity achievement.
   b. foreclosed on his identity.
   c. declared a lengthy moratorium.
   d. experienced identity diffusion.

4. In 1957, 6-year-old Raisel and her parents emigrated from Poland to the United States. Compared with her parents, who grew up in a culture in which virtually everyone held the same religious, moral, political, and sexual values, Raisel is likely to have:
   a. an easier time achieving her own unique identity.
   b. a more difficult time forging her identity.
   c. a greater span of time in which to forge her own identity.
   d. a shorter span of time in which to forge her identity.

5. An adolescent exaggerates the importance of differences in her values and those of her parents. Her parents see these differences as smaller and less important. This phenomenon is called the:
   a. generation gap.   c. family enigma.
   b. generational stake.   d. parental imperative.

6. In our society, the most obvious examples of institutionalized moratoria on identity formation are:
   a. the Boy Scouts and the Girl Scouts.
   b. college and the peacetime military.
   c. marriage and divorce.
   d. bar mitzvahs and baptisms.

7. First-time parents Norma and Norman are worried that, during adolescence, their healthy parental influence will be undone as their children are encouraged by peers to become sexually promiscuous, drug-addicted, or delinquent. Their wise neighbor, who is a developmental psychologist, tells them that:
   a. during adolescence, peers are generally more likely to complement the influence of parents than they are to pull their friends in the opposite direction.
   b. research suggests that peers provide a negative influence in every major task of adolescence.
   c. only through authoritarian parenting can parents give children the skills they need to resist peer pressure.
   d. unless their children show early signs of learning difficulties or antisocial behavior, parental monitoring is unnecessary.

8. (Thinking Like a Scientist) Which of the following statements would a 13-year-old girl be most likely to make?
   a. "Boys are a sort of disease."
   b. "Boys are stupid although important to us."
   c. "Boys hate you if you're ugly and brainy."
   d. "Boys are a pleasant change from girls."

9. In forming an identity, the young person seeks to make meaningful connections with his or her past. This seeking is described by Erikson as a striving for:
   a. individual uniqueness.
   b. peer-group membership.
   c. continuity of experience.
   d. vocational identity.

10. Rosaria is an adolescent in an immigrant family. In response to the conflict between the peer-group emphasis on adolescent freedom and the values of her family's culture, Rosaria is most likely to:
    a. rebel against her family, possibly leaving home.
    b. join a delinquent group.
    c. give in to parental control.
    d. ask to live with her grandparents.

11. Statistically, the person *least* likely to commit a crime is a(n):
    a. African-American or Latino adolescent.
    b. middle-class white male.
    c. white adolescent of any socioeconomic background.
    d. Asian-American.

12. Ray was among the first of his friends to have sex, drink alcohol, and smoke cigarettes. These attributes, together with his having been hyperactive and having poor emotional control, would suggest that Ray is at high risk of:
    a. becoming an adolescent-limited offender.
    b. becoming a life-course-persistent offender.
    c. developing an antisocial personality.
    d. foreclosing his identity prematurely.

13. Carl is a typical 16-year-old adolescent who has no special problems. It is likely that Carl has:
    a. contemplated suicide.
    b. engaged in some minor illegal act.
    c. struggled with "who he is."
    d. done all of the above.

14. Statistically, who of the following is *most* likely to commit suicide?
    a. Micah, an African-American female
    b. Yan, an Asian-American male
    c. James, a Native American male
    d. Alison, a European-American female

15. Coming home from work, Malcolm hears a radio announcement warning parents to be alert for possible cluster suicide signs in their teenage children. What might have precipitated such an announcement?
    a. government statistics that suicide is on the rise in the 1990s
    b. the highly publicized suicide of a teen from a school in his town
    c. the recent crash of an airliner, killing all on board
    d. any of the above

Key Terms

Using your own words, write a brief definition or explanation of each of the following terms on a separate piece of paper.

1. identity
2. possible selves
3. false self
4. identity versus role confusion
5. identity achievement
6. foreclosure
7. negative identity
8. identity diffusion
9. identity moratorium
10. gender identity
11. rite of passage
12. suicidal ideation
13. parasuicide
14. cluster suicide
15. internalizing problems
16. externalizing problems
17. incidence
18. prevalence
19. adolescent-limited offender
20. life-course-persistent offender
21. generation gap
22. generational stake
23. bickering
24. parental monitoring
25. peer pressure

ANSWERS

CHAPTER REVIEW

1. identity; possible selves
2. false self; acceptable false self; pleasing false self; experimental false self
3. identity versus role confusion
4. identity achievement
5. foreclosure
6. negative identity
7. identity diffusion
8. moratorium; college
9. achieved identity; foreclosed; foreclosed; identity achievers
10. 10 years
11. can; within; without; social
12. gender identity; roles; behaviors

13. sexual orientation; male–female
14. girls; literature; confusion
15. more; negative; foreclose; different from that of others; 40
16. values; social structures; customs; rite of passage
17. easier; rare
18. was not; family; school; church
19. less
20. mania; bipolar disorder; adolescence and early adulthood
21. increases; females
22. suicidal ideation; common; hormonal; genes; stress; social
23. less
24. do not; parasuicide
25. a. the availability of lethal methods
    b. the extent of parental supervision
    c. the use of alcohol and other drugs
    d. gender
    e. the attitudes about suicide held by the adolescent's culture
26. males; females
27. are
28. cluster suicides

At any age, these include chronic depression, death of a close friend, drug abuse, loneliness, social rejection, and homosexuality.

Native American males have the highest rates, followed by European-American males, African-American males, Native American females, Asian-American males, and so on.

29. internalizing; depression, anorexia, bulimia, self-mutilation, overuse of sedative drugs, and suicide; externalizing; injuring others, destroying property, and defying authority; increase suddenly
30. cognitive; identity; logically

Externalizing actions may prove harmful later on, they often harm others, and they may be signs of serious mental disturbance.

31. second decade; incidence; prevalent
32. greater

Adolescent males are three times as likely to be arrested as females, and African-American youth are three times as likely to be arrested as European-Americans, who are three times as likely to be arrested as Asian-Americans.

33. being a victim of violence; teenagers
34. adolescent-limited; life-course-persistent
35. is
36. have sex and use gateway drugs; school; antisocial; brain damage; language; hyperactive; emotional
37. is not

Children who have been abused or neglected, who have few friends, who are early substance users, or who are bullies are at higher risk.

38. generation gap; time; place
39. generational stake
40. early; mothers; early; daughters; bickering
41. late; dependency; closeness
42. communication; support; connectiveness; control
43. parental monitoring; depression
44. supportive; musical tastes, domestic neatness, and sleeping habits; world politics or moral issues
45. peer pressure; rises; 14; fall
46. longer; before; generation gap

The sequence begins with foreclosure on traditional values, continues with rejection of tradition in favor of mainstream values, is followed by a moratorium, and culminates in identity achievement by connecting with other young Asian-Americans.

The progression begins with groups of same-sex friends. Next, a loose, public association of a girl's group and a boy's group forms. Then, a smaller, heterosexual group forms from the more advanced members of the larger association. Finally, more intimate heterosexual couples peel off.

47. affect; timing; sequence; biological
48. slow down; homophobic; deny; change; conceal
49. are not; late
50. less
51. a peer of the same age and background
52. young men and sex; heterosexual couples
    a. that they have no control over their sexual impulses, especially when they have been drinking
    b. that it is more appropriate for a boy to have more than one sexual partner than for a girl

Adolescent peers are reluctant to judge a friend's behavior, their analysis may be faulty, their personal fable lets them deny responsibility, and they underestimate the difficulties of raising a child.

53. happy
54. often have
55. genetic vulnerability, prenatal insults, family disruptions, childhood discord, learning difficulties, aggressive or withdrawn behavior in elementary school, inadequate community intervention

PROGRESS TEST 1

Multiple-Choice Questions

1. **b.** is the answer. (p. 498)

    a. According to Erikson, this is the crisis of infancy.

c. & d. In Erikson's theory, these crises occur later in life.

2. **a.** is the answer. (p. 499)

   b. This describes an identity moratorium.

   c. This describes a negative identity.

   d. This describes identity diffusion.

3. **c.** is the answer. (p. 499)

4. **d.** is the answer. (p. 519)

5. **d.** is the answer. (pp. 502–503)

6. **d.** is the answer. (p. 518)

   a. The generational stake refers to differences in how family members from different generations view the family.

   b. Foreclosure refers to the premature establishment of identity.

   c. Peer screening is an aspect of parental monitoring, but it was not specifically discussed in the text.

7. **a.** is the answer. (p. 517)

8. **c.** is the answer. (pp. 516–517)

9. **b.** is the answer. (p. 503)

   a. This occurs in some cases, but not in *most* cases.

   c. Moratorium is a time-out in identity formation in order to allow the adolescent to try out alternative identities. It is generally not a solution in such cases.

   d. Young people who experience identity diffusion are often apathetic, which is not the case here.

10. **c.** is the answer. (p. 498)

    a. & b. Teenagers who try out these false selves tend to feel either worthless and depressed (acceptable false self) or experience the psychological consequences of living an identity just to impress or please others (pleasing false self).

11. **b.** is the answer. Incidence is how often a particular circumstance (such as lawbreaking) occurs; prevalence is how widespread the circumstance is. A crime that is committed by only a few repeat offenders is not very prevalent in the population. (p. 513)

12. **c.** is the answer. (p. 511)

13. **c.** is the answer. Most life-course-persistent offenders are among the earliest of their cohort to have sex. (pp. 515–516)

14. **b.** is the answer. (p. 511)

15. **c.** is the answer. (p. 517)

a. In fact, parent–child conflict is more likely to involve mothers and their early-maturing offspring.

b. The text did not compare the rate of conflict in two-parent and single-parent homes.

True or False Items

1. T (p. 504)

2. F   Parent–teen conflicts center on day-to-day details, not on politics or moral issues. (p. 517)

3. F   Just the opposite is true. (pp. 519–520)

4. T (p. 522)

5. T (p. 513)

6. F   Most self-destructive acts stem from many earlier developmental events. (p. 528)

7. T (pp. 514–515)

8. T (p. 499)

9. F   Just the opposite is true. (p. 499)

10. T (p. 510)

PROGRESS TEST 2

Multiple-Choice Questions

1. **c.** is the answer. (p. 505)

2. **d.** is the answer. (p. 511)

3. **a.** is the answer. For this reason, autonomy in their offspring tends to be delayed. (p. 518)

4. **c.** is the answer. (p. 513)

   a. This answer would have been correct if the question had stated, "If the majority of cases of a crime are committed by a small number of repeat offenders."

   b. Because it is simply the total number of cases of an event or circumstance (such as a crime), incidence cannot be less than prevalence.

5. **c.** is the answer. (p. 508)

6. **d.** is the answer. Lesbian adolescents find it easier to establish strong friendships with same-sex heterosexual peers than homosexual teenage boys do. (pp. 523–524)

7. **a.** is the answer. (p. 499)

   b. This describes an adolescent undergoing an identity moratorium.

   c. This describes identity foreclosure.

   d. This describes an adolescent who is adopting a negative identity.

8. **d.** is the answer. (p. 507)
9. **b.** is the answer. (p. 514)
10. **c.** is the answer. (p. 514)
11. **d.** is the answer. (p. 499)

   a. Identity foreclosure occurs when the adolescent prematurely adopts an identity, without fully exploring alternatives.

   b. Adolescents who adopt an identity that is opposite to the one they are expected to develop have taken on a negative identity.

   c. Identity diffusion occurs when the adolescent is apathetic and has few commitments to goals or values.

12. **a.** is the answer. (p. 516)

   c. & d. The text does not suggest that the size of the generation gap varies with the offspring's sex.

13. **d.** is the answer. (p. 504)
14. **d.** is the answer. (p. 517)

   a., b., & c. In fact, on these issues parents and teenagers tend to show substantial *agreement*.

15. **d.** is the answer. (p. 508)

Matching Items

1. g (p. 497)	**5.** c (p. 499)	**9.** f (p. 518)
2. i (p. 498)	**6.** h (p. 499)	**10.** e (p. 510)
3. a (p. 499)	**7.** d (p. 516)	**11.** b (p. 511)
4. k (p. 499)	**8.** j (p. 517)	

THINKING CRITICALLY ABOUT CHAPTER 16

1. **b.** is the answer. Apparently, Sharon never explored alternatives or truly forged a unique personal identity. (p. 499)

   a. Individuals who rebel by adopting an identity that is the opposite of the one they are expected to adopt have taken on a negative identity.

   c. Individuals who experience identity diffusion have few commitments to goals or values. This was not Sharon's problem.

   d. Had she taken a moratorium on identity formation, Sharon would have experimented with alternative identities and perhaps would have chosen that of a medical researcher.

2. **c.** is the answer. (p. 499)
3. **b.** is the answer. (p. 499)

   a. Identity achievers often have a strong sense of ethnic identification, but usually are low in prejudice.

   c. & d. The text does not present research that links ethnic pride and prejudice with either iden-

tity diffusion or moratorium.

4. **b.** is the answer. Minority adolescents struggle with finding the right balance between transcending their background and becoming immersed in it. (pp. 502–503)

   c. & d. The text does not suggest that the amount of time adolescents have to forge their identities varies from one ethnic group to another or has changed over historical time.

5. **b.** is the answer. (p. 517)

   a. The generation gap refers to actual differences in attitudes and values between the younger and older generations. This example is concerned with how large these differences are perceived to be.

   c. & d. These terms are not used in the text in discussing family conflict.

6. **b.** is the answer. (p. 499)
7. **a.** is the answer. (p. 524)

   b. In fact, just the opposite is true.

   c. Developmentalists recommend authoritative, rather than authoritarian, parenting.

   d. Parental monitoring is important for all adolescents.

8. **b.** is the answer. (p. 522)
9. **c.** is the answer. (p. 502)
10. **c.** is the answer. Adolescent girls in immigrant families are most likely to live docilely at home until an early marriage. (p. 521)

   a. & b. Boys are most likely to do these things.

   d. This may be the parents' response to problems with their children.

11. **d.** is the answer. (p. 514)
12. **b.** is the answer. (p. 515)
13. **d.** is the answer. (pp. 498, 508, 514)
14. **c.** is the answer. (p. 511)
15. **b.** is the answer. (p. 511)

   a., c., & d. Cluster suicides occur when the suicide of a local teen leads others to attempt suicide.

KEY TERMS

1. **Identity**, as used by Erikson, refers to a person's self-definition as a separate individual in terms of roles, attitudes, beliefs, and aspirations. (p. 497).
2. Many adolescents try out **possible selves**, or variations on who they are, who they might like to become, and who they fear becoming. (p. 497)

3. Some adolescents display a **false self,** acting in ways that are contrary to who they really are in order to be accepted (the acceptable false self), to impress or please others (the pleasing false self), or "just to see how it feels" (the experimental false self). (p. 498)

4. Erikson's term for the psychosocial crisis of adolescence, **identity versus role confusion,** refers to adolescents' need to combine their self-understanding and social roles into a coherent identity. (p. 498)

5. In Erikson's theory, **identity achievement** occurs when adolescents attain their new identity by establishing their own goals and values and abandoning some of those set by their parents and culture and accepting others. (p. 498)

6. In **foreclosure,** according to Erikson, the adolescent forms an identity prematurely, accepting earlier roles and parental values wholesale, without truly forging a unique personal identity. (p. 499)

7. Adolescents who take on a **negative identity,** according to Erikson, adopt an identity that is the opposite of the one they are expected to adopt. (p. 499)

8. Adolescents who experience **identity diffusion,** according to Erikson, have few commitments to goals or values and are often apathetic about trying to find an identity. (p. 499)

9. According to Erikson, in the process of finding a mature identity, many young people seem to declare an **identity moratorium,** a kind of time-out during which they experiment with alternative identities without trying to settle on any one. (p. 499)

10. **Gender identity** is a person's self-identification of being female or male, including the roles and behaviors that society assigns to that sex. (p. 501)

11. A **rite of passage** is a dramatic ceremony marking the transition from childhood to adulthood. (p. 505)

12. **Suicidal ideation** refers to thinking about committing suicide, usually with some serious emotional and intellectual or cognitive overtones. (p. 508)

13. **Parasuicide** is a deliberate act of self-destruction that does not result in death. (p. 510)

14. A **cluster suicide** refers to a series of suicides or suicide attempts that are precipitated by one initial suicide and that occur in the same community, school, or time period. (p. 511)

15. **Internalizing problems** are inwardly expressed emotional problems such as eating disorders, self-mutilation, and drug abuse. (p. 512)

16. **Externalizing problems** are outwardly expressed emotional problems such as injuring others, destroying property, and defying authority. (p. 512)

17. **Incidence** is how often a particular circumstance (such as lawbreaking) occurs. (p. 513)

18. **Prevalence** is how widespread a particular behavior or circumstance is. (p. 513)

19. **Adolescent-limited offenders** are juvenile delinquents whose criminal activity stops by age 21. (p. 514)

20. **Life-course-persistent offenders** are adolescent lawbreakers who later become career criminals. (p. 514)

21. The **generation gap** refers to the alleged distance between generations in values, behaviors, and knowledge. (p. 516)

22. The **generational stake** refers to the need of each family member, because of that person's different developmental stage, to see family interactions in a certain way. (p. 517)

23. **Bickering** refers to the repeated, petty arguing that typically occurs in early adolescence about common, daily life activities. (p. 517)

24. **Parental monitoring** is parental watchfulness about where one's child is, what he or she is doing, and with whom. (p. 518)

25. **Peer pressure** refers to the social pressure to conform to one's friends in behavior, dress, and attitude. It may be positive or negative in its effects. (p. 519)

Appendix B

More About Research Methods

Appendix B Overview

The first two sections describe important ways of gathering information about development: library research and the Internet. The final section discusses the various ways in which developmentalists ensure that their studies are valid.

NOTE: Answer guidelines for all Appendix B questions begin on page 271.

Guided Study

Appendix B should be studied one section at a time. Before you read, preview each section by skimming it, noting headings and boldface items. Then read the appropriate section objectives from the following outline. Keep these objectives in mind and, as you read the appendix section, search for the information that will enable you to meet each objective. Once you have finished a section, write out answers for its objectives.

Learning More (pp. B-1–B-2)

1. Identify several helpful resources for conducting library research on development.

Using the Internet (pp. B-2–B-4)

2. Discuss the advantages and disadvantages of using the Internet for conducting research on development.

Ways to Make Research More Valid (pp. B-4–B-6)

3. Describe the six terms or techniques pertaining to the validity of developmentalists' research.

Appendix B Review

When you have finished reading Appendix B, work through the material that follows to review it. Complete the sentences and answer the questions. As you proceed, evaluate your performance for each section by consulting the answers on page 271. Do not continue with the next section until you understand each answer. If you need to, review or reread the appropriate section in the textbook before continuing.

Learning More (pp. B-1–B-2)

1. Two collections of abstracts that review current articles from developmental journals are _____ and _____ .

2. Three journals that cover development in all three domains are _____ , _____ , and _____ .

Using the Internet (pp. B-2–B-4)

3. Internet _____ list general topics or areas, while _____ _____ sort information to help you find what you want.

4. One problem with Internet research is that there is _____ ; another is that _____ .

5. The most important piece of advice in using the Internet in research is to _____ _____ .

Ways to Make Research More Valid (pp. B-4–B-6)

6. To make statements about people in general, called a _____ , scientists study a group of research _____ , called a _____ .

7. An important factor in selecting this group is _____ _____ ; that is, the group must be large enough to ensure that the results are not distorted by a few _____ _____ .

8. When a sample is typical of the group under study—in gender, ethnic background, and other important variables—the sample is called a(n) _____ _____ .

9. When the person carrying out research is unaware of the purpose of the research, that person is said to be in a state of "_____ ." The subjects of the study _____ (should/should not) be in this condition.

10. Researchers use _____ _____ to define variables in terms of specific, observable behavior that can be measured precisely.

11. To test a hypothesis, researchers often compare a(n) _____ _____ , which receives some special treatment called the _____ _____ , with a(n) _____ _____ , which does not. To test the possible effects of this treatment, the two groups are compared in terms of some _____ _____ .

Progress Test

Circle your answers to the following questions and check them with the answers on page 272. If your answer is incorrect, read the explanation for why it is incorrect and then consult the appropriate pages of the text (in parentheses following the correct answer).

1. A valuable collection of abstracts that review current articles from a variety of developmental journals is:
   a. *Psycscan: Developmental Psychology.*
   b. *Child Development Abstracts.*
   c. *Developmental Psychology.*
   d. a. and b.
   e. a., b., & c.

2. Two journals that publish research on all three domains of development are:
   a. *The Developmentalist* and *Child Psychology.*
   b. *Developmental Psychology* and *Child Development.*
   c. *Developmental Science* and *Aging.*
   d. *Child Psychology* and *The Developmentalist.*

3. Which of the following was *not* mentioned as a disadvantage of using the Internet to conduct developmental research?
   a. There is too much information.
   b. Anyone can put anything on the Internet.
   c. Plagiarism and prejudiced perspectives are common problems.
   d. There is no way to sort through the massive amount of information.

4. The entire group of people about whom a scientist wants to learn is called the:
   a. reference group.
   b. sample.
   c. representative sample.
   d. population.

5. A researcher's conclusions after conducting a study are not valid because a few extreme cases distorted the results. In designing this study, the researcher evidently failed to pay attention to the importance of:
   a. sample size.
   b. "blindness."
   c. representativeness.
   d. all of the above.

6. Rachel made a study of students' opinions about different psychology professors. She took great care to survey equal numbers of male and female students, students who received high grades and students who received low grades, and members of various minorities. Clearly, Rachel wished to ensure that data were obtained from a:
   a. population.
   b. "blind" sample.
   c. comparison group.
   d. representative sample.

7. A person who gathers data in a state of "blindness" is one who:
   a. is unaware of the purpose of the research.
   b. is allowing his or her personal beliefs to influence the results.
   c. has failed to establish operational definitions for the variables under investigation.
   d. is basing the study on an unrepresentative sample of the population.

8. Which of the following is an example of a good operational definition of a dependent variable?
   a. walking
   b. aggression
   c. 30 minutes of daily exercise
   d. taking steps without support

9. The comparison group in an experiment:
   a. receives the treatment of interest.
   b. does not receive the treatment of interest.
   c. is always drawn from a population different from the experimental group.
   d. must be larger in size than the experimental group.

10. For a psychologist's generalizations to be valid, the sample must be representative of the population under study. The sample must also be:
    a. significant.
    b. all the same age.
    c. large enough.
    d. none of the above.

11. The particular individuals who are studied in a specific research project are called the:
    a. independent variables.
    b. dependent variables.
    c. subjects.
    d. population.

Key Terms

Using your own words, write a brief definition or explanation of each of the following terms on a separate piece of paper.

1. population
2. subjects
3. sample
4. sample size
5. representative sample
6. blindness
7. experimental group
8. comparison group

ANSWERS
APPENDIX B REVIEW

1. *Psycscan: Developmental Psychology; Child Development Abstracts and Bibliography*
2. *Developmental Psychology; Child Development; Human Development*
3. directories; search engines
4. too much information; anybody can put anything on the Internet
5. read with a critical eye
6. population; subjects; sample

7. sample size; extreme cases

8. representative sample

9. blindness; should

10. operational definitions

11. experimental group; independent variable; comparison group; dependent variable

PROGRESS TEST

1. **d.** is the answer. (p. B-1)

2. **b.** is the answer. (p. B-2)

3. **d.** is the answer. This is precisely what search engines are used for. (pp. B-2–B-3)

4. **d.** is the answer. (p. B-4)

   a. This is not a term used in scientific research.

   b. & c. Samples are subsets of the larger populations from which they are drawn.

5. **a.** is the answer. (pp. B-4–B-5)

   b. "Blindness" has no relevance here.

   c. Although it is true that a distorted sample is unrepresentative, the issue concerns the small number of extreme cases—a dead giveaway to sample size.

6. **d.** is the answer. Rachel has gone to great lengths to make sure that her student sample is typical of the entire population of students who take psychology courses. (pp. B-4–B-5)

7. **a.** is the answer. (p. B-5)

8. **d.** is the answer. (p. B-5)

   a., b., & c. Each of these definitions is too ambiguous to qualify as an operational definition.

9. **b.** is the answer. (p. B-5)

   a. This describes the experimental group.

   c. The comparison group must be similar to the experimental group (and therefore drawn from the same population).

d. The comparison group is usually the same size as the experimental group.

10. **c.** is the answer. (p. B-4)

11. **c.** is the answer. (p. B-4)

    a. These are the factors that a researcher manipulates in an experiment.

    b. These are the outcomes that a researcher measures in an experiment.

    d. It is almost always impossible to include every member of a population in an experiment.

KEY TERMS

1. The **population** is the entire group of individuals who are of particular concern in a scientific study. (p. B-4)

2. **Subjects** are the people who are studied in a research project. (p. B-4)

3. A **sample** is a subset of individuals who are drawn from a specific population. (p. B-4)

4. **Sample size** refers to the number of subjects in a specific sample. (p. B-5)

5. A **representative sample** is a group of research subjects who accurately reflect key characteristics of the population being studied. (p. B-5)

6. **Blindness** is the situation in which data gatherers and their subjects in a research project are deliberately kept unaware of the purpose of the study in order to avoid unintentionally influencing the results. (p. B-5)

7. The **experimental group** in an experiment is the group of subjects who experience the condition or treatment (independent variable) under investigation. (p. B-6)

8. The **comparison group** in an experiment is the group of subjects who are comparable to those in the experimental group in every relevant way except that they do not experience the independent variable. (p. B-6)